THE INSTITUTE FOR GOVERNMENT RESEARCH
OF
THE BROOKINGS INSTITUTION

STUDIES IN ADMINISTRATION NO. 37

THE BROOKINGS INSTITUTION

The Brookings Institution—Devoted to Public Service through Research and Training in the Social Sciences—was incorporated on December 8, 1927. Broadly stated, the Institution has two primary purposes: the first is to aid constructively in the development of sound national policies; and the second is to offer training of a super-graduate character to students of the social sciences. The Institution will maintain a series of co-operating institutes, equipped to carry out comprehensive and inter-related research projects.

The responsibility for the final determination of the Institution's policies and its program of work and for the administration of its endowment is vested in a self-perpetuating board of trustees. The trustees have, however, defined their position with reference to the investigations conducted by the Institution in a by-law provision reading as follows: "The primary function of the trustees is not to express their views upon the scientific investigations conducted by any division of the Institution, but only to make it possible for such scientific work to be done under the most favorable auspices." Major responsibility for "formulating general policies and co-ordinating the activities of the various divisions of the Institution" is vested in the president. The by-laws provide also that "there shall be an advisory council selected by the president from among the scientific staff of the Institution and representing the different divisions of the Institution."

FEDERAL REGULATORY
ACTION AND CONTROL

FEDERAL REGULATORY ACTION AND CONTROL

BY

FREDERICK F. BLACHLY

AND

MIRIAM E. OATMAN

THE BROOKINGS INSTITUTION
WASHINGTON, D.C.
1940

Printed in the United States of America
George Banta Publishing Company
Menasha, Wisconsin

AUTHORS' PREFACE

During the last fifty years there has been a remarkable and rapid development of federal intervention in the realm of private economic activity. Today six or seven hundred statutory provisions are applicable to this realm in one way or another. These provisions represent a more and more clearly defined public policy of economic regulation.

To outline a policy does not make it self-enforcing. In order that the expressed will of Congress may be carried out, it has been necessary to organize suitable agencies for the administration of various laws; to bestow powers and functions upon such agencies; to determine their relationship to other officers and agencies of government; to prescribe procedures; to develop and perfect forms of administrative action; to provide means of enforcing the acts of each agency; and to establish proper controls over such acts. These methods are all requisite to the double end sought by Congress: the protection of the individual as to guaranteed rights, and the efficient administration of federal economic policy.

Every method employed must be permissible under the Constitution of the United States, as interpreted and applied. For example, general policy must be outlined by Congress, and delegations of legislative power to administrative agencies must be specific and limited. Administrative and executive agencies cannot disregard or control the acts of the courts. Where constitutional rights are involved, any procedure established for administrative acts must safeguard such rights. Administrative officers may not be arbitrary or capricious in their acts. All these principles and many more have been respected and applied by Congress, the administrative system, and the courts, in the performance of their respective functions.

Today, as never before, the methods by which federal economic and social policies are administered are being examined and questioned for many reasons and from many quarters. The economic stresses of years past have naturally caused an increased interest in the subject of the relations between government and economic activities. As a result of such interest and the investigations to which it has led, three chief schools of thought have developed, which hold, respectively: (1) that the whole process of government administration should be under greater executive control; (2) that the process should be subjected to a more pervasive and strict judicial control; and (3) that after careful study of the whole situation, necessary changes should be made, whatever they may be.

This little book, which is largely preliminary in nature, describes briefly the organization, legal status, and relationships of the federal administrative system. The various plans that have been advocated for improvement of this system are also examined, both factually and critically.

The primary object of the book is to contribute toward an understanding of the multitude of problems in law and administration which must be solved if federal intervention in the economic realm is to be both efficient and legal. In this study no questions are raised concerning either the value of the constitutional structure within which federal administration must function, or the wisdom of Congress in adopting certain economic policies and establishing the present types of government intervention. The inquiry is confined to the much narrower problem of explaining the principal features of the administrative system through which the economic policies of Congress are carried out, and of examining and evaluating suggestions for the improvement of that system, without reference to possible changes in the Constitution.

In the preparation of this book the authors have necessarily received much assistance from others. Some of this assistance has consisted in broad discussions of questions of policy or constitutional or administrative law. Some of it has been obtained from manuscripts written by persons who kindly permitted the authors to examine their studies. Invaluable criticism has been given by many specialists in various fields. A host of government officers have been good enough to answer detailed technical questions and to supply both published and unpublished information. For all this assistance the authors are deeply grateful.

Especial thanks to persons outside the Brookings Institution are due to Mr. Thomas B. Billig of the Federal Security Agency; Mr. Robert M. Cooper, special assistant to the Attorney General of the United States; Professor Robert E. Cushman of Cornell University; Professor Oliver P. Field of Indiana State University; Mr. Robert E. Freer, chairman of the Federal Trade Commission; Professor Ralph F. Fuchs of Washington University; Professor Walter Gellhorn, director of the Attorney General's Committee on Administrative Procedure; Mr. Gregory Hankin, with the Federal Power Commission; Professor James Hart of the University of Virginia; Professor Charles Grove Haines of the University of California at Los Angeles; Mr. I. J. Lowe of the Department of Agriculture; Mr. Aldo L. Raffa, with the Railroad Retirement Board; Mr. J. Emmett Sebree, with the Board of Tax Appeals; and Mr. Ashley Sellers, head attorney, Office of the Solicitor in the Department of Agriculture.

Within the Brookings Institution, valuable assistance has been given by Mr. Charles L. Dearing, Mr. Willard C. Matthias, and Mr. Daniel T. Selko. Particular thanks are due to Mr. Lewis Meriam, who has not only acted as the chairman of the committee and general editor for this publication, but has also given much valuable advice. The other members of the committee who cooperated with the authors in the preparation of this volume are Mr. Meyer Jacobstein, Mr. Arthur C. Millspaugh, and Mr. Laurence F. Schmeckebier, to all of whom the authors wish to express their gratitude.

No person who has been mentioned is responsible in any way for the faults or shortcomings of this book, as to which the sole responsibility must belong to the authors. They are painfully conscious of the fact that a study which embraces so large a part of federal administrative law and practice cannot be perfect. It is their hope, however, that any faults of detail which may appear cannot vitiate their main contention that there is a highly developed federal administrative system which should be understood before efforts are made to change it.

Because of the nature of the subject matter, a detailed table of contents has been made, rather than an index.

Frederick F. Blachly
Miriam E. Oatman

February 1940

CONTENTS

SUPPORTING STATEMENTS

PART I
THE PRESENT SYSTEM

CHAPTER I

STATEMENT OF THE PROBLEM

I. CONFLICTING DOCTRINES

Three conflicting doctrines of public administration are now struggling for domination of the federal government. Any one, if applied in practice, would have far-reaching and momentous consequences, not only in the field of public administration, but also in such fields as jurisprudence, constitutional law, business, industry, and economic activities in general. These doctrines may be called: (1) the doctrine of executive management; (2) the doctrine of the judicial formula; (3) the revisionist doctrine.

It is the purpose of this book to explain, discuss, and evaluate these doctrines in the order in which they were named. Before this task is undertaken, however, it is necessary to point out the fact that the conflict of doctrines is not an open and dramatic battle. Few people know that it is taking place. Fewer still are acquainted with the technical principles of public administration, law, and jurisprudence, which must be understood before a rational judgment can be given as to the merits of any doctrine or the merits of legislation based thereon. Yet a comprehension of such principles should not be difficult. When they appear relevant to given phases of the discussion, the following pages will state them as simply as possible, in the hope of removing the conflict of doctrines from the remote and obscure ground where it is now being waged, to the arena of public discussion.

The doctrine of executive management. The essential feature of the doctrine of executive management is the assertion that all administrative activities of the federal government (except those of a quasi-judicial nature) should be under the control of the Chief Executive. According to this theory, the structure and the relationships of administrative authorities should be established with a view to facilitating such control.

Those who believe in this doctrine are particularly opposed to the independent position of the great regulatory boards and commissions. Such agencies, they say, are a headless fourth branch of the government, subject to no effective control. It is asserted that the very structure of these agencies involves a conflict of principles, since they perform at the same time (1) functions of administration and the determination of policy, as to which they should be responsible to the President, and (2) functions of adjudication, as to which they should be independent.

From this situation, say the proponents of the doctrine of executive management, follow certain disastrous consequences. Chief among these are: the carrying on of judicial functions under conditions which threaten the impartial performance of such functions; and the danger of arbitrary action which always accompanies irresponsibility.

The appropriate remedy is seen as a separation of the activities of policy formation, rule making, and general administration, from the function of adjudication. Those advocating the doctrine of executive management propose, therefore, that the first-named activities, which they call administrative, shall be made subject to the control of the Chief Executive and that the judicial function shall be lodged in authorities of a purely judicial nature.

The doctrine of the judicial formula. Those who propound the doctrine of the judicial formula take the position that the thing most to be feared in federal administration is "administrative absolutism," or the impairment of personal and property rights by the "great Leviathan" of the administrative machinery. In order to deprive the administration of its alleged power to injure, they would give it very little discretion; would compel it to act in so far as possible according to the judicial formula of notice and hearing followed by a decision; and would subject to judicial review practically every act which could even remotely affect rights.

Believers in this doctrine seek to apply the judicial formula even to acts long recognized as legislative in nature. Thus, they would have rules and regulations made only after publication of notice and public hearings. Although it is true that no bill now before Congress provides in general terms that all administrative rules and regulations must be based upon the evidence received at hearings, the whole tendency of the judicial formula is in this direction. The

Pure Food, Drug, and Cosmetic Act of 1938 actually contains a specific provision to this effect. Moreover, it is hoped by those who uphold the judicial formula that it can be applied to acts with which the courts have hitherto consistently refused to interfere, on the ground either that no rights are affected or that such acts involve a wide measure of administrative discretion. In other words, if this hope should be realized, acts connected with licenses, grants, civil service, and the like, or acts of a proprietary, promotional, benefactory, or facilitatory nature, are in general to be performed after notice and hearing; and if anyone deems himself injured thereby, these acts are to be subject to judicial review.

The revisionist doctrine. The revisionist doctrine sees in the present federal administrative system a fairly satisfactory adaptation of structure and relationships to function. At the same time, it advocates certain improvements. It takes the position that in establishing administrative agencies for particular purposes, Congress has acted, on the whole, both wisely and consistently. Hence the administrative structure is not a haphazard assemblage of miscellaneous parts. It is a system, and an organic system, in which specialized organs perform differentiated functions. Further evolution, however, can improve the system.

The revisionists point out such facts as the following. In the course of the past fifty years the federal government has been confronted with important new problems, particularly in the field of economic control. That it might meet these problems, the government has been compelled to assume numerous functions which it had not previously carried on, and to allocate these functions to authorities. It has necessarily established suitable organizations to carry on these newer activities, many of which involve sublegislative and subjudicial action. Among such authorities are the independent boards and commissions. Because these organizations are so largely concerned with action legislative and judicial in nature, it has been thought necessary that they should have a position of independence from the Executive.

Because the regulatory process might interfere with personal or property rights by commanding or compelling something to be done or by refusing to permit something to be done, special forms of action were developed which (1) enable the government to function in its sublegislative and subjudicial capacity, and (2) at the same time guarantee that as it does so, individual rights shall be protected. The guarantees include statutory delimitations of the scope of administrative acts and requirements as to procedure; also, when necessary, the application to these acts of such judicial controls as the statutory injunction and the review of administrative action by the courts upon the transcript of the record. Special types of enforcement methods were also developed, by which the acts of the newer authorities could be made effective.

Step by step, as new situations arose, Congress, the courts, and the administrative authorities themselves have thus been building an administrative system, which, although very diversified in detail, is clearly perceptible in its general outlines. This system is not haphazard, nor does it sacrifice to the needs or whims of the administrative authorities the rights and interests of the public or the individual. It is the result of much thought as to the constitutional problems involved, the particular circumstances to be regulated, and the best methods of handling them. The system is now reinforced by a wealth of informed experience.

The first step toward improvement, say the revisionists, is to understand the present system and to analyze, after careful study, its strengths and its weaknesses. What is needed is not destruction of the system, but its improvement. Because it has been developed piece by piece, it contains many weaknesses and even inconsistencies. Useless complexities also abound, as when the statutes make several statements of the same principles, methods, or processes, all with minor variations; whereas one statement, with any necessary exceptions, would suffice. Any inconsistency or confusion, however, is superficial rather than basic, since it is due merely to the multiplicity of methods or processes. The principles on which the administrative system rests have an organic unity which should not be disturbed, but should be recognized in the terms of the law. To speak more concretely, the law should recognize the fact that quite often administrative agencies can be subjected to the same procedure or lack of procedure, the same controls or lack of controls, the same type of enforcement or lack of enforcement, for the same type or form of action.

II. SCOPE OF PRESENT STUDY

The present study will make a brief analysis of the federal system of administration, particularly as it concerns the regulatory functions. It will then consider each of the three conflicting doctrines from the viewpoint of its effect upon that system, its constitutionality, and its general desirability from the viewpoint of sound administration. If a reasoned choice can be made among the various doctrines, it must rest upon an inquiry of this kind.

CHAPTER II

BASES OF THE PRESENT SYSTEM

Before an attempt is made to outline in detail the criticisms that have been leveled at the present system and the proposals that have been made for its improvement, a rough picture will be given of the system as it exists today.

For the understanding of any system of public administration, two elements must be carefully examined: (1) the legal framework within which the system functions, and (2) basic relationships.

I. THE GENERAL LEGAL FRAMEWORK

The legal structure within which federal public administration functions has a two-fold basis, that of the common law of England as developed and applied in this country, and that of the federal Constitution.

A. The Common Law Basis

The doctrines of the common law are all-pervasive in our legal thinking. Many of them have been written into the Constitution of the United States, and others control the interpretation of the Constitution and of other norms of law.

The most potent of the common law doctrines, in so far as the federal government is concerned, is that of sovereignty. It is this doctrine, in the minds of those who made the Constitution and in the minds of the judges who interpret it, which, in the last analysis, gives the federal government such absolute powers in respect to foreign relations, war, immigration, taxation, and customs. The principle of jurisprudence that the government cannot be sued without its consent is another expression of the common law conception of sovereignty.

It is the common law which, even though modified in various ways as time goes on, gives content to many of the words and phrases of the Constitution. What are "life, liberty, and property"? What is "commerce . . . among the several states"? They are what the courts, thinking largely in terms of the common law, have long declared them to be. It is true that statutes have provided, for example, that the labor of human beings is not a commodity, and that employees and others on railway trains engaged in interstate commerce must have certain qualifications, duties, and liabilities; and it is also true that the courts have upheld Congress in passing these statutes. But the jurisprudence which defines the various terms of the Constitution, and even the terms of statutes, is rooted in the common law of England.[1]

B. The Federal Constitution

The federal Constitution as interpreted by the courts contains several provisions that must be borne in mind in considering our administrative system. These constitutional doctrines will merely be indicated here as a basis for understanding the problems involved.

The constitutional doctrine of the separation of powers precludes Congress from making a grant of legislative power to an administrative or executive agency, unless in doing so it makes a statement of its own policy sufficiently definite to control the executive or the administrative body in the exercise of the power thus delegated.[2] Proposals for a general grant of power to make rules and regulations implementing the law must be considered in the light of this constitutional principle.

Separation of powers further implies that an administrative function cannot be given to a constitutional court.[3] These courts consistently refuse to perform such functions, and even to review the valid exercise of discretion on the part of administrative bodies.[4] This must be considered when evaluating proposals to grant administrative power to the courts in connection with review over rules and regulations.

[1] *Bowman v. Chicago & N.W. R. Co.*, 125 U.S. 465; *Cooley v. Board of Port Wardens*, 12 How. 299; but see Robert H. Jackson, "The Rise and Fall of Swift v. Tyson," *American Bar Association Journal*, August 1938.

[2] See *Panama Refining Co. v. Ryan*, 293 U.S. 388; *Schechter v. United States*, 295 U.S. 495.

[3] *Reagan v. Farmers Loan & Trust Co.*, 154 U.S. 362; *Keim v. United States*, 177 U.S. 290; *Keller v. Potomac Elec. Power Co.*, 261 U.S. 428; *Royal Farms Dairy, Inc. v. Wallace*, 7 Fed. Supp. 560; *Murray v. Hoboken Land & Improvement Co.*, 18 How. 272.

[4] *Interstate Commerce Commission v. Ill. Central Ry. Co.*, 215 U.S. 452; *Postum Cereal Co. v. California Fig Nut Co.*, 272 U.S. 693.

The constitutional provision[5] to the effect that the judicial powers of the constitutional courts extend only to cases and controversies is important as limiting the possibilities of judicial review over the acts of executive or administrative officers or agencies. As this provision has been interpreted by the Supreme Court,[6] it means both that Congress cannot withdraw from judicial cognizance any matter which from its nature is the subject of a suit at common law, equity, or admiralty; and also that Congress cannot cause or compel the constitutional courts to take jurisdiction of a matter which, from its nature, is not a subject for judicial determination. The constitutional courts will take jurisdiction only over proceedings involving rights susceptible of judicial determination, or justiciable questions as to which they can give final judgments, where there are real parties having adverse interests. They will not give advisory opinions upon a hypothetical state of facts. This constitutional provision, as interpreted by the courts, must be taken into consideration when any changes are made in the present system of judicial control over administrative acts.

The doctrine regarding legislative courts runs parallel to the doctrine regarding the jurisdiction of constitutional courts. The so-called legislative courts are specialized courts created to hear appeals from certain types of administrative action, either in first or second instance. According to judicial theory there are several distinctions between constitutional courts and legislative courts.

[5] Constitution, Art. III, Sec. 2, reads:

"The judicial Power shall extend to all Cases, in Law and Equity, arising under this Constitution, the Laws of the United States, and Treaties made, or which shall be made, under their Authority;—to all Cases affecting Ambassadors, other public Ministers and Consuls;—to all Cases of admiralty and maritime Jurisdiction;—to Controversies to which the United States shall be a Party;—to Controversies between two or more States;—between a State and Citizens of another State;—between Citizens of different States,—between Citizens of the same State claiming Lands under Grants of different States, and between a State, or the Citizens thereof, and foreign States, Citizens or Subjects.

"In all Cases affecting Ambassadors, other public Ministers and Consuls, and those in which a State shall be Party, the supreme Court shall have original Jurisdiction. In all the other Cases before mentioned, the supreme Court shall have appellate Jurisdiction, both as to Law and Fact, with such Exceptions, and under such Regulations as the Congress shall make.

"The Trial of all Crimes, except in Cases of Impeachment, shall be by Jury; and such Trial shall be held in the State where the said Crimes shall have been committed; but when not committed within any State, the Trial shall be at such Place or Places as the Congress may by Law have directed."

[6] See Supporting Statement XII, pp. 333-38 for details and cases.

It has been held repeatedly that legislative courts are created by Congress by virtue of the specific grants of legislative power conferred in Article I, Section 8, Par. 9, and Article IV, Section 3 of the Constitution,[7] instead of Article III of the Constitution.[8] They are instruments for carrying out the legislative policy of Congress. Nonjudicial, quasi-legislative and administrative powers may be imposed on legislative courts, whereas constitutional courts can exercise only judicial power. Thus, the legislative Court of Customs and Patent Appeals can be given authority to review the determinations of the Patent Office[9] and the Tariff Commission.[10] Such a court may be required to submit to the Secretary of the Treasury recommendations for the payment of claims against the United States.[11] A legislative court may be authorized to render advisory opinions to the heads of departments.[12] The legislative courts have a special type of jurisdiction. Matters which are susceptible to either legislative or executive final determination are matters in respect to which an aggrieved person has no constitutional right to a judicial remedy; hence they cannot be included in the jurisdiction of constitutional courts unless they are especially placed within this jurisdiction by statute, and likewise unless they can be presented in such form that the judicial power is capable of acting upon them. They can, however, be assigned to a legislative court for either judicial or administrative determination.[13]

This distinction between legislative and constitutional courts must be kept carefully in mind in any proposal to increase the present-day control of the courts over administrative action. Manifestly it would be possible to give legislative courts control over several wide fields

[7] Art. I, Sec. 8, Par. 9, provides that Congress has power "to constitute tribunals inferior to the Supreme Court."

Art. IV, Sec. 3, provides that Congress "shall have power to dispose of and make all needful rules and regulations respecting the territory or other property belonging to the United States."

[8] See *American Ins. Co.* v. *Canter*, 1 Pet. 511.

[9] *United States* v. *Duell*, 172 U.S. 576; *Postum Cereal Co.* v. *California Fig Nut Co.*, 272 U.S. 693.

[10] *Ex parte Bakelite Corp.*, 279 U.S. 438, 449-60.

[11] *Gordon* v. *United States*, 2 Wall. 561; *In re Sanborn*, 148 U.S. 222.

[12] *In re Sanborn*, 148 U.S. 222.

[13] See *Williams* v. *United States*, 289 U.S. 553; F. F. Blachly and M. E. Oatman, *Administrative Legislation and Adjudication* (1934), p. 128; Wilbur G. Katz, "Federal Legislative Courts," 43 *Harvard Law Review* 884; and "The Distinction between Legislative and Constitutional Courts," 43 *Yale Law Journal* 316ff.

of administrative action that the constitutional courts will refuse to review or will only review as to lack of jurisdiction or abuse of power.

The President's constitutional power of appointment and removal must be considered in connection with any proposals to place action affecting individuals in the civil service under judicial control.[14] It is very doubtful whether the courts could be given the power to pass upon the exercise of executive discretion in suspending or removing persons from office.

The due process of law provision of the Constitution, as applied to the federal government in the Fifth Amendment, must be given the most careful consideration by those who seek to make changes in forms of administrative action and in administrative procedure. Under this amendment such questions arise as: what forms of action, to be constitutional, require notice, hearing, and a right of appeal; what procedures are necessary at hearings; what tribunals can or cannot pass finally upon different types of action; what types of appeal should be given; what are the powers of the court in appellate cases; and so forth.

In establishing the present administrative system Congress, by making hundreds of adjustments to meet the common law and constitutional requirements as developed by the courts, has integrated statutory law with constitutional law. Changes in the system must take into account the need of such integration and also that which has already been accomplished.

II. BASIC RELATIONSHIPS OF THE PRESENT ADMINISTRATIVE SYSTEM

The most fundamental statement that can be made in respect to the federal administrative system is this:[15] that the particular relationships between the government and the individual largely determine the types of administrative authorities, their relationships to

[14] See Oliver P. Field, *Civil Service Law*, pp. 179-80.

[15] This statement is made as the result of detailed studies of administrative organizations, their functions, forms of action, procedures, enforcement methods, and methods by which they are controlled. See F. F. Blachly, *Working Papers on Administrative Adjudication*, printed for use of the Senate Committee on the Judiciary, 75 Cong. 3 sess.; *Administrative Law*, Hearings before [H.] Subcommittee on the Judiciary on H. R. 4236, H. R. 6198, and H. R. 6324, 76 Cong. 1 sess., p. 156.

other authorities, types of functions which they perform, the forms of administrative action, the procedures employed, the enforcement of administrative law, and the controls over it. These relationships may be classified as: (1) political or sovereign; (2) tortious; (3) contractual; (4) revenue; (5) proprietary; (6) promotional; (7) regulatory; (8) benefactory; (9) protective; (10) conciliatory; (11) judicial.[16] A brief examination will show that these different relationships are interwoven into the warp and woof of federal administration.

A. Political or Sovereign Relationships

The political or sovereign relationship of the government to the individual or business involves such activities as the making of war and peace, the command of the army and navy, the making of treaties, the control of immigration, and general control over foreign relations. Here the government, acting largely through the President, the State Department, and Congress, especially the Senate, provides in a general impersonal way for national safety and welfare. Although the individual may be seriously affected by such action, he has no redress except that which Congress may wish to give him. The procedures may be as summary as ordering a soldier into the front line trenches. The courts almost always refuse to adjudicate disputes between the government and the individual in respect to the sovereign relationship. No special agencies, as a rule, have been set up to adjudicate disputes and no special procedures have developed.[17]

B. Tortious Relationships

When the administration in its functioning wrongfully injures or does damage to an individual or business, ordinarily no legal action for recovery can be brought, since the courts have adopted the general doctrine that the sovereign cannot be sued. The only redress that the injured party has is to bring suit against the responsible officer or to make an appeal to Congress for relief, unless Congress

[16] The judicial relationship is not a subdivision of the administrative system; but it is discussed here in order to make a complete picture.

[17] There are certain exceptions to this broad statement, such as courts martial, the examining and retiring boards of the Navy, and the retiring boards and courts of inquiry in the War Department.

has made some special provision for administrative settlement, as it has done in respect to claims up to $1,000[18] based on negligence, the compensation of employees injured in government service,[19] or damages done to private property from military operations.[20] The Court of Claims has no jurisdiction over claims resulting from torts.[21]

C. Contractual Relationships

Under English common law the sovereign was non-suable. The federal courts, adopting this doctrine, held that the government could not be sued in contract. Persons therefore contracted with the government at their own risk. In case the government was guilty of a breach of contract, the injured individual could not sue the government, but was limited to petitioning Congress for redress. The Congress, by passing the Court of Claims Act of 1855, and its subsequent amendments, has waived this immunity from suit under contracts. Instead of the old sovereign relationship, a new contractual relationship was established in which the individual stands before the courts on a basis of equality with the government. He can contract or not at his pleasure, and if he contracts he can sue the government for the enforcement of the contract. No regulatory situation compels or forces him to contract with the government. Even under the Walsh-Healey Act, he can accept the conditions laid down by the government or not, just as he wishes.[22] Although a special court has been set up to handle contractual claims, no unusual processes or procedures are involved. No complicated problems of due process of law are present.

[18] 31 U.S.C. 215.
[19] 5 U.S.C. 768, 769.
[20] 5 U.S.C. 208-10.
[21] 28 U.S.C. 250.
[22] It should be noted that the regulatory situation in which the contractor finds himself under the Walsh-Healey Act and the Davis-Bacon Law, takes place after the contract is made. The agreement to this type of regulation in fact is a part of the contract. In other words, before making the contract he is in a complete position of freedom in respect to the government. After making the contract, the regulations he must conform to are just as much a specific part of the contract as provisions as to price, quality, time when work is to be finished, etc.

The control of the government in respect to contracts exercised by the Advisory Board of Contract Awards is merely for the purpose of preventing fraud on the government in respect to bids and contracts. It has nothing to do with the contractual relationship as such.

D. Revenue Relationships

Revenue relationships arise from the levy and collection of taxes and customs. Here the individual does not, as in respect to contracts, stand in a position of equality with the taxing authorities, but in the position of a subject. The state expresses its will; he must obey. Refusal to obey may involve punishment. The government may use special procedures against him, such as seizures, confiscations, distress warrants. The individual's business may be destroyed by the taxing methods employed, without possibility of redress. The constitutional provisions limiting Congress in the use of the taxing power were adopted for the purpose of placing all parts of the country on a like footing, and not for the purpose of protecting the individual.

Because of the paramount necessity of the government,[23] the courts have allowed more legislative and administrative discretion in taxation than in most fields, and have not attempted to control so narrowly the requisite processes. They have not always acted to secure due process of law and other constitutional rights as these are ordinarily interpreted. Sometimes the procedural difficulties have blocked quite effectually all channels of relief for the taxpayer.

Congress has displayed a definite intent that, despite considerations of sovereignty, justice shall be done to the taxpayer. It has therefore established several authorities to settle disputes involving revenue: the Board of Tax Appeals, the United States Customs Court, the United States Court of Customs and Patent Appeals, and the United States Processing Tax Board of Review in the Treasury.[24] These tribunals are not like the independent boards and commissions, regulatory authorities engaged in sublegislation and administration, but are merely controlling authorities passing upon administrative action already taken. Appeals lie to the Supreme Court from both the special tribunals and the ordinary courts when these act on tax cases.

[23] "Given a purpose or object for which taxation may be lawfully used and the extent of its exercise is in its very nature unlimited. It is true that . . . in most instances . . . any limitation is unsafe. The entire resources of the people should in some instances be at the disposal of the government." *Loan Association* v. *Topeka*, 20 Wall. 655, 663; see also *Springer* v. *United States*, 102 U.S. 586, 594; *Hager* v. *Reclamation District No. 108*, 111 U.S. 701, 708.

[24] Some tax cases, such as refunds, may also go to the regular courts.

E. Proprietary Relationships

As a proprietor and entrepreneur, the government acts much as a person does. The individual has no subjective rights to the property of the government, which can sell its property, lease it, allow it to be used for special purposes, grant timber rights, grazing rights, or mineral rights, as it wishes. The government can lay down conditions precedent to the sale or use of its property. Ordinarily in dealing with the government as a proprietor, the individual enters into contractual or quasi-contractual relations, or obtains his right to use property, by virtue of a grant, a lease, a permit, or a permission. When the government is acting as a proprietor, it can establish organizations to handle its property in various ways without necessarily giving thought to relationships; it does not have to establish a due process of law procedure. The courts usually take the view that in granting public lands or uses of public lands, the government is in the position of dispensing a bounty, and that although the "distribution or grant must be made in accordance with statutory requirements, the would-be beneficiary has no standing to object to a fairly wide latitude of discretion on the part of land officials."[25] Hence the courts exercise little control in land cases. The legislature has not seen fit to establish any statutory right of appeal.

Several quasi-judicial authorities which have been established in connection with the General Land Office, including the registers, the cadastral engineers, the Board of Appeals, the Commissioner, and the Secretary of the Interior as a final appellate authority, appear to be engaged in settling disputes between private individuals as well as disputes between the individual and the government.

In respect to such things as navigable streams and air waves for the use of radio, over which the federal government has dominion, the government enjoys much the same power that it does over its own property. The United States by statute[26] maintains the control in itself over all "channels of interstate and foreign radio transmission," and provides for the use of such channels, "but not the ownership thereof, by persons for limited periods of time under licenses granted by Federal authority." It can give administrative

[25] John Dickinson, *Administrative Justice and the Supremacy of the Law*, p. 277.
[26] 47 U.S.C. 301.

authorities wide discretion in granting radio station licenses, for example, by providing that "public convenience, interest or necessity" must be served thereby. Since one has no subjective rights to the use of air waves, logically a due process of law hearing in respect to applications for licenses, etc., is not constitutionally necessary. It would appear that judicial review over the refusal of such an application is discretionary with Congress.

In respect to its own enterprises such as the Tennessee Valley Authority or the Alaska Railroad or the Panama Canal, the federal government operates much as if it were a private individual or corporation. The decisions of such authorities do not have to be made as the result of notice and hearing, and they are not subject to judicial review unless they are *ultra vires* or otherwise illegal. Their contractual acts are subject to the same control as acts of private individuals.

The operations of the Post Office present several anomalies. It is organized as a government department and not as a corporation. In its arrangements with railroads and electric carriers for transporting the mail, it does not operate by the contract method; the rates and compensation are fixed by the Interstate Commerce Commission through the regulatory process. The carrier has no direct appeal against the order fixing such rates, but it may sue in the Court of Claims for the balance the carrier believes due.[27] In respect to air mail rates, etc., the Civil Aeronautics Authority fixes the rates by the regulatory method.

The services which the Post Office Department furnishes to individuals, strange as it may seem, are not placed under the monopolistic public utility formula that an individual has a right to the service, but under the privilege formula, that is, as a "privilege which the government is not obliged to supply and as an indirect form of taxation."[28] As a result judicial review is considerably circumscribed.

F. Relationships in Respect to Promotional Activities

In all promotional activity the government stands as a giver of gifts. What shall be promoted, how and when and where promotion

[27] See 39 U.S.C. 542, 570; *United States* v. *Griffin*, 303 U.S. 226.
[28] James P. Lynch, *Judicial Review of Federal Administrative Adjudication*, Doctor's dissertation, Georgetown University Law School (1939), p. 13.

shall take place, is merely a question of policy. The individual has no rights that must be protected by processes and procedures, except that promotional activity must be carried out in accordance with statutory requirements. The function of promotion is so general in nature that an individual may or may not benefit from it, depending upon his particular situation. The benefit received by one group may injure another, as may be the case in respect to the tariff, but those injured have no rights in the matter that can be tested in the courts. The only remedy is political action. No particular judicial processes and procedures and no particular types of organization are necessary. Practically no cases between individuals have to be settled, and little or no judicial control is necessary. It is significant that, in respect to the promotional activities of the federal government, there are no special administrative tribunals, unless these activities, as is the case in respect to standards, grades, etc., are combined with the regulatory activity.[29]

G. Relationships in Respect to Regulation of Business and Industry

In the regulation of business and industry three quite different types of relationships must be distinguished: (1) what may be called the policy and managerial type; (2) the police type; and (3) the type based on the establishment and enforcement of standards, grades, etc.

Policy and managerial regulation. Among the problems confronting administrators in policy and managerial regulation are unfair methods of competition, price discrimination, reasonableness of rates and services, preventing speculation, stabilizing industry, regulating competing carriers in such a way as to guarantee a well-rounded and adequate transportation system, and regulating the relationships between employers and employees. In such regulation the administration is not as a rule dealing with single, relatively simple, concrete factors, but with a complex of factors many of which are extremely intangible. Such regulation involves diverse types of economic situations, broad objectives that must be defined to meet concrete circumstances, appropriate forms of control, distinctive technical methods and procedures, and a variety of relationships.

[29] See Blachly, *Working Papers on Administrative Adjudication*, pp. 13-20.

Questions of public policy, questions of complicated economic relationships, and problems of public management arise in this type of regulation. The regulatory process involves a continuous adjustment rather than a one-time act. It necessitates the development of detailed lines of policy from rather general legislative declarations, and the application of these detailed policies to specific cases. The questions that arise do not follow the syllogism: major premise, the rule of law; minor premise, the particular facts of the case; conclusion, the decision. In many instances the basic law cannot be made sufficiently specific to form the major premise.

The position of the individual in policy and managerial regulation is distinctive; it is not one of equality, as when the individual negotiates a contract with the government; nor one of almost complete subjection, as when the government exercises its war powers; nor one of acceptance of gifts or favors, as when the government gives land or pensions. In this distinctive regulated position the individual is no longer free to deal or not deal with the government; he is forced to deal with it. His relationship, moreover, is not a single episode connected with a single and special act; it is a continuing relationship.

New legal situations have been created by the government to which an individual must conform regardless of his wishes: his rates must be reasonable; he must secure a certificate of convenience and necessity or a license before commencing operations; he must furnish safe and satisfactory service. It is largely within this field that administrative agencies are entrusted with the determination of questions involving constitutional rights and interests. It is in this field also that wide administrative discretion is exercised, subject to careful control.

Although under the regulatory process the individual must conform to the will of the government, he has, under our constitutional system, certain subjective rights that are protected against wrongful governmental action. His property cannot be confiscated by the regulatory process; it cannot be regulated without due process of law. His interests must be guarded by a process which is fair and just: there must be a declared legislative policy and a reasonably clear standard whereby administrative discretion is governed; governmental powers must not be delegated to a private person or a group of private persons; the governmental authority which makes quasi-judicial decisions must be as free from political pressure as possible; the individual must have his day in court; there must be a notice and a hearing at which he has full opportunity to present his side of the case; there must be a finding of facts to support an order; there must be an appeal to the courts if any of these rights are denied.

The creation of large independent boards and commissions, which exercise in the first instance all three powers of government, is due in the main to the special relationship between state and government inherent in policy and management regulation. It is the need for an expert treatment of this relationship which has caused Congress to create such agencies as the Interstate Commerce Commission, the Federal Trade Commission, the Federal Power Commission, the Federal Communications Commission, the United States Maritime Commission, and the Securities and Exchange Commission.

Because these authorities are carrying on functions primarily legislative and judicial in nature, they have, as a rule, been given a position of independence from the executive.[30] For the same reason, two important types of action by these agencies have been established: (1) the administrative rule and regulation, and (2) the order. Through the rule and regulation the statutes are so implemented as to make them directly applicable to general situations. Through the order procedure, congressional policy may be further defined and specifically applied to concrete situations, or decisions judicial in nature may be made. The order procedure has been made applicable to those situations where the government commands that action be taken or refuses to let action be taken; withholds an authorization, a relief, a claimed right, a privilege, or a license; determines upon rights and obligations; or declares the status of persons or things. Generally the order procedure connotes[31] a formal notice, a "due process of law" hearing, and an

---

[30] See Robert E. Cushman, *The Problem of the Independent Regulatory Commission*, Number III, The President's Committee on Administrative Management, pp. 35ff.

[31] See, for exceptions and a broader discussion of the order, Supporting Statement V, pp. 287-301.

appeal to the constitutional courts with further appeal to the Supreme Court. Nearly two hundred of the most important instances of regulation of business and industry are governed by the order procedure.[32]

Because of the special types of relationships that are involved in the regulatory process, the legislature has not permitted the common law system of control over administrative action to govern. As a rule the rights of the individual in protesting against governmental action and also the method by which the government enforces its action, are established by statute.[33] Administration under law thus has a special significance in respect to the regulatory activity.

In certain instances new economic situations have resulted in so modifying the policy and regulatory function as to give it a distinct managerial quality. Such a transformation takes place, for example, when the regulatory authority is required by statute to make adjustments among competing forms of transportation rather than among competing corporations, or when it must determine on the ground of public interest, convenience, and necessity, whether a new business is to be established or an old business discontinued.

Thus the Transportation Act of 1920[34] declared it "to be the policy of Congress to promote, encourage, and develop water transportation, service, and facilities in connection with the commerce of the United States, and to foster and preserve in full vigor both rail and water transportation." The basic principle of this act consisted in recognition of the fact that the public has the responsibility of maintaining an adequate transportation system as well as enforcing restrictive safeguards. This new policy was well summarized in 1924 by the Supreme Court in the *Dayton Goose-Creek R. Co.* v. *United States* case[35] where the court said:

. . . The new act seeks affirmatively to build up a system of railways prepared to handle promptly all the interstate traffic of the country. It aims to give the owners of the railways an opportunity to earn enough to maintain their properties and equipment in such a state of efficiency

---

[32] See Supporting Statement IV, pp. 276-86.
[33] See Supporting Statement XI, pp. 318-32.
[34] 41 Stat. L. 456, 499.
[35] 263 U.S. 456, 478.

that they can carry well this burden. To achieve this great purpose, it puts the railroad systems of the country more completely than ever under the fostering guardianship and control of the Commission, which is to supervise their issue of securities, their car supply and distribution, their joint use of terminals, their construction of new lines, their abandonment of old lines, and by a proper division of joint rates, and by fixing adequate rates for interstate commerce, and in case of discrimination, for intrastate commerce, to secure a fair return upon the property of the carriers engaged.

The 1920 act provided that construction of extensions and branch lines should be undertaken only after the issuance by the Commission of certificates of public convenience and necessity. The Emergency Railroad Transportation Act of 1933 (49 U.S.C. 15a) provides:

In the exercise of its power to prescribe just and reasonable rates the Commission shall give due consideration, among other factors, to the effect of rates on the management of traffic; to the need, in the public interest, of adequate and efficient railway transportation service at the lowest cost consistent with the furnishing of such service; and to the need of revenue sufficient to enable the carriers under honest, economical, and efficient management, to provide such service.

The Motor Carrier Act of 1935[36] also exhibits a strong tendency toward the managerial aspect of regulation. It gives the Interstate Commerce Commission power to regulate transportation performed in interstate commerce and by common and contract motor carriers in respect to entrance into and abandonment of service, consolidations, mergers, acquisition and control of other lines, rates, safety, and conditions of labor.

Under these laws and others, the regulatory authority is not primarily regulating monopoly but is managing the competitive systems of several different branches of transportation for the general social welfare. In order to demonstrate this fact it is only necessary to enumerate the chief managerial functions and then compare them with the functions now being exercised by the Interstate Commerce Commission in respect to these various transportation systems. The chief functions of management may be said to be:

[36] 49 Stat. L. 543.

1. To decide whether or not a business shall be established. If it is necessary to secure a certificate of convenience and necessity, this decision no longer rests primarily with the private individual, but with the government.

2. To decide whether to extend or reduce business operations. In the field of transportation this power is largely under government control.

3. To determine upon the amount and quality of service that is necessary to meet competition effectively. This power cannot be exercised by railway executives independently of the government.

4. To determine upon conditions of service such as speed or safety, auxiliary services such as picking up of freight, continuous service, or the abandonment of certain types of service. In all these affairs the government now has a controlling hand.

5. To determine policy toward personnel. The government now exercises a certain degree of control here.

6. To determine when and under what conditions money shall be borrowed and securities issued. This is now under the control of the government.

7. To apportion the proceeds of joint rates. Today rates of railways do not have to be apportioned according to mileage or actual service rendered, but may be distributed according to the financial needs of the carriers.

8. To fix the rates at which services are sold. Here the Interstate Commerce Commission and other government agencies have important powers.

In other words, government management has, in the transportation field especially, and in several others notably, to a very appreciable extent supplanted private management.

With the transition from regulatory intervention to managerial regulation, several important changes are taking place in the relationship of business to the government. In the first place there is a decided lessening of subjective rights to engage in and encourage private enterprises. Such subjective rights in certain instances hardly exist at all. This result is brought about, for example, by requiring a certificate of convenience and necessity as a condition precedent to the establishment of a radio broadcasting station or of an interstate motor transportation line. In these situations a person is now considered not to have any inherent right to operate such businesses.

In the second place, changed conditions may have deprived certain individual subjective rights of their old economic significance. A railway carrier, for instance, according to concepts of due process of law as developed by the courts, has a right to a reasonable return upon its investment. But if the regulatory body, operating upon this formula, establishes a rate theoretically high enough to make such return, and, as the result of the high rate, the carrier cannot compete, its investment may entirely disappear. In other words, the higher the rate it is allowed to charge, the less business it may get, with the result that it not only loses a proper rate of return upon its investment but also the investment itself. Street car systems competing with automobiles furnish a good example of this situation. When such a situation exists legal rights lose their economic significance, for the attempt to enforce a constitutional right to a reasonable rate of return in the face of a competitive situation may mean financial suicide.

The concept of a rate or tariff, set by a regulatory authority through a judicial procedure in order to bring a fair return upon a prudent investment, is not applicable to a highly competitive situation. It was really only applicable to a situation of a relatively high degree of monopoly. When the government attempts to regulate most or all of the competing agencies, it becomes even less applicable. The hearing must of necessity cease to be, if it ever was, a hearing upon questions of law, and must become an economic and social investigation in which those interested present their side of the case merely to inform the regulatory authority. Relatively few justiciable questions are involved. The questions raised are largely those of public policy and management.

To bring an attack against many forms of managerial action has now become almost impossible. What criteria are applicable as to whether or not a certificate of convenience and necessity should be granted? How can one say which of the many criteria are the most important? How can one dispute the way in which a commission has balanced the various factors? How can one limit and control such discretion? Since certain necessary transportation agencies might not be able to exist without the exercise of the managerial function by the government, they have no grounds for protesting against either the assumption of this function by the government, or the way in which it is exercised in concrete cases.

In the modern economic system, individual subjective rights to engage in any lawful enterprise must yield to general social necessity. For instance, under a completely competitive system the motor vehicles might easily destroy the railroad system of the country. But can the nation afford from the standpoint either of defense or safety or of the convenience and necessity of its citizens to allow any part of its transportation system to sink into desuetude? It is clear that the needs of the nation must, in this and other instances, be paramount.

In brief, the extreme complexity of the work of subordinate policy determination and regulation of business has had important social, economic, and legal consequences. It has led not only to the creation of special organizations to carry on this work, but also to a new body of law, new restrictions on former rights, new or highly developed forms of action, new procedures, and new methods of control.

Police type of regulation. In exercising its powers over interstate commerce in general, the postal service, shipping, waterways, public property and lands, foods, drugs, and cosmetics, etc., the federal government has developed many functions of a purely police nature in the interests of public health, safety, morals, the prevention of fraud, or the protection of governmental property. In this type of regulation the ordinary police formula has usually been applied; that is, a fixed rule of law, a charge that the law has been broken, and a decision.

The fixed rule of law is laid down before the taking of administrative action, and is made so definite that those administering the act have a precise knowledge of what constitutes a violation. In this respect there is a vast difference between police regulation and what has been described above as policy and managerial regulation. The rule of law may be established by three different methods: the legislative, the sublegislative, and the administrative. In some instances the legislature itself can establish such definite norms that they are immediately enforceable by administrative officers and courts, as for example the 28-hour law controlling the feeding and watering of livestock in transit. In other cases the subject is so technical in nature that the details are left to specially equipped administrative bodies. These may sublegislate, as when they issue general rules and regulations in respect to railroad and motor carriers, the purity and vitality of seeds, and the contents and purity of foods, drugs, and cosmetics. In the licensing system of control the administrative method is necessarily applicable. Here the administrative authorities, acting under statute or rules and regulations, establish conditions within the license itself. It must be emphasized that the rule of law in all kinds of police regulation, even the last named, is established before administrative action for enforcement takes place.

The charge that the law has been violated arises, as a rule, from the day-by-day functioning of the regulatory system, through the continuous processes of inspection and examination, analysis, etc. At times it may also arise as the result of a special investigation.[37] In many instances special authorities such as the Post Office inspectors, or the maritime, police, and border patrols, may assist in the process of discovering infractions of law. The Federal Bureau of Investigation in the Department of Justice, which has developed as a general law enforcement organization, may participate in this process. The point to be emphasized here is that no one type of organization handles the police function. There seems to be no good reason why only one type should do so.

The prosecution of those believed guilty of violations, although probably initiated by a regulatory authority, is seldom in its hands. As a general rule, prosecution is carried on before the district courts, by the United States district attorneys acting through the Department of Justice. The decisions made by the courts upon these cases are appealable.[38]

[37] For a good example of how the police activities of the federal government operate in a special field, see Food and Drug Administration, *Department of Agriculture Miscellaneous Pub. 48* (1939). See also A. C. Millspaugh, *Crime Control by the National Government* (1937).

[38] There are certain exceptions to these general principles. The most striking is in respect to unfair methods of competition where the details of what constitutes

The main reason for the procedure inherent in the police formula undoubtedly is the fact that many violations of laws or regulations are made punishable by fine, forfeiture, imprisonment, or a combination of these penalties. Because of this fact an administrative trial of the case, except in respect to hearings as to whether or not a recommendation for prosecution should be made, cannot be had.[39] For example, the Food and Drug Administration in the Department of Agriculture makes investigations and on the basis of these makes recommendations for prosecutions to the Attorney General in respect to violations of the Food, Drug, and Cosmetic Act, the Tea Act, the Naval Stores Act, the Import Milk Act, the Caustic Poison Act, and the Filled Milk Act; but the trial of such cases is before the regular district courts. Many similar examples could be cited.

The restriction of the administration in such cases to the work of investigation, inspection, and examination, protects the individual in his constitutional rights. The preliminary hearing of the case held by an administrative agency results in no action that can affect such rights adversely. The trial of the case is in the hands of the regular courts. There is, therefore, no necessity for placing such matters in an independent organization in order to eliminate political pressure. The authorities that are administering are not adjudicating and the authorities that are adjudicating are already in an independent position.

The exercise of the police regulatory power through the grant, suspension, and revocation of licenses demands some further consideration. Licenses may be divided into four main classes: (1) licenses to individuals who have responsibilities in respect to the safety, health, or welfare of others; (2) licenses in respect to the manufacturing of unhealthful or dangerous materials; (3) licenses

---

unfair methods of competition are not laid down in advance, where the formulation of policy is largely laid down in the decision, and where both the prosecution and the trial of the case are in the hands of the same authority. Other examples are: enforcement of the steamboat inspection laws by the Bureau of Marine Inspection and Navigation, and enforcement of the boiler inspection laws by the Interstate Commerce Commission. Even in these instances an appeal lies to the courts. See *United States* v. *B. & O. R. Co.*, 293 U.S. 454.

[39] The Sixth Amendment to the Constitution provides: "In all criminal prosecutions, the accused shall enjoy the right to a speedy and public trial, by an impartial jury. . . ."

as a condition precedent to doing business, for the purpose of protecting against fraud, manipulation, unfair practices, etc.; (4) licenses to protect the government itself.

1. In the type of licenses to individuals who have responsibilities in respect to the safety, health, or welfare of others, the main question is individual fitness. Examples of such licenses are those issued to pilots of steam vessels, drivers of motor vehicles, or aviators. From the viewpoint of organization a small board of technical examiners, in a government department or an independent regulatory authority, can appropriately decide the matter of fitness. Since the standards are laid down in detail, the sole question to be determined is whether the applicant can meet the standards. The tests are generally of a scientific nature, so that the examiner has objective criteria to apply to objective facts. The danger that powerful interests care whether or not any one applicant receives a license is slight. Since no large questions of public policy are involved, political pressures are at a minimum. The examiners, as a rule, have no motive for making their decisions otherwise than in an objective way. Because of these facts and because the process is neither legislative nor judicial in nature, there seems to be no reason for placing the work of issuing licenses under judicial process, or for having it performed by an authority that is independent from a government department. A simple administrative review of refusal to grant a license is evidently sufficient unless the person refused the license claims that there has been an abuse of power or a failure to follow the rules and regulations made applicable to the situation. The statutes seldom, if ever, provide for judicial review in respect to such licenses.

2. Licenses are required as a condition precedent to the manufacturing or handling of certain products that are dangerous to health or safety. Such activities include the production of viruses, serums, toxins, and antitoxins for the prevention and cure of diseases of animals and men, the manufacturing and handling of explosives, and so on. If the rules and regulations connected with such operations are violated, the licenses may be suspended or revoked. If hearings are permitted before this action is taken, it does not appear that the regulatory authority must act in accordance

with the evidence thus presented. Evidently he may use his discretion, and may give far more weight to scientific tests made by the scientific and professional personnel of the agency than to testimony adduced at the hearing. No statutory right of appeal is given.

3. Licenses, certificates, permits, etc., as conditions precedent to doing business, for the purpose of protecting against fraud, manipulation, unfair practices, etc., are rather common. Some of the more important are those required of a perishable agricultural products commission merchant, dealer, or broker, a radio station operator, a motor carrier operator, a foreign trade zone board operator, a custom house broker, and a contract market operator. In these situations the money interests may be large, and there may be a significant public interest as well as a private interest. Hence, in most cases, action to suspend or cancel such licenses is taken by the statutory order, which involves a notice and a hearing, with the possibility of an appeal to the courts.

The granting and renewal of radio station licenses present several types of particularly difficult problems of regulation. The first type involves questions of public policy, such as whether a transmitting service has merit, whether it has sufficient chain connections, whether there is too much advertising in proportion to entertainment, whether the program is sufficiently diversified, whether it is used for propaganda, personal views and attacks, etc. The second type are questions of a distinctly police nature. Some of these are: whether the station has been engaging in the piracy of other station programs; whether it has been guilty of defamation, sedition, libel, or the furthering of lotteries; whether it has allowed obscene, indecent, or profane language; or whether its advertising has to do with schemes to defraud, astrology, fortune telling, etc. The law forbids such acts and provides penalties. Cases arising under it are tried in the district courts, and legal penalties are imposed only by the courts. Even the technical questions involved in radio licensing are important. Frequencies, areas served, overlapping, and the like, must all be studied carefully in order that the licenses issued shall benefit both the holder and the public.

Perhaps the most important of all the problems which confront the Federal Communications Commission is that of freedom of expression.[40] In both the commercial and the political fields, this problem is of major significance. The public, too, has rights that must be protected—the right to truth in advertising, and the right to hear all sides of a political discussion.

It is obvious that in considering whether to grant or to renew a radio license, the Commission is not only passing on questions of scientific fact; not solely determining matters of public policy; and not merely deciding judicially as to violations of law. Any decision which it makes may embody considerations of fact, policy, and law.

Review over the acts of the Federal Communications Commission is related in part to its work and in part to the basis on which Congress established it. In the field of radio control , either of two bases for the exercise of the licensing function might be employed: (1) the federal government's dominion over air waves; or (2) its power to regulate interstate commerce. If the basis of governmental dominion were used, there would seem to be no constitutional need for due processes of law in handling such licenses. The person could take or leave the license as he wished. But if he took it, he would be subject to the disadvantage attached to the governmental dominion formula, that is, the lack of any constitutional rights or remedies.

The Congress has preferred to regulate the issuing of radio licenses by means of the interstate commerce formula, and has therefore subjected this function to such judicial processes and controls as notice, hearing, and review by the courts. The adoption of this formula raises some fundamental questions as to the expediency of judicial review. Sometimes the Commission has to decide a case that involves a complex of: (1) the broad concept of "public interest, convenience and necessity"; (2) technical physical matters in general radio control; and (3) charges that obscene, indecent, or profane language was used. Is there any room here for review by the courts beyond a mere determination whether the Federal Communications Commission has abused its discretion?

Since political, religious, or racial considerations may be brought to favor some stations and to eliminate or lessen the effectiveness of others, it would seem that the authority handling radio licenses

[40] See Louis G. Caldwell, "Legal Restrictions on the Contents of Broadcast Programs in the United States," *Report to the Second International Congress on Comparative Law*, The Hague, Aug. 4-10, 1937.

should be as free as possible from such influences. Congress has tried to secure such freedom by giving the work of issuing radio licenses to an independent regulatory commission.

4. Licenses, permits, etc., for the protection of the government or its dominion or property are issued by various authorities. A few examples may be given. The California Debris Commission, after issuing a general order as to requirements for hydraulic mining, grants to miners whose plans and specifications fall under the terms of the order, permits to commence mining. The object of this control is the protection of navigable waters. The Civil Aeronautics Authority issues, modifies, suspends, or revokes permits to foreign air carriers to engage in air transportation, thus protecting its dominion. The Federal Communications Commission issues licenses to radio operators in order to "maintain control of the United States over all the channels of interstate and foreign radio transmission; and to provide for the use of such channels, but not the ownership thereof, by persons for limited periods of time, under licenses granted by Federal authority."[41]

Classification, grades, and standards. In the functions having to do with classification, grading, and standardization of products sold and shipped in interstate commerce, the government acts in a two-fold capacity: as a promoter of business and industry, and as a regulator. The promotional activity is carried on for the general purpose of facilitating business. Those who buy, lend money on, or store wheat, for example, can deal in it with much greater ease if it is certified as to type and standard. But government certification also prevents fraud and dishonesty. The mere making of classifications, grades, and standards does not involve the exercise of the regulatory power; such power is exercised only in enforcement of the law, that is, when persons are required to follow the rules and regulations setting up classes, grades, standards. Several methods of enforcement are used.[42] The Department of Agriculture acts as an investi-

[41] 47 U.S.C. 301; 48 Stat. L. 1081.
[42] Examples of enforcement methods are:
Under the Cotton Futures Act a tax of two cents per pound is levied upon each contract of sale of any cotton for future delivery made at, on, or in any exchange, board of trade, or similar institution. In case the contracts conform to certain requirements there is exemption from the tax. (26 U.S.C. 1090-95; see also 7 U.S.C. 56.)

gational and where necessary as a prosecuting authority. It does not, however, try the cases itself, but sends them before the courts.

The Department of Agriculture not only lays down standards and sees that they are enforced, but actually certifies (in most instances through its inspectors and examiners) the class, grade, or standard in respect to all products involved. Individuals then buy, sell, contract for, store, or lend money on substances according to government certification. Persons dealing with these substances may not agree with the class, grade, or standard set by the Department and may appeal to it for a new certificate showing the actual quality of the product. The basic dispute may be between A, the buyer, and B, the seller, as to the grade of the things sold; but

---

Under the Cotton Standards Act it was made unlawful in connection with any transaction or shipment of cotton in commerce, in publication of a price or quotation, in any classification for the purpose of or in connection with a transaction or shipment in commerce, for any person to indicate for any cotton a grade or other class, which is of or within the official cotton standards of the United States, by a name, description, or designation, or any system of names, descriptions, or designations not used in such standards. (7 U.S.C. 52.) Penalties are provided for violations of this. (7 U.S.C. 60.)

Under the Grain Standards Act the use of official standards, with certain exceptions, was made compulsory for grain shipped in interstate commerce. (7 U.S.C. 76.)

Under the Warehouse Act all fungible agricultural products stored for interstate or foreign commerce in a warehouse licensed under the act have to be inspected and graded by a duly licensed person. The penalty for not having such produce graded seems to be the suspension or revocation of the license of the warehouse man. (7 U.S.C. 243-56.)

Under the Tobacco Inspection Act the Secretary of Agriculture is authorized to establish standards for tobacco, and to employ licensed samplers, weighers, and inspectors. There appears to be no compulsion upon the part of those dealing in tobacco to have this product sampled, weighed, or certified (7 U.S.C. 511e), but in case a person uses words in connection with any statement which indicates that it has been weighed, standardized, graded, etc., by the government when it has not been, a penalty is provided. (7 U.S.C. 511 i, j, k.) In case the grading, inspection, and standardization is of real commercial value, a method is thus provided for punishing those who attempt to gain such benefit illegally.

By the Standard Container Act of 1928 (15 U.S.C. 257), hampers or baskets have to be manufactured under approved specifications made by the Secretary of Agriculture. Hampers, etc., offered for sale, sold, or shipped in interstate commerce, may be proceeded against in any district court by a process of libel for condemnation. (15 U.S.C. 257e.)

Under the Naval Stores Act of 1923, the Secretary of Agriculture was authorized to establish official standards for naval stores. The act forbade and made unlawful the sale in commerce of any naval stores or anything offered as such, except under or by reference to United States standards. (7 U.S.C. 95.) Persons violating the provisions of the law may be punished by fine or imprisonment. (7 U.S.C. 96.)

since the transaction takes place on a government certificate, the contest between them involves the accuracy of this certificate, or the correctness of administrative action. The original grading, classification, standardization, etc., is in no sense a dispute but is a mere fact finding. The board or committee set up to settle the dispute merely makes a new fact finding and issues a new certificate. Such authorities, of which there are some twenty[43] in the Department of Agriculture alone, are not controlling authorities examining the jurisdiction, the processes, the evidence, the facts found, and the decisions reached by the inspectors, examiners, etc. They merely make a new finding. They are not primarily concerned with the settling of the dispute between individuals. Their scientific finding of fact does not constitute a decision in a case between two contestants. The new certificate is merely conclusive evidence of a factual situation. It is not a decision for or against a party to a judicial contest.

In the process of standardization, grading, classifying, and inspecting the government stands, as was said above, in a mixed relationship to the individual. It is undoubtedly promoting the facility of business transactions. But it is also regulating and controlling the manner in which business shall be done. It exercises powers of a police nature in enforcing its policy.

This particular mixture of functions almost inevitably involves certain types of governmental organization, certain relationships, and certain procedures. For the establishment of detailed standards, Congress must depend largely upon an administrative authority. To secure compliance with standards a large inspectional and investigational force is ordinarily essential. For the purpose of grading and classifying particular substances, there must also be a large administrative organization. Since a case involving a crime requires court action, the Department itself cannot try the case but must turn it over to the regular courts. Since those hearing appeals as to grades, classifications, etc., are not adjudicating legal matters or matters of public policy but are merely passing upon questions of fact in a purely scientific way, there is no need that their decisions shall be reviewed by the courts. Owing to the nature of the

[43] See Blachly, *Working Papers on Administrative Adjudication*, p. 13ff.

questions to be determined upon by these appeal authorities, no procedure other than that dictated by scientific requirements is necessary. It is essential, however, that such agencies be numerous enough to settle promptly the many disputes that arise as to grades and classification and that they be staffed by experts. Since questions of law are not involved in respect to these categories, but merely questions of scientific fact, an appeal to the courts is not necessary.

H. Benefactory Relationships

In this relationship the state stands to the individual as the giver of gifts and benefits. The most common of such benefits are military pensions of various sorts; social security benefits such as old age benefits and assistance; aid to the needy blind, and to dependent children; relief work through the Works Progress Administration; the relief of youth through the National Youth Administration; farm and rural relief; emergency conservation work; unemployment relief; and low cost housing.

In all such situations the individual has no rights against the government. The various actions taken by officers in respect to such matters are merely administrative rather than quasi-judicial, since rights are not involved. The rules and regulations for carrying on the work of organizations handling such activities are primarily rules of management and business procedure, and do not include a "due process of law" hearing.

The procedures are entirely administrative rather than quasi-judicial. The form of action is the administrative decision. Since benefits are being received there is no problem of enforcing the decisions of administrative authorities. Since no rights are involved, no question of a judicial appeal arises. Appeals of an administrative sort may be provided and they can be made final and conclusive with no further court review.

I. Protective Relationships

In a wide sense many activities of government are protective in nature, such as the preparation for or carrying on of war, or the administration of a tariff policy. In a narrow sense, however, the term may be used to include only those activities which protect persons or property from danger, and make safe mechanical processes and operations. In the exercise of such functions the relationship between the government and the individual may be of a mixed nature. For instance, in the slaughter of animals having hoof and mouth disease the individual may suffer from the exercise of the police power of the state at the same time that he and other cattle raisers are being protected. The particular action in any given case may protect the general social welfare rather than the immediate welfare of the individual. Whether the individual suffers an undue loss for the benefit of society in general depends entirely upon whether Congress makes an appropriation to meet his loss. The general theory of English and American law is that the government does not have to make good such loss, and in so far as it does not, the individual stands in a position of one helpless before a sovereign act. The taking or destruction of property under the police power is not subject to the constitutional restrictions surrounding either taking property for a public purpose or interference with property under the regulatory power. More and more Congress is taking the position that where great individual loss is sustained for the public safety, health, or welfare, the government should make compensation. This it has done in connection with the attempts to exterminate the cotton boll weevil and to eradicate the hoof and mouth disease.

Where the state is carrying on a general work of protection, as in maintaining lighthouses, providing for the safety of aviation, or operating the Coast Guard service, the individual has few rights against administrative action. He has no right to require such service, and in case he is injured by its functioning he has no rights against the government. Because of the absence of any direct rights in respect to the exercise of these functions there is no necessity for independent organizations, or for special relationships between administrative agencies and the executive. No special forms of action, procedures, controls or enforcement methods are essential.

J. Conciliation, Mediation, or Arbitration Relationships

At the present time most of the work of conciliation, mediation, and arbitration done by the federal govenment has to do with employer-employee relationships. Among organizations performing such functions are the United States Conciliation Service, the Davis-Bacon referees in the Department of Labor, and the National Mediation Board.

The National Recovery Administration furnished the most striking example of the attempt to settle economic disputes by way of mediation, conciliation, and administrative procedures generally rather than by judicial or quasi-judicial action. The word "compliance" was used to designate the process. Other agencies, particularly the Interstate Commerce Commission and the Federal Trade Commission, use an informal method of settling cases that approximates the mediation-conciliation method, even though the case, as in the Federal Trade Commission, is between the government and the individual. The experience of the Interstate Commerce Commission early demonstrated that differences between shippers and carriers which arose from mistake or misunderstanding, could be satisfactorily disposed of through informal intervention by the Commission rather than through the issuance of a formal complaint. In the handling of informal cases the complaint is examined and certified by the Commission and if it possesses merit, the carrier is called upon either to make a statement relative to the matter or to settle with the complainant. In case the shipper and carrier cannot agree, the informal complaint frequently develops into a formal case.[44]

The Federal Trade Commission has developed a procedure called "stipulation procedure" that is used in many cases. If a violation of law occurs through ignorance, the Commission often finds that it has only to call the attention of the offender to the illegality, to induce him to stop the practice. Instead of issuing a formal complaint, the Commission allows the individual or corporation to sign a stipulation agreeing to cease and desist from the practice. If he does so, further action is suspended. In case of refusal, there is a formal hearing.[45]

In nearly all cases where the conciliation, mediation, arbitration methods are used, the government does not use compulsion upon in-

[44] *Interstate Commerce Activities*, 1887-1937, pp. 53-56.
[45] Federal Trade Commission, *Duties and Procedure*, p. 5.

dividuals.[46] It does not make a decision which binds the parties, as does a court, an administrative tribunal, or in some cases a regulatory body. If the parties cannot be made to agree, the government usually takes no further action. This was not entirely true of the National Recovery Administration. "All of its elaborate mechanism of compliance is therefore designed, first, to establish the fact of violation of a code, and, second, to 'persuade' the violator to mend his ways and to 'adjust' complaints. Only at the end of the procedure is the case passed on to the Department of Justice or the Federal Trade Commission for the exercise of the government's power to coerce."[47]

Since no compulsion is used in the work of conciliation, mediation, or arbitration no questions of due process of law are involved in the procedure. Hence the agent or authority attempting to settle the difficulty can use almost any methods: private conferences with the parties concerned, joint conferences, hearings, etc. When no decision is made by the investigating authority, or when the authority makes a decision which does not have compulsory force, no question of appeal is involved. Since such authorities are not acting in a judicial or legislative capacity, there is no reason why they should be given a position of independence.

K. The Judicial Relationships

From the standpoint of public adminstration, the judicial relationship expresses itself in a series of controls and enforcements which affect either the individual or the act of an administrative authority. These controls and enforcements effect four principal purposes, namely: (1) they hold the administration within its field of competence and within the boundaries of the law; (2) they prevent abuse of power by the administration; (3) they enforce the rights of the individual, as determined originally by administrative action; and (4) they compel the individual to take action

---

[46] An exception to this general statement is found in the work of the National Railroad Adjustment Board. Here a division of the Board makes an award and issues an order to the carrier to make the award effective. If the carrier does not comply, the individual injured may bring a suit in the district court against the carrier. 45 U.S.C. 153.

[47] Charles Dearing and others, *The ABC of the NRA*, p. 97.

required by the administrative authority acting under law.

1. Holding the administration within its field of competence and within the boundaries of the law is accomplished in several ways. The chief of these is review of the order or other administrative determination on the ground that it exceeds the limit of the powers given by Congress to the administrative agency; that in making it, the administration failed to follow the procedures required by law; that the act is confiscatory or in violation of constitutional norms and principles; that Congress has no power under the Constitution to prescribe the performance of the administrative act; and so on. Another is incidental review when the administration seeks for enforcement.

2. Preventing abuse of power by the administration is a function of the courts when, in a controversy coming before them, it is admitted that the adminstrative authority had power to act and acted within the limits of such power, but it is charged that it committed abuses in the exercise thereof. Such abuses might include, for example: refusal of a license for political reasons; discrimination against certain religious denominations; denial of a fair hearing when a hearing is required; or capricious, willful and arbitrary disregard of evidence presented.

3. Enforcement of individual rights as determined originally by administrative action takes place (or, more accurately, may take place) when the administration has decided a controversy in such a way that a person or corporation is required to cease and desist from an unfair practice, to pay reparations, etc. In this case the individuals who will benefit from the cessation of such practice, or to whom the money is required to be paid, have a direct interest in the matter, since the enforcement of the administrative act is also an enforcement of individual rights. Provision is usually made by statute for invoking the jurisdiction of the courts under such circumstances. The facts as found by the administrative agency are usually made *prima facie* evidence, but the courts have insisted upon their right to pass finally upon questions of law, or mixed questions of law and fact. Their final decision may therefore differ from the determination of rights made originally by the administration.

4. Compelling the individual to take action which is required

by the administration acting under the law is a duty of the courts. It is a basic doctrine of federal administrative law that a proper act of the administration directed toward the performance of its legal functions will be enforced by the courts, as only by this method can the law be made effective without destroying the constitutional separation of powers. This enforcement may be requested by a person having an interest, as described above; or it may be requested by the administrative agency. If the courts are satisfied that the act is in accordance with law, they will use the injunction or some other appropriate process in order to compel the individual to conform with it.

CHAPTER III

TYPES OF AUTHORITIES AND THEIR RELATIONSHIPS

Any intelligent plan of reorganization must begin with recognition of the fact that administrative authorities are not all of one type. This fact raises an assumption that changes advisable for one type might not be desirable for another type; but even this conclusion should not be reached *a priori*. The various types must be studied and their significant characteristics must be understood before it is possible to arrive at conclusions or to recommend changes with any confidence.

The present administrative authorities belong to two principal types: (1) authorities which carry on the direct work of administration; and (2) authorities which act as controlling agents. Each of these types includes several groups or classes. There are a number of authorities which, in different connections, both administer and control.

I. AUTHORITIES WHICH ADMINISTER DIRECTLY

The present discussion is chiefly concerned with authorities exercising administrative functions that affect the economic rights, interests, or concerns of the individual. Existing authorities of this type may be divided into several classes: (1) The President of the United States and the heads of executive departments; (2) quasi-independent agencies within government departments; (3) independent regulatory boards and commissions; (4) independent regulatory authority with an administrator; (5) quasi-independent division of a department, with an administrator and committees; (6) ex officio commissions; (7) independent authorities of a non-regulatory type; and (8) government corporations, enterprises, etc.

The President of the United States and the heads of executive departments. The President of the United States, although his primary duties are executive, exercises certain powers which may be called administrative in that they touch the rights, interests, or concerns of individuals. Among these functions are: appointment and dismissal of public officers; certain controls over money and banking; and the right to take certain acts connected with tariff schedules. Even the power to issue orders and proclamations, though basically executive, may be exercised in such a way that it is equivalent to administrative action.

The heads of excutive departments are not as a rule charged personally with the regulation of business and industry. The Secretary of State, the Secretary of the Navy, the Secretary of the Treasury, and the Attorney General perform practically no functions of economic regulation. A little work of this type is done by the Secretary of War, the Postmaster General, the Secretary of the Interior, the Secretary of Commerce, and the Secretary of Labor.

The single department head who exercises important regulatory functions in the economic realm is the Secretary of Agriculture. More than forty separate statutes bestow upon this authority various duties and powers of a regulatory nature, in particular the power to issue rules and regulations and to make decisions and orders. He may delegate the details of this work to others, but he is ultimately responsible. In many cases he is the final administrative appellate authority passing upon acts of his subordinates. Suits are brought directly against him and not his agents.

Quasi-independent agencies within government departments. Upon the quasi-independent authorities within departments various names have been bestowed, such as administrations, divisions, commissions, bureaus, services, etc. These authorities derive their considerable degree of independence from such sources as the following: they are expressly established by law rather than by departmental action; their functions and procedures are largely created by law; under the law they make their own decisions or orders independent of the head of the department within which they are located; the law provides that their action may be final, or that appeals from it lie not to the head of the department but to the courts; they, rather than the head of the department, are responsible for seeing that the law under which they operate is enforced. In several instances, such authorities are appointed by the President and report directly either to him or to Congress.

The following regulatory authorities fit generally into the description above, although each one may vary from it in some particular detail: in the Treasury, the Federal Alcohol Administration, the Bureau of the Comptroller of the Currency, and the Bureau of Narcotics; in the War Department, the California Debris Commission; in the Department of the Interior, the Bituminous Coal Division, and possibly the Petroleum tender boards; in the Department of Labor, the Wage and Hour Division, the Division of Public Contracts, and the Immigration and Naturalization Service; in the Department of Commerce, the Bureau of Marine Inspection and Navigation and the Patent Office.

Independent regulatory boards and commissions. By far the most important regulatory authorities are the independent regulatory boards and commissions. The following authorities fall within this classification: the Interstate Commerce Commission; the Federal Trade Commission; the United States Tariff Commission in respect to unfair methods in foreign trade; the Federal Power Commission; the Securities and Exchange Commission; the Federal Communications Commission; the National Labor Relations Board; the United States Maritime Commission; the Board of Governors of the Federal Reserve System.

In establishing the various independent regulatory boards and commissions, Congress may be said to have followed one general pattern with many individual variations. All these agencies, except the Board of Governors of the Federal Reserve System,[1] are markedly similar in respect to organization, relationship to other public authorities, functions (in the large), forms of action, procedures, methods by which they are controlled, and enforcement methods. These similarities are, so to speak, generic, whereas there are innumerable specific differences.

All these authorities are established as boards or commissions of

[1] The Board of Governors of the Federal Reserve System, though an independent regulatory authority, is exempted from this general statement, because the highly specialized and extremely delicate nature of its functions, its forms of action, procedures, and enforcement methods, as well as the controls over its acts, are not designed upon the general pattern.

from three to eleven members.[2] This type of authority was regarded by Congress, when it considered the matter of organization, as better adapted to the performance of quasi-legislative and quasi-judicial functions than a single administrator would be.[3]

Several features of the organization of the regulatory authorities were specifically designed to keep them as free as possible from executive control or domination. In every case but one, the terms of the members of these boards and commissions were made longer than the term of the President of the United States. Furthermore, the original members of most of these agencies were appointed for terms "staggered" in such a way as to prevent, under normal circumstances, the appointment of an entire board during the same presidential term. As a further guarantee of freedom from political control, in a number of cases the law requires that no more than a bare majority of members may belong to the same party. In many instances the members of the regulatory authorities are placed beyond the President's power of removal, except for inefficiency, neglect of duty, or malfeasance in office.

No agency here discussed was placed under the control, direct or indirect, of an executive department. These authorities were and are regarded largely as agents of Congress, especially in respect to their legislative functions.[4] With few exceptions they are required to report directly to Congress rather than to the President or any other authority.

[2] For the details of their organization see Robert E. Cushman, *The Problem of the Independent Regulatory Commissions*, pp. 35 ff.

[3] See remarks of Senator Newland in the course of the hearings on the Federal Trade Commission bill: "I assume also that there should be a commission rather than one executive official, because there are powers of judgment and powers of discretion to be exercised. The organization should be quasi-judicial in character. We want traditions; we want a body of administrative law built up. . . . Such work must be done by a board or commission of dignity, permanence and ability, independent of executive authority, except in its selection, and independent in character." 63 Cong. 2 sess., S. Rept. 597, App. p. 22; 51 Cong. Rec. 11092.

See minority committee report in favor of the Cullom bill: "We desire to impress the House with an implicit belief in the present advantage of a board of interstate Commissioners. We ask you to defer radical regulation until we have tried the Commission, which, with power to hear grievances, will also be required to report annually to Congress and to suggest from time to time the legislation necessary." 17 Cong. Rec. 7275.

[4] "Of course, the fixing of rates is a legislative function, and Congress, having other things to attend to, created the great tribunal, the Interstate Commerce Com-

In order to facilitate their principal function of regulation, these authorities have been given extensive legislative, administrative, and judicial functions. The legislative functions are of four principal types: (1) the carrying on of investigations on the basis of which Congress may take action or the agency itself may issue rules and regulations; (2) the making of recommendations for new legislation in annual or other reports; (3) the formulation and adoption of rules, regulations, or requirements which have the force of law; and (4) the issuance of orders legislative in nature. Congress has frequently directed one of these bodies to make a special investigation. In many instances statutes expressly provide that in their annual reports to Congress these bodies shall or may make recommendations as to new legislation.

The making of substantive rules, regulations, and requirements is an important work of the regulatory authorities. This power, as a rule, is bestowed by specific grants in respect to concrete economic circumstances. The regulatory agencies are also given wide power to issue procedural rules which supplement and add to statutory requirements.[5]

The administrative functions of the regulatory agencies are naturally such as are necessary to make the work of regulation effective. They generally include inspection, examination, keeping accounts and records, preparing statistics, gathering evidence, hearing complaints, and the like.[6]

A very important function of the regulatory authorities is that of administrative adjudication. The agencies are sometimes required to follow a quasi-judicial process even when issuing orders

---

mission, and invested it with authority to hear and determine those questions." (Rep. Gordon, 56 Cong. Rec. 2543.) "If I understand the situation at all the Interstate Commerce Commission is a creation of the Congress of the United States. . . . I understand further that the matter of judging as to the reasonableness of rates is not an executive function . . . the matter of making rates is a legislative function, and for very proper reasons it has been delegated to the Interstate Commerce Commission, and it is certainly an erroneous statement to say that the Commission is a creature of the President." (Rep. Black, the same, 2709.)

[5] See F. F. Blachly, *Working Papers on Administrative Adjudication;* John H. Wigmore, "Federal Administrative Agencies: How to Locate Their Rules of Practice and Rulings," 25 *American Bar Association Journal* 25ff.; Theodore W. Graske, *Federal Reference Manual,* 1939.

[6] See Blachly, cited above.

that are legislative in nature and effect, such as rate orders. In many instances they are given a more directly judicial function, as when they issue an order in a dispute between individuals, or make cease and desist orders or reparation orders.

These authorities perform many of their legislative and judicial functions through a statutory order procedure, which will be discussed later. When the primary functions vested in these agencies affect rights of persons or property, their legislative regulatory acts as well as their judicial acts are generally made subject to control by the ordinary courts under certain conditions. Such acts of the regulatory authorities are usually enforced not by themselves, but by the courts, thus opening to the persons affected certain opportunities to seek judicial remedies.

From these facts, it appears that Congress has been developing, whether consciously or unconsciously, a regulatory system over many fields of economic life, which is made effective largely through the independent regulatory boards and commissions. Despite certain exceptions, these agencies resemble one another in respect to organization, relationships to the Congress, to the President, to the heads of departments, and to the courts. The same is true in respect to their purposes, functions, powers, forms of action, procedures, the methods by which their acts are enforced, and the methods by which their acts are controlled.

Independent regulatory authority with an administrator. The only example of the independent regulatory authority headed by an administrator is the Civil Aeronautics Authority, set up by the Civil Aeronautics Act of 1938[7] for the purpose of regulating, controlling, and promoting civil aeronautics. The Authority is an independent agency responsible only to Congress. It is charged with such regulatory and judicial functions as making rules and regulations, conducting investigations, issuing certificates of convenience and necessity, determining upon applications, granting permits, making orders, and the like. It is composed of five members appointed by the President, not more than three of whom can be selected from any one political party. It is evident that Congress intended that the five members constituting the Authority itself should exercise

[7] 52 Stat. L. 973.

the functions of administrative legislation and administrative adjudication.

Within the Authority is an Administrator, who is made responsible for carrying out the so-called "executive" functions of the Authority and for furthering its general policies. Although the members of the Authority are removable by the President only upon cause, the Administrator is removable at the will of the President. In other words, here is an attempt to establish a definite separation between (1) the functions of administrative legislation and adjudication, which are given to the Authority; and (2) the executive function and the function of policy, which are given to an Administrator immediately responsible to the President.

Independent of both the Authority and the Administrator is a Safety Board of three members appointed by the President, whose duty it is to make rules and regulations governing notification and report of accidents involving aircraft, to investigate such accidents, to make recommendations as to ways of preventing accidents, to make reports and general recommendations, and to assist the Authority in eliminating accidents.

Quasi-independent division of a department, with an administrator and committees. The Fair Labor Standards Act of 1938,[8] which establishes a quasi-independent agency within a government department, departs even farther from the earlier pattern than does the Civil Aeronautics Act. The Fair Labor Standards Act is not administered by a board or commission, but by a Wage and Hour Division in the Department of Labor. At the head of this Division is an Administrator appointed by the President, with no limitations upon the President's power of removal. The Administrator, in establishing wages, etc., for a particular industry, is assisted by an industry committee appointed by himself. This committee investigates questions as to minimum wage rates or other relevant problems. It makes recommendations as to classifications, which it files with the Administrator. Upon the filing of such report the Administrator, after due notice and opportunity to be heard, issues an order which approves and carries into effect the recommendations, if he finds them in accordance with the law and de-

[8] 52 Stat. L. 1060.

signed to effect its objects. The orders of the Administrator may be reviewed, upon complaint, by the appropriate circuit court of appeals or by the United States Court of Appeals for the District of Columbia. Under this system of organization, it is clear that the determination of administrative policies and the exercise of administrative powers, as well as powers of a legislative and judicial nature, are lodged in the Administrator and ultimately in the President.

Ex officio commissions. The outstanding example of ex officio commissions is the Commodity Exchange Commission. This body is composed of the Secretary of Agriculture, the Secretary of Commerce, and the Attorney General. Its functions are relatively simple. It issues orders fixing limits to the amount of trading under contracts of sale of commodities for future delivery; cease and desist orders to end violations of rules, regulations, or orders regarding contract markets; and orders excluding or debarring an association or corporation from trading in a contract market. Its functions are therefore carried out by means of administrative legislation or administrative adjudication. The wholly administrative functions connected with commodity exchange regulation are under the control of the Secretary of Agriculture. Other examples of ex officio commissions are the Foreign Trade Zones Board and the National Munitions Control Board.

Independent authorities of a non-regulatory type. Certain administrative agencies make decisions affecting the rights or interests of individuals, but do not regulate any economic field or activity. Among such agencies are: the General Accounting Office, the Civil Service Commission, the United States Employees' Compensation Commission, the Veterans' Administration, the Federal Security Agency, the Railroad Retirement Board, and the National Mediation Board.

These authorities carry on such functions as granting benefits, assisting the President and Congress in the determination of policy, assisting in the administration of the personnel system of the federal government, performing offices of mediation, and so on. They make their determinations by decision rather than by order. This means that they do not need a procedure of judicial type. Their decisions generally are self-enforcing or are enforced by administrative means. As a rule, there is no judicial control over such authorities so long as they remain within their jurisdiction and do not abuse their powers. The legal principle applying to the agencies which makes grants and gratuities is that no rights are involved and therefore no suit to protect rights can be brought.

Two agencies, which are not subject to this principle, should be noted. The deputies acting under those provisions of the Employees' Compensation Commission Act which apply to private employment in the District of Columbia and to longshoremen and harbor workers do not make grants, but settle disputes between employers and employees involving questions of right. Hence their decisions are appealable. Again, by statute the final decisions of the Social Security Board in respect to old age benefits are made reviewable in a civil action brought in the district courts.[9]

To return to the general rule: The courts are not given by statute, nor have they generally assumed, jurisdiction over civil service cases. The official doctrine is that a public office is not a property right giving rise to a case or controversy over which the courts might take jurisdiction;[10] that since civil service rules and regulations do not have the force of law, they cannot be enforced in equity;[11] and that the President has a general right to dismiss officers under the Constitution.[12]

Appeals do not lie from the decisions of the General Accounting Office. It is possible, however, for a person injured to make some collateral attack, as by bringing a suit in the Court of Claims, or applying to a court for an injunction.

Government corporations, enterprises, etc. The federal government has established numerous corporations, administrations, boards, authorities, and so on, which either directly carry on public enterprises, or act as credit-granting agencies.

Among those which carry on public enterprises are: the Tennessee Valley Authority, the Inland Waterways Corporation, the Panama Railroad Company. Such enterprises have no regulatory power as such. They carry out their operations as do private business enter-

---

[9] 42 U.S.C. 405 (g).
[10] *White* v. *Berry*, 171 U.S. 366.
[11] *Flemming* v. *Stahl*, 83 Fed. 940; *O'Neil* v. *United States*, 56 Ct. Cls. 89.
[12] See Oliver P. Field, *Civil Service Law*, pp. 179-81.

prises, and make ordinary business decisions. They enforce their decisions, etc., as do private business enterprises. Judicial forms of procedure are not necessary for the making of their determinations, which are based upon business judgment. The rights which individuals have as against these agencies are largely contractual in nature, and are enforced accordingly. When such authorities make rules and regulations, these are in the nature of the rules governing a business enterprise.

Among the long list of credit-granting agencies[13] are: the Farm Credit Administration, with several types of agencies subordinate to it; the Federal Home Loan Bank Board; and the Reconstruction Finance Corporation. These agencies, likewise, carry out their functions much as they would if they were private enterprises. Although they make rules and regulations, these are not comparable with the acts of agencies whose functions are regulatory,[14] being more like the rules of any business undertaking.

These authorities take most of their actions that affect individuals through contracts, mortgages, leases, etc. They make ordinary business decisions which are not subject to judicial review and which are enforced much as are other business transactions.

II. AUTHORITIES WHICH ACT AS CONTROLLING AGENTS

Certain administrative agents and agencies stand toward various acts of their own subordinates or of other agencies in the relationship of controlling authorities. The purposes of administrative control are: to promote efficiency in the conduct of public business; to unify the action of the various agents engaged in the administrative process; to provide an administrative method of hearing appeals from the lower administrative agents or agencies; to provide a method of advising the administrative authority which has formal responsibility for decisions; to provide for a final decision, so that

[13] For the credit-granting agencies of the federal government see 75 Cong. 1 sess., *Investigation of Executive Agencies of the Government*, Preliminary Report of the Select Committee to Investigate the Executive Agencies of the Government, S. Rept. 1275, pp. 175-87.

[14] It is true that, through rules and regulations as to lending, they may indirectly control individual action to a considerable extent. Thus, rules and regulations setting forth requirements regarding location, type of construction, connection with water, gas, and electric facilities, types of plumbing, heating, etc., as conditions precedent to securing a loan, may affect the building of homes quite as much as do the ordinary regulations made under the police power.

those contesting administrative action may know that there is no further redress except (in certain cases) through the courts; and to establish a proper basis for judicial review.

Administrative control, which is regularly exercised through the administrative appeal, is highly desirable for several reasons. It removes the case from one who may be charged with the administration of meticulous detail or with acting under specific instructions, to an authority with a wider grasp of the situation, broader viewpoints, and more general responsibilities. By so doing it takes the controversy from an agent who might possibly view it in a rather personal way, to one who can handle it impersonally. It gives to the individual who believes himself aggrieved both a new hearing and a new decision. All this can be done at very slight cost, thus eliminating the necessity for expensive litigation.

In some instances, there is the possibility of what may be called an advisory appeal, or an appeal to an authority who advises the one finally responsible for making the decision. This enables the individual to present his case to an authority (1) which has more time than the busy administrator; (2) which may have a much higher degree of technical competence; and (3) which is likely to possess more exact and better procedures for establishing the facts.

In dealing with a governmental authority, it is important to know definitely when the action of such authority becomes final. This is especially significant if some method of appealing from or controlling such action is contemplated. Since it is a general rule that the courts will not review an administrative case until there has been an exhaustion of administrative remedies, it is necessary for the individual to know just what action is the final and conclusive action of the authority concerned. When final administrative action has been duly taken by the one ultimately responsible for it, such action, if justiciable, may be made the basis for an appeal.

Administrative controlling authorities are of several types. The most important[15] are: (1) sub-appellate authorities in government departments; (2) advisory appellate authorities; (3) heads of departments; (4) administrative appellate agencies in government

[15] A description of most of these authorities and their work is found in Blachly, *Working Papers on Administrative Adjudication.*

authorities; (5) independent administrative tribunals and legislative courts.

Sub-appellate authorities within government departments. If a department is so organized that specific divisions, sections, etc., are largely responsible for particular activities, an appeal from the decision of inferior officers is taken in many instances to the head of the division or bureau instead of to the head of the department. If the case is settled satisfactorily by the division head or bureau chief, it may end there. If it is not, further appeal may lie to the head of the department.

Advisory appellate authorities. In some instances the head of a department or other regulatory authority must decide a multitude of disputes which he has no time to consider in detail or for the understanding of which he may lack technical competence. He realizes that his decision will be final, with no possibility of judicial appeal; and this fact may lead him to establish an agency of some kind which will help him to decide fairly. In view of such considerations, a number of advisory appellate authorities have been set up, largely by rules or regulations. Thus, there are fifteen or more agencies which assist in the adjustment of personnel disputes in various government authorities,[16] such as the Board of Appeals and Review in the State Department, the Examining and Retiring Boards in the Navy Department, and the Board of Review in the Tennessee Valley Authority.

These agencies have no final power to make decisions, but merely gather information, hold hearings, prepare reports, and make recommendations to the responsible authority. The latter makes the final decision. As a rule the procedures of such agencies are simple. Almost of necessity their recommendations are generally followed by the authority who is finally responsible.

Other more general advisory appellate authorities include the Board of Review in the Immigration and Naturalization Service, the Board of Appeals in the Interior Department, and the Public Contracts Board in the Department of Labor.

Heads of departments. Heads of departments often act as appellate authorities from the acts of those immediately under them. This is necessary when statutes bestow upon department heads the

[16] See the same for a list of these.

final responsibility for decisions made in the first instance by those under them. It is not necessary when the subordinate agencies are in a quasi-independent position, and their decisions and orders are made by statute directly reviewable by the courts. In such instances the head of the department is rarely given power of review. It appears, for instance, that the Secretary of the Treasury has no control over the orders of the Federal Alcohol Administrator and that the Secretary of Labor does not control the orders of the Administrator in the Wage and Hour Division.

Administrative appellate agencies in government authorities. Administrative appellate agencies in government authorities have grown up largely during the past fifteen or twenty years. Such agencies are not merely advisory, but may pass independently upon appeals from administrative decisions already made. In some instances their decision is not subject to further review. Such is the case, for instance, with the Board of Tea Appeals in the Department of Agriculture, which hears appeals from tea examiners; and with the Board of Appeals in the Veterans' Administration, which passes finally and conclusively upon veterans' claims.

Similar appellate agencies in government departments and other authorities include the Processing Tax Board of Review in the Treasury; the Board of Appeals in the Patent Office; and the Insurance Claims Council in the Veterans' Administration. These authorities hear appeals from administrative action, but their decisions are subject to review by the courts.

A somewhat different type of review authority exists in certain government departments. Such agencies review the decisions of lower authorities not in an advisory way but in a final way, subject however (theoretically at least) to further review by the head of the department, who is the person made responsible by law. In practice the appellate decisions are nearly always final from the administrative viewpoint, since the head of the department is largely guided by them. Review authorities of this kind have been established particularly in the Department of Agriculture in connection with the standardization, classification, and grading of agricultural products. They include various committees, boards, appeal inspectors, and so on.

The type of appeal handled by these authorities differs from any ordinary appeal. Review is not made upon questions of law. The reviewing authorities are not attempting to exercise judicial control over the actions of lower agents or agencies. They are merely making a scientific re-examination in order to reach a final conclusion. Their function is in no sense judicial, but is purely administrative.[17]

The appellate authorities in the government departments have a few common characteristics, but differ appreciably in respect to other significant features. The characteristics in which they resemble one another are:

1. They are all integral parts of some government unit, a feature which distinguishes them from the special independent tribunals or the legislative courts, which stand outside the active administrative organization.

2. As a rule their members are also members of the respective administrative bodies within which they are organized. The members seldom have either a fixed term of office or a permanent tenure depending upon good behavior, but are generally subject to administrative appointment and dismissal.

3. The members of such authorities are not called judges, but have various appellations.

4. It is not necessary that those who constitute such authorities be lawyers. Although the possession of "competent legal knowledge" is required of the members of the Board of Appeals in the Patent Office, and although some of the members of the Board of Appeals in the Veterans' Administration must be lawyers, appropriate technical knowledge is often considered of more value than legal knowledge.

5. Despite their lack of formal judicial status, the members of such authorities, except for the grading and classification agencies in the Department of Agriculture, do work that is judicial in nature. They do not merely give opinions or advice, or make reports, but actually decide conflicts in respect to administrative acts that have already taken place.

6. The appeal authorities neither exercise the rule-making power

[17] The same, pp. 13ff.

nor, as a body, perform administrative work. It is true, however, that in many instances individual members, when not sitting in a judicial capacity, may carry on administrative functions. For example, the Board of Appeals in the Patent Office is composed of the Commissioner of Patents, the Assistant Commissioners, and the examiners in chief, all of whom perform administrative duties when not sitting with the Board.

Independent administrative tribunals and legislative courts. Independent administrative tribunals are an important feature of the federal administrative system. The number of disputes arising between the government and the individual in connection with the administration of customs, taxation, patents, and contracts is so great, and of such a technical nature, that special authorities have been set up to hear and decide them. These authorities are organized either as administrative tribunals or as legislative courts. No matter how organized, they have certain common features:

1. They are established by statute rather than by rule or regulation.

2. They are independent of the administrative authorities.

3. All their members are appointed by the President.

4. In all except the Board of Tax Appeals the members are called judges.

5. They neither exercise sublegislative powers nor perform the ordinary administrative functions. They merely settle, in first, second, or third instance, as the case may be, disputes that arise regarding the acts or decisions of administrative authorities.

6. They do not decide controversies resulting from the relationship of private individuals to one another,[18] but solely cases in which some act of public administration is involved. In the great majority of instances the government is a party to these suits. Their procedure is much like that of ordinary courts.

7. There is nearly always an appeal from their decisions to the ordinary courts.

These independent administrative appellate authorities are at present divided into two classes: (1) an "executive or administrative

[18] There are a few exceptions to this rule. For example, the authorities which settle disputes as to patents may decide infringement cases to which only private individuals are parties.

board," the Board of Tax Appeals; and (2) the legislative courts, which include the United States Customs Court, the Court of Customs and Patent Appeals, and the Court of Claims.[19] In addition to these classes, there is the special case of the "bifurcated" Court of Appeals of the District of Columbia, which acts in certain instances as an administrative tribunal.

According to judicial theory there are several distinctions between legislative courts and constitutional courts. In the first place, it has been held that legislative courts are created by Congress by virtue of the specific grants of legislative power conferred in Article I, Section 8, and Article IV, Section 3, of the Constitution, instead of Article III of the Constitution.[20] In the second place, they are instruments for carrying out the legislative power of Congress.

Again, nonjudicial, quasi-legislative, and administrative powers may be imposed on legislative courts, whereas constitutional courts can exercise only judicial power. Thus, a legislative court such as the Court of Customs and Patent Appeals can be given authority to review the determinations of the Patent Office[21] and the Tariff Commission.[22] Such a court may be required to submit to the Secretary of the Treasury recommendations for the payment of claims due against the United States.[23] A legislative court may be authorized to render advisory opinions for the heads of departments.[24]

Finally, the legislative courts have a special type of jurisdiction. Matters which are susceptible to either legislative or executive determination are matters in respect to which there is no constitutional right to a judicial remedy. Such matters cannot, therefore, be included in the jurisdiction of a constitutional court. They can, however, be assigned to a legislative court.[25]

[19] For a brief description of these authorities see F. F. Blachly and M. E. Oatman, *Administrative Legislation and Adjudication* (1934), pp. 122-30.

[20] See *American Ins. Co.* v. *Canter*, 1 Pet. 511.

[21] *United States* v. *Duell*, 172 U.S. 576; *Postum Cereal Co.* v. *California Fig Nut Co.*, 272 U.S. 693.

[22] *Ex parte Bakelite Corp.*, 279 U.S. 438, 449-60.

[23] *Gordon* v. *United States*, 2 Wall. 561; *In re Sanborn*, 148 U.S. 222.

[24] *In re Sanborn*, 148 U.S. 222.

[25] See Blachly and Oatman, *Administrative Legislation and Adjudication*, p. 128; *Williams* v. *United States*, 289 U.S. 553; Wilbur G. Katz, "Federal Legislative Courts," 43 *Harvard Law Review* 884, and "The Distinction between Legislative and Constitutional Courts," 43 *Yale Law Journal* 316ff.

CHAPTER IV

THE FORMS OF ADMINISTRATIVE ACTION

Administrative action which affects the rights of individuals, or which gives rise to new rights, obligations, or duties, may be taken by the federal government by means of several definite forms. Each of these forms of action has its own special field of application, legal significance and effects, processes and procedures, methods of enforcement, and types of control. A fairly detailed knowledge of the principal forms of administrative action is essential to an understanding of the federal administrative process. The most significant forms are: (1) rules and regulations; (2) requirements; (3) statutory administrative orders; (4) administrative decisions; (5) statutory executive and administrative proclamations; (6) executive orders; (7) administrative stipulations; (8) consent decrees; (9) statutory administrative awards.

I. RULES AND REGULATIONS

Rules and regulations are the basic method of making the adjustments necessary for putting general statutory provisions into effective operation. They so implement and supplement the law as to make it directly applicable to the citizen. They may both establish the procedure by means of which the administration and the citizen deal with each other, and supply details of substantive law.[1] For example, the statutory law provides that traveling expenses may be deducted from gross income in figuring income tax payments. The rules and regulations of the Treasury Department lay down in great

[1] "The administration today is thus a great deal more than a mere machine for the application of law. To an increasing extent it has become a creator of law; in this sense and within the limits of their respective competences, the administrative departments and agencies resemble a group of special legislative bodies. The administration is the authority which, in an increasing number of instances, intervenes between the legislature and the ordinary citizen. The general rules and principles set forth in statutes must often be filled in, extended, and made more definite, before they can be applied in individual cases. In other words, the administration is called upon to render the law tangible to the citizen. In so doing it must exercise power which partakes of the nature of legislative power." F. F. Blachly and M. E. Oatman, *Administrative Legislation and Adjudication* (1934), pp. 4, 5.

detail what shall be considered as traveling expenses, and also provide for the way in which these items shall be listed in a tax return statement.[2] The statutes give to the Civil Aeronautics Authority the right to make rules and regulations as to air safety. This agency has adopted elaborate rules as to the strength requirements of landing gear, the kind and location of lights on airships, the qualifications of pilots, and so on.[3]

The extent of the power to issue rules and regulations. Nearly every regulatory authority is granted the power to issue rules and regulations. It is customary to include in the statutes which authorize an authority to act in a given matter, a special grant of such power. For example, the Secretary of Agriculture in respect to foreign commerce alone makes rules and regulations under more than a score of specific statutory authorizations. Such authorizations have been granted him in respect to the importation of honey bees, the quarantining of imported animals, the slaughter of such animals, the exportation of livestock and poultry, the quality and color of imported seeds, and various other matters.

When the power to make rules and regulations is granted by statute, the terms may be general or particular. Thus, the law may bestow power to "make rules and regulations under this Act," or it may restrict the power to objects and purposes named or described.

The nature of rules and regulations. Rules and regulations are essentially legislative in nature. They deal with matters laid down by statute, and in general they supply necessary details. They do what Congress can do and sometimes does. Thus, in the Federal Seed Act[4] of 1939, Congress defines and names "agricultural seeds" in some detail (though authorizing the Secretary of Agriculture to add to or to take from the list under certain conditions), but leaves to the Secretary of Agriculture, acting either alone or jointly with the Secretary of the Treasury, the power to define "weed seeds" in respect to importations, by means of rules and regulations.

The scope of the authorization to make rules and regulations naturally depends primarily upon other provisions of the statute

[2] See Bureau of Internal Revenue, *Regulations 101, Income Tax, Revenue Act of 1938,* for many examples of regulations which implement the law.
[3] See, for example, *Civil Air Regulations of the Civil Aeronautics Authority.*
[4] 7 U.S.C. 118-118z-6.

concerned, although various matters, to be considered subsequently, may affect it. If, for example, a statute provides in broad terms that a person must receive an official certificate as to qualifications and rating before he may become a mechanic engaged in building or repairing airplanes, one of two things will probably be added. The statute itself may provide for certain minimum qualifications in respect to education, age, citizenship, character, skill, experience, and technical knowledge. In this case the administrative agency (presumably the Civil Aeronautics Authority) will probably be given power to issue rules and regulations laying down such further requirements as it may consider necessary. The other and more probable alternative is that the broad provision of the statute will not be further defined but will be followed by an authorization to the Authority to make "all necessary rules and regulations to the carrying out thereof."

Rules and regulations resemble statutes in that they normally have to do with future situations rather than with past actions. The considerations which enter into rule-making relate to the future, rather than to the past.[5] Rules and regulations, moreover, are general in nature rather than specific. They govern classes of personal or property rights and situations, rather than specific acts or circumstances. Their legislative nature is thus obvious.

Procedure for making rules and regulations. Except in rare instances (to be discussed later) the statutes do not lay down requirements as to the procedure to be employed in making rules and regulations. The authority charged with the function of rule-making can generally exercise that function at its discretion. The types of procedure ordinarily employed by administrative agencies have been classed as investigational, consultative, auditive, and so-called adversary.[6]

Investigational procedure is much like an ordinary legislative investigation. It often takes the form of a hearing, but other methods of obtaining information are also employed. The purpose of this

[5] Ralph F. Fuchs, "Procedure in Administrative Rule Making," 52 *Harvard Law Review* 261.

[6] The same, p. 273; James Hart, "The Exercise of Rule-making Power," *President's Committee on Administrative Management, Report with Special Studies,* pp. 309ff.

procedure is to inform the authority which contemplates issuing rules and regulations. Investigation may be made at the request of private individuals as well as upon the initiative of the administrative authority. It may take the form of researches and inquiries made by expert agents of the authority. There may be a combination of these methods with informal hearings.

Consultative procedure also resembles a legislative inquiry. Here the issuing authority may call in experts, or those affected may request to be heard on various proposals. In many cases special interest groups are well organized and are likely to make proposals or requests concerning rules and regulations. Occasionally a draft of contemplated regulations is submitted to such a group for suggestions or objections.

No requirements are laid down by statute as to the ways in which consultation must take place, or as to the effect of suggestions or objections. The issuing authority can exercise its own discretion as to whether or not it will ask for or accept suggestions or objections; as to the form in which these, if allowed, must be presented; and as to its own acts in consequence of such consultation. Since those close to the subject matter of the regulations are usually heard or present evidence or documents, the regulatory authority may give the evidence of such persons great weight in the final formulation of the regulation. For instance, it is almost unthinkable that the Civil Aeronautics Authority would not consult with manufacturers as to the quality and structure of airship equipment before promulgating regulations on this subject.

Auditive procedure is closely related to the other types. In essence, it consists of informal hearings, such as may be held, but are not necessarily held, in connection with investigations and consultations. These informal hearings "are valuable to the extent that notice of them can be brought home to affected parties, that they are accessible to these parties, and that the questions involved are susceptible to intelligent discussion by those who do appear."[7]

So-called adversary procedure is a formal hearing at which persons appear and produce evidence. Full records are kept of the proceedings. The authority issuing the rules and regulations may

[7] Fuchs, "Administrative Rule Making," 52 *Harvard Law Review* 276.

be required by law to base its conclusions of fact upon the evidence received and to set them forth as findings.

Such procedure is legislative in nature, but judicial in form. This is shown by the fact that administrative discretion is reduced to a minimum and that failure to follow the evidence in the making of a rule or regulation may cause the same to be declared invalid if tested in the courts. In general, this type of procedure is laid down by statute, and the issuing authority must follow the statutory provisions. Appeals from the final actions of the authority lie to the courts.

The regulatory authority itself may establish a sort of adversary procedure in certain instances, when it has before it persons who favor a proposed regulation, and persons who oppose it. In this situation, and in the absence of statutory provisions such as those mentioned above, it is unnecessary for the issuing authority to conform to a strict due process of law procedure or to base its rules and regulations upon the evidence presented. This is a correct situation; whereas the statutory requirements are based upon a failure to realize that the making of rules and regulations is a legislative act and is therefore unsuitable for judicial control.

Within the past few years several statutes have provided for something that superficially resembles adversary procedure in the making of rules and regulations. The relevant provisions of a few of these laws will be discussed at this point.

The Bituminous Coal Act of 1937[8] provides: "No order which is subject to judicial review under Section 6, and no rule or regulation which has the force and effect of law, shall be made or prescribed by the Commission, unless it has given reasonable public notice of a hearing, and unless it has afforded to interested parties an opportunity to be heard; and unless it has made findings of fact." The statute does not, however, require the Commission to base its rules and regulations upon the said findings of fact.

The Federal Food, Drug, and Cosmetic Act[9] of 1938 provides:

The Secretary shall . . . hold a public hearing upon a proposal to issue, amend, or repeal any regulation contemplated [under certain sections

[8] 50 Stat. L. 72; 15 U.S.C. 829.
[9] 52 Stat. L. 1040, 1055.

of the law]. The Secretary shall give appropriate notice of the hearing, and the notice shall set forth the proposal in general terms and specify the time and place for a public hearing. . . . At the hearing any interested person may be heard in person or by his representative. As soon as practicable after completion of the hearing, the Secretary shall by order make public his action in issuing, amending, or repealing the regulation or determining not to take such action. The Secretary shall base his order only on substantial evidence of record at the hearing and shall set forth as part of the order detailed findings of fact on which the order is based. . . .

In case of actual controversy as to the validity of any order . . . any person who will be adversely affected by such order if placed in effect may at any time prior to the ninetieth day after such order is issued file a petition with the Circuit Court of Appeals of the United States for the circuit wherein such person resides or has his principal place of business for a judicial review of such order. . . .

The procedure here outlined is essentially the same as for an appeal against a true administrative order, rather than a rule or regulation.

In 1936 the laws governing the inspection of steam vessels were amended by the addition of some paragraphs[10] concerning vessels carrying inflammable liquid cargo. A Board of Supervising Inspectors was given the power to adopt rules and regulations, subject to the approval of the Secretary of Commerce. "Before any rules and regulations, or any alteration, amendment, or repeal thereof, are approved by the Secretary of Commerce under the provisions of this section, except in an emergency, the said Secretary shall publish such rules and regulations and hold hearings with respect thereto on such notice as he deems advisable under the circumstances."[11]

The Federal Seed Act of 1939[12] provides:

Prior to the promulgation of any rule or regulation under this Act due notice shall be given by publication in the Federal Register of intention to promulgate and the time and place of a public hearing to be held with reference thereto, and no rule or regulation may be promulgated until after such hearing. Any rule or regulation shall become effective on the date fixed in the promulgation, which date

[10] 46 U.S.C. 39(a).
[11] 46 U.S.C. 391 a(3).
[12] 7 U.S.C. 118 n(c).

shall not be less than thirty days after publication in the Federal Register, and may be amended or revoked in the manner provided for its promulgation.

Nothing is said in the statute as to review over such rules and regulations.

Several other actions which, although not designated by law as rules and regulations, fall by nature within this general category, have been placed by statute in the procedural framework of a regulatory order. Among such acts are the orders with marketing agreements under the Agricultural Adjustment Act,[13] the wage orders applying to entire industries under the Fair Labor Standards Act,[14] and the orders fixing limits on the amount of trading under contracts of sale of certain commodities for future delivery under the Commodity Exchange Act.[15]

Under the Agricultural Adjustment Act[16] the Secretary of Agriculture is authorized to enter into marketing agreements with processors, producers, associations of producers, and others engaged in the handling of certain agricultural commodities or products thereof, in so far as such handling is in the current of interstate or foreign commerce, and to issue orders the function of which is to regulate handlers. The statute provides:

Whenever the Secretary of Agriculture has reason to believe that the issuance of an order will tend to effectuate the declared policy of this [title] . . . he shall give due notice of and an opportunity for a hearing upon a proposed order. After such notice and opportunity for hearing, the Secretary of Agriculture shall issue an order if he finds, and sets forth in such order, upon the evidence introduced at such hearing (in addition to such other findings as may be specifically required by this section) that the issuance of such order and all of the terms and conditions thereof will tend to effectuate the declared policy of this [title] with respect to such commodity.

Although such an order has the outward appearance of a regulatory order, it is in reality a rule or regulation. The hearing is held for the purpose of formulating a rule or standard of general applicability. The action taken is not directed toward particular in-

---

[13] 7 U.S.C. 608 b-c.
[14] 29 U.S.C. 208, 210(a).
[15] 7 U.S.C. 6a.
[16] 7 U.S.C. 608 c(3) (4).

dividuals, but has the wide-reaching effect of a norm of law. The procedure is not truly judicial nor truly adversary in nature, although in its outward aspects it may appear to be so. All these circumstances tend to show that the hearing is essentially legislative, and that the so-called order is of the nature of a regulation.[17]

Under the Fair Labor Standards Act[18] an industry committee, after making investigations and possibly hearing witnesses and taking testimony, recommends to the Administrator of the Wage and Hour Division the highest feasible minimum wage rates for the industry, and reasonable classifications within the industry. Upon the filing of a report by the committee, the Administrator holds a hearing. Upon the basis of this hearing and other factors required by law (mentioned below), the Administrator approves the recommendations by order or disapproves them.

Although the action taken under this statute by the Administrator is called an order, it is manifestly a rule and regulation. It involves the same subject matter covered by the statute and supplements and implements the law. Its action is general rather than particular, affecting all who fall within certain classes specified by law.

The procedures required by the statute are not judicial in nature. This is true of the procedure of the industry committee, which acts as the original policy-determining authority. According to the regulations applicable to the functioning of the committee, it is to consider "such data as is submitted to it by the Administrator and interested persons."[19] This means that it generally holds hearings. The Administrator does not appear as an adverse party. The interested persons are not in the position of formal adversaries, although differences of views and desires will certainly appear.

Much the same things may be said as to hearings before the Administrator. The purpose of these hearings is primarily to consider any objections that may be made, or any support that may be given, to the report of the industry committee. The most nearly judicial feature of this proceeding is the fact that the order approv-

[17] See Ashley Sellers, "Administrative Procedure and Practice in the Department of Agriculture under the Agricultural Marketing Agreement Act of 1937," issued by Department of Agriculture, 1939, mimeographed.
[18] 29 U.S.C. 201-19.
[19] *Regulations Applicable to Industry Committees Pursuant to Section 5 of the Fair Labor Standards Act,* 3 Fed. Reg. 2744.

ing and carrying into effect the recommendations of the committee is to be issued only if the Administrator is convinced that these have been made in accordance with law and have been based upon the evidence received. This feature does not change the legislative character of the so-called order.

There is much confusion here, due partly to the fact that an administrative action which should be classified as a regulation is classified as an order, and partly to the fact that this legislative action is placed under many of the limitations of a judicial procedure. This confusion is made worse by the fact that those who develop policy are not able to make it effective, whereas the Administrator, who issues the order, is not responsible for its content. It is true that, from the standpoint of organization, policy lies in his hands in the final analysis, since he can refuse to approve the work of an industry committee, and even appoint a different industry committee. It is evident that these powers may be used in such a way that the policy of the Administrator will prevail, although that policy is attributed to an industry committee.

The entire process gives a misleading appearance of quasi-judicial action followed by administrative judicial review. Furthermore, it is so complex as to contain evident contradictions. The Administrator, when he holds a hearing on the recommendations of the industry committee, is required by statute[20] to base his decision to approve these by order (or to disapprove them) upon four separate considerations: (1) whether the recommendations are made in accordance with law; (2) whether they are supported by the evidence adduced at the hearing; (3) competitive conditions as affected by transportation, living, and production costs; the wages established for work of like or comparable character by collective labor agreements negotiated between employers and employees by representatives of their own choosing; the wages paid for work of like or comparable character by employers who voluntarily maintain minimum wage standards in the industry concerned; and other relevant factors; (4) whether the recommendations will carry out the purpose of the law.

[20] 29 U.S.C. 208.

When court review of the order is obtained, however, the findings of fact made by the Administrator shall be conclusive, according to the statute, "when supported by substantial evidence." The basic facts for the third group of considerations listed above may not have appeared as evidence at the hearing, but only as supporting statements to the recommendations of the industry committee; and in any case, the Administrator's evaluation of them, even when made a part of the record, is not the kind of evidence which courts recognize as a basis for findings of fact.

Finally, there seems to be no good reason why recommendations should be made before a formal hearing is held, and why even after the hearings these recommendations cannot be modified, but must be accepted or rejected as a whole.

The Commodity Exchange Act was passed for the purpose of diminishing, eliminating, or preventing excessive speculation in commodities under contract for sale for future delivery. Under this law the Commodity Exchange Commission may, by order, fix limits to the amount of "trading in futures" of various commodities which may be done by any person. Different trading limits may be fixed for different commodities, or for buying or selling operations. These acts of regulation are embodied in so-called orders. Although the orders are issued after notice and hearing, no particular procedure is laid down, and no judicial review is provided.

All the statutes just mentioned confuse legislative action with judicial action. Hence they provide for procedures and at times for controls that, although suitable for justiciable matters, are wholly inappropriate to the legislative activity of making general rules and regulations.

The legal effect of rules and regulations. Rules and regulations that are properly made, in accordance with any legally prescribed procedure and within the limits set by statute, have the force and effect of the law itself. They are often made enforceable by the courts as a part of the law. In many instances statutes provide penalties for violations of rules and regulations. Such penalties include revocation of rights, privileges, or licenses; fines and forfeitures; and even imprisonment.

II. REQUIREMENTS

A requirement is very close in nature to a rule or regulation, except that it is usually more specific and has the general connotations of a command. It is used chiefly in respect to physical objects, as when there is a requirement that certain machines be equipped with safety appliances. Although many requirements might theoretically be made under the police power, which could be exercised without the elaborate procedures and controls applied when requirements are made by administrative agencies, there are reasons why the latter arrangement is preferable. A requirement may involve heavy expenditure and much loss of time. In order to protect the individual against serious and wanton invasions of his rights, the statutes which authorize an administrative agency to make requirements often provide for notice, hearing, and judicial review. Examples are the safety requirements of the Interstate Commerce Commission[21] in respect to motor carriers (which are enforced by orders), and the requirements of the Federal Communications Commission as to radio on shipboard.[22]

III. STATUTORY ADMINISTRATIVE ORDERS

The statutory order is almost exclusively a development of the past half century. Together with rules and regulations, the order has become the chief type of administrative action used by the federal government for the regulation and control of business and industry. In nearly two hundred circumstances under which the federal government regulates and controls economic life, it takes action through the statutory order.[23] Congress specifically requires this type of action by the large regulatory boards and commissions; but various other agencies of the government also issue orders. Today about twenty-five[24] authorities, when taking action that affects the rights of individuals, use the order method.

[21] 49 U.S.C. 304 a(1), (2), (3).

[22] 47 U.S.C. 356(3).

[23] See Supporting Statement IV, pp. 276-86.

[24] These authorities are: Administrator under the Fair Labor Standards Act of 1938; the California Debris Commission; the Civil Aeronautics Authority; the Commissioner of Internal Revenue; the Commodity Exchange Commission; the Director of the Bureau of Mines; the Federal Alcohol Administrator; the Federal Communications Commission; the Board of Governors of the Federal Reserve System; the Federal Trade Commission; the Foreign Trade Zone Boards; the

The nature of the statutory order. In a broad way the statutory administrative order is usually a command, a prescription, an injunction, a declaration, a restraint, a withholding, or a refusal.[25] The order commands the taking of action, or refuses to let action be taken; it grants or withholds, suspends or revokes, an authorization, a relief, an exemption, a claimed right, a privilege, a license, a permit, a grant, a certificate, or a registration; it determines rights and obligations; it declares the status of persons and things.

To clarify the nature of an order, it should be differentiated from other types of action, particularly the rule and regulation and the administrative decision. Although the Congress in hundreds of instances has specifically mentioned these different types of action, it has never attempted to make definitions of them. A detailed examination of the statutes, however, shows that certain characteristics have usually been attached to each type, in respect to purpose, subject matter, persons affected, the procedure of making or issuing, finality, enforcement, and controls. Despite the fact that at times the types approach and even overlap, they can generally be distinguished by these characteristics.

The rule or regulation differs from the order primarily in the fact that the purpose of the former is to establish a standard of general applicability, whereas the purpose of the latter (with exceptions which will appear presently) is to take action upon an, individual situation. The subject matter of the rule or regulation is essentially that of the statute, extended and developed; the subject matter of the order is a specific situation and the application of the statute thereto. The rule or regulation does not inquire into the past or present conduct of a particular person or organization, or into a specific situation, whereas the order usually results from an inquiry into a specific problem of this type.

Procedure. It was shown above that since the making of rules and

---

Interstate Commerce Commission; the Bituminous Coal Division; the National Labor Relations Board; the National Railroad Adjustment Board; the Postmaster General; the Railroad Retirement Board; the Secretary of Agriculture; the Secretary of Commerce; the Secretary of Labor; the Securities and Exchange Commission; the Tender Boards of the Petroleum Conservation Division; and the United States Maritime Commission.

[25] It should be noted that there are several administrative actions called "orders" by the statutes which do not conform to these criteria.

regulations is a legislative act, no special procedure is constitutionally required. Hearings are seldom provided for by statute, though
they are often provided for by the administrative authority. In any
case they have the nature of discussions, presentations of evidence,
and arguments, with the purpose of assisting legislative action. In respect to the order, hearings are usually provided for by statute and
are often formal like judicial hearings, with opposing parties represented by counsel and a complete record. When making rules
and regulations the administrative authority does not act as a
judge but as a legislator. In the order procedure, particularly in
the judicial order procedure, the regulatory authority often sits as
a judge, hearing and passing upon evidence. In procedure for issuing rules and regulations, the authority hearing evidence is seldom
required to make a decision upon the evidence presented; but the
contrary is true, as a rule, in order procedure. For making rules
and regulations no special findings of fact are usually required,[26]
whereas findings of fact are the normal basis of an order. When a
hearing is provided for by statute and a finding of facts is required
in connection with rule-making, the conclusion should not be drawn
that the action is not legislative. Such provisions cannot change the
legislative act of rule-making into a judicial inquiry.[27] The parties
in an order procedure are usually contending parties asserting
specific rights. There are, strictly speaking, no parties in the procedure for making rules and regulations.

Rules and regulations do not, as the judicial order does, result
in an authoritative determination of rights or legal privileges.
Finally, rules and regulations are seldom open to direct review,
whereas the order is generally reviewable by the courts.[28]

Classification. A. For some purposes, orders may be classified
according to their legal nature.[29] By this method of classification

---

[26] "But the statute did not require special findings; doubtless because the regulation authorized was general legislation; not an administrative order in the nature
of a judgment directed against an individual concern." *Pacific States Box & Basket
Co.* v. *White,* 296 U.S. 176, 186.

[27] Fuchs, "Administrative Rule Making," 52 *Harvard Law Review* 259.

[28] Undoubtedly exceptions could be found to any of these statements. It is believed,
however, that they present a rather accurate generalized picture of the statutory
situation. See Supporting Statement IX, pp. 310-14, for further details regarding
order procedure.

[29] See *Administrative Law,* Hearings before Subcommittee No. 4 of the House
Committee on the Judiciary on H. R. 4236, H. R. 6198, and H. R. 6324, 76 Cong.

orders fall into four categories: procedural; legislative; legislative in form but judicial in effect; judicial.

1. Procedural orders are either general in nature, partaking of the nature of legislation but establishing methods of procedure to be used when cases are brought before the authority concerned; or they are specific, as when they require a given person to be present at a given time and place to testify in a given investigation, when they dismiss or postpone proceedings, when they command a corporation to appear and show cause why certain action against it should not be taken, and so on. Since they do not affect rights, the courts almost always decline to review them.

2. Legislative orders have a certain likeness to rules and regulations, in that they generally affect the public at large, or groups or classes. They implement or supplement the law according to policies laid down by Congress and within limits set by statute. The courts will act to hold the administration within its delegation of power, but not to control its action within such proper delegation. Legislative orders are a part of the law, made by administrative agencies under delegation from Congress.

3. Orders which are legislative in form but judicial in effect, such as a rate order which may deprive a railroad of property without due process of law, are issued under the terms of a legislative delegation, and are generally made reviewable by the courts. In any case, the courts will intervene to prevent the use of such orders to deprive persons of their legal rights.

4. Judicial orders are issued after notice and hearing. As a rule this procedure, as well as the authority to issue the orders, will be provided by statute. Orders of this type include injunctive and command orders, penalty orders, and so on. Because they affect rights in a direct way, such orders are always made subject to judicial review.

B. It is more generally useful to use a mixed scheme of classification, based on subject matter, legal nature, and legal effect. According to this scheme, orders may be classified as follows: legislative regulatory; procedural; administrative controlling; injunctive and

---

1 sess., pp. 169ff; F. F. Blachly, "Work Materials on Administrative Action and Procedure" (manuscript); Supporting Statement XI, pp. 318-32; Gregory Hankin, "The Fate of the Negative Order Doctrine" (manuscript).

command; reparation and analogous orders; penalty orders; orders in respect to licenses, registrations, etc.; orders *in re* declarations and designations; and negative orders. This classification will be employed and developed later in the present study.

IV. ADMINISTRATIVE DECISIONS

Hundreds of statutes provide or imply that administrative authorities shall take action in respect to particular circumstances by means of decisions. These circumstances are connected with agriculture, communications, banking, civil service, contracts, customs, foods, drugs, and cosmetics, employee compensation, the granting of credit, patents, copyrights, prints and labels, trade-marks, public lands, social security, shipping, taxation, licenses, and veterans' pensions—to name only a few examples.

There are striking differences between an order and an administrative decision. These have to do chiefly with the nature of the subject matter concerned, the authorities performing the action, the statutory set-up, the procedure, the nature of the control over such actions, and the enforcement methods used.

The order is employed, as has been seen, chiefly in the field of economic regulation. The administrative decision is used to a certain extent in the same field; thus, actions which affect banking (except those taken under the Clayton Act) are taken by decision rather than by order. A more frequent use of the administrative decision[30] is to take actions of a police nature as, for example, those which protect shipping, the public lands, navigable waters, or highways. The most important fields where the administrative decision is used are the contractual, revenue,[31] proprietary, promotional, facilitatory, and benefactory. In other words, the decision is chiefly used to perform old and historically established types of government action, or acts which do not invade guaranteed rights, rather than to accomplish the newer task of economic regulation under present-day conditions.

The administrative units which operate largely by way of the order are generally the newer regulatory agencies, whereas those which take action chiefly by means of the decision are the great

[30] Blachly, "Work Materials on Administrative Action and Procedure."
[31] The word revenue is used here to describe action involving taxation, customs, loans, and public debt. It is true that a few actions involving the public debt fall within the field of contracts.

government departments, government corporations, and so on. The following lists show the two classes of agencies. These lists do not purport to display the relationships and controls existing among the various agencies named. It is not entirely logical to name both a department and a division or other unit within that department; but the failure in logic seems necessary for the sake of presenting a true picture of the ways in which the decision and the order are employed. Since most of the agencies named use both the order and the decision under appropriate circumstances, it has been necessary in making the lists to decide which form of action is more characteristic and more important in connection with the work of each agency.

Agencies Which Act Mainly through the Order

1. Boards and Commissions (all independent agencies except as otherwise noted)
    National Labor Relations Board
    National Railroad Adjustment Board
    Railroad Retirement Board
    Federal Communications Commission
    Federal Power Commission
    Federal Trade Commission
    Interstate Commerce Commission
    Securities and Exchange Commission
    United States Tariff Commission
    United States Maritime Commission
    Civil Aeronautics Authority
    California Debris Commission, War Department
    Tender Boards, Interior Department
    Commodity Exchange Commission (ex officio)
    Foreign Trade Zones Board (ex officio)

2. Agencies under One Chief Officer
    Federal Alcohol Administration, Treasury Department
    Wage and Hour Division, Labor Department
    Bituminous Coal Division, Interior Department

Agencies Which Act Mainly through the Administrative Decision

1. Executive Departments
    State Department
    Treasury Department

War Department
Justice Department
Post Office Department
Navy Department
Interior Department
Agriculture Department
Commerce Department
Labor Department

2. Government Corporations

Commodity Credit Corporation
Federal Farm Mortgage Corporation
Federal Surplus Commodities Corporation
Federal Crop Insurance Corporation
Inland Waterways Corporation
Federal Deposit Insurance Corporation
Reconstruction Finance Corporation
Disaster Loan Corporation
Home Owners' Loan Corporation
Federal Savings and Loan Insurance Corporation
Electric Home and Farm Authority
United States Housing Authority
Tennessee Valley Authority

3. Boards and Commissions

a. Independent boards and commissions
Maritime Labor Board
National Mediation Board
National Munitions Control Board (ex officio)
Board of Tax Appeals
Civil Service Commission
Employees' Compensation Commission

b. Boards subordinate to other agencies
Board of Labor Review, Public Works Administration
Board of Veterans' Appeals
Social Security Board
Board of Grain Supervisors
Board of Patent Appeals, Patent Office
Public Contracts Board, Public Contracts Division
Board of Review of Immigration and Naturalization
Board of Tea Appeals
Processing Tax Board of Review

4. Other Agencies
   National Youth Administration
   Veterans' Administration
   Work Projects Administration
   Farm Credit Administration
   Farm Security Administration
   Rural Electrification Administration
   Puerto Rico Reconstruction Administration
   Patent Office
   Bureau of Comptroller of the Currency
   Office of Indian Affairs
   General Land Office

Another difference between the order and the decision is connected with the extent of statutory and administrative detail made applicable. In the great majority of instances the statute itself lays down the particular economic circumstances to be handled by means of the order, the processes and procedures by which the order is to be made, the methods by which it is controlled in the first and later instances, and the methods by which it is to be enforced. On the other hand, there are seldom any statutory requirements as to notice and hearing, or the so-called "due process of law" procedure, in respect to the administrative decision.

Administrative decisions generally involve a broad discretion, whereas orders, although the element of discretion is present, rest upon facts found on the basis of evidence. Because of the large degree of discretion involved in the making of decisions (owing to the subject matter with which they are concerned), there is seldom a direct appeal from an administrative decision to the courts. It has been held in many judicial opinions that a decision which lies within the discretion of the administrator and does not affect actual rights cannot give rise to a justiciable case or controversy, beyond questions of *ultra vires*, abuse of power, and the like.[32] On the other hand, since many orders affect rights, these should be subject to judicial review. The statutes generally provide for review of such orders by the courts.

---

[32] *Lloyd Sabaudo Societa Anonima per Azioni* v. *Elting*, 287 U.S. 329; *Passavant* v. *United States*, 148 U.S. 214; *Oceanic Steam Navigation Co.* v. *Stranaham*, 214 U.S. 320; *Tidal Osage Oil Co.* v. *West*, 58 App. D.C. 327, 30 F. (2d) 737; *Riverside Oil Co.* v. *Hitchcock*, 190 U.S. 316.

Administrative decisions are often self-executing or are enforced by administrative action. There are few instances where judicial action is necessary or possible. The great majority of orders which affect rights, on the other hand, are enforceable only by the courts.

There are certain exceptions to these broad statements. Such exceptions as a rule have to do with subject matter; the type of question involved (question of fact or question of law); whether, despite the usual finality of administrative decisions, in doubtful or border-line cases an express statutory right of review has been granted; the fairness of the administrative procedure; and the basis for the decision. These exceptions will be discussed in more detail in the chapter on control over administrative action.

V. STATUTORY EXECUTIVE AND ADMINISTRATIVE PROCLAMATIONS

Proclamations are essentially an executive form of action lodged in the President. In at least one instance, however, Congress has given this power to the head of a government department—the Secretary of Agriculture.

It is not possible to consider here the many executive proclamations of a general type, such as those which set the dates of public holidays. The proclamations of most interest for the purposes of this study are those in which the President states, under the terms of a law, that certain conditions which the law specifies have come into existence, and that action authorized under such conditions is thereby taken. This action generally brings into effect certain provisions of the law which are non-operative until the proclamation has been made. A proclamation of this type, though executive in source, is a part of the legislative process and is exercised under a delegation of power made by Congress.

Among proclamations of the type just mentioned are those imposing new or additional duties on goods imported from countries which discriminate against the commerce of the United States;[33] those excluding goods coming from such countries;[34] those modifying existing schedules and tariffs under trade agreements with for-

[33] 19 U.S.C. 1338(a).
[34] 19 U.S.C. 1338(b).

eign countries;[35] and those declaring that a state of war exists, made under the Neutrality Act of 1939.[36]

Other proclamations of great economic significance are those fixing the weight of the gold dollar,[37] and those prescribing an emergency period during which member banks of the Federal Reserve System shall not transact any banking business except to such extent and in accordance with such regulations, limitations, and restrictions as may be prescribed by the Secretary of the Treasury with the approval of the President.[38]

Because proclamations are normally executive in nature, they are not ordinarily subject to judicial review. When they are made under a special delegation of legislative power and are subject to conditions set by law, however, the situation is changed. It is probable that the question could be raised in a case or controversy, whether the President, in issuing a proclamation making certain statutory clauses effective, had exceeded the powers or failed to observe the conditions attached by Congress; but in general the courts have always displayed the strongest reluctance to take any action which might appear an attempt to control the exercise of executive power.

An unusual authorization concerning proclamations is found in the Agricultural Adjustment Act. This law provides that the Secretary of Agriculture, when he has reason to believe that the conditions of and the factors relating to the production, marketing, and consumption of certain commodities are such that the exercise of any one or more of the powers conferred upon him by the act would tend to effectuate the declared policy of the act, shall cause an immediate investigation to determine such facts. If he finds the existence of such facts, he shall proclaim such determination and shall exercise one or more of the powers conferred upon him.[39] It is clear that the Secretary cannot act in such a matter without a fact-finding.[40] Any strict judicial review, except as to the matter of

---

[35] 19 U.S.C. 1351, 1352.
[36] 76 Cong. 1 sess., Pub. Res. 54.
[37] 31 U.S.C. 821.
[38] 12 U.S.C. 95.
[39] 7 U.S.C. 608 (1) (b).
[40] *United States* v. *Seven Oaks Dairy Co.*, 10 F. Supp. 995.

procedure, *ultra vires*, etc., is not possible, since the terms of the act bestow upon the Secretary a wide discretion.

VI. EXECUTIVE ORDERS

Proclamations and executive orders overlap in content, and there is no hard and fast distinction between them. "Executive orders have a wide scope, ranging from the authorization of the appointment of a charwoman in a local post office (No. 6420) to prescribing rules and regulations under the Trading-with-the Enemy Act (No. 2796)."[41] Executive orders generally relate to the conduct of government business or to the organization of the executive departments. Some, however, have a much wider significance. As examples of the latter may be mentioned orders creating emergency agencies in 1933, and orders approving codes of fair competition under the National Industrial Recovery Act of the same year.

Executive orders do not usually have to be made as the result of any formal procedure or hearing. It has been held by the Supreme Court, however, that when the authority delegated to the President by Congress "depends upon determinations of fact, those determinations must be shown."[42] The court bases this requirement upon the "general principles of Constitutional government," and remarks: "We cannot regard the President as immune from the application of these Constitutional principles. When the President is invested with legislative authority as the delegate of Congress in carrying out a declared policy, he necessarily acts under the Constitutional restrictions applicable to such a delegation."[43]

Executive orders issued as a result of authority delegated to the President by Congress must fall within the scope of authority so granted. In delegating authority to the President, Congress must establish all necessary standards, norms, and rules of conduct to guide and restrict his action.[44] It appears that the President is bound by the terms of any congressional delegation, and that the courts will control his actions thereunder in respect to constitutionality of the delegation itself, excess of power, and failure to follow pre-

[41] L. F. Schmeckebier, *Government Publications and Their Use*, rev. ed. (1939), p. 322.
[42] *Panama Refining Co.* v. *Ryan*, 298 U.S. 388, 432.
[43] The same, p. 433.
[44] *Schechter* v. *United States*, 295 U.S. 495.

scribed procedure. It would seem, therefore, that the courts could control the actions of the President in respect to wrongful delegation of power by Congress, lack of jurisdiction, and lack of a fact-finding where determination depends upon such a finding.

VII. ADMINISTRATIVE STIPULATIONS

The administrative stipulation is used particularly by the Federal Trade Commission. It is in the nature of an agreement between the government and the individual. Before the service of complaint[45] by the Federal Trade Commission, it may permit the respondent to dispose of cases by stipulation. In these stipulations the respondent, after admitting the material facts, agrees to cease and desist from the unfair methods of competition involved, and further agrees that the admissions may be used against him, if thereafter the Commission has reason to believe that the respondent is violating his promise and agreement. If it so believes it issues a complaint against him.

The disposition of a case by stipulation is a privilege and not a right. It is the policy of the Commission not to accept stipulations from respondents if it has reason to believe that they have been guilty of intentional fraud or wrongdoing or of violations of the criminal sections of the Sherman Act or other statutes. Refusal to accept stipulations is also based on the probability that such respondents will not keep their agreements. The Commission reserves the right in all cases, for any reasons which it considers sufficient, to refuse to extend to the respondent the privilege of stipulation.

Since the stipulation is a voluntary agreement, no particular type of procedure is needed for preparing it and allowing the respondent to sign it. There can be no judicial review of this form of action. The stipulation as such cannot be enforced; but if the signer fails to adhere to it, formal procedure is initiated by the Commission to obtain a cease and desist order to prevent further violations of the law.

VIII. CONSENT DECREES

The consent decree is a form of action that has been developed largely in respect to the enforcement of the Sherman Act. Section 1

[45] The facts here given are stated in Federal Trade Commission, *Rules, Policy, and Acts*, Nov. 16, 1936.

of this act makes illegal every contract, combination in the form of trust or otherwise, or conspiracy in restraint of trade or commerce among the several states or with foreign nations. It also makes violations of the foregoing provisions misdemeanors, subjecting the violator to a fine not exceeding $5,000, or imprisonment, or both. Section 2 makes similar provisions in respect to persons who shall monopolize, or attempt, combine, or conspire to monopolize, any part of trade or commerce among the several states or with foreign nations. The federal district courts are given equity jurisdiction to prevent or restrain violations of this law, through the issuance of injunctions or by other suitable means, when proceedings for this purpose are instituted by the district attorneys of the United States, under the direction of the Attorney General. The Antitrust Division of the Department of Justice, after making necessary investigations, determines whether it will proceed by the criminal remedy or by the civil remedy, or by both.

The criminal remedy is essentially coercive in that it both penalizes past illegal action and operates as a deterrent against repetition of illegal conduct.

The civil remedy, on the other hand, is constructive, looking to rearrangements in the conduct of business to bring it in line with the law. An injunction not only may forbid in express terms those acts which violate the law, but may also forbid many acts which, taken by themselves, do not violate the law. An injunction may forbid many separate acts, lawful in themselves, but which operate in practical effect, when taken together with other acts, to defeat the broad purposes of the antitrust laws. More than this, an injunction may contain positive mandatory provisions requiring definite and specific rearrangements and realinements in an industry, the adoption of new techniques for carrying on business, and the doing of many affirmative acts which in and of themselves the law does not require. In other words, an injunction may contain in all of its detail a practical plan for the accomplishment of the purpose of the antitrust laws, and in so doing may contain many provisions which isolated and by themselves seem to go beyond the active requirements of the law.[46]

Two types of injunction are available: the injunction issued in a contested proceeding, and the injunction entered by consent, other-

---

[46] "Consent Decree Policy in Antitrust Suits," an address delivered by Wendell Berge, special assistant to the Attorney General, at the Fifth Annual Business Convention of the American Finance Conference, Nov. 10, 1938, mimeographed.

wise called a consent decree. The injunction in a contested proceeding is issued by the court as the result of a suit. A consent decree, on the other hand, is the result of a plan submitted by the defendants as an offer for the settlement of the litigation. The plan as submitted has usually been worked out in co-operation with the Antitrust Division of the Department of Justice. The government has a right to suggest provisions in such plans, but it cannot force their acceptance.

The procedure in respect to consent decrees is of fundamental importance. In outline, it is as follows:

The Department of Justice, on the basis of evidence that it has collected or that has been presented to it, believes that certain individuals are guilty of violations of the antitrust laws. In some cases it may concurrently begin civil and criminal suits against the person believed to be in violation of the law. The present policy of the Department of Justice in respect to these suits is described in the public statement which it issued on May 18, 1938, at the time of the institution of the proceedings before the grand jury at South Bend in the automobile finance cases:

1. The Department will not compromise in a criminal case upon an agreement by the defendants to refrain in the future from the violations with which they are charged. We cannot accept the responsibility of condoning violations of the antitrust laws because of a promise to reform.

2. The commencement of a grand jury proceeding or a criminal prosecution does not do away with the presumption of innocence which surrounds any defendant. It only means that this Department is in possession of evidence of violation of law which it deems so compelling that it cannot accept the responsibility of ignoring it and must therefore present it to an impartial judicial tribunal. While the Department must exercise a preliminary judgment as to weight of the evidence, the ultimate responsibility for the weighing of that evidence is necessarily on the grand jury and petit jury and the court.

3. In using civil and criminal proceedings concurrently (a practice which has been approved by the Supreme Court in the case of *Standard Sanitary Manufacturing Co.* v. *United States,* 226 U.S. 20) it is not the purpose of the Department to coerce or compel the prospective defendants to consent to a civil settlement on threat of criminal prosecution. The sole purpose of the criminal proceeding is to present to an impartial tribunal evidence which leads the Department to believe that the antitrust laws have been violated. At the same time it has never been the policy of the Department to bar its doors at any stage of the pro-

ceeding against businessmen who may desire to propose a practical solution which is of major and immediate benefit to the industry, to competitors and to the public and which goes beyond any results which may be expected in a criminal proceeding.

Such a solution must be voluntary. While we do not invite the submission of such proposals, it will be our policy in all cases to examine and consider any which may be made. They must offer in addition to a prohibition of the violations of the antitrust laws with which the prospective defendants are charged, substantial public benefits connected with the policy of maintaining free competition in an orderly market which could not be obtained by the criminal prosecution.

If proposals of this character are submitted to the Department, it conceives that its duty is to present them to the court before whom the proceeding is pending in order that he may determine whether a *nolle prosse* is justified in the public interest.[47]

More briefly stated, the Department of Justice will not compromise an antitrust case upon mere agreement to desist from the practices complained of. Nor will the Department suggest a compromise. The initiative must always come from the defendant.

In case the Department of Justice can come to a satisfactory agreement regarding the consent decree, it will recommend that the case be dropped and will present the proposed consent decree to the district court for approval. Although the court has the right to refuse its consent, in practice it does not do so.

The test of whether a *nolle prosse* will be recommended on the basis of a consent decree is whether that decree accomplishes more in effectuating the purposes of the Sherman Act than could be obtained through the criminal court.

If the persons against whom proceedings have been instituted present reasonable propositions, and if the court agrees to the propositions submitted, it issues a consent decree which is final and binding. Violation of such a decree may be punished as contempt of court.[48] Several advantages are claimed for consent decrees over either civil or criminal suits.

1. The injunction entered by a consent decree may provide a

[47] Department of Justice Release, Nov. 7, 1938, "Antitrust Laws Consent Decrees" (presented by the government in the Automobile Finance Cases).

[48] For examples of such decrees see *United States of America* v. *Ford Motor Company, Universal Credit Corp., et al,* Civil No. 8 in the District Court of the

workable and practical plan for effectuating the purpose of the law, and may provide for a really effective method of implementation of the law.

2. A consent decree may contain socially and economically desirable provisions for reforming the conduct of an industry which could not be accomplished forcibly by litigation.

3. In establishing a plan for the operation of business through consent decrees, it is possible to insert many provisions which, standing in isolation and by themselves, would go far beyond the actual requirements of the antitrust law.

Despite the advantages of the consent decree, there are certain dangers in connection with its use. It may be employed as a kind of bludgeon, particularly when the threat is made to bring criminal suit unless propositions are offered which satisfy the Department of Justice. Even the possibility of a civil suit, where the government may exercise a great deal of discretion in making concessions in the public interest for the sake of obtaining a consent decree, is fraught with danger. Unless a high degree of public morality and restraint is exercised by the Department of Justice, either or both of two undesirable things may happen: (1) the Department may be tempted to accept a decree which does not fully meet the requirements of the law and which does not actually remedy the situation; (2) it may be tempted to undertake work which is regulatory in nature. The last-named dangers are lessened by the necessity of approval by the court.

The consent decree, when issued by the court, is obviously a judicial act. In assisting defendants to prepare plans for submission, however, the Department of Justice is performing work legislative and administrative in nature. The acceptance of the plan by the court controls the preparation of the consent decree, and in a real sense, though not, of course, in a technical sense, subjects it to judicial review. The fact that the defendant will be in contempt of court if he violates the terms of the consent decree gives an efficacious method of enforcement.

United States for the Northern District of Indiana, and *United States of America* v. *Chrysler Corp. et al*, Civil No. 9 in the District Court of the United States for the Northern District of Indiana.

IX. STATUTORY ADMINISTRATIVE AWARDS

A statutory award settles disputes between individuals and usually provides for a payment of money. It differs from a reparation order largely in the fact that it represents the result of an endeavor to arbitrate and mediate. Awards are made by divisions of the National Railroad Adjustment Board, and by Boards of Arbitration in the National Mediation Board.[49]

The procedure used in establishing awards is of a quasi-judicial nature, since parties are heard in person, by counsel, or by representatives; notice is given to interested parties; and a rather formal hearing is held.

Awards of the National Railroad Adjustment Board in favor of the petitioner are made effective by an order issued by the division hearing the dispute. If a carrier fails to comply in due time with an order of a division, the person for whose benefit the order was made may file in the appropriate district court a petition setting forth briefly the causes for which he claims relief and the order of the division in the premises. The suit proceeds as any civil suit, except that the findings and order of the division of the board constitute *prima facie* evidence of the facts therein stated.

Awards of Boards of Arbitration within the National Mediation Board are filed in the appropriate district court. Unless a petition to impeach the award is filed within ten days after this is done, the court enters final and conclusive judgment upon the award.

It should be noticed that methods of control and methods of enforcement are not the same in the two kinds of awards. Those made by divisions of the National Railroad Adjustment Board are embodied in an order and controlled and enforced by suit upon the order. Those made by Boards of Arbitration within the National Mediation Board are controlled and enforced by impeachment before the district courts, on grounds provided by statute.

---

[49] Awards are also made by the National Labor Relations Board. These, however, are not made as the result of a mediation or arbitration but as the result of a suit before the Board which results in a cease and desist order, often combined with an award of damages or back pay.

CHAPTER V

ADMINISTRATIVE PROCEDURE

Within the past half-century various procedures have been developed by administrative agencies for performing their functions.

I. TYPES OF ADMINISTRATIVE PROCEDURES

Administrative procedures, as distinguished from forms of action, fall into four general classes: (1) administrative discretionary procedure, which ends in an administrative decision; (2) the procedure of administrative legislation, which ends in the making of a general norm or standard for the future; (3) the procedure of administrative-judicial legislation, which, though judicial in form, ends in an act legislative in nature; (4) the procedure of administrative adjudication, which results in an enforceable decision based on past facts and determining rights.

Administrative discretionary procedure. Administrative discretionary procedure is employed chiefly for carrying on a function in which the public has a direct interest, but not a justiciable interest or right. Such functions are: sovereign, proprietary, promotional, benefactory, and (to some extent) revenue. In all these fields the government is performing acts which greatly concern the individual, but which, in the absence of statutory provisions,[1] he has no right to demand or to attack.[2]

For most of these acts no procedure is prescribed by statute, or at most only the outlines of procedure are given. The procedural rules issued by the agencies or heads of departments establish methods of doing work, such as examining and passing upon petitions. These rules facilitate and regularize procedure in fields where acts of a given nature constantly recur. Among the many

[1] No such right is given, for example, under the World War Veterans' Act of 1924; hence the decisions of the Administrator of Veterans' Affairs as to compensation are conclusive and not subject to judicial review unless unsupported by evidence, wholly dependent on a question of law, or arbitrary or capricious. *Silberschein* v. *U.S.*, 226 U.S. 221; *Smith* v. *U.S.*, 83 F.(2d) 631.

[2] This statement is as nearly correct as the facts permit, but it is subject to modifications. There is a growing tendency in judicial thought today to consider that the expressed will of Congress may constitute a kind of right, though not a vested right—but certainly the right to an unbiased investigation of a claim.

agencies which publish rules of this kind in exercising their administrative discretionary functions are the Civil Service Commission and the Federal Emergency Administration of Public Works.[3] In connection with many acts, however, such as the issuing of an executive proclamation or the preparation of a bulletin describing the national parks, printed rules of procedure are neither relevant nor possible.

The most striking thing about administrative discretionary procedure is its variety. It includes any method selected by the administrator for doing a specialized type of work: customary procedures, examination, investigation, informal conferences, and so on, as well as informal hearings and formal public hearings. Although administrative discretionary procedure is used principally in the fields named above, practically all public agencies employ it to some extent, as in settling matters by informal conference in order to avoid formal proceedings.

An essential fact regarding administrative discretionary procedure is that although it may inconvenience the individual, it does not, in itself, affect individual rights. Hence it need not conform to any fixed requirements as to giving notice, holding hearings, taking evidence, and making a decision that is subject to judicial review. It is not necessary that the person who hears the evidence shall make the final decision; that the person who makes a finding of fact shall be limited to facts adduced at a formal hearing; or that the decision shall be based entirely upon the facts found, without consideration of any other factors. The statutes often require that the authority who makes a decision shall consider the general public welfare.

Except for statutory limitations, the administrator sets his own procedure according to his views of what is necessary to enable him to do his work to the best advantage and to make informed and equitable decisions. The courts will not attempt to control his discretion, nor will they control the procedure by means of which he exercises it except in so far as specific procedural requirements have been prescribed by statute.

[3] Civil Service Act and *Rules, Statutes, Executive Orders, and Regulations of Civil Service Commission;* Federal Emergency Administration of Public Works, *Terms and Conditions.*

Administrative legislative procedure. Administrative legislative procedure, in its simplest form, is the procedure used for making rules and regulations under a statute. In very few cases do the statutes, when granting to an administrative agency the rule-making power for a given purpose, prescribe the procedure which it shall employ in exercising this power. The courts have held that the "due process of law" clause of the Constitution is not concerned with the problem of procedure used in the exercise of administrative rule-making.[4]

The reasons for this freedom in making rules and regulations seem clear. (1) The act of rule-making is legislative in nature; hence the procedure employed should be comparable to the procedure of a legislature—that is, it should be a free exercise of legislative power. (2) Since rules and regulations, like statutes, do not directly affect rights until they are applied, the procedure for making them need not be controlled as, for example, judicial procedure must be. The rules and regulations are addressed "to indicated but unnamed and unspecified persons or situations; to distinguish this function from the issuance of orders or findings or the taking of action applying to named or specific persons or situations: . . . "[5] Since it is not possible to know all the persons who will or may be affected by a contemplated rule or regulation, it would be absurd to require a procedure in which they must be given notice and hearing.[6]

The absence of a legal necessity for a hearing does not mean that hearings are never given. In many instances the rule-making authority wishes to obtain as full information as possible before it formulates rules and regulations. In such case a public hearing may be advertised at which any interested persons will be heard.

Since no rights are directly affected by the rule-making power, no person has a standing in court to enjoin the making of a rule or regulation. When a rule or regulation has been made and applied

---

[4] *Pacific States Box & Basket Co.* v. *White,* 296 U.S. 176, 186; *Bi-metallic Invest. Co.* v. *State Board of Equalization,* 239 U.S. 441; *Highland Farms Dairy, Inc.* v. *Agnew,* 16 F. Supp. 575, 586-87, aff'd. 300 U.S. 608.

[5] Ralph F. Fuchs, "Procedure in Administrative Rule Making," 52 *Harvard Law Review* 265.

[6] See Gregory Hankin, "Implementation of Statutes," 27 *Georgetown Law Journal* 424, 434-39.

to him, he can obtain a judicial decision upon the following questions: whether the administrator acted within the limits set by the law; whether he abused his powers; whether the rule or regulation is inconsistent with statutory law or with the Constitution. In the few instances where a part of the procedure for rule-making is prescribed by statute, the courts will also consider whether this procedure was followed. In no case will they make or modify a rule or regulation, although they may set one aside on the grounds just named.

Administrative-judicial legislative procedure. In many instances an administrative act, legislative in nature, does have an immediate effect upon the rights of individuals. Thus, the establishment of a wage order, a railroad rate schedule, or an order for apportionment of joint rates touches at once the economic relationships of those to whom it applies. The courts clearly recognize the legislative nature of such an act, but since it is their duty to prevent property from being taken without due process of law, they also recognize the necessity of judicial control over the procedure of the administrative authority by which the act is performed.

The external form of the procedure which satisfies the courts in connection with administrative legislation of this type is judicial. It is nearly always laid down by statute, and is one type of order procedure. It applies to legislative orders authorized by law. This is the procedure used by the Interstate Commerce Commission in prescribing railroad rates, fares, charges, freights, etc.; by the Federal Power Commission in requiring extension of facilities by a natural gas company; by the Federal Communications Commission in fixing new charges, suspension of charges, and refunds, in respect to interstate and foreign communications by wire or radio; and by the same and other authorities in connection with a wide variety of circumstances.

The usual requirements of "due process" here include notice, hearing, record, fact-finding, and legislative action found and embodied in an order which establishes the new wage scale, rate, etc. The statutory requirements for hearings by the Federal Communications Commission in respect to charges for wire or radio service differ from the more common provisions in that the order of the Commission deals with a schedule filed with it by a carrier; but they are typical in other respects. A brief summary of them will be given.

Whenever a new charge is filed with the Commission, it may, either upon complaint or upon its own initiative, enter upon a hearing concerning the lawfulness of the same. Reasonable notice must be given. A record is kept of all evidence presented at the hearing, a fact-finding is made, and an order is issued which regulates the matter by prescribing maximum or minimum charges, or both. It should be noted that in the strict sense there are no parties to such a proceeding, since the Commission is not opposing the carrier, but obtaining information on the basis of which to make a legislative order.

The district courts of the United States have jurisdiction over enforcement suits brought by the Commission, the Attorney General, or any person injured by a carrier's disobedience to an order. If, after hearing, the court determines that the order was regularly made and duly served, and that the person was in disobedience of the same, it shall issue a writ of injunction or other proper process to enforce obedience.

If the carrier prefers to attack the order, rather than fight its enforcement in the courts, he may bring suit in the district court to have the order enjoined, annulled, set aside, or suspended in whole or in part.[7]

This entire procedure, with its elaborate provisions for hearings, controls, and remedies, is designed both to guarantee informed action on the part of the administration, and to protect the individual in his rights, when these are invaded by an administrative act, legislative in nature.

Administrative adjudicatory procedure. The procedure of administrative adjudication, like that of adjudication by the courts, is adapted to the reaching of a decision as to rights or duties, based on past facts. It differs from ordinary adjudication, however, in that it is not intended merely to cause right to be done or the laws of the land to be enforced in a particular instance, but rather plays a spe-

---

[7] Many legislative orders are appealed to the circuit courts of appeals. See Supporting Statement XI, pp. 318-32.

cial part in the process of administering certain statutes, especially regulatory statutes. It differs from administrative-judicial legislative procedure in that it determines the rights and duties of individuals upon a past state of facts, and ends in a decision quasi-judicial in nature. It differs from the mere administrative decision in that it is not primarily an exercise of informed discretion, since the quasi-judicial decision must be based on a fact-finding, and since rights of parties are involved.

In external form, this procedure is hardly distinguishable from that which ends in a legislative order, except that it involves opposing parties, one of which may be the United States acting through the administrative agency. The decision and order which result from such a procedure determine the rights of the parties. Statutory authorization is always necessary for making an order of this kind.

Administrative adjudicatory procedure requires notice, a hearing at which the parties present their opposing views and evidence, a record, a fact-finding, and a quasi-judicial decision based on the facts found. This decision is normally made effective by means of an order, which may be a cease and desist order, a reparation order for moneys unlawfully charged and collected, or any quasi-judicial order authorized by statute.

Orders of this type, except orders for the payment of money, are enforced and controlled as are administrative-judicial legislative orders. Because of the Seventh Amendment to the Constitution (which provides: "In suits at common law, where the value in controversy shall exceed twenty dollars, the right of trial by jury shall be preserved"), orders for the payment of money are made subject to a special procedure[8] for enforcement and control when they touch rights known to the common law. Because of the Fifth Amendment, which prohibits the taking of property without due process of law, such orders are subject to judicial control.

II. STATUTORY PROVISIONS CONCERNING PROCEDURE

The statutory provisions concerning procedure apply chiefly to the order. A few procedural requirements, mentioned above,[9] are directed to other forms of administrative action. These, however,

[8] See supporting Statement X, pp. 315-17 and XI, pp. 318-32.
[9] Chap. IV.

are exceptional; whereas the grant of power to make statutory orders is generally accompanied by provisions governing procedure. Such provisions usually cover the initiation of action, the sending of notice, the hearing, the record, and the order. Much less frequently they deal with other matters, such as the burden of proof, time limits, answers by those complained of, and rules of evidence.[10]

Notice. In the great majority of instances the statutes demand notice before an order is made. There are, however, certain exceptions to this rule. Notice is not generally required:

1. When the regulatory authority is acting for the government, which is one of the parties, but not an adverse party. This is the case when the Postmaster General fixes rates for the transportation of mail by private carriers.

2. When the order requires the sending of reports, prescribes the forms in which accounts are to be kept, and the like.

3. When the order is merely procedural in nature.

4. When the order results from an investigation (if it does not affect rights).

5. When the person concerned is furnished with a copy of the complaint, or when with the complaint he receives an order to satisfy it or show cause why he should not.

6. When the order is issued by an agency of the government acting in a sovereign capacity; as when the Council of National Defense orders the Director of the Bureau of Mines to grant or to withhold a license.

7. When an order is sent to an individual requiring him to appear personally.

8. When applications are passed upon favorably without the necessity of a hearing.

Hearing. There are several statutory statements as to the type of the hearing. They include: "hearing," "full hearing," "full opportunity for a hearing," "opportunity for a hearing," "after hearing," "hearing to show cause," "hearing upon the charges," "public hearing," and so on.

In some instances the laws specify the minimum length of time

[10] See Supporting Statement IX, pp. 310-14, and F. F. Blachly, "Work Materials on Administrative Action and Procedure" (manuscript).

between notice and hearing, the type of evidence to be received, the persons who may be heard, and the matters to be considered by the authority who makes the order, the record, and many other points of procedure.

III. ADMINISTRATIVE PROVISIONS CONCERNING PROCEDURE

The provisions of the law in respect to the hearing are in practically all cases supplemented by rules and regulations issued by the administrative authority. There is generally a statutory authorization for the making of these rules and regulations.[11]

Each agency prepares and publishes its own rules of procedure. Occasionally separate rules are made for procedure under different laws administered by the same agency.[12] In general, however, one inclusive statement is prepared, which covers hearing procedure before the agency concerned. This statement usually contemplates an adversary procedure, but it may be used in the process of making all different types of orders. This means that in many sets of procedural rules and regulations no clear distinction is made between procedure for making a legislative order and that for making a judicial order. Where such distinction is made, it refers in the main to evidence and the joinder of parties.[13]

A composite picture of the procedures of the independent regulatory authorities shows that they are much the same in substance, although a certain variety in particulars is inevitable. They

[11] See F. F. Blachly, *Working Papers on Administrative Adjudication* (1938). In some cases the language of the statute does not make a clear distinction between the procedural rules here referred to and substantive rules and regulations.

[12] The Department of Agriculture publishes many sets of rules. See for example: *Order Promulgating Rules of Practice to Govern Proceedings under the Packers and Stockyards Act,* 1921, as amended; *Order Promulgating Rules of Practice to Govern Proceedings under the Commodity Exchange Act;* Agricultural Adjustment Administration, Division of Marketing and Market Agreements, Statement No. 1, *Procedure for Marketing Agreements, Orders and Amendments Thereto; Regulations of the Secretary of Agriculture under the United States Warehouse Act of Aug. 11, 1916,* as amended; Bureau of Agricultural Economics, *Service and Regulatory Announcement No. 121,* second revision (November 1938); *Rules and Regulations of the Secretary of Agriculture for Carrying out the Provisions of the Perishable Agricultural Commodities Act,* 1930, as amended.

[13] The Interstate Commerce Commission procedure, it is true, makes some distinctions as to the type of case under consideration. Procedure is different, for example, in respect to applications under the fourth section of the Interstate Commerce Act, and in respect to applications under the Inland Waterways Corporation Act.

cover the following subject matter, with details appropriate to each subject of regulation:

1. Rules as to public sessions and hearings
2. Admission to practice before the authority
3. Parties and classes of parties
4. Appearance by attorney or in person
5. Joinder of parties
6. Complaints, types of and substance
7. Answers to complaints
8. Motions
9. Continuations and extensions
10. Hearings
11. Witnesses and subpoenas
12. Briefs
13. Documentary evidence
14. Oral argument
15. Reports of trial examiners
16. Transcript of testimony
17. Applications for further hearings
18. Reopening of proceedings
19. Reports showing compliance with the order

This analysis shows that the procedural rules issued by the various regulatory authorities implement the statutory provisions as to notice and hearing, and furnish a rather complete outline of the steps that must be taken in bringing a case. Often the procedural steps before the regulatory boards and commissions are outlined as fully and completely as are those which must be taken when recourse is had to the regular courts. Much the same can be said regarding procedure of an adversary nature before the Department of Agriculture. Procedure before other regulatory authorities within the governmental agencies may or may not be equally elaborate, depending upon statutory requirements, subject matter handled, and rights involved.

CHAPTER VI

ENFORCEMENT OF ADMINISTRATIVE ACTION

Before administrative action can be enforced, action appropriate for enforcement must be taken. Conversely, unless the government acts in a manner which requires the individual to do something, there is nothing to enforce. Other administrative acts do not need enforcement. Not until the individual has disobeyed a requirement or command, or failed in the performance of a duty established or defined by an administrative act, can enforcement be sought by the government.

I. PROMOTIONAL, FACILITATORY, BENEFACTORY, LENDING ACTION

Since no commands or denials appear in promotional, lending, facilitatory, or benefactory government action, no enforcement of such action is necessary or possible. If the government decides to establish a highway, takes action to facilitate the flow of interstate commerce, promises to make a loan, or determines that a person has a valid claim to a pension, it has nothing to enforce.

II. TORTIOUS ACTION

There is no basis for the enforcement of tortious action by the government. It is not the intent of the government to commit torts.

III. SOVEREIGN ACTION

Sovereign action which affects the individual often involves executive or administrative enforcement in one form or another, as through an army command, a seizure, a refusal to allow persons or goods to enter the United States, etc. In the last analysis, the decision may be enforced through the armed forces.

IV. CONTRACTUAL ACTION

A contractual action is enforced, as a rule, through either administrative or judicial action. Administrative enforcement is used in many instances. Often the contract itself provides a penalty for non-performance, such as forfeiture of a certain sum per diem when work is not completed on time. The administrative authorities may deduct this amount from the contract price in making settlement. If circumstances warrant leniency, administrative authorities may compromise claims made by the United States which arise from the default of the contractor.

In respect to many claims, the authority concerned requests the contractor and his security to make payment. If payment is not made the claim is turned over to the Comptroller General for settlement. In case he is not able to obtain a settlement, the Department of Justice is asked to handle the matter. It has authority either to compromise the case or to bring a suit.[1]

V. REVENUE ACTION

Revenue decisions deal with two subjects: (1) customs; (2) internal revenue.

A. Customs

Several administrative methods are used for the enforcement of customs decisions, depending largely upon the nature of the subject matter. Decisions involving purity, quality, etc. may be enforced by requiring exportation, reconditioning, or destruction.[2] Seizure is often employed as a method of enforcement. Some decisions are enforced by means of fines, penalties, or forfeitures.[3] The decisions of the United States Customs Court and the United States Court of Customs and Patent Appeals are administratively enforced.[4]

B. Internal Revenue

The federal government collects a wide variety of internal revenue taxes.[5] From the viewpoint of enforcement, these taxes fall into two main classes: (1) those involving a determination made by an administrative authority; (2) those which seldom require

[1] See O. R. McGuire, *Matters of Procedure under Government Contracts* (1935), rev. ed.
[2] See *Customs Regulations* (1937), Chap. X.
[3] The same, Chap. XXI.
[4] Rule 27 of the United States Customs Court adopted May 29, 1936: ". . . the court's judgment, . . . shall be the collector's mandate and shall constitute his authority for the reliquidation of the entry or entries covered thereby."
[5] For a list of such taxes, see the *Annual Report of the Commissioner of Internal Revenue.*

administrative determination or which (in other words) are automatic or nearly so.

The first class, of which the federal income tax is one example, requires the administrative authorities to make a wide variety of decisions, many of which may be only preliminary or auxiliary. Such questions as the following may arise: whether a person is a resident or a non-resident; whether as a taxpayer he falls within a special class, such as a corporation, a trust, a religious association, or a benevolent association; whether the thing to be taxed falls within a particular classification; what is income; what is the value of the property or commodity; what exemptions and exceptions, if any, are justified; what shall be considered as business expenses; and so on. Separate decisions on such questions ultimately result in a decision concerning the tax due from each individual concerned. It is this final decision which must be enforced if the government is to collect its taxes.

In respect to a large number of other taxes there is little or no need for decisions by administrative officers. For example, not decisions, but facts, determine the amount of a tax established by Congress on the basis of number or quantity. Other examples of taxes falling within this class will be mentioned later. In connection with these taxes, all that the administrative authority must do is to see that each taxable article is taxed. It has no discretion as to the amount of tax to be assessed or collected. By means of careful inspection and records its work of enforcement is reduced to a minimum.

1. Enforcement of taxes requiring administrative decisions

a. Income taxes. In the process of collecting the income tax and similar taxes, two principal methods of enforcement are used: (1) the regular assessment and collection of deficiencies; and (2) jeopardy assessments.

(1) Deficiencies. If the Commissioner of Internal Revenue determines that an income tax payment is deficient he sends notice of the fact to the taxpayer, who within ninety days after the mailing of notice may file a petition with the Board of Tax Appeals for a redetermination of the deficiency. Under normal circumstances, no distraint or proceeding in court for its collection shall be begun

until the expiration of the ninety-day period, nor, if a petition has been filed with the Board, until the decision of the Board has become final.

If appeal is taken to the Board, the entire amount redetermined as the deficiency by the decision of the Board (when final) is assessed and must be paid upon notice and demand from the collector. In case of non-payment, the amount due is collected by distraint or by proceedings in court. The same is true in cases of non-payment where no appeal is taken to the Board of Tax Appeals.[6]

(2) Jeopardy assessments. If the Commissioner of Internal Revenue believes that the assessment or the collection of a deficiency (which may mean the entire amount of the tax) will be jeopardized by delay, he is required to assess such deficiency immediately, together with the interest and additional amounts provided by law. Notice and demand for payment are served at once.[7]

Unless bond is given, the property of the taxpayer may be seized and sold to satisfy the demand. If, instead of giving bond, the taxpayer appeals to the Board of Tax Appeals, the Commissioner may nevertheless sell the property on a jeopardy order, by issuing an execution; although this is not likely to be done except in extreme cases. After the sale has been made, appeal may be based only upon the demand of the assessor and not upon the fact of the sale. After the decision of the Board of Tax Appeals is rendered, such decision controls the deficiency assessment.

b. Capital stock tax. The Commissioner of Internal Revenue must finally determine the amount of the tax upon the capital stock of corporations. His decision is enforced by distraint or by judicial procedure.[8]

c. Estate tax. Decisions as to the taxes due from estates of decedents are enforced by methods similar to those employed for enforcing the income tax, including the making of jeopardy assessments. If the tax is not paid on or before the date when it is due, the collector, upon instruction from the Commissioner, proceeds

---

[6] See Bureau of Internal Revenue, *Regulations 101, Income Tax, Revenue Act of 1938*, Chap. XXX, Sec. 272, Art. 272.

[7] The same, Sec. 273, Art. 273.

[8] Sec. 1109 of the Revenue Act of 1926, as amended by Sec. 619 (a) of the Revenue Act of 1928.

to collect it under the provisions of general law; or commences appropriate proceedings in any court of the United States having jurisdiction, to obtain a judgment for the sale of the property.[9] This method of enforcement is not exclusive. The Collector may issue a warrant of distraint authorizing the seizure and sale of any or all of the assets of the estate.[10]

d. Excess profits tax. All the provisions of the law applicable to income taxes are made applicable to excess profits taxes.[11]

e. Gift tax. The decisions made by the Collector of Internal Revenue are enforced in almost the same manner as are his decisions in respect to income taxes.[12]

2. *Enforcement of taxes requiring little or no administrative determination*

In a wide variety of taxes, as has previously been pointed out, the necessity for determinations by administrative authorities is reduced to a minimum. These taxes are laid upon items that can easily be recognized, measured, and counted. Congress decides that such a tax shall be collected, according to a basis which it lays down. The administrator sees that it is collected, through stamps or otherwise according to the terms of the law, without the necessity of making the complex decisions which confront him in the case of income and similar taxes.

In one class of these taxes, Congress provides for the payment of so much per pound, bottle, bale, carton, ton, etc. Such taxes are laid upon distilled spirits, wine, cordials, oleomargarine, narcotics, playing cards, crude petroleum, coal, and so on. A second class is the tax on certain items and transactions, such as messages sent by telephone, telegraph, radio, or cable; and the tax upon the lease of safety deposit boxes. Still a third class is the uniform payment required for the privilege of carrying on a business. Perhaps the unjust enrichment, unemployment compensation, and social security taxes belong in this general group of taxes.

These taxes are almost automatic or self-enforcing if the adminis-

[9] See Bureau of Internal Revenue, *Regulations 80, Estate Tax* (1937 ed.), p. 132.
[10] The same, p. 157. See also 26 U.S.C. 1580.
[11] 48 Stat. L. 771.
[12] 26 U.S.C. 559-77.

trative work connected with them is done properly. Since the facts are relatively easy to obtain, are concrete, and leave no room for equitable adjustment, there is little place for the discretion of the administrator, and the enforcement of the tax becomes largely a matter of computation and inspection.

3. *Taxes of a mixed nature*

In respect to taxes upon the transportation of oils by pipe lines, two situations exist. The tax, which is equivalent to four per cent of the amount paid for transportation to the person furnishing the same, usually falls within the almost automatic taxes. When no charge is made for transportation, whether because pipe lines and oils are owned by the same persons or for any other reason, a tax equivalent to four per cent of a "fair charge" for such transportation must be paid by the person furnishing the same. To decide what is a "fair charge" in each case involves making an administrative determination which can be enforced by the imposition of a penalty of one per cent a month, and the possibility of fine and imprisonment upon conviction by the courts of refusal to pay the tax.

VI. REGULATORY ACTS

In a preceding chapter[13] it was pointed out that enforcement methods, like many other aspects of public administration, depend to a large extent upon the function to be performed. This fact appears with especial clarity in connection with the enforcement of acts designed primarily to carry out the function of regulation of economic affairs. The two principal types of regulatory acts, decisions and orders, are used for different purposes and are consequently differently enforced.

A. Decisions

The most common way of enforcing regulatory decisions is by means of administrative action. Before this subject is discussed, the fact should be noted that in some cases no enforcement is needed. This is true of most negative decisions, such as a decision to refuse a grant, license, or permit. The decision is self-enforcing and cannot be enforced by any agency. The same thing is true of some positive decisions, such as the decision to suspend or withdraw a privilege.

[13] Chap. II.

Most positive decisions of regulatory administrative authorities fall into two classes: decisions which grant licenses, permits, authorizations, approvals, etc.; and those which require action to be taken.

The first class, namely, decisions which grant the request of the individual, are likewise self-enforcing. There is no need to compel the individual to accept that which he desires. Among such acts are: the decision to grant a certificate which permits an association to carry on business as a national banking association; to approve the consolidation of banks; to approve the issuance of preferred stocks; to grant a certificate of public convenience and necessity. It is clear that these decisions do not require enforcement.

The case is different as to decisions commanding action which the individual does not wish to take. These can be disobeyed and may consequently require enforcement.

Administrative enforcement of such decisions may be carried on either by the regulatory authority itself, or by another administrative authority. The first method is used, for example, when the Comptroller of the Currency decides that a bank is insolvent and appoints a receiver who closes the affairs of the banking association and enforces the personal liability of the stockholders. The second method is used when the Secretary of the Treasury, acting through the customs officers, enforces decisions made by the Secretary of Agriculture as to the inferior quality of agricultural seeds offered for importation by refusing to admit the same to the United States.

Judicial action is used in relatively few circumstances to enforce the decisions of administrative authorities. For example, any ship that leaves harbor in violation of the provisions of the Federal Communications Commission in respect to radio installations, shall forfeit to the United States the sum of $500 recoverable by way of suit or libel.[14]

B. Orders

No one rule governs the enforcement of all orders, since they are of such different types. It is necessary, therefore, to examine, in some

[14] 47 U.S.C. 362 (a).

detail, each type. In a previous chapter a classification of orders was made as follows: (1) legislative regulatory orders; (2) procedural orders; (3) injunctive and command orders; (4) reparation and analogous orders; (5) penalty orders; (6) orders in respect to licenses, registrations, certificates, etc.; (7) orders regarding declarations; and (8) negative orders. Each class will be considered in turn.

1. Legislative regulatory orders

The enforcement of legislative regulatory orders will be considered in three categories: (1) no enforcement; (2) administrative enforcement; and (3) judicial enforcement.

a. No enforcement. Certain legislative regulatory orders, because of their nature, are not enforceable or require no enforcement. These include: permissive, exemption, and valuation orders; orders establishing classes; and regulatory orders negative in effect.[15]

b. Administrative enforcement. Many legislative regulatory orders are enforced by means of a cease and desist order issued by the administrative authority. Other examples of administrative enforcement occur, for example, when an order prescribes rates of pay for certain classes of work done for the government, and the fiscal authorities enforce these rates.

c. Judicial enforcement. By far the most common means for the enforcement of legislative regulatory orders is the judicial. The statutes provide for several different methods of judicial enforcement of such orders, the chief of which are: (1) civil suits for enforcement, brought by the administrative agency which issued the order; (2) civil suits brought by a person injured by the disobedience of the one to whom the order was directed; (3) civil suits instigated by the United States to recover a fine, penalty, or forfeiture; (4) injunction suits, usually brought by the administrative authority concerned, to have the order enforced; (5) criminal suits to collect a fine, penalty, or forfeiture or to punish by imprisonment the one guilty of violating the provisions of an order. It should be noted that two or more methods of enforcement are often provided in respect to the same order.[16]

[15] For more details see *United States Court of Appeals for Administration*, Hearings on S. 3676, 75 Cong. 3 sess., Pt. I, chart facing p. 60.
[16] Thus, Securities and Exchange Commission orders under 1933 act; 15 U.S.C. 77t (b).

2. *Procedural orders*

As a rule no statutory provisions govern the enforcement of mere procedural orders. If, however, such orders require the attendance of witnesses or the production of evidence, disobedience may result in the enforcement of an order by a district court. Failure to obey the judicial requirements may lead to punishment by the court for contempt.

3. *Injunctive and command orders*

Injunctive and command orders take two forms: (1) cease and desist orders; and (2) enforcement orders.

a. Cease and desist orders. Cease and desist orders are enforced, if necessary, by judicial action. There are at least four distinct methods of enforcement, each of which will be considered briefly: (1) suit to enforce the order; (2) judicial finality under statutory conditions; (3) the injunctive method; and (4) criminal enforcement.

(1) Suit to enforce the order. A suit for enforcement of a cease and desist order is the standard method used in connection with such orders issued under the Clayton Act[17] by the Federal Trade Commission, the Interstate Commerce Commission, the Federal Communications Commission, and the Board of Governors of the Federal Reserve System. Until 1938 this was the method of enforcement for the orders of the Federal Trade Commission under the Federal Trade Commission Act.[18] This method was also adopted for the cease and desist orders of the National Labor Relations Board[19] and has been adopted in modified form for certain orders of the Secretary of Agriculture.

The chief characteristic of this method of enforcement consists in the fact that in case of disobedience the issuing authority, or in some instances the person aggrieved by such disobedience, must bring suit for enforcement. Except in the case of certain orders of the Secretary of Commerce[20] and the Secretary of Agriculture,[21]

---

[17] 15 U.S.C. 21.

[18] 15 U.S.C. 45. This method was changed by the act of Mar. 21, 1938, 52 Stat. L. 111, to the "judicial finality under statutory conditions" methods.

[19] 29 U.S.C. 160 (c)-(e).

[20] Orders to prevent monopolies or restraint of trade in the fishing industry, 15 U.S.C. 522.

[21] Orders in respect to monopolization or restraint of trade by associations of agricultural producers, 7 U.S.C. 292.

and orders of the National Labor Relations Board which it seeks to have enforced when all circuit courts of appeal are on vacation,[22] suit is always brought in the appropriate circuit court of appeals.[23]

(2) Judicial finality under statutory conditions. Cease and desist orders of the Federal Trade Commission concerning unfair methods of competition or unfair or deceptive acts[24] and cease and desist orders of the Secretary of Agriculture concerning various provisions of the Packers and Stockyards Act,[25] may be appealed to the courts only during time limits set by statute. After the expiration of such periods they acquire judicial finality.

The 1938 Federal Trade Commission Act does not provide for a separate enforcement procedure as did the earlier statute, but provides that the order shall become final under specified conditions, of which the most important is that no petition for review has been filed within sixty days after the order is served. This provision forces the person disobeying the order to appeal, instead of throwing upon the Commission the burden of bringing suit for enforcement.[26] Review may be had upon the transcript of the record of the proceedings held as a basis for the issuance of the order. The statute expressly provides that the court may affirm, modify, or set aside the order of the Commission. To the extent that the order of the Commission is affirmed, the court must issue its own order commanding obedience to the terms of the order of the Commission.

The enforcement procedure under the Packers and Stockyards Act differs from the procedure above chiefly in the facts (1) that a bond is required of the packer as a guarantee that he will pay the costs of the proceeding if the court so directs; and (2) that the decree of the court affirming or modifying the order shall operate as an injunction to prevent violation.

(3) Injunctive method. In respect to several cease and desist

[22] 29 U.S.C. 159-60.
[23] See Supporting Statement XI, pp. 318-32, for the details of the procedure of enforcement of cease and desist orders.
[24] 15 U.S.C. 45. This is the 1938 act amending the Federal Trade Commission Act.
[25] 7 U.S.C. 193, 194.
[26] 15 U.S.C. 45.

orders the injunctive method of enforcement is used.[27]

(4) Criminal enforcement. Several cease and desist orders are enforced by criminal procedure.[28] This method may be combined with, or used as an alternative to, civil enforcement.

b. *Enforcement orders.* Certain enforcement orders, specifying the fact of disobedience as established by a hearing, are issued to make an earlier order or an award effective. These differ from other orders in that they refer specifically to earlier regulatory acts, and not merely to the terms of the law or of general rules and regulations. There are three different methods by which such orders are enforced: (1) a cease and desist order type of suit; (2) a suit for injunction brought by the regulatory authority; (3) a suit by the person for whose benefit the order was issued.

(1) Cease and desist order. The suit based on a cease and desist order to enforce earlier regulatory action is practically the same as that described above, in connection with the cease and desist order.

(2) Suit for injunction. Several statutes provide that when any person violates the provisions of the order to compel obedience, the regulatory authority may apply to the appropriate district court for enforcement by a writ of injunction or other proper process restraining such violation. Such a suit is handled before the district courts according to the Rules of Civil Procedure governing the injunction.

(3) A few statutes provide that any party injured by the failure of another to obey an order may apply to the appropriate district court for enforcement.[29]

4. *Reparation and analogous orders*

Six authorities are authorized by statute to issue reparation and analogous orders, namely, the Federal Communications Commission, the Interstate Commerce Commission, the Secretary of Agri-

---

[27] Secretary of Agriculture: (1) in respect to monopolization or restraint of trade by associations of agricultural producers, 7 U.S.C. 292; (2) wrongful charges and practices of stockyards, 7 U.S.C. 216.

Secretary of Commerce: orders to prevent monopolies or restraint of trade in the fishing industry, 15 U.S.C. 522.

[28] Secretary of Agriculture: (1) in respect to unlawful practices of packers, 7 U.S.C. 195; (2) Commodity Exchange Commission, 7 U.S.C. 13a.

[29] F. F. Blachly, "Work Materials on Administrative Action and Procedure" (manuscript).

culture, the United States Maritime Commission, the National Railroad Adjustment Board, and the National Labor Relations Board.[30] The reparation orders of these authorities are generally enforced by either (1) *de novo* civil suit brought by the one for whose benefit the order was made or (2) review upon the transcript of the record.

a. De novo suit. In all instances, except for orders requiring reinstatement with back pay issued by the National Labor Relations Board, the enforcement of damage and reparation orders is effected by means of a *de novo* suit brought by the one for whose benefit the order was issued. With minor exceptions[31] the procedure is as follows: A petition briefly stating the facts is filed with the regulatory authority by the one deeming himself injured. It is forwarded to the one complained of with the request that the complaint either be satisfied or a written answer be made. If reparation is made, the regulatory authority relieves the one complained of from liability for this particular violation. If the one complained of does not satisfy the complaint, and there appears reasonable ground for an investigation, such investigation is made either formally or informally. If circumstances warrant, a hearing is held, and the regulatory authority makes a report in writing which gives its findings of fact, conclusions, and order. This report is published.

In case of non-compliance with the order, the person for whose benefit it was made files in the district court a petition setting forth the reason for which he claims damages and the order in the premises. Suits thus instigated proceed in all respects like other civil suits for damages, except that in the trial of such suit (1) the findings and order of the regulatory authority are *prima facie* evidence of the facts therein stated; and (2) the petitioner is not liable for costs in the district court or for costs at any subsequent stage of the proceedings unless they accrue upon his appeal. The trial is generally conducted according to the new Rules of Civil Procedure, although there is an exception in respect to damage orders under the Perishable Agricultural Commodities Act.[32]

---

[30] The reinstatement of the worker with back pay in connection with the cease and desist order is included here, although it differs considerably from the ordinary damage or reparation order.

[31] Blachly, "Work Materials on Administrative Action and Procedure."

[32] See Rule 81 (a) (4), 7 U.S.C. 499 g.

b. Transcript of the record method. The National Labor Relations Board's orders awarding reinstatement with back pay[33] are enforced by the courts upon the transcript of the record. The Board may petition the appropriate circuit court of appeals (or a district court if all circuit courts are on vacation) for the enforcement of the order. It certifies and files with the court a transcript of the record, including the pleading and testimony upon which the order was entered, and the findings and order of the Board. The court has power to grant such temporary relief or restraining order as it deems just and proper. Upon the pleadings, testimony, and proceedings set forth in the transcript, the court may make and enter a decree enforcing, modifying, and enforcing as so modified, or setting aside in whole or in part, the order of the Board. The findings of the Board as to facts, if supported by evidence, are conclusive; but on good cause shown the court may order additional evidence to be taken before the Board, which may thereupon make modified or new findings and recommendations.[34]

5. Penalty orders

Penalty orders, as has been said, are orders not of a reparation type, which penalize a person for certain kinds of illegal action. Because of the special conditions which surround licensing, this category does not include orders which revoke or suspend a license as a punishment for illegal action. Only four authorities seem to issue penalty orders: the Securities and Exchange Commission, the Interstate Commerce Commission, the Postmaster General, and the Commodity Exchange Commission.

The chief method of enforcing penalty orders is administrative. Thus, the order of the Securities and Exchange Commission sus-

---

[33] 29 U.S.C. 160.

[34] In the *Jones* v. *Laughlin Steel Corp.* case, 301 U.S. 1, 48, it was argued that the reinstatement of employees with back pay was in contravention to the provisions of the Seventh Amendment to the effect that "in suits at common law, where the value in controversy shall exceed twenty dollars, the right of trial by jury shall be preserved." The court held, however, that the amendment "has no application to cases where recovery of money damages is an incident to equitable relief even though damages might have been recoverd in an action at law. . . . . It does not apply where the proceeding is not in the nature of a suit at common law. . . . The instant case is not a suit at common law or in the nature of such a suit. The proceeding is one unknown to the common law. It is a statutory proceeding."

pending or expelling a member from a registered securities exchange is self-enforcing or is enforced by the very administrative act of suspension or expulsion. The same is true of an order of this commission removing from office an officer or director of a registered securities exchange. Fraud orders issued by the Postmaster General are also enforced administratively. The orders issued by the Commodity Exchange Commission excluding or debarring an association or corporation from trading in a contract market are likewise of the self-enforcing type.

6. Orders in respect to licenses, registrations, certificates, privileges, permits, approvals, grants, and designations

Almost no statutory provisions exist as to the enforcement of orders of the categories above; and the general provisions of the statutes as to enforcement of orders are in nearly all cases inapplicable. This fact is explained by the following reasons:

a. Licenses. If a license, etc., is granted, manifestly the regulatory authority has nothing to enforce.

b. Refusals. The same thing is true as to refusals. A refusal cannot be enforced, for there can be no violation of such an action.

c. Suspensions and revocations. In respect to suspensions and revocations, a somewhat different theory is applicable. Since licenses, etc., are generally issued for the purpose of control, they are made prerequisite to carrying on particular economic activities, and severe penalties may be attached to attempts to operate without them. Refusal to grant a license, or an order suspending or revoking one, automatically makes the individual who disregards it a violator of the law. Operation without such a document, therefore, is basically not a violation of the order of refusal, suspension, or revocation, but a violation of the law.

By their very nature such orders are self-executing; that is, the order without further administrative or judicial action places the individual in the class of one who has no right to operate. Nothing in the order as such has to be enforced. This is true even if the regulatory authorities are charged by statute with seeing that the law and orders made thereunder are obeyed. They are merely seeing that the law is enforced and are not trying to secure the enforcement of their own orders.

The few exceptional instances in which such orders have to be enforced arise when orders granting licenses, etc., impose specific conditions which must be met in operating under the permission thus granted. Since these conditions can be violated, it is necessary to see that they are enforced. For example, when orders are issued with requirements for carrying on hydraulic mining or hydraulic mining construction,[35] these requirements may be violated. Such violation may result in a forfeiture, or in enforcement by equity suit for injunction brought in the name of the United States by the United States Attorney in a district court.[36]

7. Orders in re declarations

If an order making a declaration is broadly legislative in nature and merely establishes certain classes, there is nothing to enforce, for the order is self-enforcing.

If, however, the declaration is judicial in nature, that is, places a particular individual in a class for regulatory purposes, and the individual refuses to assume the duties, liabilities, etc., belonging to the class, enforcement may become necessary.

8. Negative orders

A negative order is by its very nature non-enforceable. There can be no violation of a negative order issued because the authority deemed it had no power or jurisdiction in the matter; of an order which does not forbid or compel conduct; of an order refusing aid; or of an order which declines to relieve a person of a statutory command compelling or forbidding action.[37]

---

[35] 33 U.S.C. 673.

[36] 33 U.S.C. 679; 21 O.A.G. 10.

[37] For a new view of negative orders, see Gregory Hankin, "The Fate of the Negative Order Doctrine" (manuscript).

CHAPTER VII

CONTROL OVER ADMINISTRATION

All three primary branches of the national government, legislative, executive, and judicial, participate in the control of administration.

I. LEGISLATIVE CONTROL

The Congress not only determines the policies which the government is to follow and the functions which it is to fulfill, but it may, and generally does, establish the administrative agencies which are to carry out the policies and exercise the functions. Ordinarily it specifically sets up the positions of higher officers in administrative control of the agency, and defines the duties, responsibilities, and powers of those officers. It may go further and prescribe in some detail the internal organization of the agency. In the case of regulatory agencies it generally prescribes in broad terms the procedures which the agency is to follow in conducting its work; and it may do so in the case of non-regulatory agencies.

Each year the Congress drafts, perfects, and passes the appropriation bills which provide funds for most of the administrative agencies. Through its control over appropriations, it exercises at times the power of life or death over administrative agencies. Although this power of control is vested in the Congress as a whole, its application is ordinarily initiated or facilitated by committees which consider and report out bills for substantive legislation and which generally draft the appropriation bills. Administrative agencies, moreover, are not infrequently subjected to searching scrutiny by special investigating committees.

II. EXECUTIVE CONTROL

The executive, under his power to take care that the laws be enforced and under his powers of appointment and removal, has a strong and extensive control over administration. Although the Congress may vest certain functions in officers subordinate to the President, yet since the President has general power to remove executive and administrative officers, he can in a large measure direct and control them in the exercise of the powers vested in them by Congress, removing them in case such action seems to him advisable.

The independent regulatory authorities constitute an important exception to the President's power of direction and removal. The Congress may, if it sees fit, make these agencies largely independent of executive control and circumscribe the President's power by prescribing terms of office, and removal only for cause.

The Congress may leave to the discretion of the President, department heads, bureau chiefs, or the heads of independent agencies many details regarding organization, procedures, and business practices, although procedures with respect to finances, purchases, personnel, etc., are often governed by general law. The great executive departments are all created by statute. Thus in no small measure the power to control the administrative agencies, which is vested in the President or in subordinate administrative officers, is a power delegated to them by the Congress at its discretion, and is not exercised by constitutional right. If they are given the delegated power to organize, determine procedures, etc., they are usually given the related power to make such changes in organization, procedures, etc., as in their judgment will best serve the purposes of the law.

III. JUDICIAL CONTROL

By means of various procedures and types of suits in various courts, an extensive judicial control (which will be outlined below) is exercised over many kinds of administrative activity. The chief sources of this control are the Constitution of the United States, statutes enacted by Congress, and interpretations of law by the courts. Three chief ends are served by judicial control, as follows:

A. Holding the Administration within its Field of Competence and within the Bounds of Law

The field of competence of the administration is determined and delimited by both constitutional and statutory law. It is the function of the courts, acting always in appropriate cases that come before them, to prevent the administration from transgressing any applicable norm of law.

1. Constitutional law

Either an attempt by the legislature to bestow powers upon an administrative authority, or an undertaking by such authority to exercise power which it conceives to be within the limits of its competence, may be unconstitutional. The constitutional limitations most frequently transgressed in this way are those establishing a separation of the powers of government, and the "due process" clause of the Fifth Amendment.

The separation of powers means, among other things, that the legislative power, in the essential freedom of Congress to adopt any policy as to matters placed within the control of that power, cannot, under the Constitution, be abdicated or transferred. When an executive, administrative, or judicial officer receives a delegation of legislative power, such delegation is constitutional only when strictly limited by a declaration of policy or a determination of scope.[1] It is clearly unconstitutional for an administrative or executive officer to exercise any powers of a legislative or judicial nature, except such limited, subordinate, clearly defined powers as have been expressly granted to him.

The "due process" clause means, among a great many other things, that the courts will jealously protect the rights of the individual from administrative encroachment. This will be discussed more fully in the second part of the present chapter.

2. Statutory law

Administrative authorities are generally organized and their spheres of action and competence established by acts of Congress. If

---

[1] Thus Congress may authorize the courts to make rules of procedure (*Standard Oil Co.* v. *United States*, 221 U.S. 1); it may authorize the President to determine whether he shall invoke the provisions of a neutrality or embargo act, when such act shall cease to operate, etc. (*United States* v. *Curtiss-Wright Export Corp.*, 299 U.S. 304); it may authorize the Secretary of Agriculture to make rules and regulations in respect to forest reservations, violation of which involves criminal penalties (*United States* v. *Grimaud*, 220 U.S. 506). But Congress may not delegate to the courts, or to any other tribunal, powers which are strictly and exclusively legislative (*Wayman* v. *Southard*, 10 Wheat. 1); it may not bestow upon the President a delegation of legislative power unless the power is well defined and limited by expressions as to the will and policy of Congress (*Schechter* v. *United States*, 295 U.S. 495); it may not bestow upon administrative officers the power to make regulations which actually subvert or modify the terms of a statute (*United States* v. *Eaton*, 144 U.S. 677; *United States* v. *Antikamnia Chemical Co.*, 231 U.S. 654).

the rule of law is to be preserved, each authority must remain within the sphere of competence granted to it. Any individual who considers his rights injured by an action which he regards as being outside or beyond the competence granted by the legislature to the authority which has taken the action, may appropriately ask the courts to prevent that action from taking effect. In other words, it is a basic right of the individual whose interests are adversely affected, that the administrative authority shall be held within the bounds of its competence. Hence there is always a right to contest the competence assumed by administrative authorities.

B. Preventing Abuse of Power

Equality before the law means in this respect that the law is to be administered fairly and impartially. In public administration in the United States there must be no discrimination against, or bias in favor of, any class, race, religion, or political party.

Discriminatory action, whether favorable or unfavorable to the individual, constitutes abuse of power. Any arbitrary and unreasonable action, any action based on personal spite, hatred, or affection, is abuse of power. The concept abuse of power is capable of a considerable range of applications, and the courts extend it to cover not only the actions already mentioned, but also a failure to obey the conditions of the law. Examples of abuse of power falling within this category, when evidence is required by statute as the basis of action are: (1) making a decision without obtaining evidence; (2) refusing to consider evidence obtained; (3) making a decision clearly contrary to the evidence.

The courts are always able to take jurisdiction when the question of abuse of power is raised, even though no mention is made of this contingency in the statute governing the action which is alleged to be an abuse. The question whether abuse of power has actually taken place is a question of law to be decided by the courts.

C. Guaranteeing the Rights of Individuals

An important purpose served by judicial control over administrative activity is the guarantee and enforcement of individual rights. These rights may be classified, for the purposes of this discussion, as positive, negative, and procedural.

Many positive rights were developed by the common law and are guaranteed by the federal Constitution. The most important of these rights are those affecting the person and those affecting property.

With respect to negative rights the Constitution prohibits, among other things, unreasonable searches and seizures, the taking of private property for public use without just compensation, the levying of taxes without apportionment, and so on.

From the procedural standpoint, the most important constitutional principle is contained in the Fifth Amendment, which provides that no person shall be deprived of life, liberty, or property without due process of law. As interpreted by the courts this provision affects matters of procedure before administrative bodies, such as notice, hearing, contentions of parties, who must hear rules of evidence, findings of fact, and the like.

All these classes of rights, if the administration encroaches upon them, will be safeguarded by the courts.

IV. SPECIAL PROBLEMS IN JUDICIAL CONTROL

For three reasons, it is necessary to devote particular attention to certain aspects of judicial control. First, judicial control has the unique importance of saying the last word on constitutional and legal questions. Second, it is complex, by contrast with the relative simplicity of legislative, executive, and administrative forms of control. Third, the present controversy as to administrative organization and controls is devoted largely to the matter of judicial control.

A. Legal Basis for Judicial Control

Judicial control over administrative action rests upon a basis of law. The law—constitutional, statutory, and common—is the source of judicial control. It also sets the conditions under which such control can be exercised.

1. The legal sources

Judicial control over federal administration arises from the terms of the Constitution, from the statutes, from the decisions of the courts, and from such basic principles of common law as have been incorporated into the legal and judicial thought of this country.

a. Constitutional provisions. The separation of powers and the "due process" clause of the Constitution have already been mentioned in this connection, but only a few applications of these clauses have been or can be given because of limitations of space. The fact that the Constitution is the supreme law of the land is interpreted by the courts as meaning that all other norms of law—statutory or regulatory—must be in conformity with the Constitution.

A person who claims that the administration has invaded his constitutional rights will be protected in those rights if he can prove his claim to the satisfaction of the courts. This claim may be procedural or substantive. If procedural, the plea may be that no notice was given, that a fair hearing was not held, that the administrative authority did not allow evidence to be presented or did not follow the evidence, and so on. If substantive, the plea may be, for example, that a rate fixed by a commission, because it is confiscatory, takes property without due process of law. The courts have held that when a question of compensation is raised, a person is entitled to a judicial determination under the due process of law clause of the Fifth Amendment. In the St. Joseph Stockyards case, the Supreme Court said:

But the Constitution fixes limits to the rate-making power by prohibiting the deprivation of property without due process of law. . . . When the legislature acts directly, its action is subject to judicial scrutiny and determination in order to prevent the transgression of these limits of power. The legislature cannot preclude that scrutiny and determination by any declaration or legislative finding. Legislative declaration or finding is necessarily subject to independent judicial review upon the facts and the law by courts of competent jurisdiction. . . . Nor can the legislature escape the Constitutional limitation by authorizing its agent to make findings that the agent has kept within that limitation. . . . But to say that their findings of fact may be made conclusive when Constitutional rights of liberty and property are involved, although the evidence clearly establishes that the findings are wrong and Constitutional rights have been invaded, is to place those rights at the mercy of administrative officials and seriously to impair the security inherent in our judicial safeguards.[2]

In another recent case the court said:

If as to the value of his property the owner accepts legislative or administrative determinations or challenges them merely upon the ground

[2] 298 U.S. 38, 51, 52.

that they were not made in accordance with statutes governing a sub-ordinate agency, no constitutional question arises. But, when he appropriately invokes the just compensation clause, he is entitled to a judicial determination of the amount. The due process clause assures a full hearing before the court or other tribunal empowered to perform the judicial function involved. That includes the right to introduce evidence and have judicial findings based upon it.[3]

b. Statutory provisions. Most of the newer regulatory functions of the government[4] are subject to statutory provisions regarding judicial review. This is not true of certain acts of administrative authorities engaged in the older functions of government.

c. Judicial decisions. In connection with many of the older functions of the government, such as public lands, pensions, the postal service, alien control, certain types of revenue, civil service, control over shipping, regulations of a police nature, etc., court decisions, rather than statutes, tell when judicial review will lie. Even in respect to the newer functions, for which a system of review is laid down by statute, judicial decisions are important as determining the extent of such review. Thus, in many instances a general right of appeal from orders is given, but the courts refuse jurisdiction over orders which they consider merely procedural or interlocutory, those which establish valuations, require reports or accounts, etc.

In deciding whether or not any review will lie and the extent of possible review, the courts take into consideration such matters as the nature of the government power involved, the relationship of the state to the individual, and the type of activity which is being performed. They consider also whether the question raised is one of law, of fact, of mixed law and fact, of discretion, or of procedure. Their decision as to review will also be affected by the form of administrative action, or the nature and form of the proceeding.[5]

2. *Procedural factors*

The courts have decided (on the basis of the legal sources just discussed, applied to specific questions involving judicial control of ad-

---

[3] *B. & O. R. Co.* v. *United States*, 298 U.S. 349, 368, 369.
[4] F. F. Blachly, "Work Materials on Administrative Action and Procedure" (manuscript).
[5] See James P. Lynch, *Judicial Review of Federal Administrative Adjudication;* John Dickinson, *Administrative Justice and the Supremacy of the Law*, Chaps. VI-IX.

ministrative acts) that certain procedural factors are requisite to due process of law when the administration touches the rights of the individual in such a way that those rights may possibly be injured.

a. Statutory requirements. The first factor to be considered is that any procedure laid down by statute must be followed. In cases properly coming before them, the courts examine the legislative provisions applicable to a given administrative act, and require conformity with such provisions. For example, the courts may go into the following questions:

(1) What form of administrative action is required by the statute; as an order, a decision, an award, etc.; and the conformity or nonconformity of the action taken with the requirement.

(2) What type of procedure is required by the statute; as, for example, whether notice and hearing are required. In many instances, particularly when dealing with orders, the statute itself requires the equivalent of a due process of law procedure.[6]

(3) What authority is finally responsible for taking action.

(4) Notice of issues and contentions. In cases where the government compels action or refuses to permit action, the courts as a rule hold that notice of the issues and contentions involved must be given to the parties concerned. Such notice constitutes a necessary part of due process. Thus, in the second Morgan case the court said:

> The right to a hearing embraces not only the right to present evidence but also a reasonable opportunity to know the claims of the opposing party and to meet them. The right to submit argument implies that opportunity; otherwise the right may be a barren one. Those who are brought into contest with the Government in a quasi-judicial proceeding aimed at the control of their activities are entitled to be fairly advised of what the Government proposes, and to be heard upon its proposals before it issues its final command.[7]

(5) Who must hear? A doctrine recently developed by the Supreme Court goes on the ground that "the one who decides must hear." This somewhat strict requirement does not, however,

[6] *Morgan v. United States,* 298 U.S. 468, 473, 477.
[7] 304 U.S. 18, 19.

. . . preclude practicable administrative procedure in obtaining the aid of assistants in the department. Assistants may prosecute inquiries. Evidence may be taken by an examiner. Evidence thus taken may be sifted and analyzed by competent subordinates. Argument may be oral or written. The requirements are not technical. But there must be a hearing in a substantial sense. And to give the substance of a hearing, which is for the purpose of making determinations upon evidence, the officer who makes the determinations must consider and appraise the evidence which justifies them. That duty undoubtedly may be an onerous one, but the performance of it in a substantial manner is inseparable from the exercise of the important authority conferred.[8]

(6) Nature of the hearing. From the foregoing statement, it is easy to see that in any given instance the relationship of the government to the individual, or the purpose of the proceeding, determines the nature of the proceeding. This is set forth by the courts in many statements, of which the following is a fair sample: "The fundamental right to a fair hearing is determined by the character of the proceedings."[9] Thus, in proceedings involving sovereign, promotional, facilitatory, or benefactory action and the like, it is not necessary to have sworn testimony and cross-examination, to base findings on evidence, etc.

In regulatory action, controlled by the order, however, not only statutory provisions, but also due process of law requirements as laid down by the courts, involve a much more formal procedure. The Supreme Court has said: "The 'hearing' is the hearing of evidence and argument. If the one who determines the facts which underlie the order has not considered evidence or argument, it is manifest that the hearing has not been given."[10]

(7) Evidence. In general, the order procedure or "due process of law" procedure requires the opportunity to bring evidence. Evidence, moreover, must be made a part of the record. The administrative authority as well as the individual is required to present its evidence at the hearing. The administrative agency which makes the decision may not properly consider data taken from annual reports or from its own files unless this is formally placed in the record, or the pertinent portions of such documents are identified with par-

[8] *Morgan v. United States,* 298 U.S. 468, 481.
[9] *New England Divisions* case, 261 U.S. 184, 200.
[10] *Morgan v. United States,* 298 U.S. 468, 480, 481.

ticularity.[11] The decision must be based upon the evidence of record.[12]

(8) Reports and interlocutory determinations. Because of the great amount of work to be done by authorities which regulate an economic field or intervene in other ways, it is impossible for the highest officers of these authorities to hear all cases initially. They must depend upon trial examiners, referees, or other agents, who look into cases and report upon them. The relationship of these subordinate agents to a due process of law hearing has not as yet been clarified. The rules of administrative authorities vary considerably as to the extent to which the trial examiner is required to prepare proposed findings of fact or other intermediate reports; as to whether parties are required or requested to submit proposed findings of fact to the examiner; as to whether the examiner's proposed findings are submitted to the parties; as to the right of the parties to file exceptions to reports or findings thus submitted, and so on.

b. Jurisprudence concerning procedure. The courts have not taken a definite position upon the foregoing points, and it is possible that they will not do so, provided they are satisfied that rights are protected. They have held that the Fifth Amendment does not guarantee any "particular form of procedure; it protects substantial rights."[13] Thus, although the Rules and Regulations of the National Labor Relations Board provide that the Board may direct the trial examiner to prepare an intermediate report,[14] failure to issue such a report does not constitute error, if each party clearly understood the issues and contentions of the other parties and was given an opportunity to justify its action.[15] The second Morgan case decision indicates that the plan of a proposed report is one method by which parties may be advised of the issues and contentions of the other parties. This plan of action, however, is not of vital necessity.[16] In strict logic, if the doctrine that "the one who decides must hear"

[11] *United States* v. *Abilene & S.R. Co.,* 265 U.S. 274.
[12] See Albert E. Stephen, "The Extent to Which Fact-Finding Boards should be Bound by Rules of Evidence," 24 *American Bar Association Journal* 630.
[13] *National Labor Relations Board* v. *Mackay Radio & T. Co.,* 304 U.S. 333, 351.
[14] Sec. 38(a).
[15] *National Labor Relations Board* v. *Mackay Radio & T. Co.,* 304 U.S. 333.
[16] *Morgan* v. *United States,* 304 U.S. 1, 21.

is applied, the trial examiner might well be made a tribunal of first instance, and the administrative authority one of second instance.

3. Conditions of judicial review

There are several conditions all of which must be present before the courts can review an act of the administrative agencies. These conditions are related to or developed from the legal basis for review.

a. Legal right. The first necessary condition is the existence of a legal right, and a claim that such right has been invaded by administrative action. Chief Justice Taft has said: "A complaining litigant in the Federal Courts . . . must always be ready to point to the clause of the Federal Constitution or the statute by which he may rightly invoke the consideration of the court."[17] The principle which he wished to establish is clear. There must be a definite right, not merely a hope or desire; and it is only upon invasion of such definite right that an individual can ask the courts to control an act of the administration.

b. Justiciable controversy. The second basic principle is that a justiciable controversy must be present in order that the jurisdiction of constitutional courts may be invoked. This is necessary because the jurisdiction of such courts is limited to "cases" and "controversies" as defined by Section 2, Article III of the Constitution.[18]

A case or controversy under the Constitution is a definite and concrete dispute touching the legal relations of parties having adverse legal interests, and coming to the courts in such a way that they can decide it and give judgment. Congress cannot withdraw from

---

"The Government adverts to an observation in our former opinion that, while it was good practice—which we approved—to have the examiner, receiving the evidence in such a case, prepare a report as a basis for exceptions and argument, we could not say that that particular type of procedure was essential to the validity of the proceeding."

In the case of *Consolidated Edison Co.* v. *National Labor Relations Board*, 305 U. S. 197, 228, the court said: "It would have been better practice for the Board to have directed the examiner to make a tentative report with an opportunity for exceptions and arguments thereon."

[17] 35 *Yale Law Journal* 1, 11.

[18] *Ex parte Bakelite Corp.*, 279 U.S. 438; *Aetna Life Ins. Co.* v. *Haworth*, 300 U.S. 227; see Supporting Statement XII, pp. 333-38.

judicial cognizance any matter which by its nature is justiciable, nor can it, on the other hand, bring under the judicial power a matter which by its nature is not an appropriate subject for judicial determination. Some matters, however, which are not considered justiciable by nature can be made so by statute.

At the same time, there are matters involving public rights, which may be presented in such form that the judicial power is capable of acting on them, and which are susceptible of judicial determination, but which Congress may or may not bring within the cognizance of the courts of the United States, as it may deem proper.[19]

An unsigned note on "The Reviewability of Negative Administrative Orders," in a recent number of the *Harvard Law Review*,[20] summarizes the subject of case or controversy thus:

A "case" or "controversy" within the meaning of Article III requires adverse parties with substantial interests at stake whose interests are threatened with imminent invasion of valuable rights in an actual controversy involving concrete issues whose solution will result in a determination of legal rights or a redress of wrongs, before a court with power to determine finally the issues between the parties.

c. Parties. Before there can be a justiciable case or controversy there must be parties. The parties must be adverse in interest. The interests involved must be definite and specific, and not mere doubts as to the legality of action. Claims based only upon potential invasions of rights are not enough to warrant judicial intervention.[21]

The judicial power always makes case-to-case decisions. It does not, as do both the legislative power and the administrative power, make general determinations. The legislative power sets general standards and norms. The administrative power may be given delegated legislative authority to make broad general determinations affecting great numbers who fall within the provisions of the statute. The judicial authorities, on the other hand, make determinations in particular cases, and endeavor to avoid the decision of questions not fundamental to such determinations.

[19] *Murray's Lessee* v. *Hoboken Land and Improvement Co.*, 18 How. 272, 284.
[20] Vol. 53, p. 102.
[21] See Supporting Statement XII, pp. 333-38.

B. The Scope of Judicial Review

The question of the scope of judicial review centers about four principal topics: (1) judicial control over findings of fact; (2) control over discretionary action; (3) control over mixed questions of law and fact; and (4) control over questions of law.

1. Judicial control over findings of fact.

Findings of fact as a basis for administrative action must be considered from both an administrative and a judicial standpoint. From the administrative standpoint undoubtedly most administrative actions involve a finding of facts. Thus, in connection with its work, the administration endeavors to establish such facts as: the number of tons of coal that are to be taxed; the amount of each individual's income which is taxable at each different rate; whether cotton or tobacco is of a certain standard.

Fact-finding of the type just described is not at all the same thing as the fact-finding which the legislature requires of administrative agencies as a condition precedent to making certain orders. The latter is a part of a quasi-judicial process. The administrative act must be based upon the fact-finding, and the fact-finding must be based upon the evidence. Unless this is the case, due process is lacking.

Most fact-finding of this type is connected with either the regulatory process or the quasi-judicial process of making reparation orders. In the great majority of instances, judicial control over determinations made as the result of fact-finding is limited by statutory provisions and by judicial decisions.[22]

a. Legislative provisions. The legislative provisions which apply to judicial control over fact-finding are of three different classes: (1) those which make the fact-finding and order of an administrative authority *prima facie* evidence of the facts therein stated; (2) those which make an order (hence the fact-finding on which the order is based) final unless suspended or set aside by a court of competent jurisdiction; (3) those which make the fact-finding of

[22] Blachly, "Work Materials on Administrative Action and Procedure."

the administrative authority conclusive if supported by evidence, testimony, etc.

(1) The fact-finding and order as *prima facie* evidence. The original Interstate Commerce Act made the fact-finding of the Commission, as embodied in orders or reports, *prima facie* evidence.[23] The present law applies the same standard in respect to fact findings made in connection with the reparation orders issued by the Interstate Commerce Commission.[24] Later laws apply it to reparation orders issued by several other authorities.

In construing the original law, the court held that what are proper rates is a question of fact;[25] hence if the inquiry had been conducted on a proper basis, the court would be inclined to abstain from reviewing the conclusions of the Commission. This rule, however, would not apply when the Commission had misconstrued the act, and as a result had ignored or excluded facts and circumstances that should have been taken into consideration.[26] Even under such circumstances, it was not the duty of the courts to establish the facts or to dispose of the case on its merits, but to remand the case to the Commission. The court said:

> The questions whether certain discriminations were due or undue, were questions of fact, to be passed upon by the Commission in the light of all facts duly alleged and supported by competent evidence, and it did not comport with the true scheme of the statute that the Circuit Court of Appeals should undertake . . . to find and pass upon such questions of fact, in a case in the position in which the present one was.[27]

The courts have not always taken this "self-denying" attitude. In several cases the Supreme Court has indicated that in suits on orders the courts have power to admit, consider, and apply additional evidence. Thus, it said:

> It has been uniformly held by the several Circuit Courts and the Circuit Courts of Appeal, in such cases, that they are not restricted to the

---

[23] 24 Stat. L. 384, 385.

[24] Blachly, "Work Materials on Administrative Action and Procedure," under Reparation Orders.

[25] Compare the remark of the court: "Whether the Commission gave too much weight to some parts of [the evidence] and too little weight to other parts of it is a question of fact and not of law." *Ill. Cent. R. Co.* v. *Interstate Commerce Commission*, 206 U.S. 441, 466.

[26] *Texas & P. R. Co.* v. *Interstate Commerce Commission*, 162 U.S. 197.

[27] The same, p. 238.

evidence adduced before the Commission, nor to a consideration merely of the power of the Commission to make the particular order under question, but that additional evidence may be put in by either party, and that the duty of the court is to decide, as a court of equity, upon the entire body of evidence.[28]

Despite this obvious fluctuation, the courts have generally given considerable weight to the fact-finding of an administrative agency that is made by statute *prima facie* evidence, even though they do not consider themselves wholly bound by such fact-finding. The view which still may be called typical has been expressed as follows:

Whilst the court has in the discharge of its duty been at times constrained to correct erroneous constructions which have been put by the Commission upon the statute, it has steadily refused . . . to assume to exert its original judgment on the facts, where, under the statute, it was entitled, before approaching the facts, to the aid which must necessarily be afforded by the previous enlightened judgment of the commission upon such subjects.[29]

When suit is brought to enforce a reparation order issued by any administrative agency authorized to issue such orders, and the findings of fact made by the agency and the order based on such findings are *prima facie* evidence of the facts therein stated,[30] the suit proceeds in all respects like other civil suits for damages. The *prima facie* rule here simply means that the findings and order of the authority will stand unless successfully rebutted.

(2) Facts final unless set aside. Facts as found by administrative agency are not reviewed by courts. The Hepburn Act of 1906[31] contained several provisions which tended to limit the jurisdiction of the courts over the actions of the Interstate Commerce Commission. In the first place, it applied the provision making the findings of fact of the Commission only *prima facie* evidence to reparation cases only.[32] In the second place, it provided:

[28] *Interstate Commerce Commission* v. *Alabama Midland Ry. Co.*, 168 U.S. 144, 175.
[29] *East Tennessee, etc. R. Co.* v. *Interstate Commerce Commission*, 181 U.S. 1, 27.
[30] In all instances except one (namely, orders for reparations issued under the Perishable Agricultural Commodities Act, 7 U.S.C. 499 (g)), the validity of a reparation order is tested in suit for enforcement rather than by means of appeal.
[31] 34 Stat. L. 584.
[32] Sec. 5.

All orders of the Commission, except orders for the payment of money, shall take effect within such reasonable time, not less than thirty days, and shall continue in force for such period of time, not exceeding two years, as shall be prescribed in the order of the Commission, unless the same shall be suspended or modified or set aside by the Commission or be suspended or set aside by a court of competent jurisdiction.[33]

In the third place, it provided for penalties and forfeitures for disobedience of the act.[34] In the fourth place, the act provided that the Commission might apply to the court for enforcement of its orders and that if upon an enforcement hearing

it appears that the order was regularly made and duly served, and that the carrier is in disobedience of the same, the court shall enforce obedience to such order by a writ of injunction, or other proper process, mandatory or otherwise, to restrain such carrier, its officers, agents, or representatives, from further disobedience of such order, or to enjoin upon it, or them, obedience to the same.

The net result of these limitations is that the courts will pass only upon whether the Commission has exceeded its constitutional or statutory power, or has made an error of law. They will not pass upon questions of fact unless these are involved with questions of law. In elaborating upon these tests, the courts have held that whether a rate is so low as to be confiscatory and therefore in violation of due process of law is a constitutional question suitable for judicial determination. Again, the courts will intervene if the Commission fixes rates contrary to evidence or without evidence to support its order, or if the power has been exercised in an unreasonable or capricious manner.[35]

Despite the conditions and modifications just stated, the court cannot substitute its own judgment as to facts for that of the Commission. To adopt any other viewpoint would mean that "the Commission would become but a mere instrument for the purpose of taking testimony to be submitted to the courts for their ultimate action."[36]

[33] Sec. 4. Amendments have modified the language of this section, but not substantially changed its meaning.

[34] Secs. 1, 2, 4. By amendment, the passage cited below reads: "If, after hearing, the court determines. . . ." 49 U.S.C. 16(12).

[35] See *Interstate Commerce Commission* v. *Ill. Central R. Co.*, 215 U.S. 452; *United States* v. *Louisville, etc. R. Co.*, 235 U.S. 314.

[36] *United States* v. *Louisville, etc. R. Co.*, 235 U.S. 314, 321.

(3) Fact-finding made final and conclusive if supported by evidence, testimony, etc. Most of the newer statutes provide that the findings of fact of the regulatory authority shall be conclusive "if supported by evidence," "if supported by testimony," and the like.[37] How far the courts can control fact-finding under such statutory provisions can be determined only from an examination of cases. The decisions indicate that the courts will refrain from reviewing the facts if these appear to be based on substantial evidence. In a recent case, the court said:

In the case of statutory provisions like Section 10(e) [which provides that "the findings of the Board as to the facts, if supported by evidence, shall be conclusive"] applicable to other administrative tribunals, we have refused to review the evidence or weigh the testimony and have declared we will reverse or modify the findings only if clearly improper or not supported by substantial evidence.[38]

In another case, the court said, regarding the same provision of the law:

The findings of the Board as to the facts, if supported by evidence, shall be conclusive. But, as has often been pointed out, this, as in the case of other findings by administrative bodies, means evidence which is substantial, that is, affording a substantial basis of fact from which the fact in issue can be reasonably inferred. . . . Substantial evidence is more than a scintilla, and must do more than create a suspicion of the existence of the fact to be established. It means such relevant evidence as a reasonable mind might accept as adequate to support a conclusion . . . and it must be enough to justify, if the trial were to a jury, a refusal to direct a verdict when the conclusion sought to be drawn from it is one of fact for the jury.[39]

It is the duty of the regulatory body, rather than the courts, to appraise and evaluate the evidence received.[40] The courts must not substitute their own appraisal of evidence for that of the regulatory authority. In general, a court "will not consider the expediency or

[37] For examples of such requirements, see: Securities and Exchange Commission, under Public Utility Holding Company Act, 15 U.S.C. 79x; Federal Power Commission, 16 U.S.C. 825l(b); various agencies, 15 U.S.C. 21.

[38] Washington, Virginia & Maryland Coach Co. v. National Labor Relations Board, 301 U.S. 142, 147.

[39] National Labor Relations Board v. Columbian Enameling & Stamping Co., 306 U.S. 292, 299-300.

[40] Swayne & Hoyt, Ltd. v. United States, 300 U.S. 297; National Labor Relations Board v. Pennsylvania Greyhound Lines, Inc., 303 U.S. 261.

wisdom of the order, or whether, on like testimony, it would have made a similar ruling."[41]

b. Judicial doctrines. In addition to the general principle that rights must be safeguarded by judicial action, the courts have worked out several specific doctrines which, by and large, increase judicial control over administrative determination of facts. Of these doctrines, the most important concern jurisdictional facts and jurisdictional authority.

In respect to jurisdictional facts, the Supreme Court has said that the final determination of the existence of facts upon which the enforcement of the constitutional rights of the citizen depends "cannot be committed to an administrative agency."[42] For example, the administrative finding as to whether a particular employee falls within the admiralty jurisdiction of the United States under the Longshoremen's and Harbor Workers' Compensation Act is a jurisdictional fact, upon which the deputies acting under this act cannot finally determine. "Constitutional power to deal with the relationships involved in any particular case, therefore, depended upon the existence of certain facts, and unless those facts were found by a court no assurance could be had that the particular case lay within the sphere of the federal admiralty jurisdiction."[43]

Regarding jurisdictional authority, the courts have held substantially: "It would appear that whenever an administrative ruling is attacked on the ground that it violates the constitutional rights of the party against whom the determination was made, the reviewing court must reach its own independent judgment as to the validity of such administrative action."[44] In this connection the courts have held that they may review all fact determinations governing the jurisdictional authority of administrative agencies.[45]

These determinations as to jurisdiction are said to be so basic that their existence is a condition precedent to administrative action.

[41] *Interstate Commerce Commission* v. *Union Pacific R.,* 222 U.S. 541, 547.
[42] *Crowell* v. *Benson,* 285 U.S. 22, 56.
[43] James M. Landis, "Administrative Policies and the Courts," 47 *Yale Law Journal* 519, 523.
[44] Robert M. Cooper, "Administrative Justice and the Rule of Discretion," 47 *Yale Law Journal* 577, 591.
[45] *Ohio Valley Water Co.* v. *Ben Avon,* 253 U.S. 287, 289; *St. Joseph Stockyards Co.* v. *United States,* 298 U.S. 38, 44.

Consequently, it has been held that when the administrative agency makes a finding, regardless of whether it is purely factual or not, which incidentally involves a determination of its jurisdiction over a particular subject matter or transaction, that determination must remain open to the independent judicial review by the trial court.[46]

Determinations as to jurisdictional facts and jurisdictional authority are not, according to the courts, made upon the transcript of the record of a proceeding, but there must be a complete trial *de novo* of the matter.[47]

What, in substance, is the result of the various statutory provisions concerning the weight and effect of fact-finding by administrative authorities? From one point of view, this result is very slight. Whenever a question of constitutional right arises, it is possible for the courts to examine into every aspect of the problem before them, and to set aside the administrative fact-finding if they consider that there are grounds for doing so. From another point of view, the result is considerable. Although the administrative authority cannot compel the court to accept its view of the facts in controversies based on the Constitution, the presumption is that the authority has found the facts correctly. The courts acknowledge this presumption, and have even mentioned the fact that it is supported by the expert character of the administrative agency. Hence, instead of a clean slate, the complaining individual finds one on which the facts are already written by the administration. It is true that he may be able to overcome the presumption of administrative correctness, if his complaint is based on an alleged invasion of constitutional right; but it is necessary for him to do so, and not merely to bring some evidence which points the other way.

When no question of constitutional right is involved, the statute bestowing a right or establishing a control may make the administrative fact-finding final if based on evidence, and the courts will abide by the statute. In such cases they ask only if the act lies within the scope of power of the administrative agency, if there were abuses of power, if statutory procedure has been followed, and if evidence

[46] Cooper, 47 *Yale Law Journal* 591.
[47] See *Crowell* v. *Benson*, 285 U.S. 22, and *St. Joseph Stockyards Co.* v. *United States*, 298 U.S. 38.

were taken which can reasonably support the findings. The facts, if properly found by the administration, will stand.

2. *Judicial control over discretionary action*

A distinction must be drawn between determinations made as the result of a formal fact-finding and those which do not result from such a procedure. Questions of control over discretion arise largely in respect to administrative decisions as contrasted with administrative orders. In other words, they occur in connection with the contractual, fiscal, proprietary, promotional, facilitatory, and benefactory functions of the government oftener than in connection with the regulatory activities.

Outside the field of regulation in the narrow sense, and within the fields where discretion is chiefly exercised, the question of judicial control arises, as a rule, when the courts are asked to apply an extraordinary legal remedy. It has generally been held that even when the courts take jurisdiction under such circumstances, they will not attempt to control the exercise of discretion. Thus, in an early case it was held: "An officer is not subject to the control of the courts in the exercise of judgment and discretion."[48]

In connection with the use of the injunction[49] to control administrative activities, an important distinction is made between discretionary acts and ministerial acts. Only the latter are normally controlled by this writ, whereas discretion remains free unless abused. Thus, it was held in the case of *Tidal Osage Co.* v. *West*[50] that the decision of the Secretary of the Interior cannot be reviewed by injunction, when, in exercising the broad jurisdiction conferred upon him respecting the disposition and control of Indian lands, he must determine his power to act through the interpretation of statutes and of rules and regulations lawfully made in compliance therewith. The same case quotes with approval the following passage from an earlier decision:[51]

---

[48] *Gaines* v. *Thompson*, 7 Wall. 347.

[49] The mandamus has been abolished, but presumably the jurisprudence on the subject applies in appropriate instances to the mandatory injunction.

[50] 58 App. D. C. 327.

[51] *Riverside Oil Co.* v. *Hitchcock*, 190 U.S. 316, 324-25.

Whether he decided right or wrong is not the question. Having jurisdiction to decide at all, he had necessarily jurisdiction, and it was his duty to decide as he thought the law was, and the courts had no power whatever under those circumstances to review his determination by mandamus or injunction.

Other decisions are full of similar findings, which establish clearly the fact that the courts will not interfere with discretionary administrative acts unless under the most exceptional circumstances, such as a clear proof of abuse.[52]

3. Control over mixed questions of law and fact

When that which purports to be a finding of fact is so involved with and so dependent upon questions of law as to affect the decision of the latter, a mixed question of law and fact is present. In order to decide the legal questions, the court will examine the entire record, including the evidence if necessary,[53] and will exercise its own judgment as to both facts and law.[54]

4. Control over questions of law

The courts have broad powers to review administrative decisions based upon errors of law. In the St. Joseph Stockyards case the Supreme Court said: "The order of an administrative tribunal may be set aside for any error of law, substantive or procedural."[55] This is the generally accepted doctrine, although it is modified by the principle that slight or minor irregularities are not controlling.[56]

C. Applicability of Review

In considering the applicability of judicial control over administrative acts, two general factors must always be kept in mind:

---

[52] *Ex parte Panagopoulos*, 3 F. Supp. 222; *Litchfield* v. *Richards*, 9 Wall. 575; *Spang* v. *Roper*, 13 F. Supp. 840.

[53] *St. Joseph Stockyards Co.* v. *United States*, 298 U.S. 38, 74; Cooper (47 *Yale Law Journal* 591-92) appears to find a development of this attitude since the decision in 1904 of *Bates & Guild Co.* v. *Payne*, 194 U.S. 106.

[54] *Interstate Commerce Commission* v. *Union Pacific R.*, 222 U.S. 541; *United States* v. *Idaho*, 298 U.S. 105.

[55] 298 U.S. 38, 74.

[56] *Morgan* v. *United States*, 304 U.S. 1, 19; *National Labor Relations Board* v. *Mackay Radio and Telegraph Co.*, 303 U.S. 630.

(1) the particular economic or other relationship of the state to the individual ; and (2) the type of administrative action which is being taken because of this relationship. It should also be remembered that judicial review takes place, ordinarily, only after administrative remedies have been exhausted, and that any appeal to constitutional courts must involve a case or controversy concerning rights.

1. The relationship of the state to the individual

Judicial control, beyond that which is necessary to hold the administrative agency within its jurisdiction and prevent it from abusing its power,[57] is not applicable to situations involving proprietary, promotional, facilitatory, and benefactory action. Under such conditions, as has already been pointed out, the government is not compelling action or refusing to let action be taken in any way that affects justiciable rights.

In respect to many of the functions mentioned above, a rather elaborate system of higher administrative control has been established. For example, the Board of Veterans' Appeals and the Board of Appeals in the Department of the Interior control the acts of the agents who directly administer the functions.

Judicial control is particularly applicable in respect to contractual, revenue, and adjudicatory acts, as well as acts regulatory in nature.

a. Contractual action. Judicial review over disputes arising from contracts or administrative acts connected therewith is exercised primarily for the purpose of holding the contracting parties within the terms of the contract. The fulfilment of contracts between the government and individuals is controlled according to the same principles of law which apply to private individuals, with one major exception. This is, that the government cannot be sued without its own consent. However, such consent has been given and a special court, the Court of Claims,[58] has been established to hear appeals from acts of contracting officers.

---

[57] See *St. Louis Smelting & Refining Co.* v. *Kemp,* 104 U.S. 636; *Newhall* v. *Sanger,* 92 U.S. 761; *Davies* v. *Manolis,* 179 Fed. 818; J. B. Cheadle, "Judicial Review of Administrative Determination," 2 *Southwestern Political Science Quarterly* 1. Ernst Freund has said: "Well established principles of common law and equity permit a judicial review of administrative determinations wherever there is a question of jurisdiction and where there is an abuse of power." 27 *West Virginia Law Quarterly* 207.

[58] For the organization, functions, enforcement methods, and appeals from this

b. Revenue action. Control over revenue action takes place in respect to taxes and customs. This control differs from that exercised over certain other types of action in that it is a composite of administrative and judicial control, the latter being of a limited nature. These differences will be brought out in connection with concrete situations.

(1) Control *in re* taxation. In the field of taxation the courts are dealing with a sovereign function, since the ultimate condition of the state's ability to continue its existence is its power and ability to collect its revenues. The courts have expressed this idea in several striking ways: "The power to tax involves the power to destroy,"[59] said Chief Justice Marshall. In *Loan Association* v. *Topeka* it was said: "Given a purpose or object for which taxation may be lawfully used and the extent of its exercise is in its very nature unlimited. It is true that . . . in most instances . . . any limitation is unsafe. The entire resources of the people should in some instances be at the disposal of the government."[60]

In connection with tax administration Congress has established an original control quasi-judicial in nature but exercised by administrative authorities, namely, the Commissioner of Internal Revenue and the Board of Tax Appeals. The Commissioner of Internal Revenue acts as a higher administrative controlling authority within the tax administration itself, whereas the Board of Tax Appeals is a higher controlling authority outside and independent of the tax authorities.[61]

The Commissioner of Internal Revenue and the Board of Tax Appeals consider many problems of a character not strictly judicial and not suitable for judicial cognizance. The Board of Tax Appeals,

---

court see F. F. Blachly, *Working Papers on Administrative Adjudication* (1938), p. 140.

[59] *McCulloch* v. *Maryland*, 4 Wheaton 316, 431.

[60] 20 Wall. 665, 663; *Springer* v. *United States*, 102 U.S. 586, 594; *Hagar* v. *Reclamation District No. 108*, 111 U.S. 701, 708.

[61] "The Board of Tax Appeals . . . is hereby continued as an independent agency in the Executive Branch of the Government," 26 U.S.C. 600. See also *American Woolen Co.* v. *White*, 56 F.(2d) 716.

In the case of *Old Colony Trust Co.* v. *Commissioner of Internal Revenue*, Chief Justice Taft said: "The Board of Tax Appeals is not a court. It is an executive or administrative board, upon the decision of which the parties are given an opportunity to base a petition for review to the courts after the administrative inquiry of the Board has been decided," 279 U.S. 716, 725.

through its expert staff of lawyers and accountants, can properly evaluate and settle such matters.[62]

Appeals lie from the Board of Tax Appeals to the circuit courts of appeal only on questions of law, if the Board has acted within its jurisdiction and if there is evidence to sustain the conclusions reached.[63] Appeals from the decisions of the circuit courts of appeal lie to the Supreme Court on questions of law.[64]

(2) Control *in re* customs. Decisions made in respect to customs are far less susceptible to judicial control than those made in connection with taxation. The importer has no constitutional rights to bring goods into this country. His rights are purely statutory. The statutes have given him a right of appeal to two legislative courts: the United States Customs Court, which hears appeals in the first instance; and the United States Court of Customs and Patent Appeals, which hears them in the second instance.

The decisions of the Court of Customs and Patent Appeals, with specified exceptions, are subject to review by the Supreme Court upon certiorari or otherwise.[65]

c. Adjudicatory action. The adjudicatory action here discussed is merely that performed by administrative authorities. It has been shown in earlier chapters that such action may be closely related to the regulatory process; but it may be used in other connections, as in relation to contracts. At this moment attention will be given only to the settling of disputes between individuals by means of reparation orders. Several regulatory authorities, such as the Interstate Commerce Commission, the Maritime Commission, the Federal Communications Commission, the National Railroad Adjustment Board, the National Labor Relations Board, and the Secretary of Agriculture, issue reparation orders. These orders are judicial in nature. They deal with past actions. The contest is not between the

---

[62] Magill, "The Finality of Determinations of the Commissioner of Internal Revenue" (1930), 30 *Columbia Law Review* 147.

[63] In *Avery* v. *Commissioner*, 22 F.(2d) 6, the court said: "The Commissioner and Board of Tax Appeals have practical knowledge of the intricate details incident to tax problems and their determinations should be given effect when not clearly contrary to the will of Congress." The appellate court, they held, may not substitute its opinion for that of the Board on the facts shown in the record.

[64] *Old Mission Portland Cement Co.* v. *Commissioner of Internal Revenue*, 293 U. S. 289.

[65] 28 U.S.C. 308, 36 Stat. L. 11, 37 Stat. L. 11.

government and the individual but between two individuals. Judicial control over determinations that are made by such authorities is not exercised primarily for the purpose of holding them within their sphere of competence, or for holding them to a due process of law procedure, or for seeing that there is no abuse of power. It is exercised chiefly for the purpose of seeing that justice is done between private parties.

Although the word control is used, it is not wholly accurate in this connection. Actually there is a *de novo* suit upon the reparation order, when the individual in whose favor it was made seeks its enforcement by the courts. There is one notable exception to this, namely, orders of the National Labor Relations Board for reinstatement with back pay, in respect to which a review procedure is provided.

d. Regulatory action. The most important area in which the courts control administrative acts is doubtless that of the regulation of business and industry. Judicial review of regulatory action is based largely upon the "due process of law" clause of the Fifth Amendment to the federal Constitution, and upon the fact that Congress can exercise only enumerated powers. Under proper conditions the courts will examine the question whether Congress had a right to pass a law providing for the regulation of a given field, whether the law actually passed is in harmony with the Constitution, and whether the act of the administrator falls within all bounds of law, substantive and procedural. Questions of delegation of legislative and judicial power, as well as questions of interpretation of law, often arise in this connection. All the matters named above have been held by the courts to be fit subjects for the exercise of the judicial power, in connection with cases and controversies.

In practically every instance where a regulatory act, whether of the legislative type such as a wage order, or of the judicial type such as a cease and desist order, has an immediate effect upon the rights of the individual, one or more of the questions listed above can be raised. The authorization to make such orders is almost without exception accompanied by provisions for judicial review. Even in the absence of such provisions, however, the courts could control action which might constitute an invasion of legal rights.

CHAPTER VIII

SUMMARY OF PART I

The analyses in the preceding chapters show that the doctrine of guaranteed individual rights and limited fields of government power, and the relationships resulting from this doctrine, must be recognized as of paramount importance in the present controversy regarding the system of federal administration and administrative law.

I. THE DOCTRINE OF RIGHTS

The doctrine of rights has a common law basis. It is true that certain rights are named in the Constitution and that others are guaranteed to the individual indirectly by the separation of powers and negatively by prohibiting specified acts on the part of the government; but back of the making of the Constitution, deep in the minds of those who drafted it, those who adopted it, and those who accepted it, lay common law views which have never been wholly discarded. Congress, in exercising its legislative powers, and the courts, in interpreting the Constitution and the statutes, have been guided to a considerable extent, though often almost unconsciously, by the principles of the common law. The rights established by the Constitution have been interpreted, for the most part, according to the common law, whether such interpretation has been implicit in the process of legislation or explicit in that of judicial application. Specific constitutional or statutory provisions have superseded various common law doctrines; but the common law influence is still powerful.

The relationships between the government and the individual, as these have developed under the doctrine of rights and the various forms of law by which rights are interpreted and applied, may be separated into four principal fields. The first is a field where the government acts in a sovereign capacity, and the rights of the individual are few or non-existent. Thus, Congress may decide to declare war, to establish a new tariff, or to make two-dollar silver coins. The individual has no direct and enforceable rights in respect to any of these sovereign matters.

The next is a field where the government might exercise sovereign power, perhaps has exercised it in the past, and could (if it so chose) exercise it again in the future; but where certain limited rights for the benefit of the individual have been established by statute. The outstanding examples of rights in this field are the rights of suit in special courts in contracts, taxation, patents, and customs cases.

The third field contains constitutional rights which the government may not take away from the individual except under constitutional safeguards, such as "just compensation" or "due process of law." The latter clause, in particular, has been constantly applied to administrative regulation of private economic activity.

The fourth field is that of rights reserved to the individual, with which the government cannot interfere. For example, the federal government may not suspend the privilege of the writ of habeas corpus, unless such action is required for public safety in cases of rebellion or invasion; no bill of attainder or *ex post facto* law shall be passed; and no laws shall be made by Congress abridging freedom of speech or of the press. Among the reserved rights most important from the standpoint of administration are the following, quoted from Article I, Section 9 of the Constitution of the United States:

"No tax or duty shall be laid on articles exported from any state."

"No preference shall be given by any regulation of commerce or revenue to the ports of one state over those of another; nor shall vessels bound to, or from, one state, be obliged to enter, clear, or pay duties in another."

The various fields just mentioned are coexistent. In other words, at one and the same time the government and the individual may be, respectively: (1) sovereign, and subject; (2) granter of rights, and recipient; (3) prosecutor, and prosecuted, or regulator, and regulated (always under constitutional safeguards); (4) incapable of action, and free to exercise rights. These distinctions are not merely academic, or even wholly legal in their implications. They have immediate significance for the work of public administration.

1. When in respect to a sovereign matter, the administrator is carrying out the will of Congress expressed as law, the subject has in that particular field no rights to be enforced. Hence no controls or judicial reviews over administrative action as such are necessary. The only questions that can be raised are as to jurisdiction, abuse or misuse of power, and the like.

2. At the same time, the individual may be bringing suit against the government in the Board of Tax Appeals. He has the right to do this—a right carved out of sovereign power, as it were, and a right which can be rescinded by statute, but a right nevertheless. The administrator's action will be controlled, and the individual's rights will be defined and if necessary enforced, by the decision of the courts. Under the circumstances, the rights will be construed strictly, and the statutory procedure will be enforced rigidly.

3. When actions, such as the regulation of some kind or area of economic enterprise, are taken by the government, the third field of rights is concerned. In such actions the public authorities may exercise a considerable degree of control over the individual's conduct, but this control is not unlimited. The individual has constitutionally guaranteed rights which set limits to the action of the government. Prominent among these is "due process of law" when government action may take life, liberty, or property.

Rights in this field are protected by several different methods. First, in a case before them the courts will declare null and void, and will therefore refuse to enforce, any act of Congress which they consider to be in violation of the constitutional guarantees.

Second, according to legislative practice and judicial decisions, a legislative basis is required for actions affecting rights that may be taken by administrative authorities. The general policies, principles, standards, and norms governing regulatory action must be laid down by the legislature. As a rule, the legislature also prescribes the outlines of procedure to be employed in connection with administrative action, and the methods of enforcing and controlling such action.

Third, the administrative authorities have been organized by Congress in such a way that those which carry on regulatory activities involving a great amount of administrative legislation and adjudication are generally placed in an independent position as regards control by political officers such as the heads of government departments or the Chief Executive. Such independence is justified by the fact that many of the legislative orders and all the judicial orders of these authorities are based upon a "due process of law" notice, hearing, and fact-finding, which is essentially a judicial proceeding not suited to administrative review.

Fourth, the rights in question are guaranteed by establishing certain forms of administrative action, each of which is employed for certain special purposes, as granting or refusing an application, commanding future action in a general way, or deciding upon a past state of facts. Every separate form of action has specific applications and legal effects, is required to be taken according to certain procedures, and is subjected to particular methods of control.

Fifth, rights are protected through the establishment of procedures. Congress, influenced both by previous judicial decisions as to what constitutes a fair hearing and by its own ideas of proper procedure, has laid down by statute in a general way the procedure that must be followed by administrative bodies when rights may be affected by regulatory action. The minimum requirement, in general, is due notice and a fair hearing. Many judicial decisions have defined the nature of a hearing which is fair and which meets the requirements of due process of law.

Sixth, the laws providing for enforcement of administrative action are generally careful to protect guaranteed rights of the individual by requiring that enforcement shall be accomplished through judicial means. This requirement achieves two things: (1) while leaving the administration free to enforce its own acts where no rights are affected, it holds the administration within the bounds of law where such rights may be invaded, since the courts examine the question at issue before enforcing the act; (2) it gives to the courts the appropriate duty of imposing any fines, terms of imprisonment, or other penalties.

Seventh, the rights of the individual may be protected by congressional control over the administration. This control is exercised when Congress organizes or reorganizes administrative agencies, and grants, extends, or limits their powers. If an agency habitually acts in such a way as to threaten or to invade individual rights unless recourse is had to the courts, Congress may abolish or reorganize that agency, provide a larger or smaller staff, alter its powers, eliminate or modify certain of its remaining activities, change its relationship to other authorities, establish additional safeguards of procedure, and create more adequate administrative and judicial controls over certain of its forms of action. An important congressional control is exercised by increasing or decreasing the appropriation for a certain agency or a certain activity.

Eighth, administrative control protects individual rights. This form of control usually consists in having higher administrative authorities examine and perhaps revise the acts of those below them. The most common arrangement is that the lower authorities make decisions which become the decisions of the department, unless a dissatisfied person asks for an appeal to a higher authority. In such an instance the appeal may go up through the hierarchy, ending finally, if it cannot be settled earlier to the satisfaction of the complainant, with the head of the authority.

In many instances administrative control is exercised by means of the more or less formal process of rehearing upon complaint. The administrative authority, in reviewing the evidence or in examining additional documents or testimony, may correct its first decision. A rehearing of a case always acts as a method of control over action, even though the rehearing may be made by the same authority which performed the original action. The legal rights of the individual are always considered carefully, since the administration realizes that invasion of such rights will render it liable to control by the courts.

Finally, judicial control over administrative action protects individual rights. This control, which is exercised by the constitutional courts, by legislative courts, and by administrative tribunals, serves several purposes. It compels the administrative authorities to act always under constitutional limitations and within the field of competence granted to them by the legislature.

Judicial control operates to prevent administrative authorities from abusing their power. Abuse of power may result from basing a decision on personal hate, spite, or malice. It may result from permitting political, religious, or racial feelings or prejudices to affect the decision. The courts also recognize certain types of abuse of power in respect to evidence. Thus, the making of a decision judicial in nature without any evidence constitutes an abuse of power. The refusal to consider valid evidence, when evidence is required by statute as a condition precedent to the making of a decision, also constitutes an abuse of power. By judicial application of the concept "abuse of power," the individual is protected in his rights.

A great field of judicial control over administration, marked out principally by modern statutes and developed by the courts, is the duty of determining whether an administrative act is supported by evidence, when evidence is required as a condition precedent to valid action. In exercising such control, the courts are walking on a thin line between a field which belongs properly to administrative judgment and discretion, and a field appropriate for judicial examination. If the courts fail to walk carefully, they may find themselves making administrative decisions.

A question which is now the subject of much debate is how far the courts should examine the evidence in order to determine whether it supports the administrative act in question. If they go carefully into the details of the evidence in every case, they will burden themselves with a vast amount of work for which they have no training. Moreover, they have no machinery for handling such burdens. Even the administrative authorities, which are less rigidly bound by rules of procedure than the courts and can therefore work more rapidly, have been forced to establish elaborate organizations for sifting evidence.

Another important field of judicial control is the interpretation of the law. Within this field the courts exercise an almost supreme power. It is true that Congress may create by statute a right or privilege not established by the Constitution, and provide exclusively for an administrative determination of such right or privilege, in which case the courts will not take jurisdiction.[1] In only a few

[1] *United States* v. *Babcock,* 250 U.S. 328, 331; *Wilder Mfg. Co.* v. *Corn Products Refining Co.,* 236 U.S. 165; *Arnson* v. *Murphy,* 109 U.S. 238; *Barnet* v. *National Bank,* 98 U.S. 555; *Farmers' & Mechanics' National Bank* v. *Dearing,* 91 U.S. 29.

instances, however, has Congress left to final administrative determination questions of law; and these questions arise in fields not covered by constitutional guarantees, such as public lands,[2] tax matters,[3] pensions,[4] immigration,[5] and so on. The constitutional rights of the individual are still protected by the courts; it is still basic in federal jurisprudence that "the judicial department of . . . government is the rightful expositor of its laws."[6]

4. When a right is reserved to the individual by the Constitution in such form that Congress may not invade it, naturally the administration may not interfere with such a right. Any act of Congress which has the effect of invading a constitutional right of this kind, and any action on the part of the administration which endeavors to enforce such a law, will be set aside by the courts.

The gist of all that has been said is that acts of federal administration in general fall into two main classes: (1) acts which do not affect individual rights; and (2) acts which do affect individual rights. The former are almost never susceptible to judicial control. Acts which affect rights, on the other hand, are generally performed as the result of a procedure judicial in nature, and are subject to judicial review and judicial enforcement.

II. ADMINISTRATIVE EFFICIENCY

Efficiency in the performance of government functions, as well as the protection of private rights and public interests, must be a principal objective sought in connection with the organization, relationships, and duties of administrative agencies. Various methods of securing efficiency have been developed, some by Congress and some by the administrative agencies themselves.

In the first place, the creation by statute of special agencies charged with the regulation of particular economic fields is an important step in the direction of efficiency. The laws concerning regulation are not to be enforced in haphazard fashion at the instigation of private individuals who bring suit in the regular courts,

[2] *Dunlap* v. *Black*, 128 U.S. 40; *United States* v. *Schurz*, 102 U.S. 378.
[3] *Cary* v. *Curtis*, 44 U.S. 235.
[4] *Decatur* v. *Paulding*, 14 Pet. 497.
[5] *Lem Moon Sing* v. *United States*, 158 U.S. 538.
[6] *Bank of Hamilton* v. *Dudley*, 2 Pet. 492.

when they believe that their interests have been invaded. On the contrary, it is made the primary duty of each of the numerous regulatory agencies to enforce a law or laws, usually by means of regulations, decisions, and orders.

Congress has provided the regulatory agencies with the requisite facilities (such as staffs of expert investigators, accountants, lawyers, statisticians, and so on) for studying their problems thoroughly from all points of view. The actions and determinations of these authorities therefore stand upon a broad basis of specialized knowledge, both factual and interpretative.

Efficiency of action results also from the fact that the regulatory agencies are given sublegislative power. It is not, as a rule, necessary for them to await the slow process of legislative action in respect to the minor details of the policy they are administering, or in respect to the rules of procedure under which they carry out that policy. Their power of sublegislation enables them to meet quickly and effectively situations with which they are confronted.

Again, the procedures of the regulatory authorities, in connection with the handling of cases that come before them, are much more simple and less technical than procedures before the regular courts. The strict rules of evidence that obtain in the ordinary courts of law are not generally applied to cases before the administrative agencies. Many of the disputes which come before such authorities are settled by discussion around the table. Adjustments can be made in order to prevent long-drawn-out and expensive suits. Administrative appeals can sometimes be taken from the acts of inferior agents to those higher in the system.

A great degree of finality has been given to the fact-finding of the administrative authorities. Even when the Constitution requires that a jury trial be permitted, the facts as found by these authorities are often made *prima facie* evidence, subject to rebuttal and final determination by the jury. When rights protected by the "due process" clause of the Constitution are involved, the fact-finding of the administrative agency concerned is frequently made final and conclusive if supported by evidence. If no constitutional or common law rights are involved, the conclusiveness of fact-finding by the administration depends upon the pleasure of Congress.

Efficiency of administration increases as the facts found by it are given weight in courts, thus preventing the long delays and the hampering uncertainties which would lessen efficiency if the courts were compelled to investigate all questions of fact for themselves. It is hard to find any rebuttal to the presumption that administrators in a special field are quite as competent to find facts in that field as are the courts. Congress has recognized this principle, as a rule, by giving to the fact-finding of the various regulatory bodies and other administrative agencies the highest possible degree of finality under the respective conditions.

Congress has provided for expeditious appeal from certain administrative cases. In so doing, it has employed two methods: (1) appeal to a three-judge district court, with the possibility of direct review by the Supreme Court; (2) appeal to the circuit courts of appeals instead of to the district courts, and review by the Supreme Court by means of certiorari or certified question.

In addition to the methods used by Congress for increasing the efficiency of administrative agencies, there are several methods employed by the agencies themselves for the same purpose. Minor reorganizations and readjustments, administrative rules for the internal government of each agency, the use of mechanical aids, the careful drafting of regulations having general interest and applicability, and many other ways of increasing efficiency are worked out and adopted by those actively engaged in the work of administration.

III. CONCLUSIONS

The organization and the operations of the administrative agencies, particularly those agencies which perform functions affecting individual rights, are carefully devised to combine the protection of guaranteed rights with the promotion of administrative efficiency. The constitutional and statutory bases of administration, the forms of administrative action, the enforcement methods and controls applicable to the respective forms, and the special devices for obtaining efficiency contribute to both these ends. The system is not perfect; but it is constantly being improved as to efficiency, at the same time that its operations are devised and controlled in such a way that guaranteed rights are safeguarded.

PART II

THE REFORM OF THE PRESENT SYSTEM

CHAPTER IX

THE EXECUTIVE MANAGEMENT DOCTRINE

The central feature of the doctrine of executive management is the belief that all administrative activities of the federal government (except those of a quasi-judicial nature) should be under the immediate control of the President of the United States through the heads of a very limited number of great executive departments; and that much of the policy to be pursued by administrative agencies should be determined by the President.

Under this theory the structure and relationships of administrative authorities, as well as the functions which they perform, should be established in such a way as to make executive control organically possible.

The proponents of this viewpoint make certain unfavorable criticisms of the present system. A fair evaluation of the doctrine which they advocate necessitates a statement of their criticisms, as well as their theoretical proposals for reforming the present system. It is necessary to consider, likewise, what has already been accomplished to bring such proposals into effect and what further concrete and practical proposals (in the form of legislation or otherwise) have been advanced.

I. CRITICISM OF THE PRESENT SYSTEM

The attack upon the present system of public administration by those believing in the executive management doctrine centers around questions concerning the organization, the relationship, the functions, and the control over the actions of independent regulatory boards and commissions. The chief source of criticism of the present-day system, from a theoretical viewpoint at least, is the report of the President's Committee on Administrative Management, where the following statements appear:

These independent commissions have been given broad powers to explore, formulate, and administer policies of regulation; they have been given the task of investigating and prosecuting business misconduct; they

143

have been given powers, similar to those exercised by courts of law, to pass in concrete cases upon the rights and liabilities of individuals under the statutes. They are in reality miniature independent governments set up to deal with the railroad problem, the banking problem, or the radio problem. They constitute a headless "fourth branch" of the Government, a haphazard deposit of irresponsible agencies and uncoordinated powers. They do violence to the basic theory of the American Constitution that there should be three major branches of the Government and only three. The Congress has found no effective way of supervising them, they cannot be controlled by the President, and they are answerable to the courts only in respect to the legality of their activities. . . .

The independent regulatory commissions create a confusing and difficult situation in the field of national administration. There is a conflict of principle involved in their make-up and functions. They suffer from an internal inconsistency, an unsoundness of basic theory. This is because they are vested with duties of administration and policy determination with respect to which they ought to be clearly and effectively responsible to the President, and at the same time they are given important judicial work in the doing of which they ought to be wholly independent of Executive control. In fact, the bulk of regulatory commission work involves the application of legislative "standards" of conduct to concrete cases, a function at once discretionary and judicial, and demanding, therefore, both responsibility and independence.

The evils resulting from this confusion of principles are insidious and far-reaching. In the first place, governmental powers of great importance are being exercised under conditions of virtual irresponsibility. . . .

But though the commissions enjoy power without responsibility, they also leave the President with responsibility without power. Placed by the Constitution at the head of a unified and centralized Executive Branch, and charged with the duty to see that the laws are faithfully executed, he must detour around powerful administrative agencies which are in no way subject to his authority and which are, therefore, both actual and potential obstructions to his effective over-all management of national administration. The commissions produce confusion, conflict, and incoherence in the formulation and in the execution of the President's policies. . . . The people look to him for leadership. And yet we whittle away the effective control essential to that leadership by parceling out to a dozen or more irresponsible agencies important powers of policy and administration.

At the same time the independent commission is obliged to carry on judicial functions under conditions which threaten the impartial performance of that judicial work. The discretionary work of the administrator is merged with that of the judge. Pressures and influences properly enough directed toward officers responsible for formulating and administering policy constitute an unwholesome atmosphere in which to adjudicate private rights. But the mixed duties of the commissions render escape from these subversive influences impossible.

Furthermore, the same men are obliged to serve both as prosecutors and as judges. This not only undermines judicial fairness; it weakens public confidence in that fairness. Commission decisions affecting private rights and conduct lie under the suspicion of being rationalizations of the preliminary findings which the commission, in the role of prosecutor, presented to it-self.

The independent commission, in short, provides the proper working conditions neither for administration nor for adjudication. It fails to provide responsibility for the first; it does not provide complete independence for the second. . . .

The independent commissions present a serious immediate problem. . . . Any program to restore our constitutional ideal of a fully coordinated Executive Branch responsible to the President must bring within the reach of that responsible control all work done by these independent commissions which is not judicial in nature. . . .

. . . The multiplication of these agencies cannot fail to obstruct the effective over-all management of the Executive Branch of the Government almost in geometric ratio to their number. . . . As they grow in number his stature [the President's] is bound to diminish. He will no longer be in reality *the Executive*, but only one of many executives, threading his way around obstacles which he has no power to overcome.[1]

II. THEORETICAL PROPOSALS FOR REFORM OF THE PRESENT SYSTEM

The President's Committee on Administrative Management follows its unfavorable criticism of the present regulatory system with proposals for change in that system. As these proposals are the most far-reaching that have been advanced, they will be considered here. The first of them is that each regulatory agency shall be "set up, not in a governmental vacuum outside the executive departments, but within a department." The second is that each agency, once in a department, shall be divided into an administrative section and a judicial section. Concerning this second proposal, the report says:

[1] President's Committee on Administrative Management, *Report with Special Studies* (1937), pp. 39-41.

. . . The administrative section would be a regular bureau or division in the department, headed by a chief with career tenure and staffed under civil-service regulations. It would be directly responsible to the Secretary and through him to the President. The judicial section, on the other hand, would be "in" the department only for purposes of "administrative housekeeping," such as the budget, general personnel administration, and matériel. It would be wholly independent of the department and the President with respect to its work and its decisions. Its members would be appointed by the President with the approval of the Senate for long, staggered terms and would be removable only for causes stated in the statute.

The division of work between the two sections would be relatively simple. The first procedural steps in the regulatory process as now carried on by the independent commissions would go to the administrative section. It would formulate rules, initiate action, investigate complaints, hold preliminary hearings, and by a process of sifting and selection prepare the formal record of cases which is now prepared in practice by the staffs of the commissions. It would, of course, do all the purely administrative or sublegislative work now done by the commissions—in short all the work which is not essentially judicial in nature. The judicial section would sit as an impartial, independent body to make decisions affecting the public interest and private rights upon the basis of the records and findings presented to it by the administrative section. In certain types of cases where the volume of business is large and quick and routine action is necessary, the administrative section itself should in the first instance decide the cases and issue orders, and the judicial section sit as an appellate body to which such decisions could be appealed on questions of law.[2]

III. HOW FAR THIS THEORY OF REFORM HAS ALREADY BEEN PUT INTO EFFECT

The theory of administrative reform advanced by the President's Committee, and supported by the President,[3] has been made effective with various modifications, during the last few years, in respect to several government agencies. This has involved the use of

[2] The same, p. 41.
[3] A "Message from the President of the United States of January 12, 1937," as found in the President's Committee on Administrative Management, *Report with Special Studies*, pp. iii-v, said as to the Committee's entire program, "I endorse this program and feel confident that it will commend itself to you also with your knowledge of government, and to the vast majority of the citizens of the country who want and believe in efficient self-government."

various methods including: (1) failure to appoint a legally required commission while leaving an administrator in charge; (2) legislation, as in respect to the Wage and Hour Division in the Department of Labor, and the Civil Aeronautics Authority; and (3) reorganization. Although in no case has the exact pattern laid down by the President's Committee been followed, each of the methods named shows strong evidence of being based upon the philosophy of executive management.

A. Failure to Appoint

The President has never followed the expressed will of the Congress regarding the Federal Alcohol Administration. An act of 1936[4] abolished the office of Administrator of this agency (then in the Treasury Department), and established an independent Federal Alcohol Administration, to be composed of three members appointed by the President. These provisions were to take effect when a majority of the members of the Administration should qualify and take office. As the President has not yet made any appointments to this agency, an Administrator in the Treasury, responsible to the President, rather than the collegial authority required by law, still exercises the functions of the Administration.

B. Legislation

Although the Congress was not willing to dispense with the collegial type of organization in the case of the Civil Aeronautics Authority, it compromised by adding an Administrator. The Authority is composed of five members, appointed by the President. It is charged with such regulatory and judicial functions as making rules and regulations, conducting investigations, issuing certificates of convenience and necessity, determining upon applications, granting permits, making orders, and the like. The Administrator is charged with the functions of promotion and development. In other words, an officer directly responsible to the President is placed in charge of subordinate policy.

[4] Title V of Act of June 26, 1936, 49 Stat. L. 1939, 1964.

The Fair Labor Standards Act of 1938[5] goes even further in the direction of the views of the President's Committee. This act is not administered by a board or commission, but by a Wage and Hour Division in the Department of Labor. At the head of this Division is an Administrator appointed by the President, with no limitations as to removal. The Administrator is assisted by industry committees appointed by himself. Each committee investigates questions connected with a specific industry, including minimum wage rates and other relevant problems. It also makes recommendations as to classifications which are filed with the Administrator. Upon the filing of such report the Administrator, after giving due notice and opportunity to be heard, issues an order which approves and carries into effect the recommendations, if he finds them in accordance with law and designed to effect its objects. Under this system of organization, it is clear that the determination of subordinate policy and the exercise of legislative, administrative, and quasi-judicial powers are lodged ultimately in the President.

C. Reorganization

Pursuant to the provisions of the Reorganization Act of 1939,[6] the President abolished the National Bituminous Coal Commission and transferred its functions to the Secretary of the Interior "to be administered under his direction and supervision by such division, bureau, or office in the Department of the Interior as the Secretary shall determine."[7] By an order of June 16,[8] as amended by that of July 5, 1939,[9] the Secretary of the Interior established a Bituminous Coal Division, under the charge of a Director. The Division is to administer the functions vested in the National Bituminous Coal Commission. "The functions administered by the aforesaid Division shall be performed by and through its Director, who shall exercise all of the power and authority of the Division in the premises."

From the examples given, it is evident that a serious attempt is

[5] 52 Stat. L. 1060.
[6] Pub. No. 19, 76 Cong. 1 sess.
[7] Message from the President of the United States transmitting Reorganization Plan No. II, 76 Cong. 1 sess., H. Doc. 288.
[8] No. 1394.
[9] No. 1399.

being made to substitute the executive management theory of regulatory administration for that which has been developed during the past fifty years.

If this theory should be put into effect generally, the present-day system of economic regulation would be completely overturned. Fundamental changes would be made in the type of authority administering the regulatory functions. Such changes would tend to make regulatory legislative action (which is generally now, when rights are involved, taken by orders based on a fact-finding) a matter for the discretion of the Executive. As a corollary, there would be a weakening of that judicial control which guarantees that action affecting rights shall be taken according to proper procedure and shall be supported by evidence. Instead of the administrative situation which exists at present, in which action touching rights must be taken under a judicial or due process procedure, there would apparently be ordinary administrative action with whatever procedure the administrator might see fit to adopt, since under the plan of the President's Committee the judicial section would handle only justiciable matters. In other words, it could not assist in the formulation of minor policies and regulations through a quasi-judicial process. The judicial unit would be confined to two major types of activity. (1) It would pass upon actions already taken by the administrative branch to see that they were in accordance with the law and the rules and regulations. It would have authority to set aside a rule or regulation if that rule or regulation were not in accordance with the law, but it would have no authority to set it aside on the ground that it represented an unwise, unsound, or ill-considered exercise of the discretionary power vested in the administrator. (2) It would pass upon controversies between the administration and the individual, or between two private disputants.

Such fundamental changes should not be made without the fullest knowledge of what they involve. The administrative law of a country is a complicated network of economic, political, legal, and administrative factors. To disturb one may disturb many. Every proposed change should be subjected to thorough analysis and criticism.

IV. ANALYSIS AND CRITICISM OF THE EXECUTIVE MANAGEMENT THEORY

The executive management theory will be examined from the viewpoints of: (1) administrative and legal technique; and (2) broad public policy.

A. The Viewpoint of Administrative and Legal Technique

Any critical technical analysis of the proposals which were advanced by the President's Committee on Administrative Management and which have been to a greater or less extent embodied in recent statutes should start with the types of action performed by the independent regulatory boards and commissions. This is necessary because, as has been shown previously, the nature of the actions performed by any authority must to a large extent govern its organization, its relationship to the executive, the forms of administrative action that it should employ, its types of procedure, the methods by which its actions are enforced, and the types of control that are applicable.

The independent regulatory boards and commissions take their chief actions which affect individuals by: (1) making rules and regulations; (2) carrying out investigations; (3) prosecuting cases that come before them; and (4) issuing orders. The fundamental questions that should be raised in respect to these actions are: whether they should be taken by a single administrator or by a board or commission; whether they are of such a nature as to require a separation of functions; and whether such actions should be subjected to any particular type of control.

1. Issuing rules and regulations

Rules and regulations which are issued by the authorities in charge of economic regulation fall into two main classes: (1) procedural and (2) substantive.

a. Procedural rules and regulations. Procedural rules and regulations have to do with the procedure in conducting cases before the regulatory authority itself. They implement and supplement statutory provisions not only for the purpose of guaranteeing due process of law, but also for that of facilitating procedure and making it plain to contestants how to conduct their cases before the authority. There is every reason to believe that rules of procedure can best be formulated, as at present, by preliminary consultation with those concerned; preparation of a preliminary draft by subordinate administrative and legal agents of each authority; discussion, revision, and final promulgation by the members of the regulatory authority.

The types of cases handled by the various regulatory agencies are so different that some differences in procedure are evidently necessary. Those charged with handling the special types of cases are in the best position to know and understand what procedures will make for the most inexpensive and easy flow of business under the laws that they are administering. Whether or not there can and should be a greater degree of unity amid variety is a question that can probably be answered better in the near future than it can be at present, for there will soon be available the results of the studies now being conducted by the government departments and agencies themselves and those made by the Attorney General's Committee on Procedure. In case a rather uniform system of procedure is found to be theoretically possible, the question still remains as to how it should be made effective: by joint action of the authorities themselves, by congressional action, or by presidential action after consultation and agreement.

b. Substantive rules and regulations. The assumption of the President's Committee seems to be that the substantive rules and regulations of regulatory agencies involve executive policy and should therefore be subject to executive control. Such is not the case. These rules and regulations are legislative in nature. They are issued under delegated legislative power. They implement or supplement the law by developing the principles which the legislature has already established. They interpret the law and fill in details to make it directly applicable in the dealings of the government with the individual. For this work a collegial rather than a single administrator is best, since a board or commission can look at the matter, like the legislature itself, from various viewpoints. There is less possibility that special interests will obtain a controlling influence over several men than over one. No question of separation of powers arises in the making of substantive rules and regulations, since the act is purely legislative and no judicial functions are involved. Even when the processes employed resemble judicial procedures, this does not alter the legislative nature of the act.

In so far as minor details of policy are determined by rules and regulations, it appears reasonable to leave such details to the authority which is charged with the regulatory process. This subject will be discussed later.

Rules and regulations are not enforced as such. It is only when they are violated in a concrete case that the question of enforcement arises. They are enforced as the laws themselves are, usually by the Attorney General acting through the courts. The President has the same relationship to the enforcement of rules and regulations that he has to the enforcement of law.

Control over rules and regulations is exercised for two chief purposes: (1) to keep rules and regulations immediately in line with congressional policy; and (2) to hold them within the general limits of law.

1. Congressional policy is expressed and defined in its broad outlines by statute; but the minor details are provided by rules and regulations. Since these are made under delegated legislative power, control over them, from the standpoint of policy, is basically exercised by the Congress. It is a mistaken concept of our entire federal system, and particularly of the separation of powers, which assumes that the determination of policy should belong to the Executive. The debates upon the Constitution at the time of its adoption, the terms of that instrument, and innumerable judicial decisions, have long ago established the fact that the determination of policy is a legislative function.[10] In practice, and in constitutional principle, Congress, rather than the Executive, makes policies; Congress, rather than the Executive, delegates matters of detail to administrative agents and agencies; and Congress, as well as the

[10] See James Madison's *Debates in the Federal Convention of 1787*, especially the debates of June 1 to June 4; the Constitution of the United States, particularly the final paragraph of Art. I, Sec. 8; *Continental Illinois National Bank & Trust Co.* v. *Chicago, Rock Island & Pacific Ry. Co.*, 72 F. (2d) 443, aff. 294 U.S. 648; *Schechter* v. *United States*, 295 U.S. 495; *Panama Refining Co.* v. *Ryan*, 293 U.S. 388.

Executive, sees to it that the delegation thus made is employed to further the original policies.

Several methods are used by Congress in controlling the making of rules and regulations as to policy. Thus, in most instances it requires that rules and regulations made under specified statutes shall be published in the *Federal Register*. In matters of particular importance or difficulty, it sometimes requires that rules and regulations shall be laid before Congress for a fixed period prior to their becoming effective. It may provide that the rules and regulations issued under a given statute shall not go into effect until a specified period after publication. By all these methods Congress may obtain a knowledge of the manner in which the powers which it delegates are used; and if it is dissatisfied it can alter the terms of the delegation, withdraw it, or legislate on the crucial points. Even the veto of the President cannot prevent action which a large proportion of the members of Congress is determined to take in order to control policy.

2. Control to hold rules and regulations within the limits of law is exercised by the courts through several different methods, always when appropriate cases come before them. They may pass upon the constitutionality of the original grant of rule-making power by the legislature. They may decide whether an agency has acted beyond the scope of its powers under the law; whether it has followed the statutory procedure, if any, for the taking of particular action; or whether it has abused its powers. Control of this type is, and must be, not executive but judicial in nature.

Since policy in respect to rules and regulations is properly controlled by Congress, and legality by the courts, there is no place for executive control over this function.

2. *Investigations*

Investigations are made by the independent regulatory authorities under several conditions. Some investigations are carried on for the information of the legislature. Some are made upon the complaint of one deeming himself injured by unlawful acts of a carrier or other regulated person, business, or economic entity. Some are initiated by the regulatory authority itself, in case of suspected unlawful action. Except for those undertaken in order to obtain information requested by Congress or needed by the agency, investigations are generally made for the purpose of deciding whether or not to take steps against persons suspected of unlawful acts.

It is clearly inappropriate for the Executive to control investigations generally. His power could not extend to those ordered by Congress, unless by special legislative mandate. It should not extend to others, for obvious reasons. If it did so extend, the charge would often be made that a given investigation had been instituted or discontinued for political motives; and at times such a charge might have some basis in fact. Freedom from executive control in respect to administrative and regulatory investigations is as necessary for honest and unbiased administrative activities as it is in respect to the investigations of a grand jury.

When the Executive feels the need of obtaining information not available through the ordinary channels, he may ask Congress to make an appropriation for the purpose of carrying on a special investigation. If Congress grants this request, the investigation can be made without any real or apparent manipulation of administrative agencies for personal political objectives. So delicate is the balance here that even an executive order to a regulatory administrative agency, requiring greater or less vigor in the making of a given investigation in a controversial field, is likely to be interpreted as an act of partisan politics. Unless it appears clearly necessary as a part of the executive function of seeing that the laws are carried out, such an order should not be given.

A type of investigation which has not yet been mentioned is that made by the regulatory authority in order to determine whether to issue new rules and regulations or to issue new orders of a general nature. Such investigations, like those of the legislature for similar purposes, are a preliminary to legislative action. They should hence be free from both executive and judicial control.

It should be emphasized that the work of investigation is not in itself a special function. It is an activity carried on to further a legislative function or a judicial function. Often it has no meaning except as part of a larger activity. In connection with regulation, especially, investigation cannot and should not be separated from other phases of the process.

There is no need for the enforcement of investigations, as if they were orders or other acts commanding action. Any enforcement provisions which may exist deal with powers to subpoena witnesses, require the production of evidence, etc., but do not imply the meaningless conception of enforcing investigations.

3. The prosecution of cases

Those who advocate the executive management theory of administration are much concerned because in connection with certain administrative acts the work of prosecution is combined with that of adjudication. Such persons overlook the fact that this situation obtains in respect to only a few kinds of administrative action, and that even where it is present, rights are seldom endangered. Obviously, it does not exist in connection with rules and regulations or investigations. Since orders are of several types, it is necessary to ask which types, if any, justify uneasiness as to the combination of prosecuting activities with adjudication.

In respect to legislative regulatory orders, there can be no such thing as prosecution. In fixing a rate schedule, a wage schedule, a type of service, a valuation, forms of accounting, forms of reports, etc., prosecution is no part of the picture. The hearing is not held for the purpose of convicting anyone or even of contesting rights, but for that of establishing a course for future action.

Procedural orders, which are issued for the purpose of furthering an investigation or facilitating the conduct of a case, do not involve prosecution. There is no place for prosecution in the making of orders regarding declarations and designations, or of most orders in respect to licenses and permits. The same is true of administrative controlling orders, and generally of negative orders.

The question of prosecution arises, or appears to arise, chiefly in respect to: (1) reparation orders; (2) injunctive and command orders; and (3) certain orders suspending or revoking licenses because of violations of law or rules and regulations. Each class named must be considered separately.

a. Reparation orders. The reparation orders which are issued by regulatory authorities (the chief subject of the present study) are not an immediate or direct feature of the regulatory activity. They are, strictly speaking, acts of adjudication which are performed by regulatory agencies because such agencies possess relevant information and special skills. To use a familiar example: the law requires rates charged by railways to be reasonable and non-discriminatory. If an individual feels that he has been injured by an unreasonable or discriminatory rate, he complains to the Interstate Commerce Commission. The Commission makes an investigation and holds a hearing at which both the individual and the carrier present their sides of the case. If the Commission finds that injury has been done and that reparation should be made, it so orders. In final analysis, it is merely deciding a case between two individuals. It is not prosecuting any more than the district court does if a similar case is taken to it under the law.[11] The same thing is true of all other reparation orders.

b. Injunctive and command orders. Injunctive and other command orders present a different picture. There is no doubt that the problem of prosecutor-judge may arise in respect to orders of this type, such as are issued by several authorities.[12] This occurs when an administrative agency, such as the Federal Trade Commission, makes investigations and holds hearings for the purpose of determining whether an individual complained of has done wrong. The attorneys of the Commission bring evidence before it, in the attempt to prove illegal action on the part of the respondent. The latter brings evidence in his own defense. There may be pleadings on both sides. As the result of the hearing, the Commission may issue a cease and desist order.

At first sight, this procedure seems unfair to the respondent. Here is a definite instance where the agents of the Commission prosecute, and the Commission judges. Should there not be a separation of prosecution and adjudication, lest partiality lead to injustice?

Before answering this question, certain relevant points should be considered. The first is that the hearing is only a single phase of an almost continuous work of investigation. It represents, not the desire to win a case for the Commission, but the result of a checking

[11] See 49 U.S.C. 9, which provides that a person may elect whether to bring the case in a district court or bring a complaint before the Interstate Commerce Commission.

[12] F. F. Blachly, "Work Materials on Administrative Action and Procedure" (manuscript).

and sifting process that is directed constantly toward the administration and enforcement of the law. The second is the complexity of the problems involved. The single individual, and even the court, cannot know so well as the Commission can the significance and weight of a given action. The third is that the cease and desist order, or other injunctive and command order, is issued as a part of the regulatory process. The hearing, and the investigations behind the hearing, clarify situations left indefinite by the law. The fourth is that in this instance and in practically every other instance where prosecution and adjudication are performed by the same agency, they are not performed by the same individuals. Attorneys, field agents, trial examiners, etc., prepare the evidence and present it at the hearing. The amazingly small percentage of cases taken to the courts after such hearings is in itself strong evidence that the authority which adjudicates has no undue bias in favor of its agents who prosecute. The fifth is that review of the cease and desist order can be had in the circuit court of appeals—a guarantee against arbitrary, willful, or biased action by the Commission. The sixth is that the courts, not only under the new Federal Trade Commission Act, but under other similar acts, have repeatedly upheld the cease and desist order procedure.[13] To tear apart a closely woven fabric of regulatory activities fully protected by legal safeguards, because of a theoretical disapprobation of combined functions, seems both unnecessary and reckless. The present system needs little change in order to separate prosecution from adjudication, so long as the combination serves a useful purpose without invading guaranteed rights.

c. Orders suspending or revoking licenses. In cases involving the suspension or revocation of a license for violation of law, rules, regulations, orders, or requirements, the activity of prosecution often appears to be combined with that of adjudication. The authority which issues the license finds (usually after some sort of hearing) that there is cause for suspending or revoking it, and acts accordingly. In all instances of this kind, there should probably be some provision for hearing, order, and judicial review, the review to be on

[13] *Southern Pacific Co.* v. *Interstate Commerce Commission*, 219 U.S. 433; *Federal Trade Commission* v. *A. Mclean & Son*, 84 F. (2d) 910, cert. den. 299 U.S. 590; *Federal Trade Commission* v. *F. A. Martoccio Co.*, 87 F. (2d) 561, cert. den. 301 U.S. 691.

questions of abuse of power and relation between the evidence and the finding. It is by no means clear, however, that the licensing activity should be separated into "administrative" and "judicial" aspects, or that persons whose activities are controlled by licenses would obtain any benefits from such a separation. Likewise, it is not clear that the prosecuting aspect should or could be separated from the adjudicating aspect of this activity. Control by license, through its very nature, involves a great deal of discretion. If the discretion is not abused, and if administrative procedures are devised which will protect not only the rights, but so far as possible the interests, of the person who holds the license, substantial justice is done.

If the foregoing analysis is correct, there are relatively few instances where the independent regulatory boards and commissions exercise a prosecuting function in connection with their main activities. The question of separating the functions of prosecution and adjudication, therefore, seldom arises in a practical way. Where prosecution and adjudication are in the same hands, there appear to be sound reasons for continuing the mixture of functions and permitting appeal to the courts to ensure regularity and to prevent abuses.

4. The use of orders in administration

It has been shown in earlier chapters that the regulatory boards and commissions take most of their formal actions, affecting third parties, by means of statutory orders. The question must be asked whether the proponents of executive management are justified in regarding the present procedure for issuing orders as a mixture of powers which ought to be separated, with executive control over all except the judicial power. The answer to this question, as well as related questions of control, enforcement, and the like, must depend upon several factors.

a. The factor of judicial power. In the first place, the making of a considerable number of orders does not involve judicial power. To such orders the charge as to mixture of powers cannot apply.

Legislative regulatory orders are made under delegated legislative power and involve only this type of power. Although they are often issued under a quasi-judicial procedure, such procedure is employed solely for the purpose of deciding the content and scope of the proposed order, and not at all for the purpose of determining contested rights of individuals. Although persons having different interests may be heard, and such persons may even be called parties, they are not parties in any real sense. In holding hearings for the purpose of deciding upon a rate schedule, for example, the Interstate Commerce Commission may hear its own experts, representatives of the carriers who may be affected, and representatives of the public; but none of those heard have any rights which can be adjudicated at the hearing.[14]

Orders of the legislative regulatory type are made as a part of the work of administering and developing in detail a general policy laid down by the legislature. The formulation of policy is thus a part of the work of delegated legislation.

A few further considerations may be mentioned in connection with orders of a legislative regulatory nature.

Because such orders are inherently legislative, in issuing them a board or commission form of organization such as usually exists at present is preferable to a single administrator. To place the making of these orders in a department with a single head responsible to the President might leave the way open for arbitrary partisan action, or at least a color of such action. This would rightly lead to dissatisfaction which would not be cured even by a finding of a court that the head of the department or administrator had acted within his powers.

An important aspect of the lack of parties, mentioned above, is the fact that the regulatory agency, although it may be called a party at the hearings and in cases that subsequently arise, is not concerned to defeat the others who may be heard. It represents the public interest, which may be as well served by sustaining the contentions of those regulated as by denying them. It is in no sense a contestant, but an impartial legislative authority finding and receiving evidence upon which to base future action. By following a regular procedure, usually before trial examiners, there is opportunity for all sides of the question to be discussed.

[14] If the schedule finally adopted by order should prove to be confiscatory, the question of rights will arise. It cannot, however, arise in a judicial sense when no action has been taken by the Commission.

It is important to note that, even after holding hearings, the administrative body is not bound, as is a court, to make a decision or to issue an order.

In respect to such orders, therefore, the problem of the relationship of the judicial authority to the administrative authority does not arise, since the issuing of the order is not a judicial act.

In issuing certain orders regarding joint rates, etc., the problem of the regulatory authority is actually one of management rather than of regulation in the usual sense, although its orders for this purpose are legislative in nature. This happens when, as under the Interstate Commerce Act of 1920, the authority is required to regulate the rates of competing carriers in such a way as to preserve all said carriers. The legislative nature of the orders under discussion, which is acknowledged by the courts, does not withdraw them from judicial control if they are *ultra vires*, constitute abuses of power, or violate the constitutional requirement of due process of law. Due process of law, as defined by the courts, in this connection, demands that a legislative regulatory order shall be made after a fact-finding supported by evidence, and that the facts found shall be the basis of the order. It would be impossible for the President to control such orders without doing violence to the whole concept of due process of law. A sound system of administration demands that there shall be no interference by higher authorities with action that is based upon a proper fact-finding supported by evidence; otherwise a fact-finding loses its significance, and arbitrary discretion may easily be substituted for it. Even the courts can seldom interfere with such fact-finding if there has been a proper procedure including the requisite basis of evidence.

Should the enforcement of regulatory legislative orders be different from that now in use? These orders are not of such a nature that they can be enforced by the President. When enforcement is required, this is at present usually a matter for the courts to handle, and from what has been said the conclusion is obvious that it should remain such.

Procedural orders are issued for the purpose of furthering an investigation or conducting a case. They may be issued by any type of authority that is conducting such activities. These orders are strictly administrative in nature and seldom directly affect rights and duties. As a result no problems arise in respect to the proper type of authority for issuing such orders, the type of relationship that should obtain between the issuing authority and the executive, or the type of enforcement.

Administrative controlling orders are issued in connection with purely administrative functions; hence no problems in respect to organization, relationship, controls, or enforcement can arise.

Orders *in re* declarations and designations are either legislative or judicial, according to whether general classes are set up, or whether a specific individual is placed within a class after a hearing and upon the evidence. In so far as such orders are legislative in nature, the same theory should obtain as in respect to legislative orders establishing rules and regulations. In so far as they are judicial, they are made under a "due process of law" procedure and controlled by the courts. It is impossible to see how a "judicial section" of an agency could handle them better or differently.

b. The factor of separation of powers. In the second place, it is not necessary to assume *a priori* that there should be a separation of administrative from judicial powers even in connection with the issuance of orders that are clearly judicial in nature. These orders will be examined briefly, with the purpose of evaluating the contention of the believers in executive management that such a separation should be made.

(1) Injunctive and command orders. Injunctive and command orders take two chief forms:

(a) Where after an investigation and a hearing a person is held to be in violation of the law, and an order is issued requiring compliance with the law or enjoining disobedience thereto.

(b) Where the order is combined with some other order, such as a rate or reparation order.

In the first form, which is employed by the Federal Trade Commission, the regulatory authority, after investigation on its own initiative or upon complaint of an injured individual, issues a complaint and cites the person complained of to appear before it to show cause why a cease and desist order should not be issued against him. At the hearing the Commission's staff submits evidence regarding the violation of law. The law administered by the Federal Trade Commission is so general in nature, making unfair or discriminatory practices illegal without defining such practices, that one of two things must be done in order to make it applicable to concrete illegal practices. The Federal Trade Commission, or other authority operating under a similar law, would either have to implement the law by rules and regulations stating in detail what constitutes unfair methods of competition or discrimination, or else it would have to determine what are unfair methods of competition or discriminatory practices when deciding concrete cases.

Owing to the decision of the Supreme Court in the Gratz case that what is an unfair method of competition is a question for the courts and not the Commission, and that unfair competition is only that deemed unfair at common law, the Commission has been unable to implement the law by rule and regulation in order to say just what actions are violations of law.[15] The result has largely been that sublegislation as to what are unfair methods of competition and discriminatory practices has been developed case by case, in its orders.

In respect to such orders the assertion may be made with fairness that there are combined in the same authority the functions of investigation, prosecution, sublegislation (at the time of deciding cases), and the judicial function of issuing a cease and desist order. This is an unfortunate mixture of powers and functions which should be eliminated as far as possible; although it is only just to the Federal Trade Commission to remark that its organization and procedures are such as to minimize the dangers involved. The same thing may be said of other administrative agencies which exercise combined powers; they are eager, even anxious, to establish processes which safeguard the individual as well as the general public interest; and for the most part they have been remarkably successful in doing so.

---

[15] *Federal Trade Commission* v. *Gratz*, 253 U.S. 421. It is true that trade practice conferences were initiated in 1919 the object of which was to afford to a representative group in any industry an opportunity collectively to formulate and voluntarily to adopt, under the aegis of the Commission, rules expressing common conceptions of fair trade practices. Such rules, however, cannot be considered as having the force and effect of law.

In improving the situation of the Federal Trade Commission, any one of several methods might be chosen, although it should never be forgotten that a certain margin of power must be left with the Commission, to be utilized when clever minds discover new ways of being unfair. Congress, acting under its power to regulate interstate commerce and informed by the experience of the Commission, might define unfair methods of competition and discriminatory practices to include many things never dreamed of by the common law. It might prefer to establish more general but clearly defined statutory outlines of policy and delegations of power, leaving the Commission to do its work of regulation in freedom from the handicap of obsolescent concepts of economic justice. It might make the Commission an investigatory and prosecuting body, with or without statutory power to make rules and regulations defining unfair methods and discriminatory practices, but without the power to decide cases, which would go to a special legislative administrative tribunal and, on appeal, to the regular courts.

The second group of instances, namely, those in which an order of some other type is combined with an order of the injunctive or command type, presents no special problems. If, for example, a rate schedule is embodied in an order, and the order is accompanied by another enjoining the use of any rates save those provided in the schedule, the situation is relatively simple. Both orders are subject to controls which have been explained already. There seems to be no place for executive intervention, since, as was shown, it is not appropriate to the legislative act (the order embodying the rate schedule) and is not even proposed in connection with the judicial act. There is likewise no logical reason for separating the two acts, and insisting that since the legislative order has administrative characteristics which do not appear in the judicial order, executive and administrative controls ought to be applied to the former but not to the latter. The controls already existing are sufficient, and any others would be merely cumbersome.

(2) Reparation or analogous orders. Reparation or analogous orders include reparation for injury done, orders for the payment of money, and certain awards of a monetary nature. They are judicial in nature. The regulatory authority neither investigates, prose-

cutes, nor acts in a sublegislative capacity. It merely decides a con-troversy between two individuals just as a court might. In so doing, it does not exercise a mixture of powers. There seems to be no reason to expect fairer or more judicial action from "administrative sections" than from the agencies which now issue reparation and analogous orders. It has been shown above that some type of judi-cial appeal from these orders is possible; and for obvious reasons this possibility should remain open.

(3) Penalty orders. Penalty orders inflict some sort of non-monetary punishment or forfeiture of privilege, and so on, for violations of law, rules and regulations, orders, or the conditions and requirements laid down in a grant, license, permit, etc. The penalty may be suspension, expulsion, removal from office, closing of the mail to the use of an individual, exclusion of products from entrance into the country, and so forth. Penalty orders are judicial or administrative in nature. The law, order, rule, regulation, grant, license, or the like, has laid down the conditions that are to be obeyed. The only question before the regulatory authority is whether there has been disobedience.

It is true that agents of the regulatory authority may present evidence to show violation. But the authority or its examiners hear and decide on the evidence presented by both sides. They do not sublegislate in the process. Moreover, when justiciable rights are involved there is a strict judicial control over their actions; and even when no such rights exist the procedure is generally devised in such a way as to protect the interests of the individual and to avoid all possibility of arbitrary or capricious action.

(4) Orders in respect to licenses, privileges, grants, permits, etc. An administrative agency may take several different types of ac-tion in respect to licenses, privileges, etc. It may, according to circum-stances, grant or refuse to grant; it may renew or refuse to renew; it may amend or refuse to amend; it may suspend, revoke, or cancel. It is obvious that all these acts do not have identical significance. For this reason the procedure in taking them and the controls over them may be different.

It appears that the original grant, refusal to grant, amending of conditions, or refusal to amend, is a discretionary administrative act unless the legislature has established a specific right to such a document upon the fulfillment of certain conditions. If a specific right has been established, the question of whether the conditions have been fulfilled is evidently judicial in nature. Refusal to renew after a license, etc., has once been granted, as well as suspension or revocation, would seem judicial in nature if based on charges of misconduct or violation of a legal standard, but administrative, if based upon considerations of public policy or welfare. If, in the former instance, the standard which it is claimed has been violated has been laid down by statute, the administrative body has only to determine from evidence whether there has or has not been conformity. Such action is wholly judicial. If the legal standard consists in the rules and regulations established by the regulatory authority itself, and charges of violation are brought, the authority passes upon cases arising under its own sublegislative action. It is not, however, laying down norms of conduct at the same time that it is passing upon a case. There is no confusion of legislative with judicial action. Moreover, since in most instances there is statutory judicial review over all actions of a judicial nature, there can be little danger of arbitrary action.

(5) Negative orders. Negative orders of administrative bodies have generally received special treatment by the courts. Until recently, such orders have been held to include: determinations not to act; refusal to act because of supposed lack of jurisdiction; and general negative orders.

In the determination-not-to-act type of negative order, the regulatory authority is asked to take action but, after exercising its discretion, it determines that action is unnecessary, would be inexpedient, or might perhaps be illegal. Such a determination is generally administrative in nature. As a rule it does not directly affect rights. If it does not directly affect rights, it creates no obligation and places no burdens upon an individual; hence there is no need for control over it. When it is equivalent to a judicial decision denying substantive rights, the case is different. Here the courts will intervene to protect such rights, despite the negative form of the order.

A negative order issued because of a supposed lack of jurisdiction does not change in any way a juridical situation. The regulatory authority merely believes that it has no power to act and therefore refrains from acting. There is no appeal from such an order, unless appeal is granted by statute.

The general negative order may refuse any relief sought, may refuse to reopen a case, etc. Such orders, unless clearly arbitrary, have generally been held to be non-reviewable. Some negative orders, however, when they have denied substantial rights, have been reviewed so that such rights might be protected.

In a recent and very important opinion,[16] Mr. Justice Frankfurter has declared that "any distinction, as such, between 'negative' and 'affirmative' orders, as a touchstone of jurisdiction to review . . . serves no useful purpose." It appears, therefore, that each negative order must be considered as belonging to some other class of orders, according to its subject matter.

5. Summary as to mixture of powers

This detailed analysis shows that independent boards and commissions do not constitute "a haphazard deposit of irresponsible agencies and uncoordinated powers." They are carrying on a particular kind of activity, the regulatory activity. In doing so they take those types of action that are necessary and appropriate to their functions. Many of their acts are sublegislative in nature, consisting in the issuance of rules and regulations which have the force and effect of law. By such acts they fill in the outlines of statutes, as the Congress might have done had it possessed sufficient time and technical knowledge. For all important sublegislation of a substantive kind, there is statutory authorization.

Since the subject matter of sublegislative acts is much the same as that of the law itself and supplements and implements the law, these authorities are and should be responsible for such acts to Congress, rather than to the President. Congress can hold them responsible by such methods as: making its delegation of regulatory power rather narrow and limited; laying down detailed standards and norms for the guidance of the administrative agency; requiring

[16] *Rochester Telephone Corp.* v. *United States*, 307 U.S. 125. See Supporting Statement V, pp. 287-301; also Gregory Hankin, "The Fate of the Negative Order" (manuscript).

publication of rules and regulations in the *Federal Register;* and even providing that rules and regulations must be laid before it for approval, or must lie before it a certain number of days before going into effect.

The analysis also shows that (except for special instances where the administrative decision is more appropriate) the order is the most important form of regulatory action. Orders, which are of several distinct types,[17] are employed for the following purposes: (1) acts of administration; (2) acts legislative in nature but judicial in form; (3) acts judicial in nature and form; (4) acts which combine the functions of prosecution, legislation, and adjudication.

1. Acts of administration, which neither impose a general rule nor decide as to specific rights or duties, in no way confuse the legislative, prosecuting, and judicial functions.

2. Acts which, although taken in a judicial form, are legislative in nature, as orders in respect to rates, prices, accounting, wages and hours, pooling arrangements, etc., do not combine legislative, prosecuting, and judicial functions.

3. Acts which are judicial in nature, as the issuance of reparation orders, penalty orders, orders *in re* declarations and designations which concern a specific individual, or injunctive and command orders made to enforce a specific provision of the law, rules and regulations or other orders, do not mingle prosecuting, legislative, and judicial functions.

4. There is undoubtedly a combination of legislative, prosecuting, and judicial functions in the issuance of certain injunctive and command orders, when the Congress has failed to define its meaning, and has also failed to give to the authority which must administer an ambiguous statute the power to make rules and regulations which complete and clarify the law. The classical instance of an authority placed in this situation is the Federal Trade Commission, which, in holding hearings as to a given practice and issuing an order on the basis of the hearings, must of necessity legislate, prosecute, and adjudicate at once. To remedy this condition, it is not necessary to change the administrative organization and relationships of the Federal Trade Commission, or to redistribute its

---

[17] Supporting Statement V, pp. 287-301.

functions between separate administrative and judicial authorities. A simple amendment to the law, further defining congressional policy and giving the Commission power to issue rules and regulations, would make possible an end to the present confusion of functions.

All the actions which are taken by means of the order, except the last-named type, are in nature and procedure such that no combination of administrative, legislative, prosecuting, and judicial functions exists when these actions are performed. The charges to this effect, made by the President's Committee, and the accompanying recommendations for a redistribution of functions, were based on an incomplete analysis of the nature of the specific actions performed by the independent boards and commissions.

Even though it be granted that (with the exceptions noted above) the several actions taken by these boards and commissions do not involve such a combination of powers as would demand a reallocation of functions, some persons may still maintain that within each agency there is a combination of functions which makes a reallocation necessary or desirable. This problem will be discussed in the following part of the present chapter.

As regards the acts of regulatory agencies which affect the individual directly or indirectly, it has been shown that there are adequate controls over such acts, namely, control by Congress itself over rules and regulations; and control by the courts over those orders which affect individual rights in such a way that a justiciable controversy can arise. To substitute a control by the President over rules and regulations would cause him to interfere with the sublegislative expert authorities, without in any way expediting his own functions as Chief Executive. In other words, it would injure the work of the expert agencies and would not benefit that of the President.

B. Public Policy and the Independent Regulatory Agencies

Those who believe that executive management should replace the present type of economic regulation by independent administrative agencies support their position on grounds of public policy. They observe, quite accurately, that many of the most important problems of present-day economic life, such as the regulation under law of transportation, communications, water power, finance, fuel, trade and commerce, shipping, the tariff, securities and exchanges, and labor relations, are given over to independent and separate highly specialized authorities. Hence, they say, there is and can be no unity or coherence of policy in respect to the entire field of economic regulation. Each authority administers its own policy without reference to the policies of other authorities, or to any general line of policy.

It is remarked, further, that whereas the regulatory agencies are applying and developing broad economic and social policies, they are removed from any effective political control comparable to that exercised over other administrative agencies, which are also in some measure formulating policy. The independent boards and commissions are not tied together in respect to policy by the superior executive direction of the President of the United States, since he can exercise very little control over them except through the power of appointment. If the members of a commission are numerous, have staggered terms of office, possess a long tenure, and can be removed only for cause, his control is almost negligible. It is contended that the President, although elected to carry out and enforce certain economic and social policies, is prevented from doing so by virtue of the fact that all the important fields of economic governmental activity are withdrawn from his control. It is suggested, therefore, that sublegislation in respect to these policies be given over to the heads of departments who may be controlled by the President, or to the President himself.

It is sometimes claimed that centralization of the sublegislative function in the President would have certain favorable results. The regulations of a substantive nature promulgated by the President would have a higher sanction than those issued by an administrative authority. Presidential sublegislation would also free the regulatory authority from the position of being at the same time the maker and the enforcer of the law. A rule or regulation issued by the supreme administrative authority, the President, governing the actions of a regulatory authority, would have a more compelling force upon such authority than a rule issued by itself, even if it is bound by law to obey its own rules and regulations. The possibility is always present that the regulatory authority may change its rules and regulations in order to make them coincide with its particular philosophy or to meet the exigencies of a concrete situation. If the regulations under which an authority acts are made by the President, the regulatory authority is placed in its proper position, that of an administrator acting under superior direction.

In respect to procedural rules and regulations, it is claimed that if the President were able to make these, he could bring about a very desirable uniformity among the different agencies. This would tend to simplify and standardize procedure, thus tending to expedite hearings, guarantee a better process, and give litigants and their attorneys a better chance than they have at present to know what their rights are and the methods by which to obtain them.

Although these theoretical arguments for executive management within the field of policy are seductive, there are even stronger arguments on the other side. In the first place, the President is not and cannot be, under our Constitution, the general policy-determining agency of the federal government, despite the authority which he possesses in foreign relations and other specific fields. In his messages to Congress he may suggest policies, and he possesses a limited veto power; but in the last analysis Congress can determine policy within the field of its constitutional powers.

Since the activities of the regulatory boards and commissions are largely legislative in nature, control over these activities belongs primarily to the legislature, and in appropriate cases to the courts. It is hardly possible to detach from the closely woven fabric of subsidiary functions, forming the pattern known as the regulatory function, a single thread which should be in the hands of the executive. It is Congress that should organize the regulatory bodies, distribute functions among their various organs, and hold them responsible; for the simple reason that their basic activities are not either judicial or administrative, but consist in the formulation and amendment of rules which are actually a part of the law, or the issuing of orders legislative in nature. This work could be done by Congress itself, and the fact that Congress chooses to place it in the hands of a special regulatory agency does not alter the fact that the duties of such an agency are principally legislative.

Possibly those who desire to place the administration and policy of such bodies under executive control are interested less in sublegislation than in such matters as decisions to prosecute or not to prosecute, to expedite the handling of cases, to regulate with a light hand on the rein or with a heavy pull on the bit. These persons make the mistake of supposing that executive policy should be reflected in the every-day enforcement of the law, and the even greater mistake of looking upon the Executive in the United States as the authority charged with the determination of policy. It is conceivable that an arrangement such as they propose would enable the Executive to obtain the passage of rules and regulations reflecting his own views; but this would mean government by men rather than by law, and sublegislation controlled by an almost untouchable Executive rather than by Congress and the courts.

To the contention that large fields of public policy are dominated and controlled by the regulatory boards and commissions, the answer is that they should be. Legislative policies as to transportation, communication, shipping, public waters, labor relations, and the like, are of such a nature as to require consistent, flexible, informed, intelligent, and developing administration over long periods of time. Administration of this kind should be wholly nonpartisan and free from the domination of the party in power. Any attempt to make it reflect policy, other than the policy laid down by statute, is in essence an attempt to establish partisan or individual control of the economic realm involved.

With the increasing complexity of our social and economic structure, matters requiring legislation or sublegislation become constantly more numerous, difficult, and complicated. Under these conditions, the determination of sound policy requires thorough and continuous investigation, and particularly a regular, systematic collection of basic statistical information. The problem of what information to collect through reports and accounts, how to set up systems of reporting and accounting for the businesses regulated, how to classify information and co-ordinate it so that it will be significant in the regulatory process, is not only a problem of administration, but likewise one of sublegislation. It is also immediately tied in with the so-called judicial activity in respect to legislative regulatory orders; for the establishment of rates, wages, etc., depends not merely upon the evidence presented by opposing parties but also upon the evidence presented by the government through its experts, who appear at the hearings as representatives of the public interest. The function of investigation for sublegislative purposes cannot be separated from that of investigation for the so-called judicial functions.

In several instances, successful regulation involves a combination of general stability with a capacity for rapid readjustment. In the fields regulated by the Interstate Commerce Commission, the Federal Power Commission, the Maritime Commission, the Board of Governors of the Federal Reserve System, the Federal Communications Commission, and the Securities and Exchange Commission, the element of stability is particularly necessary, since these agencies are dealing with long-time operations and processes. The long-time policy which Congress is seeking to develop through the work of these authorities should not be disturbed by changes of administration.

Within the long-time policy, there is the need for a process of continuous readjustment. This is effected by the activities of making rules and regulations and of issuing regulatory legislative orders, both of which have the force of law. It should be pointed out that in many instances it is impossible to separate a specific act from the determination of policy. The establishment of a rate level by an order, or the granting of a certificate of convenience and necessity, may have wide repercussions in respect to detailed railroad rates, stocks, bonds, the welfare or convenience of the public, and the location of business. Under recent transportation laws, the Interstate Commerce Commission is required to further and support several different types of transportation. A determination regarding distribution of a joint rate may involve the financial integrity of a railway system, or its ability to borrow money for future developments. It is the expert agency, rather than the Executive with his other heavy burdens, that should decide such subordinate but important questions of policy.

No matter how detailed rules and regulations issued by the President might be, there must remain a very large field of activity where no general rules and regulations are applicable. This is the field of the regulatory order and of administrative discretion. From what has just been said it is evident that policy is formulated in other ways than by the rule and regulation. A number of specific decisions along a certain line may constitute a larger and more significant policy than is laid down by a rule or regulation. In fact, perhaps the most significant policy that is developed by regulatory authorities is made by orders. If it is desirable to give the President control over policy, he should therefore be given control over the regulatory order as well as over rules and regulations—an impossibility for several reasons, including the fact that such control would not always constitute due process of law.

If any type of control were given by Congress to the President or heads of departments over regulatory orders affecting guaranteed rights, undoubtedly both the law and the courts would require them to exercise it by the same due process of law procedure that is now held necessary for the exercise of this function by the regulatory boards and commissions, namely, an order based on a finding of fact from evidence. In such cases, therefore, the President's policy or that of heads of departments would be limited to the results of a fact-finding instead of being based on discretion. There would be no real executive control, but merely a transfer of functions.

There is little validity in the argument that the sublegislative function should be centralized in the President in order to co-ordinate and unify public policy. In few instances is there any conflict between different regulatory authorities.[18] This is due to the fact that their fields of action are fundamentally different.

It has been indicated above that in the matter of regulation, expert knowledge is necessary. A further argument for leaving the sublegislative and regulatory function where it is points to the fact that through concrete contacts with thousands of economic situations, the regulatory authorities develop a high degree of expertness in their work. Heads of departments are usually appointed for

[18] There are a few exceptions as to this *in re* the Federal Power Commission and the Securities and Exchange Commission. See *Investigation of Executive Agencies of the Government*, Preliminary Report of the Select Committee to Investigate the Executive Agencies of the Government, S. Rept. 1275, 75 Cong. 1 sess., pp. 337, 765.

political reasons, and their periods of service are, on the average, relatively short. This means that they are unsuited to the regulation of economic situations demanding expert knowledge and long-time consistent treatment.

Whether Congress could delegate as wide power to the President or to heads of departments as is given to the regulatory boards and commissions is a serious question. Rate-making, for example, has been declared by the courts to be a legislative function. According to the rule of the Schechter case, a legislative function can be exercised by the President only under strict and clear limitations of law. The same rule applies to the heads of departments, who are assistants of the President. In the relationship of Congress to the regulatory boards and commissions, which are arms of Congress doing work which Congress could do under the Constitution and not a separate and co-ordinate branch of government, the doctrine of separation of powers does not apply in quite the same manner that it does in the relationship of Congress to the President.

For the formulation of policy a board has many advantages over a single executive or administrative officer. In a board, all sides of the problem are likely to be considered; there will be deliberation and discussion; different interests will be represented; action will not be so hasty as that of a busy administrator trying to clear his desk. A collegial authority is less subject to the pressure of special interests than is a single administrator, for each member of a board or commission can thwart such pressure by the claim that his colleagues refuse to respond favorably. Since no such way of escape is open to the single administrator, the pressure brought upon him may be so intense as to counterbalance any advantages in speed, efficiency, and unified action, which are sometimes claimed as characteristics of action by one man.

Those who believe in retaining the present system, with constant care to improve it, argue that in respect to the regulation of various spheres of economic life we are still in a period of experimentation, a process of trial and error; and that consequently no detailed policy can be laid down, either by Congress or by a commission, too much in advance of the actual handling of the problem. The provisions of law must be implemented gradually by the regulatory authority, as the result of experience. Such implementation takes place not only through rules and regulations, but also through regulatory orders. These two different types of action are parts of one administrative process, and there seems no reason for placing them in the hands of separate authorities.

Implementation should be flexible. If it does not meet the needs of the situation, it should be altered. Moreover, new legal and judicial standards must be given prompt consideration, and the necessary changes made in order that these standards shall prevail. This work of adjustment can be done far better by the authority which administers a given field than by an Executive whose thought must be given to principle rather than to detail. The successful integration of legislative policy and sublegislative policy depends to a very large degree upon an intimate knowledge of the problems that arise day by day in the administration of law. Those who are coping with a special problem develop a high degree of expertness, and a detailed knowledge, such as could not be developed either by the President or by the busy head of a department.

In case the President were given the power of sublegislation he would have to do one of three things: (1) depend upon the expert advice of persons actually carrying on the regulatory activity; (2) depend upon outside expert advice; (3) depend upon a staff agency capable of preparing rules and regulations.

In case he depends upon the advice of persons actually carrying on the regulatory activity, little is gained by the proposed change. In case he calls in outside experts, their advice might be very far removed from the policy that is gradually being developed by the regulatory authority in the settling of concrete cases, and from the needs of the situation. In such cases, if the President attempted to force this advice upon the regulatory authority, as a standard for action, he would substitute an adopted opinion for theirs. It is hard to see what would be gained by such a substitution. If the President could set up an investigating agency capable of formulating rules and regulations, several difficulties would arise. Such an agency would have to depend largely upon information furnished either by the regulatory authorities or by a special staff of its own. In the first case, the change is merely lost motion. In the latter case, the investigating agency would hardly be near enough to the situation to formulate regulations appropriate to the actual conditions. If sub-legislation were made without an intimate knowledge of the practical situations that arise, the administration would become clogged with useless and unnecessary machinery, or would lack the machinery to carry out its functions effectively. Successful administration depends upon implementation of law based upon reality.

In the making of rules and regulations, experience as derived from reports, statistics, accounts, investigations, and examinations, must always be considered. Close integration between the agencies that develop these facts and the authorities which formulate sub-legislation is essential. Thus, rules regarding the structure and strength of landing gear for airships might well be made on the basis of fact that certain types, makes, structures gave satisfaction while others did not. This sort of thing is a matter of detail to which no President could attend. In case the President should delegate the work of sublegislation, no agency to which it might be delegated could be as responsible as the expert board or commission, as is evidenced by the results of the delegation of code-making power to the Administrator under the National Industrial Recovery Act.

Further, as has been pointed out, most rules and regulations do not involve duties of the type with which the Chief Executive is concerned. Those who claim that the sublegislative process should be in the hands of the heads of departments or of the President fail to realize to what a tremendous extent rules and regulations deal with technical details that involve mechanisms, processes, methods, types of structure, considerations of time, place, circumstance, weights, measures, etc.

According to the suggestions of the President's Committee, as we have seen, a regulatory commission which was placed in a department would be broken up into a judicial section and an administrative section. The administrative section would be a bureau or division of the department and fully responsible as such to the Secretary and to the President. To this section would be given the rule-making, administrative, and, in general, policy-determining aspects of regulation.

The first difficulty encountered in any attempt to separate the work of the regulatory authorities into administrative and judicial functions is the fact that regulation is a unified activity, which, though consisting of legislative, administrative, and judicial elements, cannot be broken up into these elements in any clear-cut way. Thus, much of the work of a commission may be classified from the viewpoint of internal organization as administrative, whereas from the standpoint of government function[19] it is a step to a legislative or judicial end. The administrative work done in connection with the budget, personnel, the keeping of accounts, the preparing of reports, the gathering and compilation of statistics, inspections, examinations, and so on, is merely ancillary to the chief function of regulation.

To separate the policy-determining function from the so-called judicial function is impossible in connection with a legislative regulatory order which affects guaranteed individual rights, since, although the procedure for the making of the order is judicial in form, the order itself is legislative in nature and effect. A separation of policy from adjudication is possible only in respect to general legislative or procedural orders which affect no rights directly, or to orders which are definitely judicial and are the result of a "due process" type of hearing. In numerous cases where a commission is finding facts or making regulatory orders based on the facts found, the action is legislative, despite the judicial appearance of the procedure. The so-called judicial function in such cases is merely an administrative fact-finding upon which to base future action. In all such cases the public interest and public policy are inseparable from the activity. The presentation of facts by agents of the commission is not an act of a party to a judicial proceeding, but an act in the service of the public.

The so-called prosecuting function does not stand by itself, but is largely a resultant of the function of investigation, examination, the requiring of reports, and so on. In other words, it is a part of the regulatory process.

[19] See statement of Joseph B. Eastman, *Reorganization of the Government Agencies*, Hearings before the Select Committee on Government Organization on S. 2700, 1937, p. 181.

The attempt to separate these functions will lead to unfortunate results, especially in the matter of regulatory orders, which cannot be handled properly whether they are sent to the judicial section because of their form or are left in the administrative section because of their nature. Thus, if the judicial section is given the power to pass upon legislative action taken in a judicial form, like rate orders, as well as true acts of adjudication, like reparation orders, it will be exercising a wide degree of policy determination and will perform important sublegislative functions. It may be given the duty and power to find the facts and to protect the public interest, but it will have no control over the machinery and organization which are necessary for that purpose.[20] It will, according to the President's Committee, have to make its "decisions upon the records prepared and presented to it by the Administrative Section."[21] Thus, although passing on questions of public policy, it will have no information upon which to base its decision except that furnished to it by the administrative section and that brought out in the hearing. The judicial section, when acting to formulate subordinate matters of policy, might be unwilling, and properly should be unwilling, to accept statistics and other factual material presented to it by a statistical unit under political control. It might convincingly say: We need the facts as developed by statistics and reports which we consider relevant, and which have been collected and classified by our own investigators, examiners, and statistical staffs, who are appointed by us and in whom we feel confidence. We cannot accept statistics gathered on the basis of an analysis that is irrelevant, that does not furnish the necessary information, or that is made by employees of a political department. In other words, a separation of judicial and administrative functions would operate in this case against the public interest.

If the judicial section were required to make its finding of fact on the evidence presented, and forbidden to seek information by means of its own agents, again the public interest would suffer. Important questions of subordinate policy would be decided merely

[20] The same, p. 180.
[21] President's Committee on Administrative Management, *Report with Special Studies*, p. 231.

upon the evidence of interested persons and of politically controlled witnesses. The free inquiry necessary to legislative action would be notable by its absence, and the procedure would tend to develop along traditional judicial lines, and to be governed by those "narrow rules which prevail in trials at common law where a strict correspondence is required between allegation and proof."[22] Such a development would destroy all possibility of formulating policy on the basis of wide social and economic considerations.

In case the judicial section were permitted to issue only orders that are strictly judicial in nature, such as reparation orders, certain types of cease and desist orders, and certain types of enforcement orders, the question of factual material still arises. How could the judicial section trust the "facts" presented by either the corporation interested, or the attorney for a government dominated by a policy of "hit them hard"? Even when the government might not be directly interested in a case, if the settlement involved were an adjudication of private rights, trustworthy factual material would be indispensable. Administrative adjudication has been recognized by the courts as requiring a certain freedom and flexibility, especially in the matter of evidence, which would be destroyed if the adjudicating agency had no power to find the facts. Furthermore, since the economic fields which are regulated are affected with a public interest, even private disputes in such fields have a particular importance, since on their proper adjudication important public as well as private consequences may depend.

Another difficulty in such an arrangement is the matter of responsibility for subordinate policy determination as between the administrative section and the head of the department. This difficulty exists at present in respect to the Bituminous Coal Division in the Department of the Interior. Legally the Secretary of the Interior is responsible, but can he exercise that responsibility in an adequate fashion? The difficulty would be increased in case the administrative section, rather than the judicial section, were given the function of issuing regulatory legislative orders. The head of a department could hardly be expected to attend all the hearings, and if orders were issued in his name they would be to all intents

[22] *Interstate Commerce Commission* v. *Baird*, 194 U.S. 25, 44.

and purposes only stamped by him. Where then would responsibility lie?

If the proposed changes in organization were made, but the work of issuing regulatory orders were left with the administrative section, because these orders are legislative in nature and involve the formulating of policy, other serious difficulties would arise. According to the theory of regulation that has developed under the Constitution, by statute, and by judicial decisions, such orders, when they touch constitutionally guaranteed individual rights, must be based upon a notice, a hearing, and a fact-finding. The finding of fact must be supported by evidence. To meet these requirements, the procedure is assimilated to judicial procedure, and the agency which carries it out must enjoy independence comparable to that of the courts. If such agency can be controlled by an administrative or executive superior, the order as based on fact-finding becomes meaningless. Such a situation is incompatible with due process of law.[23]

All these considerations show that the attempt to shut off the work of administrative adjudication into a separate section removed from the ordinary processes of administration is based on a mistaken notion of that work. Administrative adjudication has a two-fold character: it decides disputes as to rights, and it does this in view of the public interest and of all relevant facts. This does not mean "administrative absolutism"—a rather thin bogey sometimes named to cause a shudder among the credulous. Private rights are quite completely protected by the opportunity of appeal to the courts; but public interests are not sacrificed through rules of evidence too narrow to meet the needs of the situation. Since the courts have repeatedly declared that the present organization of judicial functions in the regulatory agencies meets the constitutional requirement of due process of law, there seems no good reason for

[23] "Congress by using the phrase 'whenever the Commission is of opinion, after hearing,' prescribed quasi-judicial action. . . . The provision for a hearing implies both the privilege of introducing evidence and the duty of deciding in accordance with it. To refuse to consider evidence introduced or to make an essential finding without supporting evidence is arbitrary action." *Chicago Junction Case*, 264 U.S. 258, 265.

separating the work of adjudication from that of general administration. On the other hand, there are excellent reasons why the present organization should not be disturbed, such as the advantage to each type of function of familiarity with the other on the part of the responsible administrators; the simple organizational fact that since there is not enough "pure" adjudication to keep a strong judicial section busy, the judicial section would tend to be weak; the need of unbiased evidence, already discussed.

From a practical viewpoint, there are several difficulties in connection with making the proposed changes in organization.

In case the general regulatory work is lodged in a department, those charged with it are under the budgetary control of the head of the department, who may be antagonistic to their work. If a special appropriation is made for the regulatory authority, this may be resented by the head of the department. If the appropriation is made to the department and not to the regulatory authority, the department may starve out the agency, thus reducing its efficiency and hindering it from accomplishing the task set for it by the legislature.

A further practical question arises as to where the various regulatory authorities should be placed. It might appear logical, for instance, to put the Interstate Commerce Commission, the Federal Trade Commission, and perhaps also the Federal Communications Commission, within the Department of Commerce. The difficulty would immediately arise, however, of placing regulatory and controlling functions within an organization whose chief function is promotional. Internal contradictions and conflicts within the department would result, for it is impossible when dealing with the same business or objective, to promote with one hand and regulate effectively with the other. No man can serve two masters; and the Secretary of Commerce who attempted both functions would be in constant trouble. There would naturally be pressure from the groups whose interests were being promoted to cause the Secretary to go lightly with regulation. Would anything be gained by placing boards and commissions within a department not especially interested in the functions promoted by them, as for instance by moving the Interstate Commerce Commission and the Federal Trade Commission to the Department of Agriculture or the Interior Department?

The argument for placing the independent boards and commissions within government departments in order to improve "housekeeping arrangements" is of very doubtful validity. After an organization reaches a certain size it is questionable whether any economy in "housekeeping" operations is gained by placing it in a large unit. "Housekeeping" would work out in practice as a control by the Executive which would certainly impair and might destroy the value of the regulatory authorities as agents of Congress.

To summarize: the work of regulation is largely legislative in nature. Its administrative and judicial aspects are closely related to the major work of formulating policy and establishing rules of law. Since the regulatory authorities are primarily legislative authorities, acting for Congress in exercising delegated legislative power, they should be responsible directly to Congress and should not be controlled by executive or administrative authorities. In their judicial work, or wherever they touch rights guaranteed by the Constitution (and sometimes other rights as well), they should be, and are, controlled by judicial action. No separation of their functions is advisable, since each part of their work now strengthens each other part, and any separation would but weaken their power to regulate under the law, while both protecting private rights and serving the interests of the public.

CHAPTER X

DOCTRINE OF THE JUDICIAL FORMULA

The doctrine of the judicial formula of public administration is largely the product of the Special Committee on Administrative Law of the American Bar Association. Although the criticisms of the present system made by this committee have varied from year to year, as have also its proposals and its drafts of bills[1] designed to put these proposals into effect, it is nevertheless possible to make a general statement defining its position. Such a statement follows here. Since the American Bar Association has accepted the reports and endorsed the proposals of its Special Committee on Administrative Law, the criticisms, suggestions, and drafts of bills are officially those of the Association itself.

I. CRITICISM OF THE PRESENT SYSTEM BY THE AMERICAN BAR ASSOCIATION

The chief criticism of the present system which has been offered by the Special Committee on Administrative Law of the American Bar Association[2] may be expressed in two words: "administrative absolutism." It is asserted by the Committee that there is a danger-ous and ever-growing tendency, in government generally and in federal government particularly, for the administration to act in absolute, arbitrary, and willful fashion. The only remedy for this

[1] For proposals and drafts of bills see *American Bar Association Journal,* Mar. 1, 1935; American Bar Association, *Advanced Program,* 1936, 1937, 1938 and *Report and Draft of Bill by the Special Committee on Administrative Law to the Chicago Meeting of the House of Delegates and the Board of Governors,* January 1939; H.R. 12297, 74 Cong. 2 sess.; *United States Court of Appeals for Adminis-tration,* Hearings before a Subcommittee of the Senate Committee on the Judiciary on S. 3676, 75 Cong. 3 sess., p. 21 ff.; H.R. 4236, H.R. 6198, and H.R. 6324, 76 Cong. 1 sess.; S. 915, 76 Cong. 1 sess.

For hearings see *United States Court of Appeals for Administration,* Hearings before a Subcommittee of the Senate Committee on the Judiciary on S. 3676, 75 Cong. 3 sess.; *Administrative Law,* Hearings before Subcommittee No. 4 of the House Committee on the Judiciary on H.R. 4236, H.R. 6198, and H.R. 6324, 76 Cong. 1 sess.

[2] For the sake of convenience, the names above will be shortened in later discus-sion to (respectively) "the Committee" and "the Bar Association."

disease, says the Committee, is an extension of judicial control over administrative activities.

The factors which, according to this viewpoint, tend to encourage the development of administrative absolutism, were best summarized in the report of the Committee made to the sixty-first annual meeting of the Bar Association in 1938.[3] This report drew largely on English, state, and local practice for its illustrative material; and used for its federal material chiefly the non-typical Bituminous Coal Commission, the long-dead National Prohibition Act, the Tri-State Broadcasting Company case, and a few cases where administrative action has been set aside by the courts of law. The Committee, of which Roscoe Pound was chairman, listed the following tendencies toward administrative absolutism:

1. A tendency to decide without a hearing, or without hearing one of the parties. This tendency may be observed even where the statute expressly requires a hearing.

2. A tendency to decide on the basis of matters not before the tribunal or on evidence not produced. A common form in which this tendency is manifested, is to act on secret reports of inspectors and examiners.

3. A tendency to make decisions on the basis of pre-formed opinions and prejudices.

4. A tendency to consider the administrative determining function one of acting rather than of deciding; to apply to the determining function the methods of the directing function.

5. A tendency to disregard jurisdictional limits and seek to extend the sphere of administrative action beyond the jurisdiction confided to the administrative board or commission. Also there is a tendency to extend the regulatory power of the administrative agency.

6. A tendency to do what will get by; to yield to political pressure at the expense of the law.

7. A tendency to arbitrary rule making for administrative convenience at the expense of important interests.

8. A tendency at the other extreme to fall into a perfunctory routine.

9. A tendency to exercise of jurisdiction by deputies.

10. A tendency to mix up rule making, investigation, prosecution, the advocate's function, the judge's function, and the function of enforcing the judgment, so that the whole proceeding from end to end is one to give effect to a complaint.

[3] This report appears in the American Bar Association, *Advance Program*, including Committee and Section Reports, prepared for the sixty-first annual meeting in 1938, pp. 134-71. All the quotations concerning "tendencies" are taken verbatim from this report.

Mr. O. R. McGuire, the present chairman of the Bar Association's Committee on Administrative Law, mentions another situation in which he believes that administrative absolutism prevails. He says:

Administrative absolutism prevails in this or any other government where administrative agencies charged with the administration of particular statutes relating to particular problems have uncontrolled discretion in interpreting the law and in finding the facts.[4]

The above-mentioned evils, it appears from various writings and speeches of the Committee and its members, occur unless the judicial functions of federal administrative tribunals are segregated from their legislative and executive functions; unless rules and regulations are made as the result of a quasi-judicial procedure and are subject to judicial review; unless principles of common law are applied in the hearing of administrative cases; unless cases involving grants, gratuities, personnel, or promotional activities, etc., are handled by the same procedures of hearing and appeal which apply to cases involving regulatory activities; unless there is judicial review over all types of administrative action; and unless the courts have almost complete jurisdiction to pass upon questions of fact as well as questions of law.

II. THE PROPOSALS OF THE BAR ASSOCIATION

The proposals of the Bar Association are largely embodied in bills now before Congress.[5] The main features of these bills have to do with the implementation of statutes; review over rules and regulations; the establishment of review boards; procedure before administrative authorities; and judicial review over administrative action. One such bill has been passed by the Senate[6] and is now before the House of Representatives. This discussion will consider only the bill as it finally passed the Senate, since to discuss the original bill and its various amendments would serve no useful purpose.

---

[4] Hearings on H.R. 4236, 6198, and 6324, cited above, p. 23.
[5] *Report and Draft of Bill by the Special Committee on Administrative Law . . .* , January 1939; and on H. R. 4236 and S. 915 and in amended form in H.R. 6198 and H.R. 6324.
[6] S. 915.

A. The Implementation of Statutes

The bill defines administrative rules as including rules, regulations, orders, and amendments thereto of general application issued by officers of the executive branch of the government interpreting the terms of statutes. Such rules, and amendments or modifications or supplements of existing rules implementing or filling in the details of any statute affecting the rights of persons or property, shall be issued only after publication of notice and public hearing, within one year after the date of the enactment of the statute to which they are applicable.[7]

The rules, regulations, and orders are to cover both adjective and substantive details, thus "providing a method by which subordinate officers and employees of the Government may be controlled by responsible superior authority in their administration of the statutes . . . [and] providing a method whereby business men and citizens may be advised in advance of administrative action determining particular cases as to the administrative interpretation of the statutes. . . ."[8]

Persons substantially interested in the effects of an administrative rule in force when the bill becomes law may petition the appropriate agency for reconsideration of the rule. This also involves notice and public hearing.

B. Review over Rules, Regulations, and General Orders

The United States Court of Appeals for the District of Columbia is given jurisdiction to hear and determine whether any rule, regulation, or order, issued or continued in force as provided in the act, is in conflict with the Constitution of the United States or the statute under which issued. The court has power to render a declaratory judgment holding the rule valid or invalid.[9]

C. Review Boards

According to this bill, every head of an agency[10] shall from time

[7] The same, Sec. 2 (a) (b).
[8] *Report and Draft of Bill by the Special Committee on Administrative Law* . . . , p. 21.
[9] S. 915, Sec. 3.
[10] " 'Agency' means any department, independent establishment, administration,

to time designate three employees for such intra-agency boards (including the field service of such agency) as may be necessary and desirable. Where such boards are in existence on the date of the approval of the act, they are to be re-established and to function in accordance with the act. At least one employee designated for each such board shall be a lawyer, who shall act as chairman. When the members of a board are not engaged in the hearing of administrative appeals, they are to be assigned to other duties.[11]

When any person is aggrieved by a decision[12] of any officer or employee of any agency, he may notify the head of the agency in writing of his objections, specifically requesting that the controversy be referred to a board. He shall be given a "full and fair hearing" before the board. Any person having a substantial interest may intervene. The testimony, other evidence, and all proceedings before the board must be reduced to a written record and filed in the agency concerned.

Within thirty days after the hearing the board shall make written findings of fact and a separate decision thereon, which is subject to the written approval, disapproval, or modification of the head of the agency concerned or of such person as he designates to act for him. A copy of the findings of fact and decision, showing the action, if any, of the head of the agency or his representative, shall be filed in the agency as a part of the written record in the case. A copy is mailed to the aggrieved person and the intervenors.[13]

Judicial review is made applicable to final acts of administrative authorities. Any party to a proceeding before an agency or independent agency, who is aggrieved by the final decision or order of the same, may within thirty days file a petition with the United States Court of Appeals for the District of Columbia, or with the appropriate circuit court of appeals, for review of the decision. Before filing a petition the aggrieved party may, within ten days, make

---

corporation, or other subdivision of the executive branch of the United States Government with one chief officer as the immediate head thereof." (The same, Sec. 1(3).)

[11] The same, Sec. 4(a).

[12] " 'Decision' means any affirmative or negative decision, order, or Act in specific controversies which determines the issue therein involved." The same, Sec. 1(8).

[13] The same, Sec. 4(b).

a motion to the agency or independent agency concerned for a re-hearing, tendering a statement of any further showing, which is also made a part of the record.

The court may affirm or set aside the decision or may direct the agency or independent agency concerned to modify its decision. Any case may be remanded for such further evidence as in the discretion of the court may be required.[14] The causes for which the decision may be set aside are listed in the bill and will be discussed later.

The judgments of the circuit courts of appeals are final, except that they are subject to review by the Supreme Court of the United States upon writ of certiorari or certification.[15] Provision is made for causes of action that are normally within the jurisdiction of the Court of Claims.[16]

The section of the bill dealing with exceptions and reservations provides: "Nothing contained in this act shall operate to modify or repeal any rights or procedure as now provided by law for any person to have his controversy with the United States heard and determined in any district court or circuit court of appeals of the United States."[17] The same section exempts from the provisions of the act a large number of agencies, functions, and circumstances.

III. CHANGES THAT HAVE TAKEN PLACE UNDER THE BAR ASSOCIATION THEORY

It has been shown elsewhere that several recent statutes have been influenced by the doctrine of the judicial formula. These include regulations issued under the Bituminous Coal Act of 1937; the Food, Drug, and Cosmetics Act of 1938; the Inspection of Vessels Act of 1939; and the Federal Seed Act of 1939.

IV. CRITIQUE OF THE PROPOSALS OF THE AMERICAN BAR ASSOCIATION

A. Implementation of Statutes

The proposals of the American Bar Association to the effect that all federal statutes shall be implemented by rules and regulations

[14] The same, Sec. 5(a).
[15] The same, Sec. 5(b).
[16] The same, Sec. 5(c).
[17] The same, Sec. 7.

defining both the adjective and substantive details of federal statutes, and that said rules and regulations are to be made within
one year from the enactment of any statute, after the publication of
notice and the holding of public hearings, deserve careful attention.
The ostensible purpose of this arrangement is to enable persons
who may be affected by the administration of a statute to know
what interpretation will be given to that statute by the administrative authorities, before a specific case must be determined. To this
purpose there can be no objection in principle.

In an ideal and completely logical system of administration, rules
and regulations of any sort governing the activities of individuals
should be laid down in advance of any action taken against them.
Several serious disadvantages inevitably follow if the prescriptions
controlling action are established during the decision of a particular
case, whether such decision is rendered by an administrative authority or by a court. Unless rules and regulations implement the
law, the individual will not be able to learn, until after he has
obtained a decision of the administrative body (perhaps followed
by a decision of a court), whether his acts of various kinds are
legal or illegal. He must act at his peril. This has been one of the
greatest difficulties in respect to the Federal Trade Commission Act
and the Sherman Anti-Trust Act. Since definite standards defining
what constitutes monopoly, restraint of trade, or unfair competition were not laid down either by the statutes or by administrative
regulations, companies were often forced to go ahead with their
arrangements without knowing whether these were or were not
within the law until suits had been brought against them.

Again, the prescriptions affecting both details of public policy
and individual conduct are not established under the proper circumstances when they are developed as portions of a specific decision.
They are too likely to be made under narrowly applied legal concepts, instead of as the result of a consideration and discussion of
all factors involved, economic and political as well as legal. To
decide questions of public policy in a judicial contest regarding the
legality of a specific action almost inevitably means that such questions will be settled according to the particular legal points brought
out in the briefs of opposing counsel, rather than according to all

relevant considerations. A related danger is that in case an administrative decision embodying a rule of conduct is appealed, the appellate court, while theoretically deciding only points of law, will actually be passing upon important questions of social policy. There is a real danger, under these conditions, that the courts may tend to become political agencies rather than judicial authorities.

Quite possibly an ideal system would consist of a rule of action established by a legislative body, as a basis upon which the citizen can know his rights and duties; an administrative body applying the law in practice and making decisions as to whether or not the individual has complied with a given provision; with an appeal to the courts. Next in desirability is this: that the legislature should lay down the general standards and norms; that the law should be implemented by the administrative body as to the details of policy and the duties and obligations of individuals; that the administration should merely act under prescriptions laid down in advance of action; and that the courts should hold the administration within the law as well as punish infractions of law by individuals.

Although these situations are desirable in theory, is it possible under modern conditions to realize them in practice? Long ago the legislative authority had to give up making detailed regulations, because of the increase of state functions, the complexity of the questions presented to it, their specialized nature, and the expertness necessary for their solution.[18] Because the legislature cannot prescribe all rules and regulations governing society, it has had to delegate a part of this legislative function to administrative bodies. In practice it has done so in two ways: (1) by giving such bodies the power to issue rules and regulations having the force of law; and (2) by giving them the power to issue orders having the force of law. A question of profound importance, from the viewpoint of the Bar Association's proposal, is whether all sublegislative action can be placed within the framework of the rule or regulation, doing away with the sublegislation contained in the legislative order.

The answer to this question depends upon the nature of the regulatory action. If absolute standards can be laid down, as in

[18] F. F. Blachly and M. E. Oatman, *Administrative Legislation and Adjudication* (1934), pp. 1-10.

respect to strength of material, factors of safety, quality of goods, grades of agricultural products, purity of food products, seeds, and so on, rules and regulations can be made by an administrative authority in advance of administering the act. The administrative authority applying the act, or its agents, will then merely have the function of administration under the law and the rules and regulations. There will be no need to legislate by order.

If, however, the administrative authority must administer such complex standards as "reasonable rates," "public convenience and necessity," "unreasonable discrimination," "undue preference," "actions necessary and desirable in the public interest," "adequate facilities and services," "undue and unreasonable disadvantage," "protection of investors," "maintenance of a fair and orderly market," "reasonable rates of commission," "manipulational or deceptive devices," "unfair methods of competition," "discrimination in prices," stock acquisitions which "tend to create a monopoly," "collective bargaining," "discrimination in regard to hire or tenure of employment," "unfair labor practices," which "interfere with, restrain, or coerce employees" or "dominate or interfere with any labor organization," and so on,[19] an entirely different situation obtains. The administration of statutes which lay down standards of this broad general nature cannot be done by the methods used when the law is specific or when specific rules and regulations under the law can be made to cover all cases.

It is not possible, for example, to administer these general laws by means of the usual police formula: that is, a fixed rule of law, a charge that the law has been broken, and a decision. The same thing is true of the formula employed in conditional licensing methods of regulation: the right to act under specific conditions, a charge that those conditions have not been complied with, and a decision. Moreover, the enforcement of "fair" or "reasonable" norms of conduct, and the like, is not based on measurable facts, as is the enforcement of statutes or regulations setting standards of grade or quality.

The laws in question can be administered only by a process of

[19] See Robert M. Cooper, "Administrative Justice and the Role of Discretion," 47 *Yale Law Journal* 582.

continuous adjustment, which involves the exercise of administrative discretion in both the application of existing legal norms and the formulation of new norms as new situations present themselves. This is a delicate process, which involves certain dangers unless it is properly controlled; but, when so controlled, it works to the advantage of both the individual and the public. The primary object of discretionary regulation is not that of the common law: arbitration of individual rights. Although such rights must be and are carefully safeguarded, the basic concern of Congress in marking out certain fields for regulation is to control important social and economic situations for the general welfare. This social objective is paramount when an administrative agency is charged by Congress with such functions as stabilizing the market; preventing unfair competition, price discrimination, speculation, and fraud; providing for reasonable rates and services; providing for adequate transportation, communication, and power facilities; preventing conflicts between employers and employees. In this type of regulation the government is primarily interested in the creation of juridical situations within which business can function in the interests of society.

In making this type of law effective, authorities must be established which deal with questions of public policy, complicated economic and business relationships, and even with problems of public management. The regulatory process, as has been pointed out, involves a continuous series of adjustments rather than one-time acts. The process necessitates the development of more detailed lines of policy on the basis of rather general legislative declarations, and the application of these more detailed policies to specific cases. It involves the making of investigations as an aid to further policy determination. In the last analysis, the facts discovered, the expert knowledge and informed discretion of the administrators, considerations of public policy, and the necessity of applying the law to a given situation or of deciding a specific case, are all necessary factors in administering laws of the type now under consideration.

Equally important is the fact that in many instances, whether consciously or unconsciously, there are inherent in the regulatory process factors distinctly managerial in aspect, such as:

1. Deciding whether or not a business shall be established, as

may happen when a certificate of convenience and necessity is required for the establishment of a radio station.

2. Deciding whether to extend or reduce business operations, as when the Interstate Commerce Commission permits a railroad to extend or to abandon certain lines.

3. Determining the amount or quality of service that is necessary to effectively meet competition, as when the Interstate Commerce Commission determines whether a railroad may add a pick-up service.

4. Determining upon conditions of service, such as speed, safety, auxiliary service, continuous service, etc.

5. Determining when and under what conditions money shall be borrowed and securities issued.

6. Exercising control over the proceeds of joint rates.

7. Fixing the rates at which services or goods shall be sold.

8. Determining upon the hours and conditions of labor.

In most of these regulatory and managerial situations the subject matter is too complex and diversified to be subjected to hard and fast rules and regulations. In numerous instances, many factors must be taken into consideration. Various weights must be given to these factors under specific circumstances; the necessity for regulation in the public interest signifies that as particular situations arise they must be decided upon this ground instead of by some standard already in existence. The administrative authority must look at the ends to be attained, and determine upon the methods that will best attain these ends.

In many situations of this kind the regulatory authority is in the position of a manager exercising judgment as to the probable results of future action, in view of all the factors brought out at the hearing; and is in no sense merely a clerk following detailed instructions. A public managing agency has a broad field of discretion as to the interpretation and the meaning of facts and evidence; for it is not merely deciding a case on the basis of past facts, but is administering in the public interest.

Obviously the nature of the action often makes it impossible for Congress to lay down detailed rules and regulations, and equally impossible for the administrative authority to lay them down in advance of taking action. Congress has fully recognized this, and has provided that in many important situations regulating economic life, the regulatory authority shall proceed by way of the order.[20] This is less desirable in theory than procedure by way of rules and regulations laid down in advance, but more practicable in actual operation. It does not, of course, preclude the use of general rules and regulations where circumstances permit such use; but it gives a flexibility often demanded by the work which is to be done.

The establishment of substantive rules and regulations in some circumstances is out of harmony with the judicial theory of case-to-case interpretations of general statutory provisions. The courts have held, for example, that what constitutes an unfair method of competition is a judicial question, to be answered as cases arise. If administrative rules and regulations go beyond what is decided by the courts, the case-to-case doctrine is violated. If they do not go beyond what has been decided in particular cases, they will not accomplish the desired purpose of giving information in advance of action.

Does the fact that the administrative authority can proceed by way of the order in a concrete case leave the individual unprotected? It certainly does not, since Congress has adopted adequate means for his protection, namely, the requirement that the order shall be issued only after notice and hearing, with an appeal to the courts. Through the use of the order a body of case-made law is gradually built up, which gives individuals quite as adequate a basis for action as was developed under the common law governing contracts, property, negotiable instruments, or sales.

For all these reasons, the nature of the regulatory function sometimes makes implementation within a fixed period undesirable or even impossible.

B. Constitutional Difficulties

As the Bar Association bill is studied, certain constitutional difficulties present themselves. The first of these appears in connection with the judicial control of administrative acts, in such form as this control would take under the bill.

[20] See Supporting Statement IV, pp. 276-86.

Some of the provisions of the bill, which would enable a person aggrieved by a final decision or order of an administrative agency to have such decision or order reviewed by the circuit courts of appeals,[21] seem contrary to the separation of powers established by the Constitution. In treating decisions and orders as if they were one and the same thing, the bill disregards not only established forms of administrative action, but also long-settled principles of jurisprudence and constitutional interpretation. The order, as a rule, touches guaranteed rights, can be reviewed by the courts, and is now reviewed by the courts. The decision, where in general only administrative discretion is concerned, is not ordinarily susceptible of judicial review. In almost countless instances,[22] the courts have refused to control administrative discretion or to substitute their own discretion for that of the administrator. There is no reason to suppose that they will change their position, since they cannot do so and still respect the constitutional separation of powers.

A second constitutional difficulty is the fact that the bill seems to contemplate delegations of power to issue rules and regulations, which are beyond the power of Congress to make. There are three possible uses of the rule-making power, namely, (1) the issuance of rules and regulations in respect to the internal operations of a department, as provided for originally in the act of July 27, 1789;[23] (2) the issuance of procedural rules and regulations; (3) the is-

[21] S. 915, Sec. 4(b), (c).

[22] A few examples follow: *Cohens* v. *Virginia*, 6 Wheat. 264; *LaAbra Silver Mining Co.* v. *United States*, 175 U.S. 423, 455; *Keller* v. *Potomac Electric Power Co.*, 261 U.S. 428, 444; *Postum Cereal Co.* v. *California Fig Nut Co.*, 272 U.S. 693; *Muskrat* v. *United States*, 219 U.S. 346; *Federal Radio Commission* v. *General Electric Co.*, 281 U.S. 464; *American Tel. & Tel. Co.* v. *United States*, 299 U.S. 232; *Kansas City Southern R. Co.* v. *United States*, 231 U.S. 423, 444; *Norfolk & Western Ry. Co.* v. *United States*, 287 U.S. 134, 141; *Interstate Commerce Commission* v. *Goodrich Transit Co.*, 224 U.S. 194, 211; *Interstate Commerce Commission* v. *Illinois Central R. Co.*, 215 U.S. 452; *Royal Farms Dairy, Inc.* v. *Wallace*, 7 Fed. Supp. 560; *Spang* v. *Roper*, 13 Fed. Supp. 840; *Haydel* v. *Dufresne*, 17 How. 23; *Noble* v. *Union River Logging R. Co.*, 147 U.S. 165; *Litchfield* v. *Richards*, 9 Wall. 575.

[23] 1 Stat. L. 28. This section, in its present form, provides: "The head of each Department is authorized to prescribe regulations, not inconsistent with law, for the government of his Department, the conduct of its officers and clerks, the distribution and performance of its business, and the custody, use, and preservation of the records, papers, and property appertaining to it." R.S. 161; 5 U.S.C. 22.

suance of general rules and regulations supplementing and implementing all statutes in a substantive way.

The Bar Association bill does not give separate consideration to these different uses, or even distinguish between adjective and substantive rule-making. The right of Congress to bestow upon the various government agencies the right to issue rules and regulations governing the internal operations of their own departments is beyond question. There would, moreover, probably be no question as to its right, by one fundamental statute, to give government agencies of all sorts the power to make procedural rules and regulations governing the conduct of cases.

The matter of substantive rules and regulations is quite different. They represent a delegation of legislative power which cannot be made in a broad and general way. Such delegation must be specific, and must operate to effect policies adopted by Congress, within limits set by Congress.[24] The language of Section 1(a) of the Bar Association bill is ambiguous, but it appears to be based on the assumption that the power to administer a statute includes the power to implement or fill in substantive details, even where rights of persons or property are affected. This is contrary to the Constitution as interpreted by the courts.

C. Practical Difficulties

Many practical difficulties appear in connection with the requirements of the Bar Association bill respecting the implementation of statutes. The chief of these arises from the provisions that rules and regulations are to be made after public notice and opportunity for hearing, and that they are to be issued within one year from the enactment of the statute to which they appertain. For a number of reasons such provisions seem unwise. Modern administrative rule-making is a highly technical and complicated thing which often demands much study, the extensive use of statistics in order to see whether a new rule is needed or whether one already in effect is working properly, or even a scientific investigation covering a long period of time. A blanket formulation in advance of actual experience might result in ill-considered and hasty regulations, which

[24] *Schechter* v. *United States*, 295 U.S. 495.

could be corrected only after the hearing and notice procedure, and
so *ad infinitum*.

Invariably to base rules and regulations on public hearings is a
practical impossibility. Such hearings may fail to bring out many
things that should be considered, and many points that should be
included in rules and regulations. Private individuals appearing
before a rule-making authority are concerned with their own particular business. They are not necessarily concerned with the public
interest or welfare. Public hearings are all too likely to open the
way for a display of antagonisms incidental to an adversary proceeding, rather than to retain a sense of balanced values.

In many instances, regulations merely supply a detail or govern
a matter now within the discretion of the administrative authority.
It would be dilatory and expensive to hold public hearings on such
points, since the hearings would consume the valuable time of the
administrative authority and probably would accomplish no better
results than are attained at present.

Although the Bar Association bill is silent on this point, it evidently intends the hearings to serve as a basis for the rules and
regulations. Unless it does so intend, the whole elaborate machinery
of notice and hearing seems meaningless. If it does so intend, it
attempts the impossible, since any later act of Congress bestowing
upon an administrative agent or agency a properly limited grant of
rule-making power in terms allowing him discretion as to the use of
such power would supersede, for that particular instance, the provisions of the earlier act. Furthermore, to base general rules and
regulations upon hearings, instead of upon the declared policy of
Congress and the informed discretion of the administrator, might
mean that administrative rule-making would be controlled by those
who had the wealth to employ the best lawyers, and the economic
interests which made it worth while to do so. A million poor men,
though vitally concerned, might go unheard; and the rules would
be based upon the representations made by a few men of wealth.
This is not a system to be introduced into a democratic society.

Section 2(c) of the bill provides that any existing administrative
regulation within the application of the section shall, upon the petition of any person substantially interested in its effects, be recon-

sidered by the administration after publication of notice and opportunity for a public hearing. The burden laid upon administrative
officers under this provision would be very heavy because of the
large number of matters to be considered; and the benefit would be
negligible, since most existing regulations have passed the test of
actual experience, from the viewpoint of the administrator and the
general public. If, as the bill seems to indicate, any existing rule or
regulation must be reconsidered whenever interested parties petition
therefor, administration might be prostrated. Various powerful
private interests would in all probability continually ask that rules
and regulations be changed for their benefit. This would cause a
constant pressure upon the rule-making authority and would con-
comitantly do much to weaken the proper enforcement of law. It
should be pointed out once more that the administration is working
to fulfill policies established by Congress, and that both our constitutional system and the whole meaning of representative government require that it be permitted to do its work, unimpeded by
pressures which tend to make the work impossible. Those who
desire a change in legislative policy should petition the legislature
and use all other proper political means of bringing about such a
change. It should not be possible for them, by obstructionist tactics,
to make a law inoperative. The Bar Association bill seems not only
to permit, but almost to invite, tactics which would in effect prevent
the administration of any law opposed by a well-financed pressure
group.

The foregoing arguments do not mean that the administration
should act arbitrarily. As a matter of practice, when important rules
are to be issued, the administrative authorities frequently consult the
persons or groups who will be affected by such rules. This is done
in various ways, as by the publication of tentative drafts to which
those interested may take exception or as to which they may make
suggestions; the use of questionnaires and statistics; informal conferences with individuals, associations, chambers of commerce, representative committees, and other groups or agencies; more or less
formal hearings at various places, and so on. With the modern
organization of business, labor, and special interest associations of
many kinds, there is little likelihood that the attention of rule-mak-

ing authorities will not be called to oppressive or abusive regulations. It is advisable, in the administration of many laws, that the
administration should have a knowledge of many points of view;
but there is no reason for making it mandatory upon every rule-
making authority to reopen any and every matter at any time, upon
private demand.

The recent publication by the Government Printing Office of a
volume containing nearly twelve hundred pages devoted only to
the general rules and regulations of certain bureaus of the Department of Agriculture, and the plan to publish a complete code of
Federal Regulations which will probably comprise twenty-three
such volumes, are indications of the vast amount of material com-
prised in and covered by administrative rule-making. To allow any
person substantially interested in the probable effects of a rule or
regulation to require the reconsideration of the same at any time,
and to make it mandatory upon the administrator to comply with
such requirement, is to paralyze administration.

D. Judicial Control over Rules and Regulations

The system of judicial control over rules and regulations which
is provided by the Bar Association bill may be considered from
two viewpoints: the technical and the general.

Technical criticism. Several legal and technical difficulties arise
in respect to the review of rules and regulations and general orders
by the United States Court of Appeals for the District of Columbia.
The bill provides that this court may render a declaratory judgment
holding a rule legal and valid or holding it contrary to law and
invalid; but no rule shall be held invalid except for violations of
the Constitution of the United States, or for conflict with a statute,
or for lack of authority. The provisions for a declaratory judgment
by the United States Court of Appeals for the District of Columbia
shall not operate to "prevent the determination of the validity or
invalidity of any rule which may be involved in any suit or review
of an administrative decision or order in any court of the United
States as now or hereafter authorized by law."[25]

The crippling of administrative activities which would probably

[25] S. 915, Sec. 3.

result from the foregoing provisions, should they become law, deserves mature consideration. It seems at first sight almost meaningless to bestow upon one court the power to pass upon the validity or invalidity of rules and regulations, without simultaneously withdrawing such power from other courts. But upon careful consideration, the question arises whether this jurisdictional device does not hamper administration while leaving the individual unrestrained by the decision.

Since no administrator would dare to re-enact a rule or regulation which the Court of Appeals for the District of Columbia had declared invalid, such a declaration "would be binding upon the Government, not only in the case at bar but also in all subsequent actions in any court, whereas a decision that the regulation was valid apparently would not be binding upon the opposite party to the suit, nor upon other persons affected by the regulation, in any subsequent proceeding. Thus the bill would confer upon the Court of Appeals a veto power over administrative regulations which . . . if viewed as judicial in its nature, clearly violates the fundamental maxim of justice that both parties to an adjudication should be bound thereby in like degree. These objections are intensified by the fact that the authority granted the Court of Appeals in the bill to pass upon the constitutionality of an administrative regulation is susceptible of being construed as including the power to pass upon the constitutionality of the statute under which the regulation is issued."[26]

Although the bill seeks to give to the declaratory judgment upon rules the appearance of adversary procedure, by providing that a rule brought for review shall be defended under the direction of the Attorney General, it does not provide that the petitioner for review shall have a real and substantial interest, or that the conditions shall be those of an actual case or controversy. The whole procedure appears in effect one of administrative control under a disguise of judicial control. There can be no real judicial control unless there is a real case or controversy.[27]

---

[26] Analysis of H.R. 6324 by Hon. Harold L. Ickes, Secretary of the Interior, in *Administrative Law*, Hearings before Subcommittee No. 4 of the House Committee on the Judiciary on H.R. 4236, H.R. 6198, and H.R. 6324, 76 Cong. 1 sess., p. 72.

[27] *Ashwander* v. *Tennessee Valley Authority*, 297 U.S. 288; *United States* v.

The proposed arrangement seems dangerous because it means that statutes as well as rules may be declared unconstitutional by an agency which is not performing true judicial functions. When the court finds that a rule or regulation, although in conformity with the statute which it assists to administer, nevertheless might operate to deprive a petitioner of property without due process of law or otherwise to violate his constitutional rights, it must of necessity base its declaration that the rule is invalid upon a declaration that the statute is unconstitutional. The possibility is thus opened that important constitutional questions may be presented to the Court of Appeals for the District of Columbia for its decision, although there is no such opposition of interests, in an actual case or controversy, as the Supreme Court has held absolutely essential to the proper determination of constitutional questions.

The legal remedies now existing are not to be taken away by the bill (nor could the bill deprive the Supreme Court of its constitutional jurisdiction). Thus, after the declaratory judgment by the Court of Appeals for the District of Columbia, a person whose interest lay on the other side of the question and who had a real case or controversy could still go to the courts and raise the question of constitutionality, carrying it through to the Supreme Court. The entire procedure in the Court of Appeals for the District of Columbia is thus seen to be, not a true declaratory judgment, but an administrative control, or an advisory opinion, not based on the consideration of the facts in a particular case. In considering this procedure as a form of administrative control, the question must be raised as to whether the Attorney General's office and the expert lawyers of each department may not be far better informed regarding the administrative matters involved and have far more time and resources to consider them than the overburdened Court of Appeals for the District of Columbia. As a judicial control it is unreal, for although it is practically binding on the government it is not binding on the persons whom the government seeks to regulate. Because it may appear to be what it is not, it must be regarded with suspicion.

Under the proposed arrangement, the Court of Appeals for the District of Columbia would be obliged in many instances to pass

---

West Virginia, 295 U.S. 463; *Bethlehem Shipbuilding Corp.* v. *Nylander,* 14 Fed. Supp. 201.

upon the validity of a rule or regulation in a "factual vacuum."[28] The determination will be reached entirely upon abstract considerations, or upon a factual situation so incomplete and undeveloped as to give little basis for action.

In case this court declares a rule or regulation to be legal and valid, the determination has no finality and may be entirely nullified by any other federal court having jurisdiction. In fact it is more than doubtful, for reasons already given, whether the determination of the Court of Appeals for the District of Columbia in such an advisory opinion or declaratory judgment is *res judicata*. Even a determination that a rule is invalid may be rendered inoperative by the simultaneous or earlier or later decision made in connection with an actual case or controversy, that the same rule is valid.

A question may be raised as to who benefits by this involved and expensive procedure. Certainly the administration is not helped. Since the procedure would be involved and uncertain it would not help the public. There remain to be considered special interests which, unable to defeat a bill in Congress, might be able to cripple its administration; also certain lawyers who serve such interests. These two groups might benefit, at the expense of good government and the general welfare.

General difficulties. In case this burden of rendering declaratory judgments under the Bar Association bill were thrown upon the Court of Appeals for the District of Columbia, it would be necessary to increase the personnel of the court. Increases in personnel would also be needed for the Department of Justice and practically all other agencies of the government. Whether the added cost and delay would yield any real benefits is highly questionable.

Finally, general judicial review of rules and regulations, whether real or pretended, is unnecessary. It adds nothing to the substantial effect of the remedies now available. Under existing laws, if an administrative rule or regulation threatens immediate injury to a legal right, the proper court may issue an injunction or other process which will prevent the injury from being done or becoming irremediable. Any rule which appears unconstitutional, illegal, or *ultra vires* may now be attacked when the administration seeks to

[28] Hon. Harold L. Ickes, Hearings, cited above, p. 72.

apply it, since an actual case or controversy then arises. To seek to control the work of the administration by declaratory judgments, before it appears how rules and regulations will operate in practice, seems highly inadvisable.

E. Intra-Agency Review Boards

It is asserted that the proposals of the Bar Association bill in re-pect to intra-agency review boards have several objects in view. The direct purposes are:

(1) To establish an uniform standard of procedure in (a) the single-headed agencies of the Federal administrative service and (b) the agencies which constitute the so-called independent boards, commissions, etc., for the hearing and determination administratively of controversies between the administrative officers and the citizen; (2) . . . to demand a formal hearing with mandatory duty that a full and fair hearing be accorded the aggrieved citizen so that there may be a proper record before the responsible administrative officers for action; and (3) To fix responsibility for administrative action.[29]

The indirect purposes are stated as follows:

(1) To obtain the psychological effect of that degree of care in de-ciding controversies which comes from being required to write out the findings of fact in accordance with the evidence and the reasons for the conclusion; (2) To build a better administrative service by making it impracticable, if not impossible for the untrained, the incompetent, and the lazy individual who procrastinates from day to day to remain in the Federal service in the more responsible positions demanding decision of controversies.[30]

An object not mentioned by the Special Committee of the Bar Association, but inherent in the terms of the bill, is to establish a series of administrative and judicial controls over acts of administra-tive authorities which have not been made justiciable by Congress or accepted as justiciable by the courts.

Before it is possible to criticize the requirements of the bill in respect to intra-agency boards, it is important to know in detail within which agencies such boards must be established. This can be determined only by an elaborate process of exclusion and inclu-

[29] *Report and Draft of Bill by the Special Committee on Administrative Law*, p. 30.
[30] The same.

sion based upon certain specific exceptions as to particular author-ities, exceptions as to functions, or exceptions as to circumstances, made by Section 7(b) of the bill;[31] upon the limitations contained in the definition of the word "agency" in Section 1(3); and upon the provisions of Section 4(a), (b) to the effect that "when any person is aggrieved by a decision of any officer or employee of any agency, such person may" request that the matter be referred to an intra-agency board. This very broad language, using the word decision in a general way and making no distinctions as to which decisions or other acts of certain agencies involve legal rights and which do not, makes it necessary to include in the list of agencies which would be compelled to set up intra-agency boards, several which might have been omitted if only the other sections of the bill were under consideration; also to list certain organizations in more than one category.

As a result of applying the criteria given by the bill, it appears that more than sixty boards might be established in the following agencies:

1. The Department of the Treasury
   a. The Secretary of the Treasury
   b. The Bureau of Engraving and Printing under a Director
   c. The Bureau of Narcotics under a Commissioner
   d. The Bureau of the Mint under a Director
   e. The Federal Alcohol Administration under an Administrator
   f. The Office of the Treasurer of the United States
   g. The Procurement Division under a Director
   h. The Public Debt Service under a Commissioner
   i. The Secret Service Division under a Chief
   j. The United States Coast Guard under a Commandant
   k. The Division of Savings Bonds

[31] For example, this section exempts from the operations of the act "any matter concerning or relating to the conduct of military or naval operations." It does not explain whether or not this means all acts of the War Department and the Navy Department. River and harbor work, in the appropriations bill, is listed in a section devoted to non-military activities; but under the Bar Association bill it might (or might not) be considered as included in the provision quoted.

Again, the section exempts controversies based on failure to receive employment. It apparently permits all other controversies based on personnel management, dismissal, demotion, etc., in any and every agency of the government, to be taken to intra-agency boards. Perhaps all acts connected with purchasing and supplies are likewise subject to review by the boards.

2. Post Office Department
   a. Postmaster General
   b. Assistant Postmasters General
   c. Bureau of the Chief Inspector
3. Department of the Interior
   a. Secretary of the Interior
   b. General Land Office under a Commissioner
   c. Bureau of Reclamation under a Commissioner
   d. Geological Survey under a Director
   e. Division of Grazing under a Director
   f. Office of Indian Affairs under a Commissioner
   g. Bureau of Mines under a Director
   h. Bureau of Fisheries under a Commissioner
   i. Bureau of Biological Survey under a Chief
   j. Petroleum Conservation Division under a Director
   k. Bituminous Coal Division under a Director
   l. Division of Territories and Island Possessions under a Director
   m. Alaska Railroad under a General Manager
   n. Bonneville Project under an Administrator
   o. National Park Service under a Director
4. Department of Agriculture
   a. Secretary of Agriculture
   b. Agricultural Adjustment Administration under an Administrator
   c. Agricultural Marketing Service under a Chief
   d. Bureau of Animal Industry under a Chief
   e. Bureau of Dairy Industry under a Chief
   f. Bureau of Entomology and Plant Quarantine under a Chief
   g. Food and Drug Administration under a Chief
   h. Forest Service under a Chief
   i. Division of Marketing and Marketing Agreements under an Associate Administrator
   j. Bureau of Plant Industry under a Chief
   k. Sugar Division under a Chief
   l. Commodity Exchange Administration under a Chief
   m. Rural Electrification Administration under an Administrator
5. Department of Commerce
   a. Secretary of Commerce
   b. Bureau of Marine Inspection and Navigation
   c. Inland Waterways Corporation with a President
   d. National Bureau of Standards under a Director
6. Department of Labor
   a. Secretary of Labor
   b. Public Contracts Division under an Administrator

    c. Wage and Hour Division under an Administrator
    d. Immigration and Naturalization Service under a Commissioner
7. Federal Security Agency
    a. The Administrator
    b. Civilian Conservation Corps under a Director
    c. Public Health Service under a Surgeon General
    d. Bureau of Old-Age and Survivors Insurance under a Director
    e. Bureau of Public Assistance under a Director
    f. Bureau of Employment Security under a Director
    g. National Youth Administration under an Administrator
8. Federal Works Agency
    a. The Administrator
    b. Public Roads Administration under a Commissioner
    c. United States Housing Authority under an Administrator
    d. Public Buildings Administration under a Commissioner
9. Veterans' Administration under an Administrator
10. Panama Canal with a Governor
11. General Accounting Office under a Comptroller General
12. International Fisheries Commission
13. Public Works Administration under a Commissioner
14. Work Projects Administration under a Commissioner

The following agencies appear to be exempted, in one way or another, from the necessity of establishing intra-agency boards to review the acts of officers and employees:

1. Specific exceptions by organizational unit
    a. Federal Reserve Board
    b. Bureau of the Comptroller of the Currency
    c. Federal Deposit Insurance Corporation
    d. Interstate Commerce Commission
    e. Department of State
    f. Department of Justice and Offices of United States Attorneys
    g. General Accounting Office in respect to the implementation of rules and regulations and judicial review of rules and regulations
2. Exceptions by function and circumstance
    a. War Department
    b. Navy Department
    c. Department of State
    d. Bureau of Internal Revenue
    e. Bureau of Customs
    f. Patent Office

g. Deputies under the Longshoremen's and Harbor Workers' Act

h. Secretary of Agriculture in respect to grading service in connection with purchase and sale of agricultural products

i. Civil Service Commission

j. Lending agencies in respect to lands
    (1) Farm Credit Administration
        (a) Federal Land Banks
        (b) Land Bank Commissioners
        (c) Federal Farm Mortgage Corporation
        (d) Federal Intermediate Credit Banks
        (e) Production Credit Corporations and Associations
        (f) Banks for Cooperatives
        (g) Regional Agricultural Credit Corporations
    (2) Federal loan agencies
        (a) Disaster Loan Corporation
        (b) Electric Home and Farm Authority
        (c) Export-Import Bank of Washington
        (d) Home Owners' Loan Corporation
        (e) Federal National Mortgage Association
        (f) Reconstruction Finance Corporation
        (g) Reconstruction Finance Corporation Mortgage Company
        (h) Commodity Credit Corporation

k. Library of Congress *in re* copyrights

3. Exceptions under the definition of "agency"[32]
    a. Commodity Exchange Commission
    b. Foreign Trade Zones Board
    c. Social Security Board
    d. Civil Aeronautics Authority
    e. Federal Communications Commission
    f. Federal Power Commission
    g. Federal Trade Commission
    h. Maritime Labor Board
    i. National Labor Relations Board
    j. National Mediation Board
    k. Railroad Retirement Board
    l. Securities and Exchange Commission
    m. Tennessee Valley Authority
    n. United States Civil Service Commission
    o. United States Employees' Compensation Commission

---

[32] " 'Agency' means any department, independent establishment, administration, corporation, or other subdivision of the executive branch of the United States Government with one chief officer as the immediate head thereof."—S. 915, Sec. 1(3).

p. United States Maritime Commission
q. United States Tariff Commission

Any acquaintance with the functions performed by the above-named agencies which apparently would have to establish intra-agency boards under the requirements of the Bar Association bill makes it possible to reach certain conclusions as to the requirements in question. These functions are extremely varied; so varied, indeed, that they cannot reasonably be subjected to a single type of procedure and control. The Bureau of Narcotics, for example, is charged with the enforcement of criminal laws such as the Harrison Narcotic Law, the Marihuana Tax Act of 1937, and the Narcotic Drugs Import and Export Act. In enforcing these laws it operates under the police formula. The Division of Public Contracts in the Department of Labor, on the other hand, is attempting to enforce provisions contained in contracts made by the government with private individuals in respect to hours of work, convict labor, age of employees, working conditions, etc. The act establishes no criminal sanctions, but sets up several other methods of enforcement, including a civil suit for the recovery of liquidated damages brought against the contractor who violates the stipulations of a government contract.

The Immigration and Naturalization Service is dealing with aliens who may be excluded from the United States under the sovereign power. The General Land Office and the Division of Grazing in the Department of the Interior are dealing with public lands in which individuals have no vested rights. One of the regulatory functions of the Bureau of Mines consists in revoking licenses already issued for the manufacture, sale, import, or export of explosives, because of acts of disloyalty or hostility toward the United States.

The Veterans' Administration makes decisions in respect to pensions to veterans, payments to dependents, government life insurance, and so on. The General Accounting Office makes decisions on claims by or against the government. The Secretary of Agriculture, under the Packers and Stockyards Act, issues both legislative and judicial orders.

These few examples, taken almost at random from among the

agencies which would probably be affected by the Bar Association bill, serve to indicate that it is probably not advisable to bring under one formula such unrelated subjects and acts as public lands, explosives, private rights, criminal suits, civil suits, revocation of licenses, legislative schedules, and cease and desist orders. Some of the agencies which would be required to set up intra-agency boards act chiefly through administrative decisions. Others are required by statute to perform certain acts by means of orders. For some acts, no procedures are established by law; for others, elaborate procedures are provided. Some acts are not, and by their nature cannot be, the basis of a case or controversy in a judicial sense. Others can give rise to a case or controversy. No judicial controls, beyond such general principles as that an administrator must act within his powers and must not abuse those powers, are provided for certain acts. Other acts, in particular orders of a judicial nature, are subjected to a strict control by the courts.

Some of the agencies which would be affected are integral parts of departments. Others stand upon a separate statutory basis, and their determinations which affect individuals are in no way controlled by the head of the department concerned. This is true of the Federal Alcohol Administration and the Wage and Hour Division, for example. In short, the functions, the applicable statutory, administrative, and judicial requirements, and the organizational relationships of the agencies concerned are so diversified as to make any single pattern for dealing with all their acts which may give rise to controversies appear both undesirable and impracticable.

Such a pattern, however, is provided by the Bar Association bill. Intra-agency boards, as was said above, are to deal with controversies based on acts of all agencies not in some way exempted. The bill provides for the establishment of such boards by the head of each agency concerned. When any person is aggrieved by a decision[33] of any officer or employee of any agency, he may notify the head of the agency of his objection to the action and request

---

[33] Sec. 1(8) provides: "'Decision' means any affirmative or negative decision, order or Act in specific controversies which determines the issue therein involved." Part I of the present study shows that this definition has no exact relation to law, administration, or jurisprudence, and that it is in many instances inapplicable if not meaningless.

that the controversy be referred to a board. The board must give "an opportunity at an early day for a full and fair hearing." Notice of the hearing is to be given to the aggrieved person, and other substantially interested parties shall have the right of intervention. Provision is made for the filing of written pleadings, the issuance of subpoenas for witnesses and documents, the taking of testimony in accordance with the rules of evidence that are applicable to quasi-judicial proceedings, the examination and cross-examination of witnesses, the reduction of the testimony to writing, the making of formal findings of fact upon the evidence, and the preparation of a separate written decision by the board. In other words, no matter how simple may be the nature of the controversy, this complicated procedure must be employed. Both the functions and the procedure of intra-agency boards, as established by the Bar Association bill, appear to be not only unnecessarily cumbersome, but possibly obstructive. This will become clearer as the discussion proceeds.

Functions of the board. The expression "aggrieved by a decision of any officer or employee of any agency," sets no limit to the type of action over which the boards are to have jurisdiction; nor is any limit set by the definitions given of "decision" and "controversy." The former was cited above; the latter reads: " 'Controversy' means any dispute or disagreement concerning any claim, right, or obligation for or against the United States and any refusal to grant any license, permit, or other privilege."[34] Earlier chapters of this study have shown that under the Constitution of the United States, there is no possibility through intra-agency boards, or in any other fashion, of making a justiciable controversy out of an act lying wholly within the discretion of an administrator. Many acts of this sort must fall under the formula, "any refusal to grant any license, permit, or privilege."

On the practical side, the bill does not consider the procedures which have been employed in the first place for performing the acts to be reviewed by the intra-agency boards. An act might be an order made only after a careful hearing and fact-finding; it might be a discretionary act; it might or might not involve legal

[34] S. 915, Sec. 1(9).

consequences to the petitioner. Yet all acts alike, if there is a dispute or disagreement concerning them, are to go to the intra-agency boards.

The bill does not make it clear whether the board is to redetermine the merits of the matter and substitute its discretion for that of the officer performing the act originally, or whether it is merely to determine whether the decision made by him was, in the particular set of circumstances, within the bounds of discretion given him by statute. It does not indicate whether in cases turning upon disputed issues of fact it is the duty of the board to redecide the questions of fact and substitute its own independent conclusions, or merely to determine whether in the light of the testimony, the decision of the officer is supported by substantial evidence.

If the officer is charged by law and by rules and regulations with making an order upon the basis of a fact-finding supported by evidence, and with preparing a written transcript of the record which is reviewable by the courts, may the board disregard this record and build up an independent record by a trial *de novo*, thus causing both the government and the individual the expense of twice introducing the same evidence and arguments?

The relationship of the intra-agency boards to the head of an agency within a department and to the head of the department is far from clear. Manifestly they are not, like the Board of Tax Appeals and the United States Customs Court, higher controlling authorities; for if they were, their "findings of fact and separate decision thereon" would not be subject to "the written approval, disapproval, or modification of the head of the agency concerned or of such person as he shall designate."[35] Nor are they merely advisory in nature, as is the Board of Appeals in the Department of the Interior. Are they merely fact-finding agencies, like masters in chancery or like the trial examiners of the Federal Trade Commission?

Must the head of the agency or reviewing officer confine his consideration of the case to the evidence contained in the record made before the board? May he take account of facts (within his own knowledge, based on the results of his own investigations, found

[35] The same, Sec. 4(b).

in the departmental records, or brought to his attention by subordinates), which have not been introduced into the hearing before the board? Must the decision of the board be sustained by the reviewing officer if he finds it to be based upon substantial evidence and a correct interpretation of the law, or may he set it aside in case he disagrees with the conclusion? May the reviewing officer decline to re-examine a matter decided by the board? Must the reviewing officer read the entire record before he passes upon a decision of the board?

By providing that the board shall make a separate decision upon the facts, the bill requires the head of the agency to act on a case that has been prejudged. Since he must approve, disapprove, or modify the decision of the board, the superior officer acts as a court of second instance rather than a responsible administrator. If all the matters decided by an intra-agency board were judicial in nature, this would be less objectionable. When, however, questions of promotion, dismissal, the granting of licenses or privileges, and other administrative discretionary questions arise, as they will arise under the terms of the bill, the administrator cannot be expected to assume responsibility without power. If he disregards the action of the board, the whole procedure may be merely dilatory. If he is bound by it, he is not responsible.

No provision is made in the bill for review by the superior administrator of actions of subordinates, before a case is sent to the board. If the board is considered a quasi-judicial authority, its action ought not to be invoked before exhaustion of administrative remedies. If it is an administrative authority, its recommendations are purely advisory and the head of the agency should not be bound by them.

The bill contains the following ambiguous provisions[36] as to rehearing prior to a request for judicial review of the decisions or orders of administrative agencies: "Before filing a petition such party may within ten days make a motion to the agency or independent agency concerned for a rehearing . . . and the time for appeal shall run from the order on such motion if denied or the

[36] The same, Sec. 5(a).

order made on such rehearing if a rehearing shall be had." It is not specified who grants or denies the request for rehearing, or who holds a rehearing if one is allowed.

The relationship of the intra-agency boards to the courts is far from clear. The bill provides that any person aggrieved by the final decision or order of any agency may file a petition with the United States Court of Appeals for the District of Columbia, or the appropriate circuit court of appeals, stating the alleged errors in the decision of the agency.[37] It is made the duty of the agency to prepare and file with the clerk of the court the original or a full and accurate transcript of the entire record in such proceeding. This is further evidence that no matter how trivial the basis of a controversy, the bill would subject it to a procedure comparable to a "due process of law" fact-finding and a judicial decision.

According to other provisions of the bill[38] the court will have to pass upon the questions whether the findings of fact are erroneous; whether they are or are not supported by substantial evidence; whether the decision is or is not supported by findings of fact; whether the decision was issued without due notice and a reasonable opportunity to the aggrieved party for a full and fair hearing, and so on. These provisions, if they ever became effective, might lead to serious difficulties. If the court should hold on the transcript of the record that the decision of the inferior authority was supported by the facts, but that the action of the superior authority thereon was not so supported, a difficult and embarrassing administrative situation would arise. The court would be sustaining subordinate, perhaps permanent, civil service employees and at the same time humiliating their superior officer, in many instances a politically appointed officer of high rank within his party. New and difficult problems in the relationship between responsible political officers and permanent civil servants would be introduced into administration.

Fortunately, the attitude of the parties and of the court may prevent these things from happening. Matters over which the

[37] The same.
[38] The same.

courts can take jurisdiction are already, in general, subject to statutory review; and it is hardly likely that anyone who can appeal to the courts from an order affecting his rights, will go to an intra-agency board and await action, first by the board and then by the head of the agency. Other matters, although the Bar Association bill would send them to the courts, cannot give rise to cases or controversies. Jurisdiction cannot be given by statute to constitutional courts where there is no case or controversy.[39]

The bill does not distinguish administrative action which involves rights from administrative action which does not involve rights and which is discretionary. For example, it makes the "refusal to grant any license, permit or other privilege" the subject of action by the intra-agency boards, and provides for review of such action by the circuit courts of appeals. Further, by expressly exempting controversies based on failure "to receive appointment or employment by any agency or independent agency,"[40] the bill implies that all other personnel cases may be handled by review boards with appeal to the courts. Similarly, since disputes concerning pensions are not exempted, it is apparently the intent of the bill to send them to the courts. Generally these and other matters which do not affect established rights but require only the exercise of administrative discretion, are recognized in long-settled jurisprudence as not being appropriate subjects of judicial action.

Many attempts have been made in the past to induce the constitutional courts to review disputes of this kind, but the courts have consistently held that they possess no jurisdiction to do so. The basic nature of the controversy is not changed by establishing a particular type of procedure before intra-agency boards. The significant thing is the relationship between the type of administrative action taken and the legal rights of the individual, and not the particular type of hearing upon an appeal from that action.

If judicial review is deemed necessary over actions which are not justiciable in constitutional courts, jurisdiction should be given to legislative courts.[41] The bill does, it is true, permit review by

---

[39] See Supporting Statement XI, pp. 318-32.

[40] S. 915, Sec. 7(b).

[41] F. F. Blachly, *Working Papers on Administrative Adjudication*, printed for the use of the Senate Committee on the Judiciary, 75 Cong. 3 sess.

the Court of Appeals for the District of Columbia as an alternative to review by the circuit courts of appeals;[42] but the former court would have to be enormously increased and perhaps reorganized in order to enable it to handle even a fraction of the cases which would come to it because the other courts had refused jurisdiction, if judicial review should be extended as the Bar Association bill provides.

Nothing that has been said is intended to imply that there should never be intra-agency boards to pass on disputes or disagreements. Such boards are already in existence in a number of agencies; but their decisions are not looked upon as the basis for review by constitutional courts. It should be possible to establish a board whenever such action will evidently assist in the work of administration; but it should not be mandatory to establish a board where the work could be done better through some other type of organization.

From an administrative standpoint, the intra-agency board procedure is often far too complicated for the subject matter handled. It is too cumbersome, slow, and expensive to be employed in connection with small matters. It goes far beyond any need for uniformity and simplification of administrative procedure. "By multiplying opportunities for hearings, all of which must include among other things power of subpoena, the right of cross-examination of witnesses, the filing of formal pleadings, and the making of written records, opportunity for delay is too clearly afforded. Numerous administrative and judicial hearings are provided for if a petitioner desires to take a rule or action under it through the court of ultimate resort. The holding of the number of hearings provided for would require months and perhaps years, if the right were fully exercised by ingenious council. The bill, by overextending the opportunities for delay, affords an opportunity for the use of dilatory tactics which may result in completely paralyzing administrative authority."[43]

[42] S. 915, Sec. 5(a).
[43] Letter of Stephen B. Gibbons, Acting Secretary of the Treasury, in *Administrative Law*, Hearings before Subcommittee No. 4 of the House Committee on the Judiciary on H.R. 4236, H.R. 6198, and H.R. 6324, 76 Cong. 1 sess., p. 106.

F. Procedure before Independent Agencies

According to the Bar Association bill, " 'independent agency' means any board, commission, authority, corporation, or other subdivision of the executive branch of the United States Government with two or more officers at the head thereof as board, commission, or other members."[44]

The following provisions are made concerning procedure before independent agencies:

Where any matter arises out of the activities of any independent agency, it may be provided by rule that such matter may be heard in the first instance by one of its trial examiners, who shall file with the independent agency the written record and his written findings of fact and separate decision, which shall be made in all instances, whether by the examiner or the independent agency, after reasonable public notice and a full and fair hearing as hereinbefore in this section provided. A copy or copies thereof shall be sent by registered mail to the aggrieved party. The independent agency shall enter at the expiration of thirty days such appropriate decision as may be proper unless within said thirty days the aggrieved party shall signify his written consent to the entry of the decision or shall file by registered mail with the independent agency his written objections to the findings of fact and decision of the examiner, in which event the independent agency shall not enter its decision without first according a public hearing upon reasonable notice to such party. Such hearing shall be before the members of the independent agency, if it has not less than three members, or before any three of such members. If the independent agency has less than three members, an intra-agency board shall be constituted. . . .[45]

These provisions are intended, according to the *Report and Draft of Bill by the Special Committee on Administrative Law*, "to establish an uniform standard of procedure in . . . the agencies which constitute the so-called independent boards, commissions, etc., for the hearing and determination administratively of controversies between the administrative officers and the citizen. . . ."[46]

Will the provisions of the bill accomplish this intention? They certainly do not achieve a complete uniformity, since they make the employment of trial examiners permissive rather than mandatory.

[44] S. 915, Sec. 1(4).
[45] The same, Sec. 4(e).
[46] Annotations on p. 30.

From the earlier part of the present chapter it appears, however, that uniformity is not desirable for its own sake and that it may be a positive detriment to effective administration if conditions are not uniform. Even with the use of trial examiners left optional, the procedure outlined by the bill appears to be too nearly uniform to fit all the situations in which it would be applied.

Several considerations should be borne in mind in evaluating the provisions for procedure before the independent agencies. First, most of the objections to the procedure before intra-agency boards are applicable. Second, the bill does not seem to give sufficient consideration to two facts: (1) that a great number of disputes arising from the activities of the independent agencies are now handled by conferences, informal hearings, stipulations, etc.; and (2) that orders touching constitutional rights and some statutory rights are reviewed by the courts. In the light of these two facts it would seem that it is entirely unnecessary to add a procedure which is equivalent to that of the intra-agency board and which can be had upon demand. There is no need for it from the standpoint of protection under the law, and it may easily prove to be a serious impediment to administrative efficiency.

Next, the bill fails to make distinctive provision for the several different relationships which exist between the individual and the regulatory agency, or to recognize the fact that satisfactory procedures have been developed in connection with most of these relationships. For example, in what are sometimes called complaint-and-answer cases the authority generally sits as a court and does not appear as a party. Such cases arise in respect to reparation orders and some kinds of enforcement orders. In such cases the commission determines the rights of private parties as any court might do. Some complaint-and-answer cases, however, although they decide matters of private right, have such broad ramifications that the decisions may affect many individuals who do not participate in the hearings either as complainants or intervenors, as when a stockyard is ordered to make reparation for acts hitherto common to stockyards but now found to be in violation of law.

In many cases the commission or other agency appears as a complainant because of alleged misconduct on the part of an individual or corporation subject to its regulation. Such a case arises when the Commodity Exchange Commission seeks to revoke the designation of a board of trade as a contract market, for violation of law, rules and regulations, or orders. Since such revocation is made subject to notice and hearing, the burden is laid upon the Commission of establishing the facts alleged in the complaint. Other cases arise, for example, when complaint is made to the Interstate Commerce Commission (or when the Commission institutes investigation to determine) that there is illegal control of two or more carriers by common directors; or when it is proposed by a regulatory authority to suspend a traffic rate or to establish a wage rate.[47]

Is it not highly probable that these different situations should be controlled by different types of procedure? In any case, is it not unwise to disregard the procedures which have been worked out by statutes, rules and regulations, and judicial decisions, and to propose as an alternative, whenever an individual chooses to demand it, a single type of procedure which (except for the trial examiner provision) lacks flexibility and has only a slight relation to administrative experience? The *a priori* assumption that one pattern of quasi-judicial procedure is advisable for all types of cases can hardly be justified in view of the facts at hand.

. It should not be forgotten that many orders issued by the independent regulatory agencies are in no sense "controversies between the administrative officers and the citizen," but are rather methods of realizing social and economic policies outlined by Congress. In the hearings which serve as a basis for such orders, the government appears formally as a party, but it is not in an adversary position. Regulation is a constant process of adjustments; not a series of judicial contests.

Finally, the proposed bill, although it would in all probability impede and hamper administration in ways already shown, does nothing to answer numerous concrete questions which are now occupying the attention of the many persons desirous of improving administrative procedure. Some of these questions are:

1. The selection of trial examiners. How should trial examiners

[47] For other examples, see Supporting Statement IV, pp. 276-86.

be chosen? What qualifications should they have? Should they be made more independent in their work?

2. The conduct of the hearing by trial examiners. (a) Witnesses. Should the trial examiner have power to issue subpoenas? Should the commission sign blank subpoenas for him to issue? Should all subpoenas be issued by the commission? (b) Place of hearing. Should the trial examiner have power to transfer the place of hearing? (c) Rules of evidence. Should certain definite rules of evidence be established, or should the commission depend upon the judgment of the trial examiner? Should different rules of evidence be applied when the public interest is involved from those used when the commission is merely deciding a dispute between two individuals? (d) Rulings. Should the trial examiner have full power to make rulings as questions arise, or should he make only provisional rulings? (e) Interlocutory appeals to commission. When a trial examiner is hearing a case, should interlocutory appeals to the commission be permitted? (f) Oral arguments and briefs. Should parties have an opportunity for oral arguments upon completion of the taking of testimony before the trial examiner? Should parties be permitted to file briefs as a part of the record made by the trial examiner? (g) Stipulation and fact-finding. Should the trial examiner have power to stipulate as to facts? Should parties, as a matter of right, be allowed to submit proposed fact-findings?

3. Nature of trial examiner's report. What should be the nature of the trial examiner's report? Should it be merely a fact-finding, or should it contain conclusions of law and a tentative order?

4. Review of trial examiner's report. (a) Should parties be allowed, as of right, to file exceptions to the report? (b) In case no exceptions are filed, should the commission adopt the findings of the trial examiner as its own, or should it review the evidence? (c) Does the type of action taken determine whether or not the evidence should be reviewed by the commission? (d) Should there be established in the commission a review division which examines the work of the trial examiner before it goes to the commission and suggests final action on matters to which no exceptions are taken?

5. Hearing before commission on review. (a) Should oral argu-

ments before the commission and the filing of briefs be permitted as a matter of right or at the discretion of the commission? (b) Must oral arguments be made before the full membership or may they be brought before single members? (c) In connection with rather common and routine matters of a police-judge nature, is there any necessity for bringing the case before the whole commission? (d) How far can adjudication be delegated to subordinates? Does the amount of delegation depend upon whether a case is one involving policy, or merely a dispute between individuals? (e) Should the grounds for the argument before the commission be based merely upon exceptions to the intermediate report of the trial examiner, or should they concern the whole report and record? (f) Should the trial examiner prepare for the commission a memorandum which considers the exceptions? (g) Does the commission have a positive duty to consider the whole case, even where no exceptions have been filed? May the answer here depend upon whether the public interest is involved?

6. The final order of the commission. (a) In respect to the making of the decision or order after a hearing, who shall study the record? Shall a review division, the solicitor of the agency, or the trial examiner assist the commission in examining the record? (b) Should tentative findings of fact and conclusions of law be prepared and given the parties before the final order or decision, when this is not required by law?

These and many related questions should be answered before any attempt is made to provide a uniform rule of procedure before the independent regulatory bodies. There are various opinions on almost every one of these questions. In order to reach intelligent conclusions regarding them, it is necessary to study carefully, with the questions held in mind, the procedure of every authority charged with the regulatory function. This category includes not only the independent boards and commissions, but other agencies, such as the Department of Agriculture, which are confronted with exactly the same type of problem. Such a study should naturally include the appropriate constitutional, statutory, and regulatory provisions and judicial decisions, but it should not end with these. It should inquire under what circumstances each agency is functioning; what types of actions it takes; what investigations it has made and is making or contemplating; what are its available sources of information; how many acts of every nature it performs, how many complaints it receives, how many informal adjustments it makes, and how many formal cases it hears, all within a given time; in general, what has been its experience. In this way alone will it be possible to build up an administrative procedure that stands on the solid ground of experience—a procedure that at one and the same time will make for the utmost efficiency and expedition in administration, will serve the public interest, and will safeguard the rights of the citizen.

G. Judicial Review of Actions of Independent Agencies

Provisions of the bill. The bill provides:

Sec. 5(a) Any party to a proceeding before any agency or independent agency as provided in section 4 of this Act who may be aggrieved by the final decision or order of any agency, or independent agency, as the case may be, within thirty days after the date of receipt of a copy thereof, may at his election file a written petition (1) with the clerk of the United States Court of Appeals for the District of Columbia; or (2) with the clerk of the circuit court of appeals within whose jurisdiction such aggrieved party resides or maintains his principal place of business or in which the controversy arose, for review of the decision. Before filing a petition such party may within ten days make a motion to the agency or independent agency concerned for a rehearing, tendering a statement of any further showing to be made thereon which shall constitute a part of the record, and the time for appeal shall run from the order on such motion if denied or the order made on such rehearing if a rehearing shall be had. The petition shall state the alleged errors in the decision of the agency or independent agency concerned. The Attorney General of the United States and the agency or independent agency shall each be served with a copy of the petition and it shall be the duty of the Attorney General of the United States to cause appearance to be entered on behalf of the United States within thirty days after the date of receipt by him of a copy of the petition and it shall be the duty of the agency or independent agency, as the case may be, within thirty days or such longer time as the court may by order direct, after receipt of a copy of the petition to cause to be prepared and filed with the clerk of such court the original or a full and accurate transcript of the entire record in such proceeding before such agency or independent agency. The court may affirm or set aside the decision or may direct the agency or independent agency concerned to modify its decision. Any case may be remanded for such further evidence as in the discretion of the court may be required but no objection not urged before the agency or independent agency, as the case may be, shall be considered by the court unless the failure or neglect to urge such objection shall be excused by the court for good cause shown. To facilitate the hearing of such appeals and avoid delay in the hearing of other matters before the court, such court may constitute special sessions thereof to consist of any three judges competent in law to sit as judges of a circuit court of appeals, which special sessions may be held concurrently with the regular sessions of said court. Any decision of any agency or independent agency shall be set aside if it is made to appear to the satisfaction of the court (1) that the findings of fact are clearly erroneous; or (2) that the findings of fact are not supported by substantial evidence; or (3) that the decision is not supported by the findings of fact; or (4) that the decision was issued without due notice and a reasonable opportunity having been afforded the aggrieved party for a full and fair hearing; or (5) that the decision is beyond the jurisdiction of the agency or independent agency, as the case may be; or (6) that the decision infringes the Constitution or statutes of the United States; or (7) that the decision is otherwise contrary to law.

(b) The judgments of the circuit courts of appeals shall be final, except that they shall be subject to review by the Supreme Court of the United States upon writ of certiorari or certification as provided in sections 239 and 240 of the Judicial Code, as amended (U.S.C., title 28, secs. 346 and 347).

(c) Where the cause of action is otherwise within the jurisdiction of the United States Court of Claims as provided in sections 136 to 187, inclusive, of the Judicial Code, as amended (U.S.C., title 28, secs. 241 to 293, inclusive), the petition provided in this section may be to the said Court of Claims at the election of the aggrieved party.

(d) Where a circuit court of appeals or the Court of Claims finds itself in disagreement with a previously rendered decision of another court having jurisdiction under this section, it shall certify to the Supreme Court of the United States a distinct and definite statement of the question or proposition of law upon which such disagreement rests, with a statement of the nature of the cause and of the facts on which such question or proposition of law arises, together with a statement of the reasons in support of such disagreement. Such further proceedings shall be as provided in section 239 of the Judicial Code, as amended (U.S.C., title 28, sec. 346).

JURISDICTION OF COURTS TO IMPOSE DAMAGES WHERE APPEAL WAS FOR DELAY AND FOR COSTS

Sec. 6. The courts shall have jurisdiction and power to impose damages in any case where the decision of the agency or independent agency is affirmed and the court finds that there was no substantial basis for the petition for review. In all cases the costs on review shall be allowed the prevailing party after final judgment, to be collected according to law.

EXCEPTIONS AND RESERVATIONS

Sec. 7. Nothing contained in this Act shall operate to modify or repeal any rights or procedure as now provided by law for any person to have his controversy with the United States heard and determined in any district court or circuit court of appeals of the United States.

Differences. The following provisions of the bill are not usually found in present-day review procedure.

1. A person evidently can elect the procedure provided by the bill rather than the three-judge district court procedure which is applicable at present to most orders of the Interstate Commerce Commission, general orders of the Federal Communications Commission, certain orders of the Secretary of Agriculture, and orders of the United States Maritime Commission.

2. The provisions which allow the court to affirm or set aside the decision, or to direct the agency or independent agency concerned to modify its decision, are different from the usual statutory provisions now existing. Such provisions generally allow the court, when reviewing an order, to affirm, modify, or set aside the same. In a few instances they require the court to enforce the decision if affirmed or modified.

3. The provisions in respect to the introduction of new evidence are much less specific than those of most present laws regarding the acts of administrative agencies.

4. The provisions of the bill in respect to the validity of findings of fact by the administrative authorities are quite exceptional. Thus, the conditions under which the facts as found administratively shall be set aside are given; whereas the usual statements to the effect that the findings of fact of the administrative agency shall be conclusive if "supported by substantial evidence," etc., are conspicuously absent.

5. There are added situations where the cause of action is otherwise within the jurisdiction of the United States Court of Claims.

6. There is added a provision as to what shall take place when a circuit court of appeals or the Court of Claims finds itself in dis-

agreement with a previously rendered decision of another court having jurisdiction.

7. A new provision gives the courts jurisdiction to impose damages where appeal was made without substantial basis, and to impose costs.

8. The appeal is the same from actions of intra-departmental boards and agencies as from independent agencies.

Advantages of the bill in re judicial review. The proposals of the bill evidently contain certain advantages over the general statutory provisions for judicial review.

1. The party aggrieved by a decision could elect the circuit court of appeals transcript of the record procedure instead of the three-judge district court procedure. This tends to a uniformity in respect to appeals, which is as desirable (in cases where it is constitutionally possible) when a matter has taken the form of a justiciable controversy, as it is undesirable while a matter is subject to administrative action. It also prevents a *de novo* trial of the case, which consumes time and may lead to the substitution of judicial discretion for administrative discretion. This new provision, however, is quite largely vitiated by the fact that a person may still proceed under the three-judge district court procedure or other procedure if he wishes (see Sec. 7 of bill, Exceptions and Reservations).

2. The substitution of the power of the court to direct the agency or independent agency concerned to modify its decision, for the usual formula that the court has the right to "modify" the decision, is a step in advance. Undoubtedly when the court modifies a decision of an administrative authority it substitutes its own discretion for that of the authority, and in so far as it does this it is administering rather than adjudicating.

3. The provision as to the settling by the Supreme Court of disagreements on questions of law, between decisions of different circuit court of appeals, is to be commended as a step toward securing uniformity of jurisprudence among the lower federal courts.

Disadvantages of the bill in respect to judicial review.

1. It is a mistake to attempt to place the determinations of the independent boards and commissions, which are generally taken by order, on the same appeal basis as the decisions regarding personnel,

pensions, standardization, etc., which are to be taken by intra-agency boards plus the head of the agency. The attempt is made here to place non-justiciable action in the same category as justiciable action, and to create rights by providing remedies.

2. The bill fails to distinguish different types of relationship between the government and the individual. Manifestly when the government is carrying out its proprietary, promotional, benefactory, etc., functions there is no such need for appeal to a constitutional court as there is in respect to regulatory actions which affect guaranteed rights.

3. Since the courts would almost certainly refuse to take jurisdiction over many of the cases that would be brought before them under the provisions of this bill, there might easily be complete confusion in federal administrative law for years if the bill should be passed.

4. If appeal from actions of a proprietary, promotional, benefactory, etc., nature is to be had, it must be before legislative rather than constitutional courts.

5. The provisions as to when new evidence may be presented or required are not so clear as in the usual statute.

6. It seems undesirable to state affirmatively and in detail the conditions under which the fact-finding of an authority may be set aside by the courts, without including any provision making the fact-finding of the authority conclusive, or at the very least *prima facie* evidence, if supported by the testimony. The bill, by so stating the conditions for setting aside the order, and failing to attribute any value to the fact-finding of the agency, tends to encourage the courts to review findings of fact to an extent not permitted by present statutes. Such review would enable the court to substitute its judgment for that of the administrative authorities, and would also probably have drastic and deleterious effect upon the work of the regulatory authorities. This is especially significant in respect to orders legislative in nature.

The language of the bill imposes upon the reviewing court the task of deciding whether the administrative determination of facts is illegal upon any or all of several specified grounds, quoted above. These grounds, summarized, are: clearly erroneous findings of fact; lack of evidence to support findings of fact; or a decision which is not supported by the facts as found. No positive valuation is clearly given to the fact-finding made by the administration. These provisions would operate to place upon the reviewing court the burden of examining the evidence and of formulating its own independent conclusions as to the correctness of the findings, rather than that of performing its present lighter and more appropriate task of merely ascertaining whether there is substantial evidence in the record, upon which a reasonable person could have arrived at the findings. The effect of the proposed change would be to bring about trials *de novo* on the administrative record. The courts then would be flooded with cases which they should not be expected to handle.

7. A judicial strait-jacket, such as is contemplated by the bill, would be both onerous to the courts and crippling to the administration, without offering any particular advantage to the individual. Mr. Robert M. Cooper, special assistant to the Attorney General, has stated the difficulties of this situation, as follows:[48]

It is hardly reasonable to assume that a judiciary, completely untrained in the problems of public administration, is more capable or more likely to reach proper results than experienced administrators selected primarily for their specialized knowledge, technical competence, and thorough familiarity with the intricacies of modern governmental policies. In recognition of this truth the tendency of legislative practice has been in the direction of according greater administrative finality to official action. Within the sphere of legitimate governmental functions, positive administrative adjudication constantly tends to replace the wholly negative aspect of judicial control. . . .

. . . As a practical matter the judiciary is no more fitted to enter the specialized fields of public administration, nor endowed with the technical competence necessary to solve the intricate problems arising in connection with the enforcement of modern legislative policies, than are the legislative bodies which were forced to delegate such functions to specialized tribunals. Obviously, then, the courts are in no position to supervise the exercise of discretionary authority by these specialized tribunals except in those cases where there is a clear abuse of power or authority. . . . Similarly, but to an even greater extent, the practice

[48] "Administrative Justice and the Rule of Discretion," 47 *Yale Law Journal* 577, 595 ff.

of permitting a complete trial *de novo* on certain fundamental issues which inevitably involve the exercise of discretion reaches beyond the outermost bounds of sound governmental practice.

In a similar vein, Dr. Charles Grove Haines has said:[49]

. . . Many of the statutes providing for administrative procedure were designed to provide remedies in fields in which the customary legal procedures had failed to render effective, expeditious, and inexpensive justice. Regardless of this fact the employment of counsel and the assurance of formal judicial procedure according to common law standards are demanded by the opponents of administrative justice. Thus the simple, direct and expeditious handling of affairs by administrative officers is held up to scorn no matter how much more advantageously individual and social values may thereby be protected and preserved.

H. Is There Administrative Absolutism?

In view of all the facts and all the jurisprudence brought together in the present chapter and in Part I of this study, it appears that the "tendencies toward administrative absolutism" so feared by certain promoters of the Bar Association bill are largely nonexistent. When the statutes require a hearing, the courts already insist that this requirement be fulfilled. A tendency to act upon evidence not produced, or to make decisions upon the basis of pre-formed opinion or prejudice (admitted that such a tendency is human and not confined to administrators) is corrected by the judicial principle that the government cannot act on evidence not produced at the hearing,[50] and by the careful inquiry of the reviewing court as to whether the evidence supports the fact-finding or the order; or, when administrative discretion as such is exercised, whether the discretion was used in a willful, arbitrary, and capricious manner. There can be no disregard of jurisdictional limits, since *ultra vires* acts are set aside.

It is not altogether clear what is meant by the charge that there

---

[49] Presidential Address delivered at the thirty-fifth meeting of the American Political Science Association, Washington, D.C. Dec. 29, 1939, *American Political Science Review*, February 1940.

[50] *Robinson* v. *Baltimore & O. R. Co.*, 222 U.S. 506; *United States* v. *Abilene & S. R. Co.*, 265 U.S. 274.

is a tendency to apply to the determining function the methods of the directing function. The administrative judicial order, it is true, both determines and directs; but so does a court order for reparations. All that can be said on this point is that orders and other administrative acts which affect rights are generally surrounded by statutory requirements for procedure and review which operate to protect those rights very completely. It is hardly possible to yield to political pressure at the expense of the law, under these conditions.

Arbitrary rule making for administrative convenience is a charge that cannot be proved. Although the courts will ask only: "Did the administrator have the power to make this rule under the laws?" —and not: "Was the administrator wise in making this rule?"—it is a matter of record that great efforts are made to consult those who will be affected, when a substantive rule of far-reaching importance is contemplated. The accompanying charge of "perfunctory routine" is a matter of opinion; nor is it possible to see how overloading the administration with obstructive complaints regarding every trifling rule would lighten the pressure and enable the work to be done in less "perfunctory" fashion.

The exercise of jurisdiction by "deputies," or better, subordinate officers (despite the declaration in the Morgan case[51] that "the one who decides must hear") cannot be avoided to a certain extent and for certain kinds of disputes. Unless the administration is to be a model of the Circumlocution Office made famous by Dickens, many disputes which do not involve rights, and some which do involve rights, must be handled by assistants, at least in first instance. The task of fact-finding in thousands of cases is so large that it is beyond the powers of any small group of men to hold all necessary hearings. When thousands of cases must be handled each year, it is obvious that the function of taking evidence must be delegated. Careful distribution of powers and establishment of relationships can make this arrangement fair to all concerned, and satisfy the courts. The Bar Association bill itself recognized this fact in its provisions regarding trial examiners, incomplete as these provisions are.

[51] *Morgan v. United States*, 298 U.S. 468, 481.

The mixture of functions as to which so much complaint is made is for the most part absent from administrative judicial actions. Where it is present, this is due in general to one of two causes: (1) the shifting nature and delicate balance of the problem, as, what is an "unfair trade practice"; or (2) the uncertainty as to the trial examiner's functions. The first cause could be mitigated, but not removed, by giving to the Federal Trade Commission (or any agency operating under a similarly difficult and somewhat vague law) a more adequate rule-making power. The second could be removed by administrative action, joint or several, or by legislative action, more clearly and completely defining the functions and relationships of the trial examiner.

The "uncontrolled discretion in interpreting the law and in finding the facts" is partly imaginary and partly a result of the constitutional separation of powers. It is necessary, if law is to be enforced, that the administrative authorities interpret it in the first instance and exercise their own judgment as to what the law means. The discretion of the administrator is never absolute, however, for it is always subject to check by the courts which will consider whether it is exercised subject to the conditions set by the law, to the requirements of the Constitution, and to standards of impartiality and reasonableness. Without transgressing the separation of powers, the courts cannot substitute their judgment as to expediency for that of the administrator acting within his legal sphere.

Where, in all this picture, is administrative absolutism? With very few exceptions, every legal and constitutional right is already protected by a procedure accepted by the courts as satisfying the substantial requirements of "due process," and is further protected by the possibility of judicial review.

The desire to extend a judicial form of procedure, with judicial review, to legislative and discretionary action on the part of the administrative authorities, is based upon a trust in the judicial formula, combined with a distrust of administrative experience, both of which are carried so far as to cause forgetfulness of the constitutional separation of powers. Not the administration alone, but the courts as well, interpret the Constitution as meaning that there is a sphere of administrative action over which the constitutional courts have no control except as to the question of regularity. To call this sphere "absolutism" is to forget that the separation of powers is designed explicitly to prevent one branch of government from becoming absolute and usurping the functions of the others. No progress would be made by seeking to substitute a real and all-pervading judicial absolutism for the imaginary "administrative absolutism" which is charged but not proved by supporters of the judicial formula.

I. General Considerations

Finally, the doctrine of the judicial formula is wrong in its fundamental objectives. Even if its doubtfully constitutional features and its most rash departures from the established system of constitutional and administrative law were eliminated, its animating purpose, the desire to subject every possible disagreement between the individual and the administration to complete control by the courts, is opposed to the inevitable, necessary, and useful evolution of administrative procedures and administrative and judicial controls that have been a notable feature of federal government during more than half a century. The theory is based on the moribund conception that law cannot prevail or justice be done except through the courts. It fails to accord to administrative authorities and procedures the degree of power and of finality which the courts themselves, applying the laws under the Constitution of the United States, have recognized as belonging to those authorities and procedures. Because it looks backward and tries to revive the very system of judicial regulation of business and industry which proved so impossible as to lead to the establishment of administrative regulatory bodies, it should be discarded. Because it destroys and does not construct, because it offers no real protection to the citizen but does menace effective administration, because it rests upon dead theory instead of evolving reality, the doctrine of the judicial formula should be rejected.

CHAPTER XI

THE REVISIONIST DOCTRINE

The revisionist doctrine is the result of long and far-reaching investigation. The doctrine of executive management is based on the assumption that all administrative activities of the federal government, except quasi-judicial activities, ought to be centralized under the President. The doctrine of the judicial formula is based on the assumption that a strict judicial control is needed in order to prevent "administrative absolutism" and to protect the individual. The revisionist doctrine is based on no assumption. It employs the inductive method, seeking only to know the facts and to base any suggestions for change upon facts rather than predilections. If the facts, when collected and examined, show inconsistencies, bottlenecks, other impediments to efficient administration, or arbitrary and unfair procedures which fail to protect the interests and rights of the individual, the revisionist method will seek to have such faults corrected. If organic relationships appear as the root of unsatisfactory functioning, changes in such relationships will be suggested.

I. METHOD OF APPROACH

In most of the numerous revisionist studies already available or now being made, the following methods of approach have been used:

1. An investigation of the historical development of federal activities in the promotion and control of business enterprise.

2. An examination of the economic fields controlled by the federal government.

3. An examination of the constitutional system in so far as this affects powers and their distribution, relationships of government authorities, due process of law, rights of individuals, and judicial control.

4. An examination of the statutory law governing all important aspects of public administration.

5. An examination of the rules and regulations of administrative authorities, particularly their rules of procedure.

6. An examination of the practical operation and effects of administrative activities in economic fields.

7. An examination of administrative determinations, decisions, orders, and other acts.

8. An examination of judicial decisions, particularly in respect to questions of delegation of powers, relationships of authorities to one another, and the criteria of due process of law as applied to administrative acts.

II. APPLICATION OF METHODS

The methods named above have been applied to the specific field of this study, by means of preliminary general investigations followed by the endeavor to answer all detailed questions which have presented themselves as relevant or necessary. Although the organizational unit has not been found applicable as a final category, each organizational unit has received particular attention and study. As an example of the manner in which this work has been done, the authors will explain briefly their investigation of the Federal Trade Commission. From the historical to the juridical, each of the methods listed above was applied to this agency. Specific questions that were asked include, among many others: its organization and structure; its relationships to other agencies or branches of government; the economic, political, social, and historical background leading to its creation; its functions; its procedures; the extent and nature of its day-by-day work; the methods by which its acts are enforced; the types of appeals or remedies available against its acts.

The foregoing and various other questions have been considered, as they might be appropriate, in connection with every agency studied. In so far as possible, working sheets have been prepared in which the same questions have been answered in respect to all agencies studied. By reading a given column in one of these working sheets, it has been possible in many cases to present a composite picture, or to make a statement of general application. Sometimes a group of statements must be made; sometimes one general statement can be formulated, subject to specified exceptions. These statements summarize the facts found.

The facts as found have been classified and analyzed in various ways, with a view to throwing light upon the central question of broad function or basic objective. Thus, administrative acts have been classified as: rules and regulations; orders; decisions; executive and administrative proclamations; awards and requirements; stipulations; and consent decrees. Under these larger classes, sub-classes have been developed. These sub-classes have been of particular value in connection with orders, which have revealed themselves as serving several different purposes and consequently as requiring different procedures and different controls. Both the sub-classes and the larger classes, when viewed functionally, have shown specialized characteristics which demand consideration before any action is taken or recommended in the general field studied.

Many supporting statements have been prepared, some of which are reproduced in an appendix to the present study. A large number of charts and diagrams have been made, in order to give a visual picture or to present a large field of subject matter in outline form. Some of these have been reproduced elsewhere.[1] Finally, all available material prepared by other persons interested in the same general field has been examined carefully.

On the basis of these studies, and on no other basis, the authors have felt themselves able to recommend or to oppose certain courses of action which are now attracting general attention. It is these studies, rather than any preconceived ideas as to the needs of public administration, which have placed the authors in the ranks of those who seek to revise the present system rather than to destroy it, maim it, impede its operations, or supplant it.

---

[1] See F. F. Blachly, *Working Papers on Administrative Adjudication*, printed for the use of the Senate Committee on the Judiciary, 75 Cong. 3 sess.; *United States Court of Appeals for Administration*, Hearings before a Subcommittee of the Senate Committee on the Judiciary on S. 3676, 75 Cong. 3 sess., especially charts following pp. 16 and 60; analysis of H.R. 6324 by F. F. Blachly, with eight supporting statements, in *Administrative Law*, Hearings before Subcommittee No. 4 of the House Committee on the Judiciary on H.R. 4236, H.R. 6198 and H.R. 6324, 76 Cong. 1 sess., p. 156 ff.; F. F. Blachly, "Work Materials on Administrative Action and Procedure" (manuscript).

III. SUMMARY OF FINDINGS

Historical studies of the activities of the federal government show that since 1887, when the Interstate Commerce Commission was established, there has been a remarkable development in the scope of governmental intervention.[2] The last few years, as everyone knows, have seen a rapid expansion not only of the regulatory functions of government, but also of functions having to do with social welfare, unemployment, old age security, and the like. As a matter of historical record, we have passed, during a period of hardly more than fifty years, from a system of little federal intervention to one in which many of the most important economic relationships are largely subject to federal control. The rapidity of this development, coupled with the fact that it has taken place bit by bit, and not as the result of a concerted drive by a single party, group, or class with an all-embracing program, is highly significant. The necessity of providing appropriate administrative machinery has been an immediate and pressing problem.

An examination of the economic fields controlled by the federal government reveals the fact that nearly every kind of economic activity[3] is affected in some degree by government intervention. It shows also that in connection with such activities the federal government stands in many different legal relationships to the individual.[4] Sometimes it regulates and controls, as in respect to banking; securities; holding companies; security exchanges; transportation; shipping; aeronautics; communications; monopolies; restraint of trade; unfair methods of competition; advertising; labor relationships; labor standards; prison labor; agricultural production; commodity exchanges; packers and stockyards; poultry; perishable agricultural products; fishing; ores; bituminous coal; explosives; alcohol; foods, drugs, and cosmetics; viruses, serums; and various other matters.

[2] See for brief summary: *Investigation of Executive Agencies of the Government*, Preliminary Report of the Select Committee to Investigate the Executive Agencies of the Government, S. Rept. 1275, 75 Cong. 1 sess., Chaps. XII and XIII; see also Service Monographs of the Institute for Government Research of the Brookings Institution, for developments in various fields. The authors have had the benefit of reading some preliminary reports written by Dr. Robert E. Cushman, who is completing a study on the history of the regulatory commissions.

[3] See Supporting Statement IV, pp. 276-86.

[4] See *Investigation of Executive Agencies*, cited above.

In many instances the federal government acts for the promotion and encouragement of industry and commerce. For such purposes it grants patents, copyrights, and the exclusive use of trademarks; employs various measures of protection against foreign competition; assists in solving problems connected with industrial production and technology; and offers many other encouragements to trade and commerce, such as information as to market conditions, measures of financial stabilization, and protection against abnormal price fluctuations. Its several loan activities do much toward the distribution of capital and purchasing power.

At times the government is dealing with individuals in respect to its own property or domain or dominion, as in the case when it takes action in respect to public lands, public streams, forests, "air waves" or bands of frequencies, and so on. This is the case, also, when it takes action regarding such enterprises as the Panama Canal, the Alaska Railroad, and the Tennessee Valley Authority.

Through its civil pension, employee compensation, and retirement systems, the federal government is providing for the welfare and old age of its civil employees. By its veterans' benefits, such as pensions, allowances, insurance, domiciliary, medical, and hospital care, it is providing for its soldiers and sailors.

Within the past few years the government has been encouraging and helping the provision of old age benefits, old age assistance, aid to the needy blind, and aid to dependent children. It has also been active in various forms of relief, such as unemployment relief, work relief, and farm and rural relief.

Because of the different legal relationships involved in carrying on these various activities, it is impossible to prescribe without careful preliminary examination a simple and uniform pattern for all types of authorities, relationships of authorities to one another, procedures, forms of control, and enforcement methods. The stupendous number and vast extent of these activities will not permit such treatment. Careful study and analysis show that not only is *a priori* prescription impossible, but that it is equally impossible to reduce the factual material to any kind of system by using such criteria as definite field of enterprise, specific purpose, or government agency concerned. The only categories which apply to all the facts alike, which give them meaning and significance from the administrative and juridical viewpoints, and into which they all fit easily, are: broad general function, legal nature and effect, and form of administrative action. As these categories have been discussed as fully as space permitted in Part I of this study, they will not be handled here.

Examination of the constitutional system reveals many important facts, of which the most significant for our present purpose is that all acts of the administration are subject to the limits set by the Constitution of the United States. These limits include: a separation of powers which prevents, for example, an extremely broad delegation of legislative power to a co-ordinate branch of government, but which is applied less rigidly when the recipient of the delegation is an arm or agency of the legislature; a definite statement of the powers bestowed upon the United States with reservation of all other powers to the states or to the people; a requirement of "due process of law" procedure when administrative action may invade personal or property rights guaranteed by the Constitution, but the possibility of flexible and informal procedure when such rights are not affected; and the basis of a "case or controversy" if a matter arising out of administrative action is to be appealed to a constitutional court. The fields of economic action which may be entered by Congress are limited by the powers bestowed upon it through the Constitution. The power to regulate commerce among the several states has been chiefly used as a basis for economic regulation; but other powers, especially the taxing power, the power to establish post offices and post roads, and the power to issue patents and copyrights, have also been employed in this connection.

Statutes, under the Constitution, are the immediate basis of government intervention in business and industry. It is by statute that a declaration of legislative policy is made and a type of activity is authorized. Statutes likewise establish an agency to perform each activity, bestow the power to perform it upon some existing agency, or authorize the President, department head, or some other high officer to make the organizational changes necessary in order that the activity in question shall be carried out. If a new agency is set up, its organization, relationships, powers, forms of action, and procedures are more or less fully prescribed. Provisions for enforcement and control of administrative action are generally contained in the statute by which an agency is established or by which its special powers are bestowed.[5] If administrative action gives rise to cases and controversies concerning rights, the constitutional courts will take jurisdiction; otherwise control can be given to administrative agencies or tribunals or to legislative courts.[6]

There is less uniformity in statutory law than might be anticipated. It is true that the whole body of law dealing with public administration reveals a system, but it is a system to which not all agencies and acts belong. Each statute must be examined for differences from, as well as likenesses to, the more common provisions. It often happens that the same statute provides for several different types of action, hearings, enforcement methods, and controls.[7]

Rules and regulations both implement the law as to substantive detail, and provide for such matters of procedure as are not covered by statute. Statutory authorization is practically always given for the issuance of substantive rules and regulations, and is often given for the issuance of "rules and regulations under this Act." No rule or regulation may be broader in scope than the limits of the power which has been delegated and which can constitutionally be delegated. Rules and regulations are of the nature of legislation.

The operation and effects of administrative activities cannot be described briefly in the form of a series of fact-findings; but certain facts regarding them can be given. A very large percentage of administrative activities give rise to no disputes touching rights. A very large percentage of the disputes which do arise are settled

[5] Blachly, *Working Papers on Administrative Adjudication.*

[6] *Murray* v. *Hoboken Land & Improvement Co.*, 18 How. 272; *Chicago & N.W. R. Co.* v. *Whitton*, 13 Wall. 270; *Federal Radio Commission* v. *Nelson Bros. Bond & Mortgage Co.*, 289 U.S. 266; *Oceanic Steam Nav. Co.* v. *Stranahan*, 214 U.S. 320; *Federal Radio Commission* v. *General Electric Co.*, 281 U.S. 464; *Luckenbach S.S. Co.* v. *United States*, 272 U.S. 533.

[7] See for example the Agricultural Marketing Agreement Act of 1937, which provides for eight different types of hearings, Sec. 1(a) to 1(h) (i); or the Securities Act of 1933, the Securities Exchange Act of 1934, and the Public Utility Holding Company Act of 1935, each of which deals with several different situations handled in different ways.

in a way satisfactory to all concerned by means of correspondence, investigations, inquiries, interviews, informal hearings, etc. Dr. Sharfman gives the following figures regarding the informal and formal cases handled by the Interstate Commerce Commission during a five-year period:[8]

Year	Informal Complaints	Formal Complaints
1929	7,339	1,520
1930	6,651	1,412
1931	6,352	1,021
1932	4,159	971
1933	3,164	741

In the *Third Annual Report of the National Labor Relations Board* for the fiscal year ending June 30, 1938 it is stated[9] that of all representation cases on docket during that year, 57.8 per cent were closed before formal action and 13.6 per cent were closed after formal action. In the *Annual Report of the Federal Trade Commission* for the same fiscal year, it appears that out of a total of 12,943 cases on docket, only 1,442 were closed by a contested cease and desist order[10]; the others were ended by consent, stipulation, etc., or dismissed for lack of merit or some other reason.

These few examples do not touch the far more numerous administrative acts which never give rise to docketed disputes. They do, however, indicate a fact which appears ever more distinctly as the investigator learns more about the work of administration: that even when complaints are made, the vast majority of them can be, and are, settled without recourse to formal procedure.

The end or culmination of the administrative process, stated in the most general terms, is the enforcement of law. In more specific terms, it is a definite act, such as a decision or an order. Although the nature of the final act, especially when it may touch guaranteed rights, is generally expressed in statutes, underlying the statutes is a necessity of adapting method to objective which in reality determines what that final act shall be. If the objective is control by means of licenses, the most common and most essential final act will be the administrative decision as to whether a

[8] I. L. Sharfman, *The Interstate Commerce Commission*, Pt. III, Vol. A, p. 9.
[9] P. 40.
[10] Pp. 95 and 97. These figures include "rescinded cases."

person is or is not qualified to receive a license. If the objective is control over an economic field, the final act will be a regulatory or judicial order adapted to the special circumstances. Part I of this study has examined in considerable detail the forms of action generally used in administration and has found that each form has a distinctive relation to purpose.

Judicial decisions throw much light upon the administrative process, especially the constitutional and statutory limitations and bases, the relationships among authorities and branches of government, the adequacy of administrative procedures, and the extent of judicial control. The constitutional courts will not determine abstract questions, questions of a hypothetical nature, or matters which come up in such a form that they are not "cases or controversies." They will not decide administrative questions, or substitute their own judgment for that of administrative officers who have acted within the limits of their powers. The courts will, however, prevent *ultra vires* actions, abuses and misuses of power, and invasions of guaranteed rights.

IV. MATERIALS NOW AVAILABLE FOR STUDY OF PROBLEMS

Within the past few years a great amount of material has been made available on many phases of public administration. This material has been handled from the viewpoints of history, economics, administrative legislation and adjudication, forms of administrative action, procedure, and controls over administrative action.[11]

V. CRITICISMS AND SUGGESTIONS

This long methodological process has finally reached the point at which some critical evaluations will be possible if they are possible at all. Before evaluations are undertaken, a brief recapitulation will be made of the outstanding features of our present system of administration.

A. Summary of the Present System

The theoretical basis of the federal administrative system is a doctrine of rights, powers, and relationships as between the government and the individual. Some of the rights guaranteed to citi-

---

[11] For materials available see Supporting Statement I, pp. 271-73.

zens existed under the common law; these and others were incorporated into the Constitution of the United States; still others, such as the right to sue the government in contract, have been created by statute. All the specific powers of the federal government were bestowed upon it by the Constitution; jurists disagree as to the metaphysical entity called "sovereignty," but this study need not consider that particular controversy. The relationships have been established by the Constitution, by statutes, by administrative rules and regulations, and by judicial interpretation.

It is necessary to remember always that the Constitution does not create or guarantee individual rights against every act of government. Thus, the individual has no rights, unless Congress chooses to create them, against acts which exercise the war power, the right of control over navigable rivers, dominion over public lands, and many other powers of the federal government. If Congress decides to create rights in respect to such matters, these are not common law or constitutional rights but statutory rights, and any remedies which accompany them lie within the discretion of Congress.

On the other hand, the Constitution guarantees many individual rights which may not be invaded by any agent or agency of government. The constitutional right to freedom of speech, press, and assembly has long been considered the cornerstone of our free government, and is protected by the constitutional courts. From the standpoint of administration, the right most likely to be invaded and to require protection by administrative or judicial action is security in life, liberty, and property as guaranteed by the Fifth Amendment; that is, protection against deprivation except by due process of law.

Guaranteed rights are protected by the courts in many ways. The courts have held that even Congress must remain within its field of competence as defined by the Constitution and as interpreted judicially; that it may pass no law summarily depriving the individual of life, liberty, or property, without a hearing that satisfies judicial requirements under the circumstances; that it may not delegate legislative power in a broad and general way, but only under careful limitations as to policy and extent; that any powers exercised by other agents or agencies of government, but derived from acts of Congress rather than immediately from the Constitution, shall be appropriately defined and safeguarded in order that rights may be protected. The question has been raised many times whether the courts or Congress should be considered the guardian and interpreter of the Constitution; but for our present purpose it is sufficient to say that these functions are held by the courts as their peculiar province.

In so far as sublegislative action is concerned, due process of law is held to demand a definite statutory basis, including norms, standards, or policies laid down by the legislature. Due process of law does not always require a particular method of procedure or of control in respect to sublegislative action; but such action must always remain within the terms of delegation. There must be "due process of law" procedure where rights may be immediately affected.

In order that rights may be protected as against general administrative activities, such activities must have an adequate legislative basis, must fall within the jurisdiction of the authority acting, and must not be abusive, arbitrary, or capricious. Moreover, where personal or property rights are concerned, notice and hearing are generally prerequisite to action.

Judicial and quasi-judicial action are carried on under the limitations which the Constitution lays down. Constitutional courts can handle only "cases and controversies," and the Supreme Court can be given no other jurisdiction save that which is bestowed upon it by the Constitution. Legislative courts, on the contrary, may be vested with broader jurisdiction and may even review administrative acts involving no real case or controversy, should Congress so require. Administrative agencies, when performing acts judicial in nature, must safeguard the rights of the individual by means of a procedure that conforms in all essentials to the requirements of "due process," although many formalities employed in courts of law may be omitted. Due notice; an opportunity to be heard, to present evidence, and to know the opposing evidence and arguments; and an impartial appraisal and decision, are required as necessary.

Under these general principles the various administrative agents and agencies carry on their work. But these principles do not operate automatically or abstractly. Administrative acts are of many kinds, and various types of action affect rights in various ways. In order that rights may be protected, different procedures and processes of law must be employed for different forms and types of action. Some actions concern military operations, foreign relations, or activities of a police nature. Others may happen to be of a tortious nature. Some may involve contracts. Others may involve the taxing power. Many involve proprietary relationships. By means of others the government is seeking to promote the general welfare. An important class is concerned with the regulation of business and industry. Within the past few years the government has been acting more and more often to bring about conciliation, mediation, or arbitration. It is even possible to assert (although the authors do not here make this assertion) that in some instances, as in respect to Postal Savings, and perhaps in respect to the Railroad Retirement Act or even some phases of the Social Security Acts, the government is acting as a trustee. In many instances the government is granting gifts, favors, gratuities, or bounties.

All this variety of function has led to a variety of treatment. In general, it is Congress that sets up administrative organizations, determines their relationships and inter-relationships, establishes their procedures, and provides methods of enforcing and controlling their actions, based upon the relationship of the administration to the individual and his rights. Some of these powers may be delegated to the head of a department or to the Chief Executive.

Such, in brief, is the general federal system of administration.

Unless certain amendments were made to the Constitution, the basis of this system—guaranteed and enforced rights, separated powers, and so on—could not be changed. There appears to be very little demand for change of so drastic a nature. It is also safe to say that as a rule the application of the general principles of federal administration to concrete situations works out satisfactorily, although many improvements are possible. Most of the fields of regulatory activity, in particular, are so organized and controlled that there is little need to fear invasion by the administration of rights guaranteed to individuals. A few types of action, however, are not properly or sufficiently controlled. Examples that may be named are: certain types of revenue and contractual action, and tortious action. The present study cannot deal with these.

B. Revisionist Criticisms and Recommendations

Those who hold the revisionist attitude agree quite generally, on the basis of the studies made by them, that certain features of the present system of public administration should be improved in specific ways. The most important of these features may be best discussed under the headings: forms of administrative action; administrative procedures; enforcement of administrative acts; and control over administrative action.

1. Forms of administrative action

It has been shown in Part I of this study that administrative action takes place by means of certain specialized forms. The principal forms, each of which was discussed and explained, are rules and regulations, orders, and decisions. Some attention was given to proclamations, requirements, stipulations, and consent decrees, which will not be discussed here because there is very little controversy or difference of opinion in respect to them.

These various forms of action have been established in rather piecemeal fashion. Although they have become differentiated in nature and use, further development, definition, and clarification are necessary. It should be recognized by statute, by administrative practice, and by judicial decisions that each form of action has or should have its own realm of applicability, procedural requirements, legal nature and effects, and methods of enforcement; also that methods of control should depend upon and vary with the applicability and legal effects of every separate form. In particular, statutes should not list "rules, regulations, decisions, orders, or other acts," as if these formed a single category. It is only fair to remark that at present such lists are generally accompanied by special provisions regarding the procedures and controls applicable to certain forms of action. Revisionists suggest that the differentiation which has already taken place shall be continued and emphasized.

The expression "rules and regulations" should be reserved for general sublegislative norms made under statutory authorization. It is advisable to make a clear distinction in nomenclature between substantive and adjective norms, the latter being called rules of procedure. This distinction is already made by statute in a number of cases, and is commonly used in administration.

The making of rules and regulations should not be subjected by statute to a hard and fast procedure. It is recognized as sound administrative practice to make rather wide investigations, have consultations, and at times even hold hearings, when rules and regulations of an important, difficult, or technical nature are to be made. Such types of assistance in the sublegislative process, however, should be discretionary with the administrative authorities themselves. As a general rule there should be no mandatory requirement of formal notice and hearing, since such a requirement would often prevent the speedy action necessary and would always tend to interfere with the exercise of administrative discretion, without necessarily informing or aiding it.

There should be no possibility of judicial review over rules and regulations prior to any attempt to enforce them. Even a declaratory judgment by a "bifurcated" court, such as the Court of Appeals for the District of Columbia, should not be possible, since any such appeal destroys the responsibility of the administrator and puts the courts into administration. Whether judicial or administrative, any court action involving a rule not yet in operation is obviously far less likely than administrative action to reflect the needs of the situation. This does not imply or necessitate a disregard for individual rights. When a person finds his rights directly injured or immediately endangered by an administrative act taken or about to be taken under a rule or regulation, and not before such a situation arises, he should be able to invoke first administrative and then judicial remedies. The remedies, of course, include the injunction to prevent the administrative agency from enforcing or applying the rule or regulation alleged to be illegal.

The word "decision," as has been shown, is used by statutes, administrative authorities, and courts in a variety of ways, but chiefly in respect to administrative actions of a discretionary nature, or actions in respect to which for one reason or another there is little formal procedure or judicial control. Such actions are in essence decisions to act in a given way, to grant or refuse a request, to take no action, etc. It is suggested that the name, "decision" be limited to actions of this type. If the administrative agency seeks to compel action or refuses to let action be taken it should use the order, with its accompanying procedures and controls.

If only acts of discretion, sovereign acts which are not controllable by the courts, and other acts of the nature indicated are called decisions, the language of statutes and codes should be made to correspond to this classification. As a general rule, there should be no statutory procedure for the making of decisions or judicial procedure for the control of decisions. The present controls over abuses of power and *ultra vires* action will remain in full effect because they have root in the Constitution.

The order, as was explained in Chapter IV of this study, has become the most important form of action employed to regulate economic situations where the government compels or forbids certain action on the part of the individual, which may affect his guaranteed or vested rights. Several subdivisions of the order have been developed. Some so-called orders are merely procedural or interlocutory in nature. Both law and administrative practice should bestow upon these forms of action a nomenclature (for example, procedural order, interlocutory order) which describes their functions. The courts have generally refused to review orders of this type, but the statutes are sometimes vague in their language. It should always be kept in mind when a law is passed or a code revised and adopted, that procedural and interlocutory orders and all non-final orders, because they do not affect rights, should not be subjected to any special procedure as regards their issuance, or to judicial review. The courts themselves may be trusted to make any requisite exceptions to this rule, as when it is claimed that an order to produce certain documentary evidence invades guaranteed rights, and a judicial determination of the question thus raised appears necessary.

Legislative regulatory orders, from the viewpoint of procedure and control, fall into three main classes: (1) orders which resemble a rule or regulation in that they are general in nature and implement or supplement the law directly, such as orders establishing classes; (2) orders which, although legislative in nature, directly affect the rights of individuals, such as orders establishing a specific rate, wage, quota, or allotment; (3) orders which, though they do not immediately affect rights, may serve as a basis for future action which does affect rights, such as orders establishing the valuation of railways, or prescribing accounting systems.

Judicial review over orders of the first and third classes, which do not affect rights without further action, should be confined to such questions as whether the authority which made the order remained within its delegation of power and whether it abused its power. In respect to orders of the second class, the case is entirely different. The type of order which, though legislative, does immediately affect rights, should be placed under certain safeguards in respect to the weight of evidence, etc. In general, this is now the case. Control is usually given to the courts, though sometimes an option is given of appeal to the courts or to a higher administrative tribunal.

Orders which are judicial in nature, such as reparation, cease and desist, and penalty orders, should be issued only after notice and hearing. The hearing should result in a finding of fact on which the order is based. There should generally be judicial review.

It is advisable that the wording of statutes should recognize the distinctions, now well established by jurisprudence, between judicial orders, orders which, though legislative, immediately affect rights, and orders of a procedural or general legislative type. At present the statutes are often very general in their language, which may purport to enable "any person aggrieved by an order" to appeal to the courts. Since the courts have defined "aggrieved" and limited "order" in such a way as to preclude review of orders which do not affect rights, it would be fairly simple to bring the form of the law into harmony with jurisprudence and with the facts of administrative practice.

Special uses of both the decision and the order are found in respect to licenses and permits. It is a general rule that to grant or to withhold such an instrument *de novo* lies within the discretion of the administrator, which will not be controlled by the courts unless he has used his power in an arbitrary, capricious, or abusive way. Since no rights are vested, no rights can be enforced. The case is somewhat different when a person has received a license, grant, or permit, and has invested in a radio station, airplane, etc. Although the courts usually hesitate to speak of vested rights even under such circumstances, Congress has been so anxious to protect investors from loss that it frequently gives the right to a "due process" notice and hearing, with review by the courts, if the administrator proposes to suspend, revoke, or deny renewal of a license or permit. Whenever provision is made for a penalty, other than suspension, revocation, or failure to renew, if the terms of a license or permit are violated, the decision procedure is inadequate. In such case there should be notice, hearing, fact-finding, order, and judicial control.

A question of growing importance is to what extent the expressed policy of Congress should create rights in fields traditionally controlled by the discretionary decision. If grants or other privileges are to be made to persons who fall within certain classes or who fulfill certain conditions, does the person who can prove that he falls within the class or meets the conditions have a right to the grant or privilege? According to traditional jurisprudence, the reply must be negative. According to the revisionist school of thought, much study is needed before any decision is reached as to the advisability of giving positive rights under circumstances of this kind.

2. *Administrative procedures*

Earlier in the present study it was pointed out that even a cursory examination of the economic situations controlled by administrative action indicates that no one type of procedure is applicable to all. The government may be making grants of its own lands, or giving privileges in respect to its lands, its property, or its dominion. It may be granting a favor, a privilege, or a benefaction, with or without attaching conditions to the grant. It may be managing its own employees. It may be acting under its limited police power.

It may be allowing or forbidding the importation of certain articles. It may require that reparation be made; it may impose, remit, or lessen fines, penalties, or forfeitures. It may issue orders of a general nature for the regulation of business and industry.

Each of these types of action, and many others, may involve a different relationship of the state to the individual. The procedure employed in each instance, according to the revisionist view, should be adapted to the specific relationship, as expressed in the performance of a general function. It should also meet any constitutional or statutory requirements.

If "due process of law" as defined by the courts is required under the Constitution or by statute in order to protect guaranteed rights, there should be a rather formal hearing procedure and an order supported by the facts found; although the rules of evidence need not be so strict as those of a court. The nature of the trial examiner's functions, and the attitude to be taken by this officer, should be clarified by rules of procedure. Whenever a trial examiner is acting, he should probably take a position of judicial impartiality, seeking only to learn the facts. In connection with some functions, although neither the Constitution nor the statutes may require a "due process" type of hearing, this type is nevertheless advisable for the purpose of making a complete record for future reference. The functions as to which such a procedure is advisable when guaranteed rights are not involved will naturally vary somewhat from time to time as conditions change.

Function, in the broad sense, subject matter, type of action, constitutional and statutory requirements, and expediency, are not the only points which should be considered in respect to administrative procedure. In connection with each separate activity certain other questions should be raised, such as the following: How many complaints are made? How many of these are now pressed through all available procedures? Does the government appear as an adverse party? What extent of interest or amount of money is or may be involved? May administrative action impose a money penalty or any disciplinary or penal measure? Is there a continuous inspection service by means of which the administrative authorities are kept currently informed? Is speed in making the decision or settling the case an important element? Even when in strict legal doctrine no constitutional rights are involved, as may be the case in respect to old age and survivors' insurance under the Social Security Act, is there a general understanding that each individual who pays into the treasury money which goes into the trust fund actually possesses certain rights in respect to the fund? Do the various activities performed by the same agency require a variety of procedures?

A few examples taken more or less at random will illustrate the importance of some of these questions from the procedural viewpoint. The Bureau of Marine Inspection and Navigation inspects vessels; grants licenses and certificates to officers and seamen, usually on the basis of written examinations; investigates marine casualties; tries officers and seamen to determine whether or not licenses or certificates should be revoked or suspended; imposes or remits or mitigates fines, penalties, and forfeitures for violations of navigation laws; and administers the "load line" laws. It is evident that the same procedure could not reasonably be applied to all the activities mentioned. Peculiar features of the decisions and orders of the Bureau of Marine Inspection and Navigation are that the cases are under admiralty and that the matter of time is often of great significance. A seaman may be charged with an offense or with gross negligence which, if proved, would make it inadvisable that he be allowed to retain his position; but unless the case can be tried while the vessel is in port, he may be allowed to remain in the crew or, if a captain, to command the ship on another voyage. Time here is the essential element.

The Secretary of Agriculture administers some forty or more laws having to do with the various phases of business and industry.[12] The methods employed for this work include licensing; requiring reparations; the making of marketing agreements; the establishment of marketing quotas; the establishment of sugar quotas; the quarantining of diseased livestock and poultry; the fixing of standards; the prohibition of certain imports; the marking and grading of meat and meat-food products; the requirement of labels for

[12] See *Administrative Law*, Hearings before Subcommittee No. 4 of the House Committee on the Judiciary on H.R. 4236, H.R. 6198 and H.R. 6324, 76 Cong. 1 sess., pp. 96 ff., for a summary of these.

certain products; the seizure of impure foods and drugs; the imposition of penalties; and so on. It is an evident impossibility to prescribe a single procedure suited to all these varied activities.

The Railroad Retirement Board acts much as a trustee might in administering the Railroad Unemployment Insurance Act of 1938. When deciding who are entitled to benefits under this act, the Board is not an adversary party. Obviously its procedure does not have to be the same under such circumstances, as if it were opposing every claim made, or seeking to prove guilt or to secure the imposition of a penalty.

One more example must suffice. The regulation and control of banking by the Comptroller of the Currency, the Board of Governors of the Federal Reserve System, and the Federal Deposit Insurance Corporation takes place largely by means of examinations and administrative decisions. It may perhaps be argued that this particular type of regulation, without the formal procedures used in making most other regulations where rights are affected, is a special instance due to the agreement made by the bank as a condition precedent to becoming a member of the Federal Reserve System. But even without such an agreement, would any bank, so long as it hopes to continue in operation, desire a public hearing as to whether it is insolvent or whether its president has abused his trust?

The foregoing examples demonstrate the impossibility of establishing a single type of procedure which will apply to all activities and all forms of action. Examination shows, however, that certain procedural principles can be established.

If the activity is such that it requires the issuance of rules and regulations, no special procedure should be (or is usually) required by law. The administrator, exercising his discretion, must decide whether hearings shall be held as a means of obtaining information. Any hearings which take place should be recognized as legislative rather than judicial in nature. Evidence from any sources and in any form should be welcomed, so long as it is relevent and informative. There should be no attempt to follow judicial rules of evidence. No formal fact-finding should be required. The rule or regulation as finally issued should be based upon the statutory authorization to make the same, and not necessarily upon the results of any hearings. These principles hold for both adjective and substantive rules and regulations.

The general regulatory legislative order, which has a wide and non-specific field of application, should not be the result of judicial procedure. Because its scope is usually narrower than that of the rule or regulation, and because it often concerns great economic interests, it is nearly always advisable, however, that hearings be held before an order of this sort is issued. The law should not require hearings, but should leave the administrator free to issue a legislative order at his discretion. The administrator must be able to act rapidly, if necessary, so long as he does not deprive persons of rights without due process of law.

In practice, hearings are held when important legislative orders are under consideration. The rules of judicial procedure and of judicial evidence should not be applied to such hearings. The facts sought are generally economic in nature, and can be obtained from many sources and by means of many methods. Statistics and reports prepared by those who may be affected, and by agents of the regulatory authority, should be offered as sources of information; but there should be no appearance of adversary procedure, nor should the interests which are to be regulated on the one hand, and the regulatory authority on the other, appear as adversary parties.

Although it is not a principle of procedure, there may be no irrelevance in stating here the principle that a friendly attitude on the part of the administrative authority often saves trouble in the long run. In strict law, the administrator may act within his delegation of power as he sees fit; but in common sense he should seek to be thoroughly informed and to make it clear to the interests which are being regulated why he issues each order.

The specific regulatory order addressed to a given individual or corporation is a different matter. The courts recognize the legislative nature of a rate order, for example; but they hold that, since it may operate to take property without due process of law, it must be safeguarded to prevent this effect. Therefore it should be issued only after notice, hearing, and fact-finding. The facts must be supported by the evidence, and the order must be based upon the facts.

The rules of evidence need not be so strict as in a court; and the regulatory authority is not necessarily an adversary party. The record must show, nevertheless, that the procedure was just and fair and that it afforded to the person to whom the order was addressed an opportunity to present both evidence and pleading. Revisionists agree with the courts upon these points, but would allow the administrator more informality and freedom than the courts are inclined to permit in the introduction of published statistics and similar material as evidence.

When the action to be taken is an enforcement order, a reparation order, or an order imposing a penalty, the procedure should approximate the judicial. This is due partly to the fact that orders of this kind are judicial in nature and have an immediate effect upon rights; and partly to the partisan nature of the dispute, in which either a person who claims injury or the regulatory authority appears as complainant and the person or corporation regulated appears as defendant. The fact that the "same agency prosecutes and judges," has resulted in much unfavorable criticism; but the history of the regulatory agencies, in general, indicates that when they sit to hear cases they display no more bias in favor of their own attorneys than a court displays in favor of the public prosecutor. No change in procedure seems to be needed in this connection. The chief difference between procedure in a formal case which may lead to an order of the type named, and procedure in a court, should be a greater freedom of the administrative tribunal to call for relevant evidence instead of merely hearing such evidence as is tendered.

It is possible to find isolated rulings which appear to display bias on the part of the administrative agency; but these instances are so exceptional that they should not be cited as evidence that the whole system of administrative jurisprudence is wrong in principle. This system is both necessary and effective; hence it should not be destroyed when it fails to function satisfactorily; it should, rather, be improved. If rulings that are unfair to the public are due to the terms of a statute, the obvious remedy is to amend the law. If a board or commission is manifestly prejudiced or incompetent, the President may remove its members for causes provided by law, and may appoint abler persons. Congress can always destroy such an agency if this extreme step seems necessary, and can create another agency, differently organized. Since the administration, in the long run, is under the power of Congress, it tends to act responsibly and fairly rather than otherwise.

The cease and desist order is likewise judicial in nature, but it has certain special characteristics not possessed by the judicial orders just discussed. It has a more direct effect in determining a future course of action. It is issued under circumstances which make impossible a complete separation of judicial activities from regulatory and prosecuting activities. Several methods have been suggested for improving procedure in such a way as to minimize this difficulty. Most revisionists are in favor of: (1) separating as far as possible, within the regulatory organization, the persons who perform the activity of examination and prosecution from those who are charged with making the decision; (2) asking Congress to define more narrowly what are unfair methods of competition in order to decrease the number of instances when sublegislative rules must be made at the same time that a case is being decided; (3) giving the regulatory authority more power to lay down substantive rules and regulations in advance of taking action to determine whether a cease and desist order should be issued. Any or all of these means would make it possible for the procedure to be more nearly judicial in character.

A more radical change, which, though not procedural, may be mentioned at this point, is favored by certain revisionists. This is an attempt to prevent misrepresentations as to kind and quality of goods, by statutory requirements that goods sold shall conform to standards laid down by the Bureau of Standards or by other appropriate government agencies, and by the provision of penalties for violation. Penal statutes might also prohibit false statements as to geographic origin or trade status of goods, or as to alleged endorsements, or favorable results of tests and questionnaires. By both of these methods the regulatory agency would be relieved of part of a heavy burden. If the practices mentioned were made misdemeanors punishable by fine or imprisonment, there would simply be a trial upon the facts and a definite penalty, instead of an order to cease and desist. In other words, police methods of control over certain phases of business might eliminate some of the present difficulties.

It appears particularly desirable to differentiate the cases which come before the Federal Trade Commission. A great many of these, which are little more than police cases involving established principles, might well be settled finally and conclusively (subject to appeal to the courts) by a trial examiner. By such procedure the Commission itself would be left free to handle important cases involving monopolistic practices or new practices not covered by statute. These are but suggestions as to a possible approach and are not intended as definite recommendations, for which much more study would be needed.

The question is sometimes raised whether orders such as reparation orders, which merely involve a suit between two individuals, should be handled by administrative tribunals. In favor of this arrangement it is said that the regulatory authority has much information related to the subject, and that it is expert and expeditious in dealing with the materials and questions involved. On the other hand, it is argued that the government is not a party, that the case is purely judicial in nature, and that suit before the regulatory authority is often a loss of time, since in case the order is not obeyed the person in whose favor it was made must bring suit in the district court to enforce it. Whether or not it would be better to bring such suits directly before the regular district courts is a question that should be decided only after careful investigation of all relevant factors, including the number of complaints docketed, the number settled informally or dismissed, the number handled by formal procedure, the number which end in a reparation order, the number of such orders which are obeyed, and the number of suits brought for enforcement.

General problems of procedure arise in respect to the larger regulatory agencies which handle thousands or tens of thousands of cases each year. Because of the volume of work in such agencies, which cannot all be handled by the higher authorities, it is necessary for some subordinate officer, such as a trial examiner or referee, to hold hearings, pass upon questions of evidence, etc., and often draft the decision or order. In some agencies the activities can be and are subdivided in such a way that the field work and the factual investigation are performed by one set of officers, and the legal work is done by another.

A few of the problems that should be studied in connection with the larger agencies will be stated briefly: What should be the position and the duties of the investigatory agency and its relationship to the solicitor's office? How far should individual investigating agents assist in the preparation of cases? If they assist materially in the preparation of a case, should they also act as expert witnesses? Should the trial examiner ever prosecute a case? Is it possible to keep the prosecuting function separated sufficiently from the judging function? If so, by what means?

Should there be a review division which goes over the findings of trial examiners and their preliminary or intermediate reports? In case such a review division exists, how should it be related to the solicitor's office? In case the review division makes great changes in the report of the trial examiner, what is the examiner's responsibility? Should he be allowed to present his opinion at the final hearing, or should it be superseded by that of the review division? What should be the relationship of the review division to the commission, and the relationship of its action to the commission's action? Should it prepare a proposed final order? In case it does not prepare such an order, is there sufficient reason for a review procedure? In cases it does prepare a proposed order for the commission, should this be submitted to the parties before a hearing is held by the commission, so that they may present evidence and oral arguments or briefs which bear directly upon the proposal? Would it be better for the commission to hold a hearing, issue an order which may or may not be based on the work of the review division, and then if requested hold a rehearing?

No attempt will be made here to answer these and many other questions which have arisen in connection with the procedure to be employed in hearing administrative cases. This much is certain, however: that economic circumstances, forms of action to be taken, and guaranteed rights, must all be kept in mind if satisfactory answers are to be reached. Any endeavors to solve these problems should be postponed until all the evidence is in, particularly: (1) the results obtained by the Attorney General's Committee on Procedure; (2) the work now being done on procedure in many of the departments and government agencies; and (3) an analysis now almost completed by the Brookings Institution of all statutory provisions governing procedure. Any attempt to formulate a program before these works are completed and thoroughly digested is, to say the least, premature.

3. Enforcement of administrative acts

Under our present laws and rules affecting administration there is a wide variety of enforcement methods.[13] They appear unnecessarily numerous and complex, and at first sight it seems that they should be revised. No detailed examination of the enforcement system has been made by the authors of this study, however, except in connection with administrative orders. So complicated is this field alone that it is necessary to turn to each type of order to find out how it is enforced; and even within types there may be several different means of enforcement.[14]

Revisionists are not urging any change as regards non-enforceable orders. It was shown in Part I that a permission or an exemption, and usually a grant or favor, will not require enforcement. Valuation orders, orders establishing classes, and orders refusing to act, are likewise non-enforceable, by their very nature. There is nothing to criticize here.

In several instances administrative enforcement is applicable. This is the case in respect to such actions as the suspension or revocation of licenses. Administrative enforcement takes place, also, when one agency makes an order and another enforces it, as when the Civil Aeronautics Authority fixes rates for transportation of mail by airplane, and the Post Office Department makes payment in accordance with the order establishing the rates. There appears to be no

---

[13] See *United States Court of Appeals for Administration*, Hearings before a Subcommittee of the Senate Committee on the Judiciary on S. 3676, 75 Cong. 3 sess., Exhibit 2, for enforcement of orders; *Administrative Law*, Hearings before Subcommittee No. 4 of the House Committee on the Judiciary on H.R. 4236, H.R. 6198, and H.R. 6324, 76 Cong. 1 sess.

[14] Chap. VI, above.

reason for changing these methods of enforcement, since all rights which may be involved are protected by various methods, such as suit in the Court of Claims.

Judicial enforcement of orders is frequently required by statute. This kind of enforcement may be subdivided into several types: (1) civil suit for enforcement brought by the agency issuing the order; (2) civil suit brought by the person injured because of the failure of the person to whom the order is addressed to obey it; (3) civil action by the government to recover a fine, penalty, or forfeiture provided for by law; (4) injunction suit to have the order enforced; (5) mandatory injunction suit to compel obedience (until the new Rules of Civil Procedure became effective this was a mandamus suit); (6) criminal suit to collect a fine, penalty, or forfeiture, or to punish by imprisonment the one guilty of violating the law or the provisions of an order; (7) finality of the order, with appeal.

It may be that each of these methods has its place under certain circumstances. It is also within the probabilities that a detailed examination would indicate the advisability of a considerable simplification. When a given form of administrative action is used to control several different economic circumstances, the question should at least be raised whether one enforcement procedure would not be sufficient. For example, since seven or eight authorities issue cease and desist orders, investigation might show that all such orders should be enforced by one generally applicable method.

Much time and energy would be saved and many suits would be prevented by a general law providing that whenever a court modifies or sustains an order brought before it for review, its decision shall operate to enforce said order, and to place any person who disobeys the same in contempt of court. Those who seek to revise and strengthen the present system of administration have for some time sought to obtain greater uniformity of controls and enforcement methods, and a more consistent body of administrative jurisprudence, through the establishment of a United States Court of Appeals for Administration, with specified jurisdiction. Such a court would be given power to enforce orders or decisions which it sustains.

4. Control over administrative action

a. Legislative control. It is not necessary for our purpose here to discuss legislative control over administrative action, which has been covered earlier in the present study.

b. Administrative control. Administrative control gives rise to several important problems. The first of these concerns review of the action of lower authorities by higher administrative authorities. Several typical situations exist here. The first is a clear line of hierarchical responsibility and an original action taken without a "due process of law" procedure. Under such circumstances it seems desirable that there should always be a series of administrative appeals up through the hierarchy to the final responsible officer. This is not only sound administration, but is also necessary if there is to be a judicial appeal, since as a general rule administrative remedies must be exhausted before the courts will take jurisdiction. In many agencies it is well to establish an advisory board because of the number of cases involved, the technical nature of the subject, or the desire of individuals affected to have their case reviewed by disinterested persons.[15]

In the second typical situation, certain administrative organizations are placed within government departments or other authorities, but the sublegislative and adjudicatory actions of such organizations are not made subject to control by the heads of the departments or authorities. Such is the situation of the Wage and Hour Division in the Department of Labor, and the Federal Alcohol Administrator in the Treasury Department. There appears to be no reason for subordinating these agencies, which do highly specialized work, to higher administrative control.

Authorities of a third type, though organized as integral parts of government departments, make decisions as the result of an elaborate process judicial in nature. In such cases there is little to be gained by having the decisions appealed to the head of the bureau or the head of the department, although this is sometimes done. For example, appeals from decisions made by the Director of the Bureau of Marine Inspection and Navigation lie to the

---

[15] For examples of such advisory authorities see Blachly, *Working Papers on Administrative Adjudication.*

Secretary of Commerce. It seems inadvisable that a decision made as the result of a detailed fact-finding should be subject to administrative review, unless it is clear that the fact-finding is merely informative and that the decision is discretionary rather than judicial. If judicial decisions are made subject to administrative appeal, there is an ever-present danger that political considerations may dominate the appellate authority and that under the guise of reviewing the case the head of the department may be exercising the pardoning power, or that he may be unduly severe in order to make an example of one person and thus frighten others. It would seem that when a fact-finding and a decision based thereon are judicial in nature, appeal should lie to the district courts, or to some special tribunal established by law.

c. Control by legislative courts. One of the most important current problems connected with administration is that of final review over administrative actions which cannot be reviewed by the constitutional courts. In order to solve this problem a case to case study is necessary; but studies already made furnish the basis for certain conclusions, as follows:

1. In respect to standardization, grading, classification, meat inspection, etc., it appears that since the questions involved are matters of scientific fact, the review boards, committees, or appeal inspectors which exist at present are sufficient. The essential thing under these conditions is that review shall be made by an expert and unbiased authority. In respect to serums, viruses, explosives, and many other matters where the issue is factual, the same thing is true.

2. Actions in connection with the use of the mails have been held by the courts to be matters of administrative discretion, since the use of the mails is a privilege rather than a right. Because of the importance of mail service, a statute should make it a right. Any administrative act to restrict this right for cause should be made reviewable by the district courts or by a United States Court of Appeals for Administration.

3. The highly discretionary nature of administrative actions involving the fining, suspension, or removal of public officers and employees sometimes appears to be in conflict with the ideal of impartial treatment. Perhaps the best solution of this dilemma is the

one now very generally adopted by governmental agencies; that is, the establishment of advisory committees, boards, etc.[16] If the question is one of abuse of power for religious, political, or racial reasons, it should be possible to obtain an easy and inexpensive appeal to an independent superior authority such as the Civil Service Commission, or perhaps to a legislative court.

4. Army and Navy veterans' claims constitute a large class of cases which are settled finally and conclusively by administrative action, except for claims in respect to insurance. A careful system of adjudication has been worked out for the handling of veterans' claims. This system seems quite adequate, although detailed changes may make for greater efficiency.

5. Land cases of various sorts at present are handled almost exclusively by administrative appeal. The system seems to be functioning adequately, but appeal to a legislative court might give more general satisfaction.

6. A problem of great importance at present is that of grants-in-aid to the states. In judicial theory at least, when grants or gifts are made no appeal will lie to the courts, since there is no basis for a case or controversy. However, in many instances (such as highway grants, social security grants, etc.) the statute makes the grant contingent upon fulfillment by the state of certain conditions. If the conditions are met, the grant should be made. If it is denied, the charge may be brought that such denial is used as a political weapon. It seems reasonable that some sort of review should be provided on the question whether the statutory conditions have been fulfilled. Considerable doubt exists, however, whether review by the regular courts is available, except perhaps as to questions of abuse of power. Such questions could be handled by a legislative court.

7. Problems of an even more serious nature arise in connection with old age and survivors' insurance under the Social Security Act. First, as the act sets up the system of so-called insurance, it is difficult to see where any rights are involved upon which a case or controversy may rest;[17] yet an appeal to the district courts is pro-

[16] The same.

[17] The money to meet the social security expenditures is collected as a tax and paid into the treasury. It is then transferred to a special fund. Out of this fund money is disbursed, not in direct proportion to what the individual has paid in, but rather on an actuarial principle. It is hard to find here a contractual basis for

vided by statute. Second, in the administration of this law a very large number of cases will certainly arise, where the money involved in each case is not very large, but where the small sum to which each individual feels himself entitled is of paramount importance to him. A fair, quick, inexpensive procedure is essential. Third, the government is not an adverse party. In reality, though not in law, it is almost in the position of a trustee. It has no interest adverse to that of the claimant and no desire to defeat his claim (aside from questions of fraud). It merely wishes to see that the money is distributed in accordance with the law.

For these reasons an attempt should be made to settle cases with as little expense and as rapidly as possible, without long drawn out legal battles. Evidently a careful series of administrative reviews is necessary. These should so guard the rights of the individual that he will feel satisfied that justice has been done him. Since despite these reviews, he may be better satisfied if he has a chance to bring the matter before a court, it might be well to have his claim adjudicated finally by a legislative court after exhaustion of administrative remedies. It is quite certain that cases cannot be handled by the constitutional courts unless they are regarded as involving either substantive or procedural rights.

d. A higher legislative court. From what has been said as to the different situations in which interests rather than constitutional rights are involved, it appears that thought should be given to the establishment of a legislative court to act in final resort upon many of the controversies arising from such situations. Before any attempt is made to set up a court of this kind, however, detailed studies should be made of the way in which the present administrative controls are functioning in practice. If they are adequate, further judicial review may merely clog and delay administration without accomplishing any definite results. On the other hand, popular demand for a day in court, if such a demand should be found to exist, would indicate the wisdom of establishing a review tribunal. The whole subject deserves careful attention.

---

the payments to individuals. The provision reserving the power to Congress to alter, review, or amend any of the provisions of the act would tend to show that there is no contractual basis. See *White* v. *United States,* 270 U.S. 175; Williams v. *United States,* 23 F. (2d) 792.

e. Judicial review by the constitutional courts. It has been shown earlier in this study that from the standpoint of the jurisdiction of constitutional courts, administrative acts fall into two great general classes: (1) those which cannot give rise to a case or controversy, or those over which the constitutional courts will not take jurisdiction; and (2) those which do give rise to a case or controversy, or those over which the constitutional courts will take jurisdiction.

The fields where they will take jurisdiction are largely regulated or controlled by means of statutory orders, decisions in respect to taxes, and certain other decisions. Nearly one-half of all the decisions which are appealed to the constitutional courts deal with taxation.

Revisionists find the following difficulties or faults in the present system of appealing administrative acts to constitutional courts: (1) appeals are permitted, apparently without plan or consistency, to many different courts. Some lie to the regular district courts, some to three-judge district courts, many lie to the circuit courts of appeals, and some to the United States Court of Appeals for the District of Columbia alone.[18] Acts of similar legal significance and nature are sometimes given to one court and sometimes to another. Earlier acts governing appeal from orders gave jurisdiction to a three-judge district court, whereas nearly all the statutes passed during the last twenty-five years have given appeals dealing with comparable subjects to circuit courts of appeals. In many cases the question has been raised whether the three-judge district court or some other court had jurisdiction. This leads to great confusion.

Again, cases of like nature are tried sometimes *de novo* and sometimes on the transcript of the record. The *de novo* method is the older one. Nearly all recent statutes provide for trial upon the transcript of the record. It is generally agreed[19] that a *de novo*

---

[18] See Supporting Statement XI, pp. 318-32 for appeals from orders. See also *United States Court of Appeals for Administration*, Hearings before a Subcommittee of the Senate Committee on the Judiciary on S. 3676, 75 Cong. 3 sess., charts following pp. 16 and 60, prepared by F. F. Blachly and J. Emmett Sebree, in respect to judicial control over numerous decisions and orders. The list was not intended to include all appealable determinations, but only those which by the terms of the bill were to be given to the proposed United States Court of Appeals for Administration. Several recent acts providing for appeal are not included.

[19] The Special Committee of the American Bar Association says: "Obviously, it should not be intended that a reviewing Circuit Court of Appeals must try the facts *de novo*, weigh the evidence, and conclude whether the court would have

trial is neither necessary nor desirable, except where required by the Constitution, that it causes delay and expense, and that it places the court in the position of substituting its discretion for that of the administrative discretion.

Since nearly one hundred courts hear appeals on administrative determinations, there is no uniformity of decisions. It is practically impossible to obtain uniformity, even on similar questions, when these are presented to so many different courts. Not only the actual decisions, but a bewildering variety of dicta upon practically identical points must operate to encourage needless litigation in the various courts. With reference to court action upon decisions of the Board of Tax Appeals, for example, the following remarks have been made:

> . . . Whatever unity and harmony is found in the Board's decision on related questions is overcome when several coordinate higher courts speak in divers and various expressions on the same subject. . . .
>
> . . . Litigation in the Board is thus fomented and encouraged, settlement of cases before trial is in such cases unlikely, or, if made, is more difficult and the Board's docket and calendar are cluttered with repeated controversies of the same question made more difficult by the task of choosing between conflicting superior views. There are instances where the same opinion of the Board in a single group of cases is appealed to several available courts for the sake of one advantage or another, perhaps in the hope of obtaining at least one favorable decision. Necessarily the question is not settled until all appeals are decided and conflicts resolved by the Supreme Court. During the interim and pending the decision of the Supreme Court new cases accumulate and collection or refunds are retarded.[20]

In many instances the statutes do not provide for the judicial review of administrative actions; hence it is necessary to examine numerous judicial decisions to see whether review will lie. Fairly often the statutes provide for judicial review of orders, without making exceptions of certain classes, such as procedural and interlocutory orders, which the constitutional courts consistently refuse

---

found the facts as the board has found them. Under such a rule judicial discretion is substituted for administrative discretion." *Report and Draft of Bill by the Special Committee on Administrative Law to the Chicago Meeting of the House of Delegates and the Board of Governors,* January 1939, p. 42.

[20] *United States Court of Appeals for Administration,* Hearings . . . , p. 8, statement by Mr. J. Emmett Sebree.

to review. In at least one instance[21] there are three different statements in respect to review over orders of one authority, although there is nothing in the nature of the orders to justify this multiplicity.

The statutes contain a great variety of different procedures for appeals to the courts. These cover such points as: before what court the suit is to be brought; the filing of the petition; the filing of the transcript of the record; pleadings; testimony; proceedings; the legal significance of the transcript; objections; conclusiveness of fact-finding; the introduction of additional evidence; the modification of the fact-finding; the filing of the modified fact-finding; exclusiveness of jurisdiction; the nature of the judgment; and further review. If several appeals based on transcript of the record go before the same court, there may be as many procedures as appeals, each varying only slightly from the others. In some instances one statement governs both enforcement procedure and appeal procedure. In others there are separate statements for the two.

The net result of the multiplicity of appellate tribunals, different types of appeal, different types of procedures before reviewing courts, different court rules, differences in statement, etc., is to cause great confusion, uncertainty, and complexity in the whole system of appeals from administrative acts. Even the best of lawyers may not know before what court to bring particular cases, or what procedures to employ. They must study, as need arises, the rules which govern each type and class of appeals.

No unified jurisprudence concerning administrative law can be built up under the present system, for the Supreme Court cannot possibly handle all administrative cases that should be settled. Under its discretionary right to grant or not grant certiorari, it may refuse to take many cases in which a problem of administration or administrative law is involved.

VI. A COURT OF APPEALS FOR ADMINISTRATION

In order to obviate these difficulties it is suggested that a single constitutional court shall handle justiciable appeals from adminis-

[21] The Securities and Exchange Commission, acting under the Securities Act of 1933, the Securities Exchange Act of 1934, and the Public Utility Holding Company Act of 1935.

trative acts. A bill for this purpose is now before Congress.[22]

By the terms of this bill, there is to be established a United States Court of Appeals for Administration. This is to be a constitutional court, with jurisdiction to review cases and controversies between the government and the individual. In other words, it will be chiefly concerned with control over administrative orders and those administrative decisions which affect rights. In this capacity, it will review most of the justiciable actions of the great regulatory authorities and the decisions of the Board of Tax Appeals. It will not be given jurisdiction over patent and customs cases, because there is no reason to interfere with the jurisdiction of the highly specialized and efficient Court of Customs and Patent Appeals in such matters.

The court is to be composed of a chief justice and ten associate justices, selected for qualifications and fitness. They are to be appointed by the President, by and with the advice and consent of the Senate, and are to receive salaries of $12,500 a year. The court is to be located in the District of Columbia, but is to be ambulatory in nature. Special divisions may be established for the purpose of hearing and deciding appeals.

The jurisdiction conferred upon the court is comprehended in one general statement. It is to cover the final appealable orders of the various authorities named therein. Procedure before the court is to be on the transcript of the record. No objection, assignment of error, or question of law relating to an order or decision shall be considered by the court unless it shall have been urged before the authority or tribunal issuing the decision or order. Either party may ask to introduce additional evidence. The court has discretionary power to permit this, and may order the evidence to be taken before the administrative authority, which as the result of new evidence may make modified or new fact-findings. The review of the court is limited to questions of law. The findings of fact of the administrative authority or tribunal are conclusive if supported by evidence.

[22] For the original bill to establish such a court, see *United States Court of Appeals for Administration*, Hearings . . . ; see also S. 916, 76 Cong. 1 sess., A Bill to establish a United States Court of Appeals for Administration, etc. This bill is found in Supporting Statement XIV, pp. 349-56.

Upon review the court shall have power to affirm, modify, set aside, or reverse the order or decision appealed from, or to remand the case for rehearing. The judgment of the court is final, subject to review by the Supreme Court upon certiorari. Upon the affirmation or modification of an order or decision, the court has power to render a decree enforcing obedience to its mandate.

This bill furnishes a sound basis for control over the large field of administrative action in respect to which cases or controversies may arise. It is possible that further study will indicate the advisability of changing the bill in a few particulars, as by eliminating the power of the court to modify the decision of the administrative authority or by adding the determinations of certain recently created agencies to the statement concerning jurisdiction.

This type of court would eliminate the difficulties which result from the present multiplicity of review authorities. Through such a court review procedure would be systematized and jurisprudence would be unified. The advantages of expert knowledge would be obtained, while every right of the individual would be preserved. The whole work of federal administration would rise in public esteem and gain in public confidence, for the good reason that it could operate more efficiently under a consistent and unified law and jurisprudence than under the present miscellany of statutes and decisions.

VII. CONCLUSIONS

To summarize: The revisionists see in the present system of federal administration a vast complex of organizations performing a multitude of functions, employing a wide variety of methods and procedures, and subjected to numerous types of control. All this activity must be carried on within a constitutional framework which is based on individual rights and which guarantees to the individual adequate protection of those rights. The administrative system has developed step by step to meet everyday needs. Because it has been based upon a common law and constitutional theory of rights and remedies, it has an internal coherence, despite certain inconsistencies and weaknesses. Because it corresponds closely with the structure and relationship of the federal government, this coherence should be preserved. Changes which are made should not be intended to destroy the administrative system, but merely to improve it.

The first step toward improvement is a thorough understanding of the present system. This can be secured only by the most painstaking research, involving the economic structure in its relationship to public law and administration. Such research is being carried on by many persons and organizations. Not all the evidence is in as yet, but enough has been accumulated to show that progress can be made in the following directions:

1. In maintaining the independence of authorities which are carrying out long-time regulatory processes.

2. In further development of the system of administrative legislation and adjudication.

3. In establishing a high constitutional administrative court to hear appeals from administrative action involving a case or controversy.

4. In more exact differentiation of the various forms of administrative action, particularly as regards applicability to specific situations; legal nature and effect; procedural requirements; methods of enforcement; and control over each type of action.

5. In simplifying administrative judicial procedure, and, where possible, in making it more uniform. Particular attention should be given to the trial examiner and his relationship to the regulatory authority.

Such changes as those just named should be made one by one, after considerable study of the detailed problems that will arise in each instance. Great care should be taken to make every alteration fit into the general plan of the constitutional, judicial, and administrative system. Considered and harmonious development based upon scientific research will not only leave the system intact, but will add to its strength and stability, while broadening and developing it to meet the expanding needs of a living democratic society.

SUPPORTING STATEMENTS

SUPPORTING STATEMENT I

MATERIALS AVAILABLE

As a result of research on the problems connected with federal administration during the past few years a rather large and significant literature has already developed or will soon be completed. These studies are beginning to furnish the basis for a real analysis and solution of the many problems raised by various proposals.

From the historical viewpoint the monographs on government services of the Institute for Government Research of the Brookings Institution are of great value. Professor Robert E. Cushman of Cornell is just completing a historical survey of the independent boards and commissions.

From the organizational viewpoint the Brookings study of the reorganization of the federal government, *Investigation of the Executive Agencies of the Government* (Preliminary Report of the Select Committee to Investigate the Executive Agencies of the Government, Senate Rept. 1275, 75 Cong. 1 sess.), contains a vast amount of material on federal organization as well as on the history and functions of various agencies. For the organization and functioning of the regulatory agencies and other administrative tribunals, the *Working Papers on Administrative Adjudication* (printed for the use of the Senate Committee on the Judiciary, 75 Cong. 3 sess.), by F. F. Blachly of the Brookings Institution is of value. This study contains classifications of administrative adjudicatory authorities, and a discussion of their legal basis, organization, functions, procedures, enforcement methods, and appeals from their actions. See also *The Administration of Federal Finances*, 1937, by Daniel T. Selko, and *Personnel Administration in the Federal Government*, 1937, by Lewis Meriam, all published by the Brookings Institution.

Special studies on certain problems of organization from the viewpoint of administrative management were made by the President's Committee on Administrative Management and published in *Report with Special Studies*, 1937.

Studies of particular agencies are also of value, such as I. L.

Sharfman's *The Interstate Commerce Commission*, 1931-1937, published by the Commonwealth Fund, and Gerald C. Henderson's *The Federal Trade Commission*, 1924.

Some of the basic problems in connection with administrative legislation and adjudication are discussed in *Administrative Legislation and Adjudication*, by F. F. Blachly and M. E. Oatman, published by the Brookings Institution in 1934.

Forms of administrative action and procedure are described in several studies recently issued in mimeograph form by the Department of Agriculture. These consist in brilliant studies by Ashley Sellers, the chief attorney in the office of the Solicitor of the Department of Agriculture, as follows: "Administrative Procedure and Practice in the Department of Agriculture under the Agricultural Marketing Act of 1937"; "Administrative Procedure and Practice in the Department of Agriculture under the Packers and Stockyards Act, 1921"; "Administrative Procedure and Practice in the Department of Agriculture under the Commodity Exchange Act"; "Administrative Procedure and Practice in the Department of Agriculture under the Perishable Agricultural Commodities Act, 1936"; "Administrative Procedure and Practice in the Department of Agriculture, 1940."

The Brookings Institution is just completing a detailed study of Administrative Action and Procedure. In this study each statutory provision governing actions which affect the individual is studied in respect to the economic circumstances under which the action takes place, the type of action it is, the legal nature and effect of the action, the processes and procedures connected with the action, how the determinations of the administrative authorities are enforced, and how they are controlled.

The Code of Federal Regulations of the United States of America, published by the Government Printing Office, contains all regulations having general applicability and legal effect, issued by all federal executive and administrative agents and agencies, in force on June 1, 1938.

The Attorney General's Committee on Administrative Procedure has made some noteworthy detailed studies of the procedures in several governmental agencies, including the United States Maritime Commission, the Federal Communications Commission, the

Bureau of Marine Inspection and Navigation in the Department of Commerce, the Federal Trade Commission, the administration of the Grain Standards Act in the Department of Agriculture, the Federal Reserve System, the Veterans' Administration, the Railroad Retirement Board, the Walsh-Healey Act administered by the Division of Public Contracts in the Department of Labor, the Federal Alcohol Administration, and the administration of the Packers and Stockyards Act in the Department of Agriculture. Some thirty or thirty-five other studies are being prepared by the committee, which will be available in the near future.

Several books issued by the Brookings Institution, although basically economic in nature, also deal with some of the administrative problems. Among these should be mentioned: *The American Transportation Problem*, 1933, by Harold G. Moulton and Associates; *The Co-operative Marketing of Livestock*, 1931, by Edwin G. Nourse and Joseph G. Knapp; *Marketing Agreements under the A.A.A.*, 1935, by Edwin G. Nourse; *Labor Relations Boards*, 1935, by Lewis L. Lorwin and Arthur Wubnig; *Three Years of the Agricultural Adjustment Administration*, 1937, by Edwin G. Nourse, Joseph S. Davis, and John D. Black; *Government and Economic Life*, Vol. I, 1939, by Leverett S. Lyon, Myron W. Watkins, and Victor Abramson.

Several hearings contain valuable information bearing on current proposals for change. Among the more important of these are: *United States Court of Appeals for Administration* (Hearings before a Subcommittee of the Senate Committee on the Judiciary on S. 3676, 75 Cong. 3 sess.), which contains charts and diagrams showing existing systems of judicial review and enforcement methods, as well as proposed systems of review and enforcement; *Administrative Law* (Hearings before Subcommittee No. 4 of the House Committee on the Judiciary on H.R. 4236, H.R. 6198, and H.R. 6324, 76 Cong. 1 sess.); and *National Labor Relations Act and Proposed Amendments* (Hearings before the Senate Committee on Education and Labor on S. 1000, S. 1264, S. 1392, S. 1550, S. 1580, and S. 2123, 76 Cong. 1 sess.). Numbers 46-63 of the series entitled *Work Materials*, published in 1936 by the Division of Review of the National Recovery Administration, also throw a great deal of light on the administrative process.

SUPPORTING STATEMENT II

SUBJECT MATTER OF FEDERAL REGULATION

The federal government regulates and controls a very wide number of businesses and business relationships. They are as follows:

1. Banking.
2. Aeronautics.
3. Contracts.
4. Employees' compensation.
5. Trusts and monopolies.
6. Alcohol.
7. Customs.
8. Foods, drugs, and cosmetics.
9. Commodity exchanges.
10. Communications.
11. Explosives.
12. Foreign trade zones.
13. Bituminous coal.
14. Labor relationships.
15. Labor standards.
16. Packers and stockyards.
17. Marketing.
18. Standards, grades, qualities of agricultural products.
19. Advertising.
20. Postal regulation.
21. Preventing restraint of trade, unfair methods of competition.
22. Regulation of poultry.
23. Perishable agricultural products.
24. Securities.
25. Security exchanges.
26. Regulation of holding companies.
27. Regulation of sale of oil.
28. Regulation of shipping.
29. Unfair foreign trade practices.
30. Regulation of patents, trademarks, copyrights.
31. Prison labor.
32. Agricultural production.
33. Social security.
34. Viruses, serums, toxins.
35. Use of navigable streams.
36. Use of water power.
37. Transportation.
38. Fishing industry.
39. Public lands.
40. Federal government employee relationships.

SUPPORTING STATEMENT III

METHODS OF REGULATION

The federal government uses from thirty to forty methods in its regulation and control of business and industry.

1. Contracts.
2. Licenses.
3. Grants.
4. Permits.
5. Authorizations.
6. Certificates of convenience and necessity.
7. Standardization, classification.
8. Grading.
9. Inspection and examination.
10. Grants-in-aid.
11. Loans.
12. Control through stock ownership.
13. Control by having directors on boards of corporations.
14. Fixing rates, charges, types and standards of service.
15. Direct competition.
16. Regulated monopoly.
17. Regulated competition.
18. Regulation of use of public domain, public waters, air, etc.
19. Prohibiting importation or allowing importation under certain conditions.
20. Approving marketing agreements.
21. Prohibiting lotteries.
22. Regulating payments into social security funds.
23. Regulating prison competition with industry.
24. Requiring specified types of accounts.
25. Recapture of property after a period of years.
26. Taxation.
27. Prohibiting sales or transactions in interstate commerce.
28. Prohibiting shipment of goods in interstate or foreign commerce.
29. Prohibiting use of the market.
30. Requiring federal incorporation.
31. Exercise of police power.
32. The direct regulatory process.
33. The managerial process.
34. Requiring certain actions as a condition precedent to the doing of business, e. g., requiring continuous access to information as a condition precedent to right to do business in commodity exchanges and security exchanges.

SUPPORTING STATEMENT IV

ECONOMIC CIRCUMSTANCES UNDER WHICH STATUTORY ADMINISTRATIVE ORDERS ARE ISSUED

Type of Order	Authority Issuing	Specific Economic Circumstances
I. Legislative regulatory orders: A. Rate, fare, or charge orders.	Interstate Commerce Commission.	In re railroad rates, fares, charges, freights, etc., 49 U. S. C. 15. Motor carriers, 49 U. S. C. 316–319. Joint routes, rates, rules, regulations, and practices in re common-carrier service upon certain rivers, 49 U. S. C. 153 (e). Orders fixing rates and compensation for carrying mail, 39 U. S. C. 542. Rates for transportation of mail matter by urban and interurban electric railway common carriers, 40 Stat. L. 742, 748.
	Secretary of Agriculture.	Prescribing rates and practices in re stockyard services, 7 U. S. C. 206, 207, 211, 212, 216, 217. Change or suspension of rates for stockyard services, 7 U. S. C. 206, 207.
	Federal Communications Commission.	In respect to interstate and foreign communications by wire or radio: (1) orders on new charges, suspension of charges, pending hearings, and refunds, 47 U. S. C. 203–205 and 47 U. S. C. 401–405; (2) orders fixing just and reasonable charges, 47 U. S. C. 205.
	Federal Power Commission.	In respect to rates and charges by electric companies engaged in interstate commerce, 16 U. S. C. 824: (1) suspension of new rates.
	Civil Aeronautics Authority.	In re rates for transportation of mail, 52 Stat. L. 973, 998.
	Secretary of War.	Order establishing reasonable tolls over bridges crossing navigable streams, 33 U. S. C. 503–507.
B. Wage orders.	Administrator under Fair Labor Standards Act of 1938.	Orders establishing minimum wages and maximum hours, 52 Stat. L. 1060. Orders providing for wages of learners, apprentices, and handicapped workers, 52 Stat. L. 1068.

Type of Order	Authority Issuing	Specific Economic Circumstances
C. Price orders.	Bituminous Coal Division.	In respect to the establishment of maximum prices for coal, 15 U. S. C. 833 (c). Due and reasonable maximum discounts or price allowances, 15 U. S. C. 833 (h).
	Bituminous Coal Division and district boards.	In re coal prices established by district boards, 15 U. S. C. 833 (a), (b), (c).
	Secretary of Agriculture.	In re fixing of minimum price to be paid to producers or associations of producers of agricultural products: (1) orders with marketing agreements, 7 U. S. C. 608c (8); (2) order with or without marketing agreements, 7 U. S. C. 608c (9).
D. Quota and allotment orders.	Secretary of Agriculture.	Orders in re sugar and liquid sugar, 7 U. S. C. 1115–1116.
E. Orders for the extension of facilities.	Federal Power Commission.	Extension or improvement of facilities, 52 Stat. L. 821, 824.
	Interstate Commerce Commission.	Order requiring railroads to provide adequate facilities or extend lines, 49 U. S. C. 1, par. (21).
F. Exemption orders.	Bituminous Coal Division.	Exemption from duty or liability under Bituminous Coal Code, 50 Stat. L. 83, 15 U. S. C. 834.
	Securities and Exchange Commission.	Exemption from provisions of the Public Utility Holding Company Act, 15 U. S. C. 79c (a), (b), (c).
G. Interchangeable mileage.	Interstate Commerce Commission.	In re interchangeable mileage for script coupon ticket, 49 U. S. C. 22, par. (2).
H. Orders in re accounting.	.....do.......	Orders in re accounts, records, memoranda, etc., of railroads, 49 U. S. C. 20. Order in re forms of accounts, records, and memoranda of motor carriers, 49 U. S. C. 320.
	Federal Power Commission.	In re accounts, 16 U. S. C. 825. In re rates of depreciation, 16 U. S. C. 825a.
I. Orders in re reports.	Interstate Commerce Commission.	In re filing of monthly reports of earnings and expenses and periodical reports, 49 U. S. C. 20 (1), (2), (5), (6).
	Federal Power Commission.	In re filing of periodic and special reports, 16 U. S. C. 825c.

Type of Order	Authority Issuing	Specific Economic Circumstances
J. Orders in re valuation.	Interstate Commerce Commission.	In re valuations of railways, 49 U. S. C. 19a.
K. Orders in re consolidations, mergers, acquiring control, etc.	.....do.......	In re consolidation, purchase, lease, acquiring control, etc., 49 U. S. C. 5 (4).
L. Orders restricting voting power.	.....do.......	Orders restricting the exercise of voting power in respect to stock or share of capital in order to prevent subjecting of one carrier to the control of another, 49 U. S. C. 5 (11).
M. Orders to prevent control by common directors.	.....do.......	Order requiring person to take action that may be necessary to prevent control by common directors, etc., 49 U. S. C. 5 (6)-(10).
N. Orders determining fact of competition.	.....do.......	Order to determine questions of fact as to competition or possibility of competition between railroads and water carriers, 49 U. S. C. 5 (19), (20), (21).
O. Orders in re pooling arrangements.	.....do.......	Orders in re pooling arrangements, division of traffic or earnings, 49 U. S. C. 5 (1).
P. Orders requiring allocation and apportionment of costs.	Securities and Exchange Commission.	In re allocation and apportionment of costs among members of a mutual service company, 15 U. S. C. 79m (c), (d).
Q. Orders for simplification.	.....do.......	Limiting the operations of a holding company to a single integrated public utility system, 15 U. S. C. 79k (b).
R. Orders establishing classes.	.....do.......	Establishing classes of persons or matters for the purpose of making rules, regulations, or orders, 15 U. S. C. 79t (c).
S. Orders revoking or modifying other orders.	.....do.......	Order revoking an exemption order, 15 U. S. C. 79c (c). Order revoking or modifying order previously made in re simplification of holding-company systems, 15 U. S. C. 79k (b) (2).
T. Declaration of status.	.....do.......	Order declaring a person to be a holding company, a subsidiary company, or an affiliate or declaring a class of

Type of Order	Authority Issuing	Specific Economic Circumstances
		which such person is a member to be affiliated, 15 U. S. C. 79b (b).
U. Permissive orders.	.....do.......	Order permitting registrant to file a preliminary registration statement, 15 U. S. C. 79e (c).
V. Orders fixing limits.	Commodity Exchange Commission	Orders fixing limits on amount of trading under contracts of sale of commodities for future delivery, 7 U. S. C. 6a.
W. Orders establishing rules and regulations.	Secretary of Agriculture	Orders in respect to the issue, amendment, or repeal of regulations, 52 Stat. L. 1040, 1055.
II. Procedural orders:		
A. Orders for investigation.	Interstate Commerce Commission	Orders for investigation and hearing as to rates, routes, routing of traffic, etc., 49 U. S. C. 15 (1).
B. Orders requiring the attendance of witnesses.	Secretary of Labor	Orders requiring the attendance of witnesses and the production of evidence, 41 U. S. C. 39.
C. Orders to dismiss proceedings.	Securities and Exchange Commission	Order to dismiss an application for review of disciplinary proceedings taken by a registered security association against a member thereof, 52 Stat. L. 1073.
D. Orders to show cause.	.....do.......	Order to show cause why a declaration by a registered holding company should become effective, 15 U. S. C. 79g (b).
E. Orders requiring the furnishing of information.	Railroad Retirement Board.	Order requiring all employers, employees, officers, boards, or other agency to furnish information, 45 U. S. C. 228j.
F. Orders in re altera ion of rules.	Securities and Exchange Commission.	Alterations of rules and regulations of a registered securities association when it fails to make a requested alteration or to supplement them, 52 Stat. L. 1070, 1074.
III. Administrative controlling orders.	.....do.......	Abrogation of rules and regulations made by an inferior authority by a superior authority, 52 Stat. L. 1070, 1074.
IV. Injunctive and command orders:		
A. Cease and desist orders.	Secretary of Agriculture.	Orders in re monopolization or restraint of trade by associations of agricultural producers, 7 U. S. C. 292.

Type of Order	Authority Issuing	Specific Economic Circumstances
	Commodity Exchange Commission.	In respect to unlawful practices of packers, 7 U. S. C. 191–195. In respect to charges or practices in re stockyards, 7 U. S. C. 210–211. In re violations of rules and regulations or orders in re contract markets, 7 U. S. C. 13a.
	Secretary of Commerce.	Orders to prevent monopolies or restraint of trade in the fishing industry, 15 U. S. C. 522.
	National Labor Relations Board.	In re unfair labor practices with affirmative order, 29 U. S. C. 160 (b)–(e).
	Federal Trade Commission.	In re unfair methods of competition and unfair or deceptive acts or practices in commerce, 15 U. S. C. 45. Order terminating discrimination, 15 U. S. C. 13 (a) (b). (See "Unfair Practices Act," 10 *So. Cal. L. Rev.* 18. Evidently "order terminating discrimination" is same as a "cease and desist" order of sec. 21 of this title.) (See "The Patman Act in Practice," 35 *Mich. L. Rev.* 707; Symposium, 21 *Iowa L. Rev.* 175.) Lease, sale, contract for sale of commodities, or fixing a price, discount, or rebate thereon on agreement not to use goods of a competitor, 15 U. S. C. 14, 21. In re acquisition by one corporation of stock of another, 15 U. S. C. 18, 21. In re interlocking directors and officers, 15 U. S. C. 19, 21.
	Interstate Commerce Commission.	Orders under the Clayton Act: (1) discrimination in re services or facilities, 15 U. S. C. 13, 21; (2) acquisition by one railroad corporation of stock of another, 15 U. S. C. 18, 21; (3) interlocking railroad directors or officers, 15 U. S. C. 19, 21.
	Federal Communications Commission.	Orders under Clayton Act: (1) discrimination in re services or facilities, 15 U. S. C. 13; (2) acquisition by one corporation of the stock of another, 15 U. S. C. 18, 21; (3) interlocking directors and officers, 15 U. S. C. 19, 21.
	Board of Governors of the Federal Reserve System.	Orders under the Clayton Act: (1) acquisition by one corporation of stock of another, 15 U. S. C. 18, 21; (2) interlocking directors and officers, 15 U. S. C. 19.

Type of Order	Authority Issuing	Specific Economic Circumstances
B. Enforcement orders.	Interstate Commerce Commission.	Order compelling carrier or broker to comply with the provisions of the Motor Carrier Act or requirements, 49 U. S. C. 304 (d). Order enforcing obedience to law prohibiting control or management in a common interest of any two or more motor carriers, 49 Stat. L. 556, 52 Stat. L. 1236, 1240. Order requiring person in violation of law to take steps to prevent continuance of violation, 49 U. S. C. 5 (5)–(10).
	Civil Aeronautics Authority.	Order requiring obedience to law and requirements thereunder, 52 Stat. L. 973, 1018.
	National Railroad Adjustment Board.	Order directed to a carrier to make an award of the division effective. Such an order may also include a reparation order, 45 U. S. C. 153 (o).
V. Reparation and analogous orders.	Interstate Commerce Commission.	Reparations for injury done by carriers, 49 U. S. C. 8, 9, 13, 16.
	Federal Communications Commission.	Orders for the payment of money or award of damages, 47 U. S. C. 206–209, 407.
	Secretary of Agriculture.	Orders for damages under the Perishable Agricultural Commodities Act, 7 U. S. C. 499g. Orders for reparations under the Packers and Stockyards Act, 7 U. S. C. 209, 210.
	United States Maritime Commission.	Orders for the payment of money for violation of Shipping Act, 39 Stat. L. 736–738, 46 U. S. C. 1114.
	National Railroad Adjustment Board.	In re disputes between an employee or group of employees and a carrier or carriers growing out of grievances or out of interpretation or application of agreements concerning rates of pay, rules, or working conditions where award concerns a requirement for the payment of money, 45 U. S. C. 153.
VI. Penalty orders.	Securities and Exchange Commission.	Suspending or revoking the registration of a registered securities association, 52 Stat. L. 1070, 1074. Order to suspend or expel a member from a registered securities association, 52 Stat. L. 1070, 1075.

Type of Order	Authority Issuing	Specific Economic Circumstances
	Interstate Commerce Commission. Postmaster General.	Removal from office of any officer or director of the registered securities association, 52 Stat. L. 1070, 1075. Safety orders in re railroads, 49 U. S. C. 26. Orders in re serviceability and condition of boilers, 45 U. S. C. 29. Fraud orders, 39 U. S. C. 259, 732.
	Commodity Exchange Commission.	Excluding or debarring an associaton or corporation from trading in a contract market, 7 U. S. C. 10a.
VII. Orders in re licenses, registrations, certificates, privileges, permits, approvals, grants:		
A. Orders in re licenses.	Secretary of Agriculture.	Order revoking license of poultry dealers, 7 U. S. C. 218a (d). Order suspending or revoking license of perishable agricultural commission merchant, dealer, or broker, 7 U. S. C. 499h (a).
	Federal Communications Commission.	Suspension of license of radio operator, 47 U. S. C. 303 (m) (1), (2). Order revoking a station license, 47 U. S. C. 312 (a).
	Council of National Defense.	Revocation of a license to deal in explosives, 50 U. S. C. 131–132. Refusal of a license to deal in explosives, 50 U. S. C. 132.
	Interstate Commerce Commission.	Suspension, change, revocation of a motor carrier license, certificate, or permit, 49 U. S. C. 304 (d), 312; 52 Stat. L. 1236, 1238, amending above sections.
	Foreign Trade Zones Board.	Revocation of grant of privilege of establishing, operating, and maintaining foreign trade zones, 19 U. S. C. 81a–81s.
	Secretary of the Treasury.	Order suspending or revoking license as a customhouse broker, 19 U. S. C. 1641 (b).
	Secretary of Agriculture.	Order suspending stockyard dealer or market agency registrant who is insolvent or who has violated the law, 7 U. S. C. 204.
B. Orders in re registrations.	Securities and Exchange Commission.	Order refusing to let registration become effective, 15 U. S. C. 77h (b).

Type of Order	Authority Issuing	Specific Economic Circumstances
		Stop orders in re registration statements, 15 U. S. C. 77h (d).
		Orders denying registration of a national security exchange, 15 U. S. C. 78 (e).
		Orders denying or revoking registration of a broker or dealer, 15 U. S. C. 78o (b).
		Order postponing the effective date of a registration, 15 U. S. C. 78o (b). (This is related to order above.)
		Order suspending registration. (This is related to registration of broker or dealer order.) 15 U. S. C. 78o (b).
		Order canceling registration where broker or dealer for whom an application is pending is no longer in existence or has ceased to do business, 15 U. S. C. 78o (b).
		Denial of an application to declare that a registered holding company has ceased to be a holding company, 15 U. S. C. 79e (d).
C. Orders in re certificates.	Bituminous Coal Division.	Revocation of a certificate of right to exemption from taxes, 15 U. S. C. 830, 835, 836.
	Tender boards	Denial of certificate of clearance for the shipment of petroleum products, 15 U. S. C. 715d and Executive Orders No. 6979 and No. 6980.
	Interstate Commerce Commission.	Refusal to grant a certificate of convenience and necessity, permits, licenses, 49 U. S. C. 306, 307, 309, 311.
		Suspension, revocation, or change of a certificate of convenience and necessity, permit, or license, 49 U. S. C. 312.
	Civil Aeronautics Authority.	Certificate of public convenience and necessity for air carrier, 52 Stat. L. 973, 987.
D. Orders in re privileges.	Postmaster General.	Orders refusing privilege of mails. "Fraud Orders." (See "Penalty Orders," above.)
	Secretary of Agriculture.	Order withdrawing privilege to trade in a contract market, 7 U. S. C. 9.
E. Orders in re permits.	Interstate Commerce Commission.	Order permitting continuance of vessel in operation or to install a new service, 49 U. S. C. 5 (20).
	Federal Alcohol Administration.	Denial or revocation, suspension, or annulment of a basic permit, 27 U. S. C. 204.

Type of Order	Authority Issuing	Specific Economic Circumstances
F. Orders in re approvals.	California Debris Commission.	Granting or denying permit as to interlocking directorate, 27 U. S. C. 208. Order with requirements authorizing or refusing to permit hydraulic mining to be carried on, 33 U. S. C. 669–673. Order without requirements as to construction permitting hydraulic mining to be carried on, 33 U. S. C. 673.
	Federal Power Commission.	Cancellation of a preliminary permit upon failure of permittees to comply with conditions thereof, or for other good cause, 16 U. S. C. 798.
	Interstate Commerce Commission and joint boards.	Suspension, changes in, or revocation in re permits to motor carriers, 49 U. S. C. 304, 305, 312. Refusal of application for permit, 49 U. S. C. 309 (b).
	Commissioner of Internal Revenue.	Revocation of permits for the manufacture or dealing in denatured alcohol, 27 U. S. C. 154–156. Revocation of permit to manufacture for false description of denatured liquors, 27 U. S. C. 154.
	Civil Aeronautics Authority.	Modification, suspension, or revocation of permits to foreign air carriers, 52 Stat. L. 973, 991, 1024.
	Federal Power Commission.	Order approving assumption of liabilities by interstate public utilities, 16 U. S. C. 824c. Disapproval of assumption of liabilities by interstate utilities, 16 U. S. C. 824c. Order refusing approval for abandonment of facilities or service of interstate natural-gas company, 52 Stat. L. 821, 824.
	Bituminous Coal Division.	Suspending or revoking prior approval of co-operative marketing of coal, 15 U. S. C. 842.
	Interstate Commerce Commission.	Refusal of approval of consolidation, merger, purchase, lease, operating contract, or acquisition of control of railways, 49 U. S. C. 5 (4). Order approving and authorizing consolidations, mergers, purchases, leases, operating contracts, or acquisition of control, 52 Stat. L. 1236, 1239.
	Civil Aeronautics Authority.	Refusal of approval for consolidation, merger, purchase, lease, operating contract, or acquisition of control of air carriers, 52 Stat. L. 973, 1001.

Type of Order	Authority Issuing	Specific Economic Circumstances
G. Orders in re grants.	Interstate Commerce Commission.	Refusal of approval for an air carrier to have and retain an officer or director who is an officer, director, or member, or who as a stockholder holds a controlling interest in any other person who is a common carrier or is engaged in any phase of aeronautics, etc., 52 Stat. L. 973, 1002. Orders refusing to grant an application for the issue of securities, 49 U. S. C. 20 (a).
VIII. Orders in re declarations and designations:		
A. Declarations.	Securities and Exchange Commission.	Declaration that a registered holding company has ceased to be a holding company, 15 U. S. C. 79e (d). Orders declaring a person to be a holding company, a subsidiary company, or an affiliate, or declaring a class of which such person is an affiliated member, 15 U. S. C. 79b (b). Order revoking an order declaring a person to be a holding company, subsidiary company, or affiliate, 15 U. S. C. 79b (b). Order permitting or refusing declaration to become effective, 15 U. S. C. 79g (b).
B. Designations.	Secretary of Agriculture. Commodity Exchange Commission.	Refusal to designate a board of trade as a contract market, 7 U. S. C. 7, 8. Suspension or revocation of a board of trade as a contract market, 7 U. S. C. 8.
IX. Orders in re adjustment, mediation, and arbitration.	Secretary of Agriculture.	Marketing agreement orders in respect to anti-hog-cholera serum and hog-cholera virus, 49 Stat. L. 781. Marketing agreement orders in respect to milk, fruits, tobacco, vegetables, soybeans, and naval stores: (1) orders with marketing agreements; (2) orders with or without marketing agreements, 7 U. S. C. 608 (c).
X. Negative orders:		
A. Order determining not to act.	.....do.......	Orders in respect to the issue, amendment, or repeal of regulations, 52 Stat. L. 1040, 1055.

Type of Order	Authority Issuing	Specific Economic Circumstances
B. Negative order issued because of supposed lack of jurisdiction.	Interstate Commerce Commission.	Issuance of a negative order solely because of supposed lack of power, 49 U. S. C. 305 (h).
C. General negative orders.	Civil Aeronautics Authority.	Orders in re regulation of aviation, 52 Stat. L. 973, 1024.
XI. Exclusion orders.	President of United States.	Orders excluding articles from entry into the United States, regarding which there have been unfair practices, 19 U. S. C. 1337. NOTE.—The law does not speak of order, but the President in practice excludes by order. (See *Frischer & Co.* v. *Elting*, 60 F. (2d) 711, cert. den., 282 U. S. 649.)

THE NATURE AND CLASSIFICATION OF STATUTORY ADMINISTRATIVE ORDERS

The statutory order, which is almost, if not entirely, a development of the past fifty years, has become the chief type of administrative action in the regulation and control of business and industry by the federal government. In nearly two hundred specific circumstances where Congress has provided for such regulation, it has required authorities to take action through the order. Although Congress has usually required this type of action to be used by the large regulatory boards and commissions, other agencies of the government are also included, so that today twenty-five or more authorities take action that affects individuals largely by this method.

I. THE NATURE OF THE STATUTORY ORDER

In a broad way the statutory order usually has the nature of a prescription, a command, an injunction, a declaration, a restraint, a withholding, or a refusal. It commands the taking of action, or refuses to let action be taken; it grants or withholds an authority, a relief, a claimed right, a privilege, or a license; it determines upon rights and obligations; it declares what shall be the status of persons and things.[1] The order is used principally for the control of economic situations in which the state regulates individuals and corporations.

The regulatory authorities, which act chiefly through this form of action, are concerned with large questions of public economic policy and management, such as the regulation of wages, banking, aviation, alcohol, commodity exchanges, communications, power and fuel, international trade, transportation, coal, labor relationships, use of the mail, stockyard services, packers and processors, agricultural production and marketing, trade practices, securities and security exchanges, holding companies, oil production and ship-

---

[1] It should be noted that there are several administrative actions called by the statutes "orders," which do not conform to these criteria.

ment, and shipping.[2] In most instances where the order is used, the state is dealing with situations where the public interest is of great importance.

Through the order, regulatory authorities are frequently dealing with limitations upon the use of economic power. In many cases they are seeing that economic power is exercised within new statutory legal norms and standards. Again, they are dealing with complicated relationships between individuals or groups. In other circumstances, the order method is used to deal with violations of law, and in still others the order is used as a method of settling disputes. In many cases the right to engage in or to continue in, or to extend business operations is within the power of regulatory authorities and is controlled by the order. In most instances the order has the force and effect of law and is enforceable even as the law.

It cannot be too strongly expressed that the order is not the type of action by which the government carries out its own proprietary, promotional, fiscal, contractual, and benefactory functions. The order is used almost exclusively in connection with regulatory activity.

The order may be distinguished from other types of administrative action in several ways. With certain exceptions, notably orders establishing procedure, the following description applies: the order does not, as does the rule and regulation, implement the statute, but rather applies it. It is not, like the substantive rule or regulation, general in nature, but is usually much more specific, although at times it applies to classes and groups of individuals. It seldom, like the procedural rule and regulation, is concerned with merely adjective matters. It is not issued as a result of mere administrative discretion, but generally it is, and must be, based upon a finding of facts. It is this fact-finding and the procedure incidental to it that makes the order, even when legislative in nature, appear to be a judicial act. The order, unlike the rule and regulation, is usually directly controllable by the courts, rather than being controllable only upon a collateral attack.

The order differs fundamentally from the decision in several particulars. In the first place, as has been said before, the order

---

[2] See Supporting Statement IV, pp. 276-86.

is used chiefly in the regulatory field, while the decision is used in almost all other fields.

In the second place, the order is largely used to control situations which the legislature itself might well control had it time and expert knowledge. The decision is much more purely administrative in nature. It is true that the decision is often used in the field of regulation, but regulation in the police sense, as safety regulations, control of shipping, plant quarantine, preventing the spread of contagious diseases, etc. The decision is also used as a type of administrative action where the government deals with the individual in connection with its own functioning, as in taxation, customs, contracts, etc. The decision rather than the order is used in respect to nearly all those activities where the government is taking action that is of benefit to the individual, such as pensions, compensations for injuries, social security payments, etc.

Finally, the order is pre-eminently a statutory creation. The statute as a rule expressly mentions that the order procedure shall be used in the control of various economic situations. It is true that the order procedure is used for situations that are not expressly governed by the statute, by some agencies and under certain circumstances. These exceptions, however, do not invalidate the general statement. As a rule, unless the order procedure is especially mentioned by the statute, the administrative authority is under no compulsion to have a notice, a formal hearing, and a finding of fact as the basis for its decision.

II. TYPES OF ORDERS

Orders might possibly be classified in several different ways according to the particular type of information desired. At times it may be useful to know under what economic circumstances various types of orders are issued. It might be useful for some other purposes to classify orders according to issuing authority. For other reasons it might be useful to know whether they are administrative, legislative, or judicial in nature. They might also for some purposes be classified according to type of procedure, appealability, or enforcement.

The most general basis for classification, however, seems to be threefold: subject matter, legal nature, and legal effect. These factors determine almost entirely whether the order is legislative, administrative, or judicial in nature, and control largely the procedure for issuing the order, its enforcement, and the conditions and extent of review by the courts.

The subject matter of the order is of prime importance in determining into what class it should fall, since it shows what the government is attempting to accomplish. Is it exercising a wide power of regulation through the order, such as might be exercised by the legislature had it time and technical equipment for the detailed work of regulating rates, services, wages, hours of work, ordering the extension of facilities, etc.? Is it merely attempting to facilitate the conduct of a case by ordering an investigation or the attendance of witnesses, dismissing proceedings, or ordering a party to show cause or to furnish information? Is the administrative authority merely trying to control a subordinate governmental or quasi-governmental agency? Is it commanding obedience to laws, regulations, or orders, or forcing individuals to cease disobedience? Is it settling disputes as to damages or injuries? Is it exercising its police power to secure safety, public health, or morals? Is it making, renewing, withholding, suspending, revoking various kinds of grants for diverse purposes? Is it making adjustments between different groups or individuals, or is it mediating or arbitrating their differences? Is it determining that it has no power to act or that it will not act in a matter?

The legal nature of the order must be considered from several viewpoints: whether it is dealing with past or future situations; whether it is final or non-final; whether it is incidental to administrative action or is the end of administrative action; whether it is interlocutory and further action is required; whether it is procedural or not; whether it is affirmative or negative in nature; whether it is discretionary in nature; what methods of appeal and enforcement are applicable.

The legal effect of the order is of almost equal importance for the classification of orders. Here likewise several points of view must be considered. Does the order change an existing juridical situation or establish a new juridical situation in a way favorable or unfavorable to the individual? Does it establish new rules for the future? Does it directly or only indirectly or potentially affect rights? Does the order lay down requirements or does it merely grant permission? Does it affect only those in the employment of the government or does it affect the rights of third persons? Is the effect of the order positive or is it merely negative?

Using then, subject matter, legal nature, and legal effect as a basis, statutory orders may be divided into the following classes: (1) legislative regulatory orders; (2) procedural and interlocutory orders; (3) administrative controlling orders; (4) injunctive and command orders; (5) reparation and analogous orders; (6) penalty orders; (7) license, certificate, and similar orders; (8) orders *in re* declarations and designations; (9) adjustment, mediation, and arbitration orders; and (10) negative orders.

Legislative regulatory orders. A legislative regulatory order is often akin to a rule or regulation, since in many cases it reaches beyond individuals and may operate more or less directly upon groups or classes of the public. Sometimes, however, an order of this type is not general in its application. As a rule the goal to be attained by the legislative regulatory order is an economic one, which in most instances involves the question of public interest, convenience, or necessity in one form or another.

The subject matter of legislative regulatory orders has to do with such things as rates, wages, hours and conditions of labor, prices, extension of facilities, consolidations, unfair methods of competition. The regulatory authorities issuing such orders may be required to apply such standards as "reasonable rates," "public interest, convenience, and necessity," "unreasonable discrimination," "adequate facilities and services," "fair and orderly markets," "protection of investors," "unfair labor practices," "discrimination in prices," etc. In the making of such orders the regulatory authority of necessity must exercise a broad discretion, since it is entrusted with enforcing the statute "in such a way as to produce the results sought by the legislature."[3]

Because of the subject matter controlled by such orders, they gen-

---

[3] Robert M. Cooper, "Administrative Justice and the Rule of Discretion," 47 *Yale Law Journal* 581.

erally have a fairly definite legal nature. They are nearly always of future applicability, and are final. Occasionally they do not become final until after the completion of a statutory period or the fulfillment of some other condition; and in a few instances they are not final; but this is exceptional.

Legislative regulatory orders generally create new juridical situations or change old ones. In so doing they may have a direct effect upon individual rights, as when a person is placed in the position of a holding company; new wage scales are established; a rate schedule is set up; a consolidation is permitted, etc. Valuation orders, orders establishing regulatory norms of general application, or orders creating classes, may only potentially affect rights.

Legislative regulatory orders may be subdivided into more than a score of classes.[4]

Procedural orders. Procedural orders are issued for the purpose of furthering an investigation or conducting a case. They are generally administrative in nature rather than legislative or judicial. They do not affect rights, and as a rule they impose duties only indirectly. Therefore no particular type of procedure is necessary before they are issued and they are generally non-reviewable.[5]

Such statutory procedural orders include orders for investigation, orders requiring the attendance of witnesses, orders to dismiss proceedings, orders under certain circumstances to show cause, orders requiring the furnishing of information, or orders altering rules and regulations.

Administrative controlling orders. The statutes provide for a few administrative controlling orders issued by a higher authority for the purpose of controlling the action of an inferior authority. These orders are final and binding upon the inferior authority. No particular procedure is required in respect to them, since they do not affect the rights or duties of third parties. For the same reason, they are subject to no review.

---

[4] See Supporting Statement VI, pp. 302-04.

[5] *Securities and Exchange Commission* v. *Andrews,* 88 F. (2d) 441; *Illinois Central R. Co.* v. *Public Utilities Commission,* 245 U.S. 493; *Isbrandtsen-Moller Co.* v. *United States,* 300 U.S. 139, 141; *Federal Power Commission* v. *Metropolitan Edison Co.,* 304 U.S. 375.

Injunctive and command orders. Injunctive and command orders take two forms: cease and desist orders and enforcement orders. The cease and desist order is judicial in nature and is similar to an injunction by a court, with the difference that the administrative authority issuing it has no power to enforce it, but must depend upon further court action to this end. In some places the law provides civil or criminal penalties for violation of the order. The administrative authority has no power to punish for contempt. The cease and desist order is chiefly used to prevent violations of the law or rules or regulations, or to prevent the continuance of practices held to be illegal. Such orders are final as far as the regulatory authority is concerned, and in several instances the statutes give them judicial finality after certain time limits have expired or other conditions have been fulfilled. They affect rights by enjoining certain acts, and they often change the economic situation of the individual. Such orders are always reviewable. The courts must be asked to enforce them in case of disobedience.

In several instances the cease and desist order is combined with other orders, such as rate or reparation orders. Thus, a regulatory authority may establish a rate and then issue an order requiring a carrier to cease and desist from violations, to the extent to which it finds that violations exist. The National Labor Relations Board may issue an order requiring a person to cease and desist from an unfair labor practice, and may by the same order take affirmative action, including reinstatement of employees with or without back pay.

Enforcement orders are issued for the purpose of compelling obedience to the law. Such orders do not change juridical situations, but merely enforce situations already existing. The orders are final in nature and would appear to be judicially controlled in all cases, directly or indirectly.

Reparation and analogous orders. Such orders include reparation for injury done, orders for the payment of money, and certain awards of a monetary nature. These orders are affirmative, apply to past situations, and are judicial rather than legislative in nature. The order, with the finding on which it is based, is made only *prima facie* evidence before a court in an enforcement suit brought by the individual for whose benefit the order was made. Where common law rights are involved in a suit, as in respect to reparation orders of the Interstate Commerce Commission, the making of such orders *prima facie* instead of final seems to be a constitutional requirement.[6] Where no common law rights are involved, reparation orders can be made final.

The legal effect of the reparation or similar order is to change an existing juridical situation and to place a burden upon the person to whom the order applies. In only one case is such an order directly appealable. Review may be had indirectly, however, if the person who is ordered to make reparation refuses to do so and presents his side of the controversy when the one for whose benefit the order was made brings action for its enforcement. Such orders are enforceable only by further judicial action.

Penalty orders. Penalty orders always inflict some sort of non-monetary punishment or forfeiture of rights for violations of the law, rules and regulations, or orders. This may be suspension, expulsion, removal from office, denying the use of the mails, exclusion of products from entrance into the United States, and so on.

Such orders are always affirmative and final and change an existing juridical situation to the disadvantage of individuals. As a rule there is a statutory right of review. Where this does not exist, the courts have often nevertheless taken jurisdiction. Such orders are usually enforced in an administrative manner, and it is not necessary to invoke the general enforcement statutes.

Orders in re licenses, certificates, privileges, permits, approvals, and grants. The administrative agency may take several different types of action in respect to licenses, privileges, etc. It may, according to circumstances, grant or refuse to grant; it may renew or refuse to renew; it may amend or refuse to amend; it may suspend or revoke. It is obvious that not all of these acts are identical in significance. For this reason they are performed by different types of action. When the action is an exercise of administrative discretion,

---

[6] The Seventh Amendment to the Constitution provides: "In suits at common law, where the value in controversy shall exceed twenty dollars, the right of trial by jury shall be preserved. . . ."

it is generally taken by an administrative decision. When individual rights are involved, the order procedure is generally used. In the majority of cases the granting or refusal of a license, etc., is regarded as discretionary; hence an order procedure is not required by law even though the statutes provide that suspension or revocation of the same type of license can be accomplished only by means of an order. There are a few exceptions to this, however, in respect to refusal.[7]

In several instances no order is required by statute, even though there may be a notice and hearing, and though the grant, etc. may be made contingent upon a finding of certain facts.[8]

In at least two instances the order is used in respect to approvals,[9] but in both cases terms and conditions or requirements are to be laid down in the order, which would seem to make it more than a mere approval.

The renewal or refusal of renewal, like the original grant or refusal, is seldom subject to order procedure; but suspension or revocation is often subject to this type of procedure.[10]

Nearly all orders in respect to licenses, grants, etc. are final in nature, apply to future situations, and affect individuals favorably or unfavorably.

In the great majority of cases, licenses, grants, etc., are self-executing and are enforced through the administrative act itself of

---

[7] Director of Bureau of Mines, refusal of a license to deal in explosives, 50 U.S.C. 131-32; Federal Alcohol Administration, refusal to grant a basic permit, 27 U.S.C. 204(b); refusal of permit for interlocking directorates, 27 U.S.C. 208; Federal Power Commission, refusal to grant permit to issue securities or assume liabilities, 16 U.S.C. 824 c(a); Interstate Commerce Commission, grant of the right to issue securities or assume obligations, 49 U.S.C. 20a; Securities and Exchange Commission, denying registration of a national security exchange, 15 U.S.C. 77f(e); denial of an application to declare that a registered holding company has ceased to be a holding company, 15 U.S.C. 79e(d).

[8] See *in re* poultry dealer license, 7 U.S.C. 218a; refusal of a license to perishable agricultural commodities market, broker, or dealer, 7 U.S.C. 499d; refusal to designate a board of trade as a contract market, 7 U.S.C. 8.

[9] Civil Aeronautics Authority, *in re* consolidation, merger, and acquisition of control, 52 Stat. L. 1001; California Debris Commission, *in re* the carrying on of hydraulic mining, 33 U.S.C. 669-73.

[10] See F. F. Blachly, "Work Materials on Administrative Action and Procedure" (manuscript).

granting, refusing, suspending, or revoking. No other agency is called upon to act for the purpose of making the order effective. Unless an appeal is taken, the person whose application for a license, etc. has been refused, or whose license, etc. has been suspended or revoked, may be in the position of one who is operating without a license and so is subject to prosecution under the law. The authority need not apply to a court to enforce its order, but merely prosecutes the person who does not act in accordance with his changed juridical situation.

Orders in re declarations and designations. Orders making declarations and designations may be either legislative or judicial in nature. They are legislative, for example, when they establish general classifications which only indirectly affect rights or do not affect them at all. The orders of the Securities and Exchange Commission establishing classes of persons or matters, for the purpose of making applicable rules and regulations or orders, are of this type.[11] Such orders, like legislative orders generally, may be issued without formal procedure and are not ordinarily subject to judicial control.

Orders in respect to designations, classes, and the like, which determine whether a particular person falls or does not fall within a given class, are judicial in nature if membership therein touches his rights, as by adding to his burdens, responsibilities, or liabilities. When an administrative agency is authorized to issue orders of this type, opportunity for judicial review of the orders is given. If an order takes a person out of such a class, a favor is granted, and there is no need for appeal. When being placed within a certain class is obviously an advantage to the person concerned, no appeal will lie. On the other hand, if being withdrawn from such a class may cause injury, an appeal will lie. Orders making designations and classifications are enforced by administrative action.

Agreement and adjustment orders. Orders in re agreements and adjustments[12] are issued only by the Secretary of Agriculture. Such orders are made for two purposes: (1) preventing undue and excessive fluctuations and unfair methods of competition and unfair

---

[11] 15 U.S.C. 79t (c).

[12] These orders might be classified as legislative regulatory orders, but are considered here in some detail because of their peculiar nature. Certain commodities are exempted from this procedure; 7 U.S.C. 602, 854.

trade practices in marketing, as in respect to the anti-hog-cholera serum and hog-cholera virus; and (2) maintaining such balance between the production and consumption of agricultural commodities, and such marketing conditions therefor, as will reestablish prices to farmers at a level that will give agricultural commodities a purchasing power with respect to articles that farmers buy, equivalent to the purchasing power of agricultural commodities in the base period. There are elaborate statutory provisions in respect to the making and signing of marketing agreements and the issuing of orders by the Secretary.

These orders are basically legislative in nature. There is no true juridical conflict, since the interests are not susceptible of being reduced to strict party interests.[13] The parties to such an agreement or order are therefore not well defined as in a legal conflict.[14]

To determine the judicial nature and legal effect of such orders, it is necessary to analyze the procedure employed in making them. In the first place an attempt is made to accomplish the ends which the law outlines by a process of agreement, rather than a process of administrative compulsion, despite the fact that the law provides for a proceeding that is comparable to a due process hearing. The first steps are usually informal conversations between the commodity marketing groups involved and the corresponding sections of the Agricultural Adjustment Administration. Not until considerable support for a proposal emerges is there a formal stage of procedure.

In the formal procedure two stages are in evidence, the making of the marketing agreement and the issuance of the order. Normally an order or agreement is proposed by the Secretary of Agriculture, or his subordinates, in the Agricultural Adjustment Administration,

---

[13] "To think of this conflict [of the interests at the hearing] as being merely between two groups, one advocating the proposal for a marketing agreement [or order] and the other opposing it, is to over-simplify the picture. Actually, in most cases both support and opposition arose from complex groupings of interests. In these it is possible to find many odd combinations—and divisions—of growers and processors. There were brought to light not only antagonisms of interests between growers and the agricultural trades, but many inter-grower and interagricultural trade group conflicts as well." Edwin G. Nourse, *Marketing Agreements under the A.A.A.* (1935), pp. 34-35.

[14] On the whole subject of the nature of these orders see Ashley Sellers, *Administrative Procedure and Practice in the Department of Agriculture under the Agricultural Marketing Agreement Act of 1937* (1939), pp. 11-34.

although provision is also made for proposals by other persons. A hearing is held upon the proposal.

In respect to the marketing agreement, upon the conclusion of the hearing, if the Secretary so decides, he announces his "tentative approval thereof." The agreement is then placed on file with the hearing clerk for public inspection and for signature by the persons eligible to become parties thereto. No further hearings are held, but if the statutory number of signatures is obtained, the Secretary determines by order whether the agreement is to become effective.

The order "with or without marketing agreement" is issued when a proposed agreement, on which a hearing has been held, does not receive the requisite legal proportion of signatures. In this case, before issuing the order, the Secretary of Agriculture must make certain determinations of fact, which are approved by the President.

The marketing regulatory order is not based upon the principle of majority consent or agreement, but is based upon the regulatory principle, the principle of compulsion. Both types of orders are enforced by applying the penalties for disobedience. From the juridical viewpoint, both orders are legislative in nature, of future applicability, and final. Since both orders may affect rights adversely, both are appealable.

Negative orders. Statutory negative orders may take several forms: (1) determining not to act; (2) refusal to act because of supposed lack of jurisdiction; and (3) a general negative order.

In the determining-not-to-act type of negative order the regulatory authority is asked to take action, but issues an order refusing to do so. Such an order is administrative in nature. It is final and as a rule only indirectly affects rights. It does not place any obligation or burden upon an individual, but may at times tend to deny a right or privilege. Where it does so affirmatively, it may be affirmative in effect although negative in form, and may therefore be appealable.

A negative order issued because of a supposed lack of jurisdiction does not change in any way a juridical situation. The regulatory authority merely believes that it has no power to act and so refrains from acting. Theoretically there would be no appeal from such action as it in no way injures rights or imposes burdens. The one statute, however, which mentions such an order provides that any party in interest may file a bill of complaint with the appropriate district court convened under the provisions of the Urgent Deficiencies Act; and that if the court determines that the Commission has such powers, it may by mandatory injunction enforce the taking of such jurisdiction.[15]

There is one statute[16] which provides that any order, affirmative or negative, issued by the Civil Aeronautics Authority (with exceptions) is subject to appeal. Since this is a general provision, it may be well at this point to discuss the problem of the negative order, from the viewpoint of situations under which it is issued, its legal nature, legal effect, and the possibility of exercising control over it.

According to Mr. Justice Frankfurter,[17] there are three situations under which such orders are issued: (1) when the order may have the effect of forbidding or compelling action, but only after some subsequent action is taken; (2) when the order declines to give relief from statutory commands forbidding or compelling conduct; and (3) when the order does not forbid or compel conduct, but fails to forbid or compel conduct by a third person.

Examples of the first situation are valuation orders of the Interstate Commerce Commission, or its determination that a railway line is not a street, interurban, or suburban electric railway within the meaning of the exemption provisions of the Railway Labor Act. Such an order is one, to quote Mr. Justice Brandeis,

which does not command the carrier to do, or to refrain from doing, any thing; which does not grant or withhold any authority, privilege or license; which does not extend or abridge any power or facility; which does not subject the carrier to any liability, civil or criminal; which does not change the carrier's existing or future status or condition; which does not determine any right or obligation.[18]

Because of the legal nature of such orders they are not appealable: first, because there is no "case or controversy" within the meaning of Article III, Section 2 of the Constitution; second, be-

---

[15] 49 U.S.C. 305(h).
[16] 52 Stat. L. 1024.
[17] *Rochester Telephone Corporation* v. *United States*, 307 U.S. 125.
[18] *United States* v. *Los Angeles & Salt Lake R. Co.*, 273 U.S. 299, 309-10.

cause resort to the courts is premature until an actual injury takes place or is imminent; third, because "Congress has been loath to authorize review of interim steps in a proceeding."[19]

In the second set of circumstances, the statute itself places restrictions upon the free action of the individual and as a rule provides for punishment for violation of these restrictions. The risk of disobedience arises not from the order but from the statute. To free himself from these statutory restrictions the individual subject to the act asks to be held to be outside the statute or requests the dispensing power of the regulatory authority. Examples of such acts are exemption from duty or liability under the Bituminous Coal Code[20] or exemptions from the provisions of the Public Utility Holding Company Act.[21]

In some instances the statute lays down conditions precedent to exemption, as in the Public Utility Holding Company Act.[22] It would seem in these instances that a finding of fact that the conditions were not present for exemption would be an order of such a nature as to warrant judicial review. In other cases, such as exemption under the Bituminous Coal Code, no conditions precedent are laid down by statute, but the Commission seems to have wide discretion. Since, however, an order denying an exemption leads to serious economic consequences, it appears that an appeal might lie.[23] In both these instances there may be a "case" or "controversy." Since in both the matters discussed, the statutes provide generally for appeals from "orders," there is statutory authorization for the challenge of the regulatory authorities' action.

In general, when the order must be based upon a finding of fact, when adverse legal consequences follow from the order, or when penalties may be imposed as a result of disregarding the negative action of the regulatory authority, it appears that a review may be had either according to specific provisions of law, or under equity jurisdiction in the absence of a statutory provision. When the regulatory authority is entrusted with granting affirmative relief, at

---

[19] See *Rochester Telephone Corporation* v. *United States*, 307 U.S. 125.
[20] 50 Stat. L. 83; 15 U.S.C. 834.
[21] 15 U.S.C. 79c(a), (b), (c).
[22] 15 U.S.C. 79c(a), (b).
[23] See *Lehigh Valley R. Co.* v. *United States*, 243 U.S. 412.

discretion, but refuses to do so, the court itself cannot interfere by granting the relief sought, since to do so would be to substitute its discretion for that of the administrative authority.

In the third situation the order fails to forbid or compel conduct by a third person. Examples of such orders are: denial of a complaint asking for the setting aside of railroad demurrage rules of carriers, or refusal to require stockyards to change their practices or establish better services.

The legal effect of such orders is to leave the situation on a *status quo ante* basis. The regulatory authority has a right as a "tribunal appointed by law and informed by experience," to make such a primary decision in connection with its regulatory work. The making of a decision refusing to change an existing situation is an exercise of discretion and is administrative rather than judicial in nature. As a rule no legal rights are involved in such a decision unless one contends that the principles of law which led the authority to dismiss the complaint were wrong. In such cases a review by the courts would probably lie. The court would have power to dismiss the bill if the regulatory authority acted within proper legal principles. If the authority proceeded on erroneous legal principles, it would be ordered by the court "to proceed within the framework of its own discretionary authority on the indicated correct principles."[24]

[24] *Rochester Telephone Corporation* v. *United States,* 307 U.S. 125. See also Gregory Hankin, "The Fate of the Negative Order Doctrine" (manuscript).

SUPPORTING STATEMENT VI

TYPES OF ORDERS

I. Legislative regulatory orders:
    A. Rate, fare, charge or tariff orders.
    B. Wage orders.
    C. Price orders.
    D. Quotas and allotments.
    E. Orders for the extension of facilities.
    F. Exemption orders.
    G. Orders in re interchangeable mileage.
    H. Orders in re accounting.
    I. Orders in re reports.
    J. Orders in re valuations.
    K. Orders in re consolidations, mergers, control.
    L. Orders restricting voting power.
    M. Orders to prevent control by common directors.
    N. Orders determining fact of competition.
    O. Orders in re pooling arrangements.
    P. Orders requiring allocation and apportionment of costs.
    Q. Orders for simplification.
    R. Orders establishing classes.
    S. Orders revoking or modifying other orders.
    T. Declarations of status.
    U. Permissive orders.
    V. Orders fixing limits.
    W. Orders establishing rules and regulations.

II. Procedural orders:
    A. Orders for investigation.
    B. Orders requiring the attendance of witnesses.
    C. Orders dismissing proceedings.
    D. Orders to show cause.
    E. Orders requiring the furnishing of information.
    F. Orders in re alteration of rules.

III. Administrative controlling orders:
    A. Order of superior authority abrogating rules and regulations of an inferior authority.

IV. Injunctive and command orders:
    A. Cease and desist orders.
    B. Enforcement orders.

  V. Reparation and analogous orders:
     A. Reparation orders.
     B. Damage orders.
     C. Awards for payment of money.
 VI. Penalty orders:
     A. Suspension or revocation orders.
     B. Suspension or expulsion orders.
     C. Removal from office.
     D. Safety orders.
     E. Fraud orders.
     F. Excluding or debarring orders.
VII. License, registration, etc., orders:
     A. License orders:
        1. Refusal to grant.
        2. Suspension.
        3. Revocation.
     B. Registration orders.
        1. Refusal to grant.
        2. Suspension.
        3. Revocation.
     C. Orders in re certificates:
        1. Refusal to grant.
        2. Suspension.
        3. Revocation.
     D. Orders in re privileges:
        1. Refusal to grant.
        2. Suspension.
        3. Withdrawal of privileges.
     E. Orders in re permits:
        1. Refusal to grant.
        2. Suspension.
        3. Withdrawal or revocation of permits.
        4. Annulment of permits.
        5. Permits with requirements.
        6. Orders changing or modifying permits.
     F. Orders in re approvals:
        1. Approvals.
        2. Disapprovals.
        3. Refusal of approval.
        4. Suspension.
     G. Orders in re grants:
        1. Orders making grants.
        2. Orders refusing a grant.

VIII. Orders in re declarations and designations:
     A. Orders making a declaration.
     B. Orders refusing a declaration.
     C. Orders revoking a declaration.
     D. Suspension of a declaration.
  IX. Orders in re adjustments, mediation, and arbitration.
   X. Negative orders.
  XI. Exclusion orders.

SUPPORTING STATEMENT VII

AUTHORITIES ISSUING STATUTORY ADMINISTRATIVE ORDERS

Administrator of the Wage and Hour Division
Board of Governors of the Federal Reserve System
California Debris Commission
Civil Aeronautics Authority
Commissioner of Internal Revenue
Commodity Exchange Commission
Director of the Bituminous Coal Division in the Department of the Interior
Director of the Bureau of Mines
Federal Alcohol Administrator
Federal Communications Commission
Federal Power Commision
Federal Trade Commission
Foreign Trade Zones Board
Interstate Commerce Commission
National Labor Relations Board
National Railroad Adjustment Board
Postmaster General
President of the United States
Railroad Retirement Board
Secretary of Agriculture
Secretary of Commerce
Secretary of Labor
Secretary of the Treasury
Secretary of War
Securities and Exchange Commission
Tender boards in the Department of the Interior
United States Maritime Commission

SUPPORTING STATEMENT VIII

LEGAL NATURE AND EFFECT OF STATUTORY ADMINISTRATIVE ORDERS

I. Legislative regulatory orders:

    A. General rule: As a rule legislative regulatory orders are final and are of future applicability. They create new juridical situations or change existing juridical situations by establishing new standards, norms, or requirements which impose duties and obligations or limitations or controls upon the individual. As a result they are appealable.

    B. Exceptions to general rule: (1) Certain legislative orders are final and of future applicability but they only indirectly or potentially affect rights. Consequently as a rule they are nonappealable. (2) Certain orders may be final and of future applicability but since they are permissive no rights are affected and therefore they are nonappealable.

II. Procedural orders: Procedural orders are incidental to administrative action. They do not directly or substantially affect rights and are, therefore, nonappealable.

III. Administrative controlling orders: Administrative controlling orders are of two types:

    A. Those that are given by a superior administrative authority to a subordinate authority. These, while final and of future applicability, do not directly affect rights of third persons and so are nonappealable.

    B. Those that are issued by a regulatory authority to a private authority assisting in the regulation of the business or industry. These may or may not affect private rights. As a rule there is only a potential injury, and for this reason such orders are generally not appealable.

IV. Injunctive and command orders: Such orders are final and of future applicability. They affect personal or property rights by forbidding or requiring certain acts. They are judicial in nature, except that the administrative authority which issues them does not have power to enforce obedience to them or to punish for contempt in case of disobedience. Such orders are always appealable.

V. Reparation and analogous orders: Such orders are final and have to do with past rather than future situations. They are judicial in nature in that they settle controversies between private individuals. They are made only *prima facie* evidence in suits to enforce them, since to make them conclusive where common law rights are involved would interfere with the possibility of a jury trial as guaranteed by the Seventh Amendment to the Constitution, which provides: "In suits at common law, where the value in controversy shall exceed twenty dollars, the right of trial by jury shall be preserved, and no fact tried by a jury, shall be otherwise re-examined in any Court of the United States, than according to the rules of the common law." They change juridical situations and affect existing rights and although not directly appealable, a review over them may occur when the one for whose benefit the order was made brings a suit for enforcement.

VI. Penalty orders: Penalty orders are final and of future applicability. They change a juridical situation and affect existing rights; as a rule they are appealable.

VII. Orders in re licenses, registrations, certificates, privileges, permits, approvals, and grants: Such orders are nearly always final and of future applicability. In respect to juridical situations such orders may be divided into three groups:

    A. Orders which change a juridical situation and affect individual rights. Such orders are issued in respect to suspension, withdrawal, refusal to re-grant, and revocation. Many of these orders are appealable by statute and others by virtue of judicial decision.

    B. Orders which do not change a juridical situation. Where the statute itself withdraws the right to freely engage in business and lays down conditions precedent to doing so, and the regulatory authority refuses to grant permission by refusing a license, registration, certificate, etc., the order of refusal is in the nature of a negative order. The person making application has no rights that are interfered with by the regulatory authority. It is the legislative rather than the regulatory body that has interfered with what was formerly a right. Such orders are rarely appealable as no case or controversy exists between the government and the individual.

    C. Orders which approve a request are as a rule final and of future applicability and change a juridical situation but do not interfere with rights and so are not appealable.

VIII. Orders in re declarations and designations: Practically all of these orders are final and of future applicability. In respect to their legal effect there are three possibilities:

    A. Where a juridical situation is changed favorably. In such case there is no appeal for the person has received a favor.

    B. Where there is a change in the juridical situation so that rights may be indirectly or potentially affected. In such cases there is no appeal, as the injury is not direct.

    C. In some instances the order is negative in effect, since the right to do a thing has been withdrawn by the statute and made contingent upon the approval of a regulatory authority. Refusal on the part of the regulatory authority does not interfere with rights; therefore there is no appeal.

IX. Orders in re agreements: The typical order of this class is the order with a marketing agreement. Such orders are of future applicability but become final only after the completion of the statutory process. Even when there has been no agreement by those concerned, the orders as issued by the Secretary of Agriculture have an obligatory and binding effect. These marketing orders are legislative in nature in that they usually affect large numbers of people and large territories; the goal is an economic one; the material introduced at the hearings is chiefly economic in nature rather than legal; there is no true adversary proceeding; there are no adverse interests but a variety of interests; the persons concerned are not well defined; formal procedure is not necessarily required and if used is for the sake of administrative efficiency rather than because of the requirements of "due process of law." Review is not directly upon the order, but upon a ruling of the Secretary as to a prayer for exemption or for modification. In taking the case in equity, however, the district court may remand the matter to the Secretary, with directions to "make such ruling as the court shall determine to be in accordance with law," or "to take such further proceedings as [in the opinion of the court] the law requires." Under the latter clause, the court may certainly give directions for the modification or rescission of the order.[1]

[1] Ashley Sellers, "Administrative Procedure and Practice in the Department of Agriculture under the Agricultural Marketing Agreement Act of 1937," pp. 28-34.

X. Statutory negative orders: In a few instances special provisions are
     made by statute regarding negative orders. These statutory
     negative orders are final. They do not directly change the
     juridical situation of the individual but may do so potentially.
     Questions of right are only indirectly involved. The only right
     that one would seem to have in respect to the issuance, amend-
     ment, or repeal of regulations under the Food, Drug, and Cos-
     metic Act is that any order issued shall be in accordance with
     law. The only right that the individual has under the Motor
     Carriers Act in respect to the issuance of a negative order be-
     cause of supposed lack of power is to ask the court for a manda-
     tory injunction compelling the Interstate Commerce Commis-
     sion to take jurisdiction. A negative order issued by the Civil
     Aeronautics Authority may or may not interfere with rights.
     All of these orders are by statute made appealable. In strict
     theory they probably should not be.

XI. Exclusion orders: Such orders are final and change a juridical
     situation. They are nonappealable.

SUPPORTING STATEMENT IX

PROCEDURE IN ISSUING STATUTORY ADMINISTRATIVE ORDERS

It is basic in federal public law that no administrative action affecting the rights, duties, and obligations of private individuals or corporate persons may be taken without statutory authorization. In the great majority of cases such action is taken by the order procedure.

This procedure, in almost all instances, is basically laid down by statute, and has to do generally with how and by whom action is to be initiated, the necessity for a notice and hearing, and the making of the order. In some instances, also, something is said as to the burden of proof, answers by those proceeded against, the reduction of testimony to writing, and rules of evidence.

This basic statutory procedure, it must be pointed out, is largely implemented by the procedural rules and regulations of the administrative authorities having charge of carrying out the law.

I. INITIATION OF ACTION

There are three main ways by which administrative order action affecting individuals or corporations may be initiated: (1) upon complaint by those deeming themselves injured, (2) upon the initiation of the regulatory authority itself, or (3) upon the initiative of the person falling within the sphere of regulation or who is being regulated.

Upon complaint. Administrative order procedure is initiated by a complaint made, for example, by those deeming themselves entitled to better service, lower rates, fares, charges, freights, or tolls, from the regulated public utilities; by those believing that they are being treated unfairly or are discriminated against; by interested parties or governmental agencies who wish to prevent a violation of law; or by those seeking monetary reparation for damages. In most instances the statute providing for initiation of action upon the complaint of an individual also provides for initiation by the regulatory agency. In several instances public authorities may act as complainants.

Where the initiation of action is upon complaint, the regulatory agency acts somewhat in the nature of a judge, deciding a conflict between opposing parties.

Upon the initiation of the regulatory authority. The most general type of initiation of administrative order procedure is by the regulatory authorities themselves. By statute they are almost universally given this right except where they are dealing with applications for licenses, registrations, certificates, privileges, permits, approvals, grants, etc. This right is given them, as a rule, even though a right of complaint is granted by statute.

The regulatory authority may initiate action:

1. Where it believes the law is being violated or where violations are called to its attention.

2. It may also initiate action itself upon complaint, as explained above.

3. Since a regulatory authority is as a rule charged with the protection of the public interest, it may initiate action to further that interest, such as seeing that rates, charges, and fares are reasonable and that services are adequate.

4. It may initiate action in order to further its regulatory task by holding hearings before establishing accounting and reporting methods, for example, or making requirements as to the furnishing of statistics, and so on.

5. The regulatory authority may initiate action in order to further some functions required of it by Congress, such as making a valuation of the railroads, making an investigation of the packing industry, the electric industry, or any monopoly.

Where the regulatory authority initiates action it may do so in any one of several capacities: (1) prosecuting; (2) sublegislative; and (3) investigational.

1. As a prosecuting authority: Where, as a result of its investigations, or upon complaint, supplemented by its own investigations, the regulatory authority, believing that the law is being violated, issues an order to show cause or requires the one regulated to answer charges or complaints, it is in a sense acting as a prosecuting

authority. The hearing on whether or not there has been a violation is judicial in nature.

2. Sublegislative authority: The regulatory authority acts very much in a legislative capacity when it determines to hold hearings as to the reasonableness of rates, charges, fares, tolls, etc., or as to whether services are adequate, as to whether new accounting and reporting systems or new requirements as to safety should be laid down. The initiation of such action is legislative and has nothing to do with prosecution. Perhaps the largest field of regulatory activity is along these lines.

3. Investigational authority: The regulatory authority may hold hearings in order to see how the law is functioning, to obtain general information, or to gather information upon which Congress may act.

Initiation of action by the one falling within the sphere of regulation or who is being regulated. The ones regulated, as a rule, only initiate administrative action when they wish some favor of the regulatory authority, such as an exemption, the right to consolidate, pool, or merge, the granting of a registration, a clearance, a certificate of convenience and necessity, the privilege of using the mails in a certain way, permits to use United States property, the right to abandon facilities, or some type of grant, declaration, etc. It may be noted that the great majority of such initiations occur within the field of licenses, registrations, permits, approvals, grants, etc.

In cases where the initiation of action is in the hands of those regulated, the regulatory authority generally acts to a very large extent in a discretionary capacity. In many instances rather wide public interests may be involved, as for instance a request for the abandonment of a railroad line or a certificate of convenience and necessity in respect to a motor carrier. Since the initiating individual is not alone concerned, very often the hearing is public in nature.

II. NOTICE

In the great majority of instances order procedure demands a notice. There are certain statutory exceptions to this rule, however:

1. When the regulatory authority is acting for the government, which is one of the parties, but not an adverse party, as for instance in fixing rates for the transportation of mail.

2. Orders in respect to reports or accounts.

3. Where the order is merely procedural.

4. Where the service of the complaint acts as a notice.

5. At times where the order results from an investigation.

6. Where the one regulated is furnished a copy of the complaint and asked to satisfy it or show cause why he should not.

7. Where the order is issued by an agency of the government acting in a sovereign capacity.

8. Where no hearing is required before the issuance of an order.

9. Where there is an order requiring an individual to personally appear.

10. In some cases where applications, etc., are passed upon favorably without the necessity of a hearing.

There are several statutory statements as to the requirement of a notice. The most common type simply provides for a "notice." Other statements are that there shall be a "reasonable notice," "due notice," "appropriate notice," etc. In some instances, where important general rights are involved, the statutes provide for a "public notice." All of these statements seem to mean much the same thing.

III. HEARING

While it is the general rule that statutory orders require a hearing or an opportunity to be heard, there are certain exceptions. They are:

1. Orders in respect to accounts and reports.

2. Orders revoking or modifying other orders.

3. Certain types of procedural orders.

4. In a few instances the order issues as the result of an investigation rather than a hearing.

5. In respect to a few sovereign actions.

6. Where certificates of convenience and necessity, permits, licenses, etc., are revoked or changed upon the application of the one regulated.

7. In certain instances where the government acts in a proprietary way or in respect to the public domain.

8. Suspension or revocation of a prior approval.

9. Where the order is made by statute to depend upon the result of an administrative finding.

10. Where an order revokes a former order which placed burdens and obligations upon the one regulated.

11. Certain negative orders.

There are several different expressions in the statutes governing the requirement of a hearing, such as "full hearing," "hearing," "full opportunity for a hearing," "opportunity for a hearing," "after hearing," "hearing to show cause," "hearing upon the charges," "public hearing," "opportunity to be heard."

A comparison of these various statements as to hearing with the subject matter concerned seems to indicate that for the most part they can be used interchangeably, except perhaps "hearing to show cause," "hearing upon the charges," and "public hearing," each of which relates to a particular type of action or a particular economic situation.

IV. OTHER REQUIREMENTS

Although the provisions regarding who may initiate action and regarding notice and hearing are the most common procedural requirements established by statute, others occasionally appear. In a few instances the statutes determine who shall bear the burden of proof. A few say something concerning answers by the party complained of. A few statutes deal with rules of evidence in a negative way by providing that the common law rules of evidence shall not apply. No statute specifically lays down rules of evidence.

Some statutes expressly provide that testimony shall be reduced to writing, but much more often this must be implied from the statements regarding appeal, which provide that the authority that has issued the order must transmit to the court a transcript of the record. There is practically always a direct statement regarding the issuance of the order, although in a few instances this must be inferred from the fact that there is a notice and hearing procedure.

Such are the statutory provisions regarding procedure. For more detailed provisions one must look to the rules and regulations of the regulatory authorities themselves. The statutory requirements at least furnish the broad basis upon which regulatory procedure rests.

SUPPORTING STATEMENT X

STATUTORY PROCEDURE BEFORE REVIEW AUTHORITIES

Type of Procedure	Reviewing Court
Rules of Civil Procedure	United States District Courts District Court of the United States for the District of Columbia
Statutory Injunction Procedure— NOTE I	Three-judge district courts
Transcript of the Record Procedure—NOTE II	United States Circuit Courts of Appeals United States Court of Appeals for the District of Columbia
General Rules of Procedure of the Court of Claims—NOTE III	Court of Claims of the United States

NOTE I

Examples of Statutory Injunction Procedure: "No interlocutory injunction suspending or restraining the enforcement, operation, or execution of, or setting aside, in whole or in part, any order made or entered by the Interstate Commerce Commission shall be issued or granted by any district court of the United States, or by any judge thereof, or by any circuit judge acting as district judge, unless the application for the same shall be presented to a circuit or district judge, and shall be heard and determined by three judges, of whom at least one shall be a circuit judge, and unless a majority of said three judges shall concur in granting such application. When such application as aforesaid is presented to a judge, he shall immediately call to his assistance to hear and determine the application two other judges. Said application shall not be heard or determined before at least five days' notice of the hearing has been given to the Interstate Commerce Commission, to the Attorney General of the United States, and to such other persons as may be defendants in the suit: *Provided,* That in cases where irreparable damage would otherwise ensue to the petitioner, a majority of said three judges concurring, may, on hearing, after not less than three days' notice to the Interstate Commerce Commission and the Attorney General, allow a temporary stay or suspension, in whole or in part, of the operation of the order of the Interstate Commerce Commission for not more than sixty days from the date of the order of said judges pending the application for the order or injunction, in which case the said order shall contain a specific finding, based upon evidence submitted to the judges making the order and identified by reference thereto, that such irreparable damage would result to the petitioner and specifying the nature of the damage. The said judges may, at the time of hearing such application, upon a like finding, continue the temporary stay or suspension in whole or in part until decision upon the application. The hearing upon such application for an interlocutory injunction shall be given precedence and shall be in every way expedited and be assigned for a hearing at the earliest practicable day after the expiration of the notice hereinbefore provided for. An appeal may be taken direct to the Supreme Court of the United States from the order granting or denying, after notice and hearing, an interlocutory injunction, in such case if such appeal be taken within thirty days after the order, in respect to which complaint is made, is granted or refused; and upon the final hearing of any suit brought to suspend or set aside, in whole or in part, any order of said commission the same requirement as to judges and the same procedure as to expedition and appeal shall apply." 28 U.S.C. 47.

"A final judgment or decree of the district court in the cases specified in section 44 of this title may be reviewed by the Supreme Court of the United States if appeal to the Supreme Court be taken by an aggrieved party within sixty days after the entry of such final judgment or decree, and such appeals may be taken in like manner as appeals are taken under existing law in equity cases. And in such cases the notice required shall be served upon the defendants in the case and upon the attorney general of the State. The district court may direct the original record instead of a transcript thereof to be transmitted on appeal. The Supreme Court may affirm, reverse, or modify as the case may require, the final judgment or decree of the district court in the cases specified in section 44 of this title. Appeal to the Supreme Court, however, shall in no case supersede, or stay the judgment or decree of the district court appealed from, unless the Supreme Court or a justice thereof shall so direct, and appellant shall give bond in such form and of such amount as the Supreme Court or the justice of that court allowing the stay, may require. Appeals to the Supreme Court under this section and section 47 of this title shall have priority in hearing and determination over all other causes except criminal causes in that court." 28 U.S.C. 47a.

Remark: The procedure above is different in several points from that prescribed by the new Rules of Civil Procedure, which, however, govern in so far as they are applicable.

NOTE II

Example of Transcript of the Record Procedure: "(a) Any person aggrieved by an order issued by the Commission in a proceeding under this title to which such person is a party may obtain a review of such order in the Circuit Court of Appeals of the United States, within any circuit wherein such person resides or has his principal place of business, or in the United States Court of Appeals of the District of Columbia, by filing in such court, within sixty days after the entry of such order, a written petition praying that the order of the Commission be modified or set aside in whole or in part. A copy of such petition shall be forthwith served upon any member of the Commission, and thereupon the Commission shall certify and file in the court a transcript of the record upon which the order complained of was entered. Upon the filing of such transcript such court shall have exclusive jurisdiction to affirm, modify, and enforce or set aside such order, in whole or in part. No objection to the order of the Commission shall be considered by the court unless such objection shall have been urged before the Commission. The finding of the Commission as to the facts, if supported by substantial evidence, shall be conclusive. If either party shall apply to the court for leave to adduce additional evidence, and shall show to the satisfaction of the court that such additional evidence is material and that there were reasonable grounds for failure to adduce such evidence in the hearing before the Commission, the court may order such additional evidence to be taken before the Commission and to be adduced upon the hearing in such manner and upon such terms and conditions as to the court may seem proper. The Commission may modify its findings as to the facts, by reason of the additional evidence so taken, and it shall file such modified or new findings, which, if supported by substantial evidence, shall be conclusive, and its recommendation, if any, for the modification or setting aside of the original order. The judgment and decree of the court, affirming, modifying, and enforcing or setting aside, in whole or in part, any such order of the Commission, shall be final, subject to review by the Supreme Court of the United States upon certiorari or certification as provided in sections 239 and 240 of the Judicial Code, as amended.

"(b) The commencement of proceedings under subsection (a) shall not, unless specifically ordered by the court, operate as a stay of the Commission's order." 15 U.S.C. 78y.

NOTE III

The only orders reviewed directly by the Court of Claims deal with rates for the transportation of mail; and these are sent to the Court not by statute, but by judicial decision.

SUPPORTING STATEMENT XI

METHODS OF CONTROL OVER STATUTORY ADMINISTRATIVE ORDERS

There are eight different situations in respect to the review over administrative orders: (1) no review; (2) review upon enforcement only; (3) review by the Court of Claims; (4) review by district courts; (5) review by three-judge district court; (6) review by the circuit courts of appeals and the United States Court of Appeals for the District of Columbia; (7) review by the United States Court of Appeals for the District of Columbia alone; (8) administrative appeal only.

I. NO REVIEW OVER THE ORDER

There is no statutory control, except perhaps as to lack of jurisdiction or abuse of power, over the following orders:

I. Legislative orders:
    A. Orders in re accounting:
        Interstate Commerce Commission:
            1. Orders in re accounts, records, memoranda, etc., of railroads, 49 U. S. C. 20.
            2. Order in re forms and contents of accounts, records, and memoranda of motor carriers, 49 U. S. C. 320.
        Federal Power Commission:
            1. In re accounts of public utilities and licensees, 16 U. S. C. 825.
    B. Orders in re reports:
        Interstate Commerce Commission:
            In re filing of monthly reports of earnings and expenses and of periodical reports, 49 U. S. C. 20 (1), (2), (5), (6).
        Federal Power Commission:
            In re filing of periodic and special reports, 16 U. S. C. 825c.
    C. Orders in re valuation:
        Interstate Commerce Commission:
            Orders in re valuation of railways, 49 U. S. C. 19a.

D. Orders in re consolidations, mergers, acquiring control, etc.:

    Interstate Commerce Commission:

        In re consolidations, mergers, purchase, lease, acquiring control, etc., 49 U. S. C. 5 (4).[1]

E. Orders determining fact of competition:

    Interstate Commerce Commission:

        Order to determine questions of fact as to competition or possibility of competition between railroads and water carriers, 49 U. S. C. 5 (19), (20), (21).

F. Orders in re pooling arrangements:

    Interstate Commerce Commission:

        Orders in re pooling arrangements, division of traffic or earnings, 49 U. S. C. 5 (1).

G. Permissive orders:

    Securities and Exchange Commission:

        Order permitting registrant to file a preliminary registration statement, 15 U. S. C. 79e (c).

II. Procedural orders:

A. Orders for investigation:

    Interstate Commerce Commission:

        Orders for investigation and hearing as to rates, routes, routing of traffic, etc., 49 U. S. C. 15 (1).

B. Orders requiring the attendance of witnesses:

    Secretary of Labor:

        Orders requiring the attendance of witnesses and the production of evidence, 41 U. S. C. 39.

C. Orders dismissing proceedings:

    Securities and Exchange Commission:

        Order dismissing proceedings to review disciplinary action taken by a registered security association against a member thereof, 52 Stat. L. 1073.

D. Order to show cause:

    Securities and Exchange Commission:

        Order to show cause why a declaration by a registered holding company should become effective, 15 U. S. C. 79g (b).

---

[1] Does the fact that the Commission lays down terms and conditions and modifications in the public interest make the order appealable?

E. Orders requiring the furnishing of information:
>   Railroad Retirement Board:
>>   Order requiring all employers, employees, officers, boards, or other agencies to furnish information, 45 U. S. C. 228j.

F. Orders in re alteration of rules:
>   Securities and Exchange Commission:
>>   Alteration of rules and regulations of a registered securities association when it fails to make requested alterations or supplement them, 52 Stat L. 1074.

III. Administrative controlling orders:
>   Securities and Exchange Commission:
>>   Abrogation by a superior authority of rules and regulations made by an inferior authority, 52 Stat. L. 1074.[2]

IV. Orders in re licenses, etc.:

A. Orders in re registrations:
>   Securities and Exchange Commission:
>>   1. Order postponing the effective date of a registration, 15 U. S. C. 78o (b).
>>   2. Order canceling registration where a broker or dealer for whom an application is pending is no longer in existence or has ceased to do business, 15 U. S. C. 78o (b).[3]

B. Orders in re permits:
>   California Debris Commission:
>>   1. Order with requirements authorizing or refusing the carrying on of hydraulic mining, 33 U. S. C. 669-673.
>>   2. Order without requirements as to construction permitting hydraulic mining, 33 U. S. C. 673.
>   Federal Power Commission:
>>   Cancelation of a preliminary permit upon failure of permittees to comply with the conditions thereof, or for other good causes, 16 U. S. C. 798.

V. Orders in re declarations and designations:

[2] This is questionable as regards possibilities of review.
[3] There might possibly arise the question whether or not it was a fact that a person had ceased to do business.

Securities and Exchange Commission:
1. Order declaring that a registered holding company has ceased to be a holding company, 15 U. S. C. 79e (d).
2. Order revoking an order declaring a person to be a holding company, subsidiary company, or affiliate, 15 U. S. C. 79b (b).
3. Order permitting a declaration to become effective, 15 U. S. C. 79g (b).

II. REVIEW UPON ENFORCEMENT ONLY

I. Injunctive and command orders:
Division of the National Railroad Adjustment Board:
Order directed to a carrier to make an award of the division effective. Such order may also include a reparation order, 49 U. S. C. 153 (o).
II. Reparation and analogous orders:
Interstate Commerce Commission:
Reparation for injury done by carriers, 49 U. S. C. 8, 9, 13, 16.
Federal Communications Commission:
Orders for the payment of money or award of damages, 47 U. S. C. 206-209, 407.
Secretary of Agriculture:
Orders for reparation under the Packers and Stockyards Act, 7 U. S. C. 209, 210.[4]
United States Maritime Commission:
Orders for the payment of money, 46 U. S. C. 829, 1114.
National Railroad Adjustment Board:
In re disputes between an employee or group of employees and a carrier or carriers growing out of grievances or out of interpretations or application of agreements concerning rates of pay, rules, or working conditions where award concerns a requirement for the payment of money, 45 U. S. C. 153.

III. REVIEW BY COURT OF CLAIMS

I. Legislative orders:
A. Rate, fare, or charge orders:
Interstate Commerce Commission:
1. Orders fixing rates and compensation for carrying mail, 39 U. S. C. 542. See *U. S.*

[4] Also alternative method.

v. *Griffin*, 303 U. S. 226, 334, 335, 338,
and 28 U. S. C. 41 (6).

    2. Rates for transportation of mail matter by
urban and interurban electric railway common carrier, 39 U. S. C. 570. See also
U. S. v. *Griffin*, 303 U. S. 226, 334, 335,
338, and 28 U. S. C. 41 (6).

IV. REVIEW BY ONE-JUDGE DISTRICT COURT OR THE DISTRICT COURT OF THE UNITED STATES FOR THE DISTRICT OF COLUMBIA

I. Legislative orders:

    A. Rate, fare, charge, etc., orders:

        Interstate Commerce Commission:

            Orders fixing rates and compensation for carry-
ing mail; jurisdiction in equity, 39 U. S. C.
570. See 28 U. S. C. 41 (6).

    B. Cease and desist orders:

        Secretary of Agriculture:

            Orders in re monopolization or restraint of
trade by associations of agricultural producers,
7 U. S. C. 292.

        Secretary of Commerce:

            Orders to prevent monopolization or restraint
of trade in the fishing industry, 15 U. S. C.
522.

    C. Reparation and analogous orders:

        Secretary of Agriculture:

            Orders for damages under the Perishable Agri-
cultural Commodities Act, 7 U. S. C. 499g.

II. Penalty orders:

    Postmaster General:

        Fraud orders, 39 U. S. C. 259, 732.[5]

III. Orders in re licenses, etc.

    Tender boards:

        Denial of certificate of clearance for the shipment of
petroleum products, 15 U. S. C. 715d and Executive
Order Nos. 6979 and 6980.

    Federal Alcohol Administrator:

        Granting or denying permits as to interlocking direc-
tors, 27 U. S. C. 208.

    Commissioner of Internal Revenue:

        1. Revocation of permits for the manufacturing or deal-

[5] Bill in equity.

ing in denatured alcohol, 27 U. S. C. 154-156.

2. Revocation of permit to manufacture because of false description of denatured liquors, 27 U. S. C. 154.

Secretary of Agriculture:

1. Marketing agreement orders in respect to anti-hog-cholera serum and hog-cholera virus. Review upon ruling, 7 U. S. C. 852, 853, 854.[6]

2. Marketing agreement orders in respect to milk, fruit, tobacco, vegetables, soybeans, and naval stores. Review upon ruling, 7 U. S. C. 608c.[6]

3. Orders with or without marketing agreements, 7 U. S. C. 608b.

V. REVIEW BY THREE-JUDGE DISTRICT COURT

There is control by a three-judge district court under the Urgent Deficiencies Act in the following cases:

I. Legislative regulatory orders:

A. Rate, fare, charge, etc., orders:

Interstate Commerce Commission:

1. In re railroad rates, fares, charges, freights, 49 U. S. C. 15.

2. Rate orders of motor carriers, 49 U. S. C. 316-319.

3. Joint routes, rates, rules, regulations, and practices in re common carriers upon certain rivers, 49 U. S. C. 153(e).

Secretary of Agriculture:

1. Prescribing rates and practices in re stockyard services, 7 U. S. C. 206, 207, 211, 212, 216, 217.

2. Change or suspension of rates for stockyard services, 7 U. S. C. 206, 207, 211, 212, 216, 217.

Federal Communications Commission, in respect to interstate and foreign communications by wire or radio:

1. Orders on new charges, suspension of charges and refunds, 47 U. S. C. 203, 205, and 401-405.

2. Orders fixing just and reasonable charges, 47 U. S. C. 205.

[6] Review in equity.

B. Orders for the extension of facilities:
> Interstate Commerce Commission:
>> Orders requiring railroads to provide adequate facilities or to extend their lines, 49 U. S. C. 1 (21).

C. Interchangeable mileage:
> Interstate Commerce Commission:
>> In re interchangeable mileage or script coupon ticket, 49 U. S. C. 22 (2).

D. Orders in re consolidations, mergers, acquiring control, etc.:
> Interstate Commerce Commission:
>> In re consolidations, mergers, purchase, lease, acquiring control, etc., 49 U. S. C. 5(4).

E. Orders restricting voting power:
> Interstate Commerce Commission:
>> Orders restricting the exercise of voting power in respect to stock or share of capital stock in order to prevent subjecting one carrier to the control of another, 49 U. S. C. 5(11).

II. Injunctive and command orders:

A. Cease and desist orders:
> Secretary of Agriculture:
>> Orders in respect to charges or practices of stockyards, 7 U. S. C. 210-211.

B. Enforcement orders:
> Interstate Commerce Commission:
>> 1. Order compelling carrier or broker to comply with the provisions of the Motor Carrier Act or requirements, 49 U. S. C. 304(d).
>> 2. Order enforcing obedience to law prohibiting control or management in a common interest, 49 Stat. L. 556.
>> 3. Order requiring person in violation of law to take steps to prevent continuance of violation, 49 U. S. C. 5 (5)-(10).

III. Reparation orders:
> Secretary of Agriculture:
>> Orders for reparations under the Packers and Stockyards Act, 7 U. S. C. 209, 210.[7]

---

[7] There are evidently two methods of control. The other is to refuse to pay and then contest the suit to force payment by the individual benefiting by the order.

IV. Penalty orders:
    Interstate Commerce Commission:
        Safety orders in re railroads, 49 U. S. C. 26.
V. Orders in re licenses, registrations, certificates, privileges, permits,
    approvals, grants:
    A. Orders in re licenses:
        Secretary of Agriculture:
            1. Order revoking license of poultry dealers,
               7 U. S. C. 218d.
            2. Order suspending or revoking license of a
               perishable agricultural commission mer-
               chant, dealer, or broker, 7 U. S. C. 499
               h (a).
        Federal Communications Commission:
            Order revoking a station license, 47 U. S. C.
            312 (a).
        Interstate Commerce Commission:
            Suspension, change, revocation of a motor-
            carrier license, certificate, or permit, 49
            U. S. C. 304 (d), 312; 52 Stat. L. 1238-
            1239, amending the above.
    B. Orders in re certificates:
        Interstate Commerce Commission:
            1. Refusal to grant a certificate of convenience
               and necessity, permit, or license to com-
               mon carriers by motor vehicle, 49
               U. S. C. 306, 307, 309, 311.
            2. Suspension, revocation, or change of a cer-
               tificate of convenience and necessity, per-
               mit, or license, 49 U. S. C. 312.
    C. Orders in re permits:
        Interstate Commerce Commission:
            1. Order permitting continuance of vessel in
               operation or the installation of a new
               service, 49 U. S. C. 5 (20).
            2. Suspension, change in, or revocation of per-
               mits to motor carriers, 49 U. S. C. 304,
               305, 312.
            3. Denial of application for permit made by
               motor carriers, 49 U. S. C. 309 (b).
    D. Orders in re approvals:
        Interstate Commerce Commission:
            1. Refusal of requests for consolidations, merg-

ers, purchase, lease, operating, contract,
or acquisition of control of railway, 49
U. S. C. 5 (4).

2. Order approving and authorizing consolidations, merger, purchase, lease, operating
contracts, or acquisition of control of
motor carriers, 52 Stat. L. 1239.

E. Orders in re grants:

Interstate Commerce Commission:

Order refusing to grant an application for the
issue of securities in respect to railroads, 49
U. S. C. 20 (a).

VI. REVIEW BY THE CIRCUIT COURTS OF APPEALS AND THE UNITED STATES COURT OF APPEALS FOR THE DISTRICT OF COLUMBIA

I. Legislative regulatory orders:

A. Rate, fare, or charge order:

Federal Power Commission:

In respect to rates and charges by electric companies engaged in interstate commerce, 16
U. S. C. 824 (d), (e).

Civil Aeronautics Authority:

In re rates for transportation of mail, 52 Stat.
L. 998.

B. Wage orders:

Administrator under the Fair Labor Standards Act
of 1938, 52 Stat. L. 1064.

C. Price orders:

Director Bituminous Coal Division:

1. Orders in respect to the establishment of
maximum prices for coal, 15 U. S. C.
833 (c).

2. Due and reasonable maximum discounts or
price allowances, 15 U. S. C. 833 (h).

D. Orders for the extension of facilities:

Federal Power Commission:

Extension or improvement of facilities, 52 Stat.
L. 824.

E. Exemption orders:

Director Bituminous Coal Division:

Exemption from duty under Bituminous Coal
Code, 15 U. S. C. 834, 836 (b).

Securities and Exchange Commission:

Exemptions from provisions of the Public Utility
Holding Company Act, 15 U. S. C. 79c (a),
(b), (c), 79x (a).

F. Orders in re accounts and rates of depreciation:
Federal Power Commission:
1. Orders in re accounts, 16 U. S. C. 825
(a)-(c), 825a, b, c, 825l (a), (b).[8]
2. Orders in re rates of depreciation, 16
U. S. C. 825a, 825l (b), (c).

G. Orders requiring allocation and apportionment of costs:
Securities and Exchange Commission:
In re allocation and apportionment of costs
among members of a mutual service company, 15 U. S. C. 79m (c), 79x (b).

H. Orders for simplification:
Securities and Exchange Commission:
Limiting the operations of holding companies to
a single integrated public utility system, 15
U. S. C. 79k.

I. Orders establishing classes:
Securities and Exchange Commission:
Establishing classes of persons or matters for
purpose of making rules, regulations, or orders, 15 U. S. C. 79t (c), 79x.

J. Order revoking or modifying other orders:
Securities and Exchange Commission:
1. Order revoking an exemption order, 15
U. S. C. 79c (c), 79x.
2. Order revoking or modifying order previously made in re simplification of holding company system, 15 U. S. C. 79k
(b), (2), 79x.

K. Orders in re declaration of status:
Securities and Exchange Commission:
Order declaring a person to be a holding company, a subsidiary company or an affiliate or
declaring a class of which such person is a
member or affiliate, 15 U. S. C. 79b (b),
79x.

L. Orders fixing limits:
Commodity Exchange Commission:
Orders fixing limits on amount of trading un-

---

[8] This is questionable, but statute does provide for notice and hearing.

der contracts of sale of commodities for future delivery, 7 U. S. C. 6a, 9.

M. Orders establishing rules and regulations:
Secretary of Agriculture:
Orders in respect to the issue, amendment, or
repeal of regulations, 52 Stat. L. 1055,
1056.

II. Administrative controlling orders:
Securities and Exchange Commission:
Abrogation by a superior authority of rules and regulations made by an inferior authority, 52 Stat. L. 1074,
15 U. S. C. 78y.[9]

III. Injunctive and command orders:
A. Cease and desist orders:
Secretary of Agriculture:
In respect to unlawful practices of packers, 7
U. S. C. 191-195.
Commodity Exchange Commission:
In re violations of rules and regulations or orders in re contract markets, 7 U. S. C. 13a.
National Labor Relations Board:
Orders in re unfair labor practices with affirmative order, 29 U. S. C. 160 (b)-(h).
Federal Trade Commission:
1. In re unfair methods of competition and
unfair or deceptive acts or practices in
commerce, 15 U. S. C. 45, 45 (c).
2. Orders terminating discrimination, 15
U. S. C. 13 (a), (b), 21.
3. Orders in re lease, sale, contract for sale of
commodities or fixing a price discount or
rebate thereon, or agreement not to use
goods of a competitor, 15 U. S. C. 14, 21.
4. Orders in re acquisition by one corporation
of stock of another, 15 U. S. C. 18, 21.
Interstate Commerce Commission:
1. Acquisition by one railroad corporation of
the stock of another, 15 U. S. C. 18, 21.
2. Interlocking railroad directors or officers, 15
U. S. C. 19, 21.
Federal Communications Commission:
1. Discrimination in re services or facilities, 15
U. S. C. 13a, 21.

[9] This appeal is questionable.

2. Acquisition by one corporation of the stock of another, 15 U. S. C. 18, 21.

Board of Governors of the Federal Reserve System:

1. Acquisition by one corporation of the stock of another, 15 U. S. C. 18, 21.

2. Interlocking directors or officers, 15 U. S. C. 19, 21.

B. Enforcement orders:

Civil Aeronautics Authority:

Order requiring obedience to law and the requirements thereunder, 52 Stat. L. 1018, 1024, 1025.

IV. Penalty orders:

Securities and Exchange Commission:

1. Suspending or revoking the registration of a registered securities association, 52 Stat. L. 1075, 15 U. S. C. 78y.

2. Order suspending or expelling a member from a registered securities association, 52 Stat. L. 1074, 15 U. S. C. 78y.

3. Removal from office of any officer or director of the registered securities association, 52 Stat. L. 1075, 15 U. S. C. 78y.

Commodity Exchange Commission:

Order controlling, excluding, or debarring an association or corporation from trading in a contract market, 7 U. S. C. 10a.

V. Orders in re licenses, etc.:

A. Orders in re licenses:

Foreign Trade Zones Board:

Revocation of grant privilege of establishing, operating, or maintaining foreign trade zones, 19 U. S. C. 81a-81s.

Secretary of the Treasury:

Order suspending or revoking licenses as a custom-house broker, 19 U. S. C. 1641 (b).

B. Orders in re registrations:

Securities and Exchange Commission:

1. Order refusing to let a registration become effective, 15 U. S. C. 77h (b), 77i (a), (b).

2. Stop orders in re registration statements, 15 U. S. C. 77h (d), 77i (a), (b).

3. Orders denying registration of a national

security exchange, 15 U. S. C. 78f (e),
78y.

4. Order denying or revoking a registration to
a broker or dealer, 15 U. S. C. 78o
(b), 78y.

5. Order canceling registration, 15 U. S. C.
78o (b), 78y.

6. Denial of an application to declare that a
registered holding company has ceased to
be a holding company, 15 U. S. C. 79e
(d), 79x.[10]

C. Orders in re certificates:

Director Bituminous Coal Division:

Revocation of a certificate to a right of exemption from taxes, 15 U. S. C. 830-836.

Civil Aeronautics Authority:

Order in re certificate of public convenience
and necessity for air carriers, 52 Stat. L.
987, 1024-1025.

D. Orders in re privileges:

Secretary of Agriculture:

Order withdrawing privilege to trade in a contract market, 7 U. S. C. 9.

E. Orders in re permits:

Federal Alcohol Administration:

Denial of or revocation, suspension, or annul-
ment of a basic permit, 27 U. S. C. 204.

Civil Aeronautics Authority:

Modification, suspension, or revocation of permits to foreign air carriers, 52 Stat. L. 991-
992, 1024.

F. Orders in re approvals:

Federal Power Commission:

1. Orders approving the assumption of liabilities of interstate public utilities, 16
U. S. C. 824c, 825l (b).[11]

2. Order disapproving the assumption of liabilities by interstate utilities, 16 U. S. C.
824c, 825l (b).

[10] Is questionable if appeal lies.
[11] This is questionable.

3. Order refusing approval for abandonment of facilities or service of interstate natural-gas company, 52 Stat. L. 824, 825.

Director Bituminous Coal Division:

Suspending or revoking prior approval of co-operative marketing of coal, 15 U. S. C. 842.

Civil Aeronautics Authority:

1. Refusal of approval for consolidation, merger, purchase, lease, operating contract, or acquisition of control of air carriers, 52 Stat. L. 1001-1002, 1024.

2. Refusal of approval of an air carrier to have and retain an officer or director who is an officer, director, or member, or who, as a stockholder, holds a controlling interest in any other person who is a common carrier or is engaged in any phase of aeronautics, etc., 52 Stat. L. 1002-1003.

G. Declarations:

Securities and Exchange Commission:

1. Orders declaring a person to be a holding company, a subsidiary company, or an affiliate or declaring a class of which such person is an affiliated member, 15 U. S. C. 79b (b), 79x (a).

2. Order refusing to let a declaration become effective, 15 U. S. C. 79g (b), 79x.[12]

Secretary of Agriculture:

Refusal to designate a board of trade as a contract market, 7 U. S. C. 7, 8.

Commodity Exchange Commission:

Suspension or revocation of designation of board of trade as a contract market, 7 U. S. C. 8.

VI. Negative orders:

Secretary of Agriculture:

Order determining not to act, 52 Stat. L. 1055, 1056.

Civil Aeronautics Authority:

Negative orders in re regulation of aviation, 52 Stat. L. 1024.

[12] This is questionable.

VII. REVIEW BY THE UNITED STATES COURT OF APPEALS FOR THE DISTRICT OF COLUMBIA ALONE

I. Legislative orders:
    A. Quota and allotment orders:
        Secretary of Agriculture:
            Orders in re sugar and liquid sugar, 7 U. S. C. 1115, 1116.

II. Orders in re licenses, etc.:
    A. Orders in re licenses:
        Federal Communications Commission:
            Suspension of license of radio operator, 47 U. S. C. 303 (m), (1), (2) 402 (b) (3).

VIII. ADMINISTRATIVE APPEAL ONLY

I. Legislative orders:
    A. Price orders:
        Secretary of Agriculture:
            In re fixing of minimum price to be paid to or maximum quantities to be marketed by producers or associations of producers of agricultural products.
                1. Orders with marketing agreements, 7 U. S. C. 602, 608, 608 (c).[13]
                2. Orders with or without marketing agreements, 7 U. S. C. 608 c.[13]
    B. Orders in re licenses:
        Director of the Bureau of Mines:
            1. Revocation of a license to deal in explosives, 50 U. S. C. 131-132.
            2. Refusal of a license to deal in explosives, 50 U. S. C. 134.

[13] The judicial appeal is on the ruling and not on the order.

SUPPORTING STATEMENT XII

THE JURISDICTION OF CONSTITUTIONAL COURTS

Courts established under the specific power given in Section 2 of Article III of the Constitution are called constitutional courts. They share in the exercise of the judicial power defined in that section and can be invested with no other jurisdiction. Their jurisdiction is limited to the classes of cases and controversies there named. *Ex parte Bakelite Corporation* (279 U.S. 438), *Aetna Life Insurance Co.* v. *Haworth* (300 U.S. 227).

A case or controversy under the Constitution is a definite and concrete dispute touching the legal relations of parties having adverse legal interests, and coming to the courts in such a way that they can decide it and give judgment. *Aetna Life Insurance Co.* v. *Haworth* (300 U.S. 227); *Marbury* v. *Madison* (1 Cranch 137); *Muskrat* v. *United States* (219 U.S. 346); *In re Pacific Ry. Commission* (32 Fed. Rep. 241, 255); *Chisholm* v. *Georgia* (2 Dall. 419); *Cohens* v. *Virginia* (6 Wheat. 264).

" We do not consider Congress can either withdraw from judicial cognizance any matter which, from its nature, is the subject of a suit at the common law, or in equity, or admiralty; nor, on the other hand, can it bring under the judicial power a matter which, from its nature, is not a subject for judicial determination. At the same time, there are matters, involving public rights, which may be presented in such form that the judicial power is capable of acting on them, and which are susceptible of judicial determination, but which Congress may or may not bring within the cognizance of the courts of the United States, as it may deem proper." *Murray* v. *Hoboken Co.* (18 How. 272, 274); *Fong Yue Ting* v. *U. S.* (149 U. S. 698, 715); *Tutun* v. *U. S.* (270 U. S. 568).

The courts will take jurisdiction if the proceeding "involves a right which in its nature is susceptible of judicial determination, and if the determination of it by the Court of Claims and by this

333

court is not simply ancillary or advisory, but is the final and indisputable basis of action by the parties." *La Abra Silver Mining Co. v. United States* (175 U. S. 423, 457).

The courts will take jurisdiction of justiciable questions as to which they can give final judgments. *La Abra Silver Mining Co. v. U. S.* (175 U. S. 423); *Gordon v. U. S.* (117 U. S. 697); *I. C. C. v. Brimson* (154 U. S. 447, 487).

The court will determine only matters actually in controversy essential to the decision of the particular case before it. *U. S. v. Alaska Steamship Co.* (253 U. S. 113); *California v. San Pablo and Tulare R. R. Co.* (149 U. S. 308, 314); *U. S. v. Hamburg-American Line* (239 U. S. 466, 475, 476).

Before there can be a justiciable case or controversy there must be parties. *Old Colony Trust Co. v. Commissioner of Internal Revenue* (279 U. S. 716); *Massachusetts v. Mellon* (262 U. S. 447, 487); *New York v. Illinois* (274 U. S. 488).

The parties must be adverse in interest. *South Spring Hill Gold Mining Co. v. Amador Medeon Gold Mining Co.* (145 U. S. 300); *Fairchild v. Hughes* (258 U. S. 126); *Massachusetts v. Mellon* (262 U. S. 447, 487).

The interest of the plaintiff must be definite and specific. *New Jersey v. Sargent* (269 U. S. 328); *Massachusetts v. Mellon* (262 U. S. 447).

The plaintiff must have a substantial interest in the matter brought for adjudication. *Fairchild v. Hughes* (258 U. S. 126); *Massachusetts v. Mellon* (262 U. S. 447).

There must be a definite cause for action, and not mere doubts as to the legality of a proposed action. *Willing v. Chicago Auditorium Association* (277 U. S. 274).

The courts will not give advisory opinions upon a hypothetical state of facts. *Nashville, C. and St. L. R. v. Wallace* (288 U. S. 249, 262, 264); *Ashwander v. Tennessee Valley Authority* (297 U. S. 288, 325), *Aetna Life Insurance Co. v. Haworth* (300 U. S. 227, 239).

The courts are not always given jurisdiction when the United States creates a right in individuals against itself. *U. S. v. Babcock* (250 U. S. 328, 331); *U. S. ex rel. Dunlap v. Black* (128 U. S.

40); *Ex parte Atocha* (17 Wall. 439); *Gordon* v. *U. S.* (7 Wall. 188, 195); *De Groot* v. *U. S.* (5 Wall. 419, 431-433); *Comegys* v. *Vasse* (1 Pet. 191, 212).

The courts will not take jurisdiction of an appeal from an administrative determination which is the exclusive remedy provided in a statute that creates a right. *U. S.* v. *Babcock* (250 U. S. 328, 331); *Wilder Mfg. Co.* v. *Corn Products Refining Co.* (236 U. S. 165); *Arnson* v. *Murphy* (109 U. S. 238); *Barnet* v. *National Bank* (98 U. S. 555); *Farmers' and Mechanics' National Bank* v. *Dearing* (91 U. S. 29).

The courts will take jurisdiction when Congress provides for review of the action of commissioners and boards created by it while exercising only quasi-judicial powers, by a transfer of their proceedings and decisions to judicial tribunals for examination and determination *de novo*. *Stephens* v. *Cherokee Nation* (174 U. S. 445). See also *Calder* v. *Bull* (3 Dallas 386); *Sampeyreac* v. *U. S.* (7 Pet. 222); *Freeborn* v. *Smith* (2 Wall. 160); *Garrison* v. *N. Y.* (21 Wall. 196); *Freeland* v. *Williams* (131 U. S. 405); *Essex Public Road Board* v. *Skinkle* (140 U. S. 334).

A case may be based upon an appeal from administrative action, provided that the necessary features for invoking the judicial power are present. *Old Colony Trust Co.* v. *Commissioner of Internal Revenue* (279 U. S. 716); *In re Pacific Ry. Commission* (32 Fed. Rep. 241, 255); *Muskrat* v. *U. S.* (219 U. S. 346).

In order that there may be a case regarding administrative action, it is not necessary that the proceedings, to be judicial, shall be entirely *de novo*. *Old Colony Trust Co.* v. *Commissioner of Internal Revenue* (279 U. S. 716); *Tagg Bros. and Moorhead* v. *U. S.* (280 U. S. 420).

Where there is no final administrative order, but only a report or direction, or preliminary or procedural or interlocutory order, the courts will not take jurisdiction. *U. S.* v. *Atlanta, Birmingham and Coast Railroad Co.* (282 U. S. 522); *U. S.* v. *Illinois Central Railroad Co.* (244 U. S. 82, 89); *Chicago Junction case* (264 U. S. 258); *Ames Baldwin Wyoming Co.* v. *National Labor Relations Board* (73 F. (2d) 489); *Securities and Exchange Commission* v. *Andrews* (88 Fed. R. 2d, 441); *Shannahan* v.

U. S. (303 U. S. 596); *Lehigh Valley Ry. Co* v. *U. S.* (243 U. S. 412).

Negative orders of administrative agents or agencies are not in general subject to judicial review, when they do not affect the existing legal situation. *Piedmont and Northern Ry.* v. *U. S.* (280 U. S. 469); *Lehigh Valley Ry. Co.* v. *U. S.* (243 U. S. 412); *U. S.* v. *Griffin* (303 U. S. 226); *Great Northern Ry Co.* v. *U. S.* (277 U. S. 172); *Procter and Gamble Co.* v. *U. S.* (225 U. S. 282, 292); *I. C. C.* v. *U. S. ex rel. Campbell* (289 U. S. 385); *Standard Oil Co.* v. *U. S.* (283 U. S. 235); *Alton R. Co.* v. *U. S.* (287 U. S. 229); *Baltimore and Ohio Railroad* v. *Brady* (288 U. S. 448).

But when an order negative in form is affirmative in effect, and denies a substantial right, the courts will take jurisdiction. *Baltimore and Ohio Railroad* v. *U. S.* (298 U. S. 349); *Atchison, Topeka and Santa Fe Ry. Co.* v. *U. S.* (284 U. S. 248). Compare *Rochester Telephone Corp.* v. *U. S.* (307 U. S. 125). This rule is not to be extended to insignificant matters, *U. S.* v. *Northern Pacific Ry. Co.* (288 U. S. 490).

The courts may be called in by Congress to ascertain contested facts on which an alien's right to be in this country has been made by Congress to depend. *Fong Yue Ting* v. *U. S.* (149 U. S. 698, 713, 714); *Murray* v. *Hoboken Co.* (18 How. 272, 284); *In re Fassett* (142 U. S. 479, 486); *Passavant* v. *U. S.* (148 U. S. 214).

The general right of a citizen to have the government administered according to law does not give him a right to bring suit with the object of securing by indirection a determination whether a statute, if passed, or a constitutional amendment, if adopted, will be valid. *Fairchild* v. *Hughes* (258 U. S. 126); *Giles* v. *Harris* (189 U. S. 475); *Tyler* v. *Judges of Court of Registration* (179 U. S. 405); *Texas* v. *I. C. C.* (258 U. S. 158, 162); *Stearns* v. *Wood* (236 U. S. 75).

Generally speaking, the award of execution is an essential part of the judicial power. See opinion prepared by Taney for *Gordon* v. *U. S.* (2 Wall. 561, published in 117 U. S. 697); *La Abra Silver Mining Co.* v. *U. S.* (175 U. S. 423, 457).

But where there is a concrete case admitting of an immediate and definitive determination of the rights of the parties in an adversary proceeding upon the facts alleged, the judicial function may be appropriately exercised, although the adjudication of the rights of the litigants may not require the award of a process or the payment of damages. *Aetna Life Insurance Co.* v. *Haworth* (300 U. S. 227, 241); *Nashville, C. and St. L. R. Co.* v. *Wallace* (288 U. S. 249, 263); *Tutun* v. *U. S.* (270 U. S. 568, 576); *Fidelity National Bank v. Swope* (274 U. S. 123, 132); *Old Colony Trust Co.* v. *Commissioner of Internal Revenue* (279 U. S. 716, 725).

Article III, Section 2, of the Constitution does not extend the judicial power to every possible injury to persons, but only "to a case in law or equity, in which a right, under such law, is asserted in a court of justice. If the question cannot be brought into court, then there is no case in law or equity." *Cohens* v. *Virginia* (6 Wheat. 264); *Smith* v. *Adams* (130 U. S. 167); *La Abra Mining Co.* v. *U. S.* (175 U. S. 423, 455).

The judicial power does not extend to the determination of abstract questions. *Ashwander* v. *Tennessee Valley Authority* (297 U. S. 288, 324); *Nashville, C. and St. L. R. Co.* v. *Wallace* (288 U. S. 249, 262, 264); *New York* v. *Illinois* (274 U. S. 488); *Aetna Life Insurance Co.* v. *Haworth* (300 U. S. 227, 242).

Claims based merely upon potential invasions of rights are not enough to warrant judicial intervention. *Arizona* v. *California* (283 U. S. 423, 462); *Ashwander* v. *Tennessee Valley Authority* (297 U. S. 288, 324); *New York* v. *Illinois* (274 U. S. 488).

The courts will not take jurisdiction of a moot case. *Singer Mfg. Co.* v. *Wright* (141 U. S. 696); *U. S.* v. *Alaska S. S. Co.* (253 U. S. 113); *Barker Painting Co.* v. *Painters Union* (281 U. S. 462).

The judicial power does not extend to an issue of constitutional law framed by Congress for the purpose of invoking the advice of this court without real parties or a real case. *Keller* v. *Potomac Elec. Power Co.* (261 U. S. 428, 444); *Hayburn's case* (2 Dall. 409, 410, note): *U. S.* v. *Ferreira* (13 How. 40, 52); *Ex parte Siebold* (100 U. S. 371, 398); *Gordon* v. *U. S.* (117 U. S. 697); *B. and O. R. R. Co.* v. *I. C. C.* (215 U. S. 216); *Texas* v. *I. C. C.* (258 U. S. 158).

The constitutional courts will not decide administrative questions. *Keller* v. *Potomac Elec. Power Co.* (261 U. S. 428, 444); *Postum Cereal Co.* v. *California Fig Nut Co.* (272 U. S. 693); *Muskrat* v. *U. S.* (219 U. S. 346); *Federal Radio Commission* v. *General Electric Co.* (281 U. S. 464).

The discretion of the court may not be substituted for that of administrative officers who have kept within the bounds of their administrative power. *Amer. Tel and Tel. Co.* v. *U. S.* (299 U. S. 232); *Kansas City Southern Ry. Co.* v. *U. S.* (231 U. S. 423, 444); *Norfolk and Western Ry. Co.* v. *U. S.* (287 U. S. 134, 141); *I. C. C.* v. *Goodrich Transit Co.* (224 U. S. 194, 211).

SUPPORTING STATEMENT XIII

THE WALTER-LOGAN BILL

76TH CONGRESS
1ST SESSION

S. 915

IN THE SENATE OF THE UNITED STATES

JULY 27 (legislative day, JULY 25), 1939
Ordered to be printed as passed by the Senate

AN ACT[1]

To provide for the more expeditious settlement of disputes
with the United States, and for other purposes.

*Be it enacted by the Senate and House of Representatives of
the United States of America in Congress assembled,*

DEFINITIONS

SECTION 1. As used in this Act, unless the context otherwise
requires—

(1) "Administrative rules" include rules, regulations, orders,
and amendments thereto of general application issued by officers
in the executive branch of the United States Government interpreting the terms of statutes they are respectively charged with
administering.

(2) "Administrative officers" means officers and employees
in the executive branch, except the President of the United States.

(3) "Agency" means any department, independent establishment, administration, corporation, or other subdivision of the
executive branch of the United States Government with one
chief officer as the immediate head thereof.

---

[1] After a bill has been passed by one house the caption "a bill" is changed to
"an act."

(4) "Independent agency" means any board, commission, authority, corporation, or other subdivision of the executive branch of the United States Government with two or more officers at the head thereof as board, commission, or other members.

(5) "Circuit court of appeals" means the United States Circuit Court of Appeals and the United States Court of Appeals for the District of Columbia.

(6) "Days" means calendar days, exclusive of Sundays and national holidays.

(7) "Person" includes individuals, corporations, partnerships, or other organizations.

(8) "Decision" means any affirmative or negative decision, order, or Act in specific controversies which determines the issue therein involved.

(9) "Controversy" means any dispute or disagreement concerning any claim, right, or obligation for or against the United States and any refusal to grant any license, permit, or other privilege.

IMPLEMENTING ADMINISTRATIVE RULES

SEC. 2. (a) Hereafter administrative rules and all amendments or modifications or supplements of existing rules implementing or filling in the details of any statute affecting the rights of persons or property shall be issued by the head of the agency and by each independent agency respectively charged with the administration of any statute only after publication of notice and public hearings. All such rules shall be published in the Federal Register within ten days after the date of their approval by the head of the agency or the independent agency concerned, and shall not become effective until such publication, except when the President declares that a public emergency exists.

(b) Administrative rules under all statutes hereafter enacted shall be issued as herein provided within one year after the date of the enactment of the statute subject to the adoption thereafter of further rules from time to time as provided in this act.

(c) Any person substantially interested in the effects of an administrative rule in force on the date of the approval of this Act may petition the head of the agency or the independent agency which administers any statute under which the rule was issued for a reconsideration of any such rule; and the head of such agency or the independent agency shall, after publication of notice and public hearing, if requested within ten days thereafter, determine whether such rule shall be continued in force, modified, or rescinded. All amendments of such rules shall be in accordance with the procedure provided in subsection (a) of this section and all action of the head of such agency or the independent agency on such petitions and all new or amended rules shall be published in the Federal Register as prescribed in said subsection (a) for the publication of rules.

(d) No person shall be penalized or subjected to any forfeiture or prosecuted for any act done or omitted to be done in good faith in conformity with a rule which has been rescinded or declared invalid by any final judgment entered as hereinafter provided, unless the act was done or omitted to be done more than thirty days after the publication in the Federal Register of the rescission or final determination of the invalidity of such rule.

JUDICIAL REVIEW OF RULES

SEC. 3. In addition to the jurisdiction heretofore conferred upon the United States Court of Appeals for the District of Columbia, that court shall have jurisdiction, upon petition filed within thirty days from the date any administrative rule is published in the Federal Register, to hear and determine whether any such rule issued or continued in force in accordance with section 2 of this Act is in conflict with the Constitution of the United States or the statute under which issued. No rule shall be held invalid except for violation of the Constitution or for conflict with a statute or for lack of authority conferred upon the agency issuing it by the statute or statutes pursuant to which it was issued or for failure to comply with section 2 of this Act. A copy of the petition, and copies of all subsequent pleadings shall be served upon the Attorney General of the United States, who shall direct the defense of the rule. The court may refer such petition and any reply thereto for the taking of such evidence as shall be material and relevant thereto. The court shall give preference to such petitions and shall have no power in the proceedings except to render a declaratory judgment holding such rule legal and valid or holding it contrary to law and invalid. If the rule is held contrary to law and invalid, the rule thereafter shall not have any force or effect except to confer immunity as provided in section 2 of this Act. Nothing contained in this section shall prevent the determination of the validity or invalidity of any rule which may be involved in any suit or review of an administrative decision or order in any court of the United States as now or hereafter authorized by law.

STATUTORY APPROVAL AND AUTHORITY FOR ADMINISTRATIVE BOARDS AND PRESCRIBING THEIR PROCEDURE

SEC. 4. (a) Every head of an agency shall from time to time designate three employees of his agency for such intra-agency boards (including the field service of such agency) as may be necessary and desirable. Where there are intra-agency boards existing on the date of approval of this Act, they shall be reestablished and function in accordance with this Act. Wherever practicable, such boards shall be designated in various sections of the United States to hear any controversy which may have there arisen. At least one employee designated for each such board shall be a lawyer, who shall act as chairman of the board. When the members of any board are not engaged in the hearing of administrative appeals as hereinafter provided, such employees shall be assigned to other duties in the service of the agency concerned. No member of a board who has participated in a particular case or in the preparation, draft, or approval of any rule which may be involved, shall sit in appeal of the case or application of the rule. Each board shall be impartial, free, and independent in the hearing and determination of administrative appeals.

(b) When any person is aggrieved by a decision of any officer or employee of any agency, such person may notify the head of the agency in writing of objections thereto, specifically requesting that the controversy be referred to a board, constituted as hereinbefore provided, for hearing and determination. Such notice shall be given not more than twenty days after the date of receipt of a registered letter notifying him of the decision, act, or failure to act. Such written objections shall be referred promptly to an intra-agency board for the agency concerned. At a time and place to be designated and communicated to the aggrieved person, he shall have an opportunity at an early day for a full and fair hearing before said board, at which time there shall be introduced into the record the testimony and any documents or objects relating to the appeal before said board. Any person having a substantial interest in the controversy shall have the right to intervene herein. A stenographer shall be assigned to the hearings before the board to take and transcribe the testimony. All testimony, other evidence, and all proceedings before the board, shall be reduced to a written record and filed in the agency concerned and a copy thereof shall be furnished to the aggrieved person upon his written request therefor at a charge not exceeding the actual cost thereof. Within thirty days after the day the evidence and arguments are closed, the board shall make written findings of facts and separate decision thereon, which shall be subject to the written approval, disapproval, or modification of the head of the agency concerned or of such person as he shall designate in writing to act for him. A copy of the findings of fact and decision, showing the action if any, of the head of the agency concerned or his representative, shall be filed in the agency as a part of the written record in the case and a copy shall be mailed to the aggrieved person and to the intervenors, if any. The United States shall take such action as may now or hereafter be provided by law to enforce the decision of the agency unless there be pending judicial review thereof as hereinafter provided.

(c) The chairman of any board, upon request of any party to the proceedings, shall require by subpena the attendance and testimony of witnesses and the production of documents and all other objects before said board without other showing than required by the rules in United States district courts for the issuance of subpenas by such courts. Any witness subpenaed or whose deposition is taken shall receive the same fees and mileage as witnesses in courts of the United States, to be paid by the party at whose instance the witness appears or deposition is taken. In the event of disobedience of a subpena issued as herein provided, the chairman, or any party to the proceedings, may apply to any district court of the United States of the jurisdiction in which the witness may be found for an order requiring his attendance and testimony and the production of all documents and objects described in the subpena. The chairman of the board shall be authorized to administer oaths to witnesses and there shall be a right of examination and cross-examination of witnesses.

(d) When the matter in controversy is such that the delay incident to the hearing and decision of the case would create an emergency contrary to the public interest and there is administrative action or inaction, prior to or without such hearing and determination, resulting in the destruction of the property or damage to the aggrieved person involved in such controversy, the findings of fact and decision when made by the board shall state the amount of pecuniary damage suffered by the aggrieved person and upon approval thereof by the head of the agency concerned, the amount of damages so approved, if acceptable to the aggrieved person, shall be certified to the Congress for an appropriation with which to pay the same.

(e) Where any matter arises out of the activities of any independent agency, it may be provided by rule that such matter may be heard in the first instance by one of its trial examiners, who shall file with the independent agency the written record and his written findings of fact and separate decision, which shall be made in all instances, whether by the examiner or the independent agency, after reasonable public notice and a full and fair hearing as hereinbefore in this section provided. A copy or copies thereof shall be sent by registered mail to the aggrieved party. The independent agency shall enter at the expiration of thirty days such appropriate decision as may be proper unless within said thirty days the aggrieved party shall signify his written consent to the entry of the decision or shall file by registered mail with the independent agency his written objections to the findings of fact and decision of the examiner, in which event the independent agency shall not enter its decision without first according a public hearing upon reasonable notice to such party. Such hearing shall be before the members of the independent agency, if it has not less than three members, or before any three of such members. If the independent agency has less than three members, an intra-agency board shall be constituted in the manner provided in subsection (a) of this section, upon which the member or members of such agency may serve at his or their election.

(f) No hearing shall be permitted before any agency or independent agency seeking affirmative relief against the United States concerning any controversy which arose more than one year prior to the date on which there was filed with such agency or independent agency a written request for such hearing as provided in this section.

JUDICIAL REVIEW OF DECISIONS OR ORDERS OF ADMINISTRATIVE AGENCIES

SEC. 5. (a) Any party to a proceeding before any agency or independent agency as provided in section 4 of this Act who may be aggrieved by the final decision or order of any agency, or independent agency, as the case may be, within thirty days after the date of receipt of a copy thereof, may at his election file a written petition (1) with the clerk of the United States Court of Appeals for the District of Columbia; or (2) with the clerk of the circuit court of appeals within whose jurisdiction such aggrieved party resides or maintains his principal place of business or in which the controversy arose, for review of the decision. Before filing a petition such party may within ten days make a motion to the agency or independent agency concerned for a rehearing, tendering a statement of any further showing to be made thereon which shall constitute a part of the record, and the time for appeal shall run from the order on such motion if denied or the order made on such rehearing if a rehearing shall be had. The petition shall state the alleged errors in the decision of the agency or independent agency concerned. The Attorney General of the United States and the agency or independent agency shall each be served with a copy of the petition and it shall be the duty of the Attorney General of the United States to cause appearance to be entered on behalf of the United States within thirty days after the date of receipt by him of a copy of the petition and it shall be the duty of the agency or independent agency, as the case may be, within thirty days or such longer time as the court may by order direct, after receipt of a copy of the petition to cause to be prepared and filed with the clerk of such court the original or a full and accurate transcript of the entire record in such proceeding before such agency or independent agency. The court may affirm or set aside the decision or may direct the agency or independent agency concerned to modify its decision. Any case may be remanded for such further evidence as in the discretion of the court may be required but no objection not urged before the agency or independent agency, as the case may be, shall be considered by the court unless the failure or neglect to urge such objection shall be excused by the court for good cause shown. To facilitate the hearing of such appeals and avoid delay in the hearing of other matters before the court, such court may constitute special sessions thereof to consist of any three judges competent in law to sit as judges of a circuit court of appeals, which special sessions may be held concurrently with the regular sessions of said court. Any decision of any agency or independent agency shall be set aside if it is made to appear to the satisfaction of the court (1) that the findings of fact are clearly erroneous; or (2) that the findings of fact are not supported by substantial evidence; or (3) that the decision is not supported by the findings of fact; or (4) that the decision was issued without due notice and a reasonable opportunity having been afforded the aggrieved party for a full and fair hearing; or (5) that the decision is beyond the jurisdiction of the agency or independent agency, as the case may be; or (6) that the decision infringes the Constitution or statutes of the United States; or (7) that the decision is otherwise contrary to law.

(b) The judgments of the circuit courts of appeals shall be final, except that they shall be subject to review by the Supreme Court of the United States upon writ of certiorari or certification as provided in sections 239 and 240 of the Judicial Code, as amended (U. S. C., title 28, secs. 346 and 347).

(c) Where the cause of action is otherwise within the jurisdiction of the United States Court of Claims as provided in sections 136 to 187, inclusive, of the Judicial Code, as amended (U. S. C., title 28, secs. 241 to 293, inclusive), the petition provided in this section may be to the said Court of Claims at the election of the aggrieved party.

(d) Where a circuit court of appeals or the Court of Claims finds itself in disagreement with a previously rendered decision of another court having jurisdiction under this section, it shall certify to the Supreme Court of the United States a distinct and definite statement of the question or proposition of law upon which such disagreement rests, with a statement of the nature of the cause and of the facts on which such question or proposition of law arises, together with a statement of the reasons in support of such disagreement. Such further proceedings shall be as provided in section 239 of the Judicial Code, as amended (U. S. C., title 28, sec. 346).

JURISDICTION OF COURTS TO IMPOSE DAMAGES WHERE APPEAL WAS FOR DELAY AND FOR COSTS

SEC. 6. The courts shall have jurisdiction and power to impose damages in any case where the decision of the agency or independent agency is affirmed and the court finds that there was no substantial basis for the petition for review. In all cases the costs on review shall be allowed the prevailing party after final judgment, to be collected according to law.

EXCEPTIONS AND RESERVATIONS

SEC. 7. Nothing contained in this Act shall operate to modify or repeal any rights or procedure as now provided by law for any person to have his controversy with the United States heard and determined in any district court or circuit court of appeals of the United States.

(b) Nothing contained in this Act shall apply to or affect any matter concerning or relating to the conduct of military or naval operations; the trial by courts martial of persons otherwise within the jurisdiction of such courts martial; the conduct of the Federal Reserve Board, the Office of the Comptroller of the Currency, the Federal Deposit Insurance Corporation, the Federal Trade Commission, the Interstate Commerce Commission; the conduct of the Department of State; the conduct of the Department of Justice and the offices of the United States attorneys, except as otherwise herein specifically provided; or any matter concerning or relating to the internal revenue, customs, patent, trade-mark, copyright, or longshoreman and harbor workers' laws; or any case where the aggrieved party was denied a loan, or may be dissatisfied with a grading service in connection with the purchase or sale of agricultural products or has failed to receive appointment or employment by any agency or independent agency. Sections 2 and 3 of this Act shall not apply to the General Accounting Office.

Passed the Senate July 18, 1939.

Attest:

Secretary.

THE ADMINISTRATIVE COURT BILL

76TH CONGRESS
1ST SESSION

S. 916

IN THE SENATE OF THE UNITED STATES

JANUARY 24 (legislative day, JANUARY 17), 1939

Mr. LOGAN introduced the following bill; which was read twice and referred to the Committee on the Judiciary

---

A BILL

To establish a United States Court of Appeals for Administration, to receive, decide, and expedite appeals from Federal Commissions, administrative authorities, and tribunals, in which the United States is a party or has an interest, and for other purposes.

Be it enacted by the Senate and House of Representatives of the United States of America in Congress assembled,

TITLE I—UNITED STATES COURT OF APPEALS FOR ADMINISTRATION

SECTION 1. There is hereby created under the authority of article III of the Constitution of the United States a United States Court of Appeals for Administration (hereinafter referred to as the court). The court, and the justices thereof, shall have all the powers and duties of the appellate courts of the United States and the judges or justices thereof. It shall be organized and constituted as follows:

(a) The court shall be composed of a Chief Justice and ten associate justices who shall be selected solely with regard to their qualifications and fitness to perform the special duties of the court.

(b) The chief justice and the associate justices shall be appointed by the President, by and with the advice and consent of the Senate. They shall hold office during good behavior and may be retired as provided in section 714 of the Revised Statutes, as amended.

(c) The chief justice and each associate justice shall receive a salary of $12,500 per year payable monthly out of the Treasury of the United States, and shall be allowed and paid his necessary expenses of travel and his reasonable expenses (not to exceed $10 per day) of maintenance incurred upon any official business of the court at any place other than the District of Columbia.

(d) The court shall have a seal with such device as it may order.

(e) The court shall be located in the District of Columbia where it shall hold one term annually, commencing on the first Monday in October; but whenever, in the opinion of the chief justice, the convenience of the public or of the parties may be promoted, or delay or expense prevented thereby, a division of the court may hold special sessions in any part of the United States.

SEC. 2. (a) Any seven justices shall constitute a quorum of the entire court.

(b) The chief justice shall preside over all sessions of the entire court, and, unless he shall otherwise direct, of any division in which he may participate. In case of inability to attend any session of the court he shall designate an associate justice to preside over that session.

(c) In case of a vacancy in the office of chief justice, or of his inability to perform the duties of his office, the court shall choose from their number an associate justice, who shall act as chief justice until such disability is removed or a chief justice is appointed and duly qualified.

SEC. 3. The court shall be organized by the chief justice as follows:

(a) The chief justice and associate justices may each constitute a division of the court for the purpose of hearing and deciding appeals coming before the court.

(b) Special divisions, consisting of three or more justices, may from time to time be formed by the chief justice for the purpose of hearing and deciding appeals when, in the judgment of the chief justice, such special division is necessary to effect the expeditious administration of justice or a hearing by more than one justice is required by law. The chief justice shall designate the presiding justice of each division.

(c) The court may from time to time be divided by the chief justice into sections when in his judgment such division will expedite the administration of justice and permit the handling of related cases by justices who are expert and experienced in the subject matter thereof. The justices to constitute each section shall from time to time be designated by the chief justice with due regard for their several qualifications by way of learning, experience, and special training for the work of the section to which they are assigned.

(d) The decision of any division shall be reduced to writing and a copy thereof distributed to the chief justice and to each associate justice of the court. It shall be reviewed by the court whenever, in the opinion of the chief justice, such review is necessary, or upon the written request of any associate justice. If no review is requested by an associate justice or deemed necessary by the chief justice, the decision of a division shall be deemed the decision of the court and shall be final; but, subject to the rules of the court, any party of record adversely affected by the judgment may file a petition for a review of such decision by the entire court.

JURISDICTION OF THE COURT

SEC. 4. (a) The court shall have exclusive jurisdiction to review on appeal all final orders and decisions, now subject to review by the Federal courts, of the administrative authorities and tribunals indicated in paragraph (b) of this section and shall exercise such other jurisdiction as Congress may from time to time confer upon it. All such jurisdiction now vested in the United States circuit courts of appeals, the United States Court of Appeals for the District of Columbia, the United States district courts, and the United States District Court for the District of Columbia is hereby abolished as to all such final orders and decisions issued one hundred and twenty days after the effective date of this Act.

(b) The jurisdiction of the court shall extend to all the final orders and decisions of the following administrative authorities or tribunal:

(1) The United States Board of Tax Appeals;

(2) The Processing Tax Board of Review in the Treasury Department;

(3) The Interstate Commerce Commission, except as to orders for the payment of money;

(4) The Federal Communications Commission, except as to orders for the payment of money;

(5) The Commodity Exchange Commission;

(6) The Federal Power Commission;

(7) The Federal Trade Commission;

(8) The National Bituminous Coal Commission;

(9) The National Labor Relations Board;

(10) The Securities and Exchange Commission;

(11) The United States Maritime Commission except as to orders for the payment of money;

(12) The Secretary of Agriculture in respect of orders (except orders for the payment of money) issued under the Packers and Stockyards Act, under the Perishable Commodities Act, orders issued as Chairman of the Commodity Exchange Commission, and orders issued to prevent monopolization, restraint of trade, and unduly enhancing prices of associations of producers of agricultural products;

(13) The Federal Reserve Board, in respect of orders under the antitrust laws;

(14) The Secretary of Commerce, in respect of orders to prevent monopoly or restraint of trade in the fishing industry;

(15) The Post Office Department, in respect of orders requiring publications to be sent by freight;

(16) The Federal Alcohol Administration in the Treasury Department;

(17) The Civil Aeronautics Authority;

(18) Administration of the Wage and Hour Division of the Department of Labor.

DEFINITIONS

The words "final order or decision" as used in this section mean an order or decision issued after due notice and an opportunity to be heard, which requires no further action by the authority issuing it to render it effective as an enforcible order of that authority.

Sec. 5. (a) Any party to a proceeding aggrieved by an administrative order or decision reviewable by the court may, within sixty days after such order or decision is issued, entered, or promulgated, file with the clerk of the court a petition for review, praying that such order or decision be modified, set aside, or reversed.

(b) Upon filing a petition for review a copy of such petition shall be forthwith served by the petitioner upon the administrative authority or tribunal issuing the order or decision complained of and upon the respondent on review, if any. Such authority or tribunal shall certify, and shall file with the court a transcript of the record upon which the order or decision complained of was entered. The transcript shall contain the notice or petition, the pertinent pleadings, if any, the relevant evidence, the findings of fact, and the order or decision appealed from, and shall be prepared and transmitted to the court in the manner which the court may by its rules prescribe.

Sec. 6. No objection, assignment of error, or question of law relating to an order or decision shall be considered by the court unless it shall have been urged before the authority or tribunal issuing the order or decision appealed from, except upon good cause shown, the court otherwise directs.

Sec. 7. If on hearing of a petition for review, either party shall apply to the court to adduce additional evidence and shall show to the satisfaction of the court that such additional evidence is material and that there were reasonable grounds for failure to adduce such evidence before the authority or tribunal, the court may order additional evidence to be taken before the administrative authority or tribunal and the authority or tribunal may modify its findings as to facts by reason of the additional evidence, and it shall file such modified new findings which, if supported by substantial evidence, shall be conclusive, and it may file its recommendations for the modifying or setting aside of the original order or decision.

Sec. 8. (a) The review of the court shall be limited to questions of law, and the findings of fact of the administrative authority or tribunal, if supported by substantial evidence, shall be conclusive.

(b) Questions coming before the court may be certified to the Supreme Court of the United States as provided in section 239 of the Judicial Code, as amended.

Sec. 9. Upon review the court shall have power to affirm, modify, set aside, or reverse the order or decision appealed from, or to remand the case for rehearing as justice may require.

Sec. 10. The judgment of the court shall be final, subject to review by the Supreme Court of the United States upon certiorari in the manner provided in section 240 of the Judicial Code, as amended.

Sec. 11. (a) Upon affirmation or modification of an order or decision, the court shall have the power to render a decree enforcing obedience to its mandate by proper process, mandatory or otherwise.

(b) The court or the Supreme Court shall have power to impose damages in any case where the order or decision is affirmed and it appears that the petition for review was filed merely for delay.

Sec. 12. (a) The filing of a petition for review shall not operate as a stay of execution of the order or decision appealed from unless otherwise provided by statute, but the appellant may, upon good cause shown at or before the time of filing the petition for review, petition the court for such stay of execution which may be granted at the discretion of the court. Notice and a copy of the petition for stay of execution shall be forthwith filed with the administrative authority or tribunal issuing the order or decision and shall operate as a temporary stay of execution pending the action of the court on such petition.

(b) In any case where a stay of execution is granted, the court may require a bond in such amount as it may consider reasonable and adequate.

SEC. 13. The court is authorized to adopt rules respecting review of the orders and decisions coming before it and the conduct of proceedings upon review, and the proceedings of the court and its divisions shall be conducted in accordance with such rules of procedure and practice as the court may prescribe. The court may also authorize and fix the amount of the fees to be charged by the clerk.

SEC. 14. (a) The chief justice, with the approval of a majority of the court, may appoint and fix the salaries of a chief clerk, who shall act as clerk of the court, and such deputy clerks as in the opinion of the chief justice may be necessary; a reporter who shall be in charge of the collection and reporting of decisions of the court and each division thereof; a legal staff, not to exceed one attorney to each division; and such law clerks as in the opinion of the chief justice may be necessary.

(b) The chief justice and each associate justice may appoint and prescribe the duties of a secretary at an annual salary not to exceed $3,000.

(c) The chief clerk shall receive a salary not to exceed $7,500 per annum. The deputy clerks shall receive a salary not to exceed $2,500 per annum. The reporter shall receive a salary not to exceed $5,000 per annum. The attorneys shall each receive a salary not to exceed $7,500 per annum. The law clerks shall each receive a salary not to exceed $3,600 per annum.

(d) The chief justice, with the approval of a majority of the court, shall have authority, subject to the provisions of the civil-service laws and the Classification Act of 1923, as amended, to appoint such stenographers, clerks, and other employees as are necessary in the execution of its functions.

SEC. 15. The court may make such expenditures (including expenditures for rent and personal services at the seat of government and elsewhere, for office furniture and supplies, law books, periodicals, and books of reference, and for printing and binding) as may be necessary for the execution of its functions and as from time to time may be appropriated for by Congress. All expenditures of the court, including all necessary expenses for transportation incurred by the employees of the court upon any official business of the court at places other than in the District of Columbia, shall be allowed and paid on the presentation of itemized vouchers therefor approved by the chief clerk of the court.

SEC. 16. The court shall provide for the publication of reports of its decisions in such form and manner as may be best adapted for public information and use, and such authorized publications shall be competent evidence of the decisions of the court therein contained in all courts of the United States without any further proof or authentication thereof.

SEC. 17. (a) If any person fails or neglects to obey any order of a commission or administrative authority which may be reviewed on appeal as provided in this Act, when such order has become final and no stay of execution has been granted by the court, and while the same is in effect, whether a petition for review has been filed or not, the commission or any party injured thereby, or the United States by its Attorney General, may apply to the appropriate district court of the United States for the enforcement of such order. If, after hearing, that court determines that the order was regularly made and duly served, that it has become final, and that the person is in disobedience of the same, the court shall enforce obedience to such order by writ of injunction or other proper process, mandatory or otherwise, to restrain such person or the officers, agents, or representatives of such person, from further disobedience of such order, or to enjoin upon it or them obedience to same. And the court may assess a fine not to exceed $100 per day (unless otherwise provided by law) for each day such person fails or neglects to obey such order.

DEFINITIONS

(b) As used in this Act—

(A) The word "person" shall include any natural person, corporation, partnership, trust, or association.

(B) The word "order" shall include any requirement or award.